JAVA FOR
EVERYONE

JAVA FOR EVERYONE

Cay Horstmann

San Jose State University

WILEY

John Wiley & Sons, Inc.

VICE PRESIDENT AND EXECUTIVE PUBLISHER	Donald Fowley
EXECUTIVE EDITOR	Beth Lang Golub
EDITORIAL ASSISTANT	Michael Berlin
PRODUCTION SERVICES MANAGER	Dorothy Sinclair
PRODUCTION EDITOR	Janet Foxman
EXECUTIVE MARKETING MANAGER	Christopher Ruel
CREATIVE DIRECTOR	Harry Nolan
SENIOR DESIGNER	Madelyn Lesure
PHOTO EDITOR	Lisa Gee
MEDIA EDITOR	Lauren Sapira
PRODUCTION SERVICES	Cindy Johnson
COVER PHOTO	© Gavriel Jecan/Corbis

This book was set in Stempel Garamond by Publishing Services, and printed and bound by World Color USA/Versailles. The cover was printed by World Color USA/Versailles.

This book is printed on acid-free paper. ∞

Library of Congress Cataloging-in-Publication Data:
Horstmann, Cay S., 1959-
 Java for everyone : compatible with Java 5, 6, and 7 / Cay Horstmann.
   p. cm.
 Includes bibliographical references and index.
 ISBN 978-0-471-79191-1 (pbk.)
 1. Java (Computer program language) I. Title.
 QA76.73.J38H675445 2010
 005.13'3--dc22
                                        2009042601
 ISBN 978-0-471-79191-1 (Main Book)
 ISBN 978-0-470-41848-2 (Binder-Ready Version)

Printed in the United States of America

10 9 8 7 6 5 4 3 2

PREFACE

This book is an introduction to Java and computer programming that focuses on the essentials—and on effective learning. The book is designed to serve a wide range of student interests and abilities and is suitable for a first course in programming for computer scientists, engineers, and students in other disciplines. No prior programming experience is required, and only a modest amount of high school algebra is needed.

Here are the key features of this new book:

Present fundamentals first.

The book takes a traditional route, stressing control structures, methods, procedural decomposition, and arrays. Objects are used when appropriate in the early chapters. Students start designing and implementing their own classes in Chapter 7.

Practice makes perfect.

Of course, programming students need to be able to implement nontrivial programs, but they first need to have the confidence that they can succeed. This book contains a substantial number of self-check questions (at the end of each section), "Practice It" pointers that suggest exercises to try after each section, simple programming assignments, and a variety of online practice opportunities, including guided lab exercises, code completion questions, and skill-oriented multiple-choice questions.

A visual approach motivates the reader and eases navigation.

Photographs present visual analogies that explain the nature and behavior of computer concepts. Step-by-step figures illustrate complex program operations. Syntax boxes and example tables clearly present a variety of typical and special cases in a compact format. It is easy to get the "lay of the land" by browsing the visuals, before focusing on the textual material.

Visual features help the reader with navigation.

Guidance and worked examples help students succeed.

Beginning programmers often ask "How do I start? Now what do I do?" Of course, an activity as complex as programming cannot be reduced to cookbook-style instructions. However, step-by-step guidance is immensely helpful for building confidence and providing an outline for the task at hand. The book contains a large number of "How To" guides for common tasks, together with additional worked examples and screencast videos on the web.

A Tour of the Book

The core material of the book is:

Chapter 1. Introduction
Chapter 2. Fundamental Data Types
Chapter 3. Decisions
Chapter 4. Loops
Chapter 5. Methods
Chapter 6. Arrays and Array Lists
Chapter 7. Objects and Classes

Input/output and exception handling are presented in Chapter 8. Sections 8.1 and 8.2 are sufficient for processing simple text files. Chapter 9 covers inheritance, polymorphism, and interfaces. Chapter 10 gives an introduction to the Java Collections

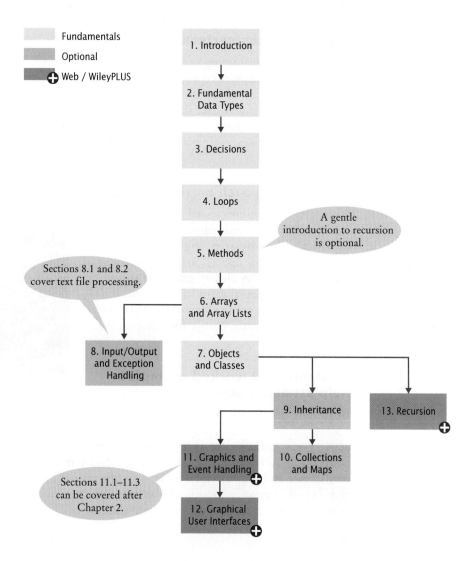

Figure 1
Chapter Dependencies

Framework from the point of view of a programmer who wants to use the collection classes effectively, without going into excessive implementation detail.

➕ Three additional chapters are available on the Web.

Chapter 11.   Graphics and Event Handling

Chapter 12.   Graphical User Interfaces

Chapter 13.   Recursion

These chapters can also be incorporated into a custom print version of this text; ask your Wiley sales representative for details. If you are interested in a two-semester text, consider a custom book with Chapters 1–9 from this book and selected chapters from Horstmann's *Big Java*.

Figure 1 shows the dependencies between the chapters.

Appendices   Appendix A lists character escape sequences and the Basic Latin and Latin-1 subsets of Unicode. Appendices B and C summarize Java operators and reserved words. Appendix D documents all of the library methods and classes used in this book.

Additional appendices available on the Web contain quick references on Java syntax, HTML, Java tools, binary numbers, and UML, plus a style guide for use with this book. Many instructors find it highly beneficial to require a consistent style for all assignments. If this style guide conflicts with instructor sentiment or local customs, however, it is available in electronic form so that it can be modified.

Web Resources

This book is complemented by a complete suite of online resources and a robust WileyPLUS course.

Go to www.wiley.com/college/horstmann to visit the online companion site, which includes

- Source code for all examples in the book.
- Worked Examples that apply the problem-solving steps in the book to other realistic examples.
- Lecture presentation slides (in PowerPoint format).
- Solutions to all review and programming exercises (for instructors only).
- A test bank that focuses on skills, not just terminology (for instructors only).

WileyPLUS is an online teaching and learning environment that integrates the digital textbook with instructor and student resources. See page xiv for details.

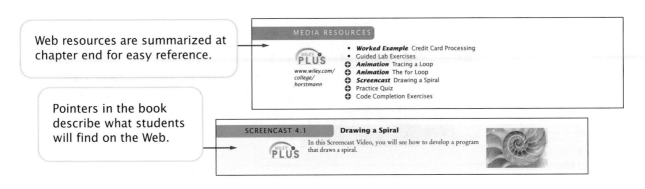

Web resources are summarized at chapter end for easy reference.

MEDIA RESOURCES

WILEY PLUS
www.wiley.com/college/horstmann

- **Worked Example** Credit Card Processing
- Guided Lab Exercises
- ➕ **Animation** Tracing a Loop
- ➕ **Animation** The for Loop
- ➕ **Screencast** Drawing a Spiral
- ➕ Practice Quiz
- ➕ Code Completion Exercises

Pointers in the book describe what students will find on the Web.

SCREENCAST 4.1   **Drawing a Spiral**

WILEY PLUS   In this Screencast Video, you will see how to develop a program that draws a spiral.

A Walkthrough of the Learning Aids

The pedagogical elements in this book work together to focus on and reinforce key concepts and fundamental principles of programming, with additional tips and detail organized to support and deepen these fundamentals. In addition to traditional features, such as chapter objectives and a wealth of exercises, each chapter contains elements geared to today's visual learner.

Throughout each chapter, **margin notes** show where new concepts are introduced and provide an outline of key ideas.

Annotated **syntax boxes** provide a quick, visual overview of new language constructs.

Annotations explain required components and point to more information on common errors or best practices associated with the syntax.

Analogies to everyday objects are used to explain the nature and behavior of concepts such as variables, data types, loops, and more.

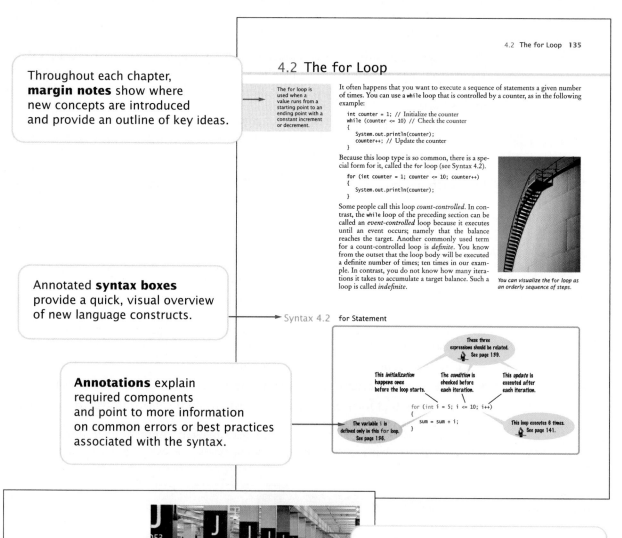

4.2 The for Loop   135

4.2 The for Loop

The for loop is used when a value runs from a starting point to an ending point with a constant increment or decrement.

It often happens that you want to execute a sequence of statements a given number of times. You can use a while loop that is controlled by a counter, as in the following example:

```
int counter = 1; // Initialize the counter
while (counter <= 10) // Check the counter
{
    System.out.println(counter);
    counter++; // Update the counter
}
```

Because this loop type is so common, there is a special form for it, called the for loop (see Syntax 4.2).

```
for (int counter = 1; counter <= 10; counter++)
{
    System.out.println(counter);
}
```

Some people call this loop *count-controlled*. In contrast, the while loop of the preceding section can be called an *event-controlled* loop because it executes until an event occurs; namely that the balance reaches the target. Another commonly used term for a count-controlled loop is *definite*. You know from the outset that the loop body will be executed a definite number of times; ten times in our example. In contrast, you do not know how many iterations it takes to accumulate a target balance. Such a loop is called *indefinite*.

You can visualize the for loop as an orderly sequence of steps.

Syntax 4.2   for Statement

These three expressions should be related. See page 139.

This *initialization* happens once before the loop starts.

The *condition* is checked before each iteration.

This *update* is executed after each iteration.

```
for (int i = 5; i <= 10; i++)
{
    sum = sum + i;
}
```

The variable i is defined only in this for loop. See page 136.

This loop executes 6 times. See page 141.

Like a variable in a computer program, a parking space has an identifier and a contents.

Memorable photos reinforce analogies and help students remember the concepts.

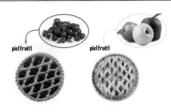

A recipe for a fruit pie may say to use any kind of fruit. Here, "fruit" is an example of a parameter variable.

HOW TO 1.1

Describing an Algorithm with Pseudocode

This is the first of many "How To" sections in this book that give you step-by-step procedures for carrying out important tasks in developing computer programs.

Before you are ready to write a program in Java, you need to develop an algorithm—a method for arriving at a solution for a particular problem. Describe the algorithm in pseudocode: a sequence of precise steps formulated in English.

For example, consider this problem: You have the choice of buying two cars. One is more fuel efficient than the other, but also more expensive. You know the price and fuel efficiency (in miles per gallon, mpg) of both cars. You plan to keep the car for ten years. Assume a price of $4 per gallon of gas and usage of 15,000 miles per year. You will pay cash for the car and not worry about financing costs. Which car is the better deal?

Step 1 Determine the inputs and outputs.

In our sample problem, we have these inputs:
- **purchase price1** and **fuel efficiency1**, the price and fuel efficiency (in mpg) of the first car
- **purchase price2** and **fuel efficiency2**, the price and fuel efficiency of the second car

We simply want to know which car is the better buy. That is the desired output.

Step 2 Break down the problem into smaller tasks.

For each car, we need to know the total cost of driving it. Let's do this computation separately for each car. Once we have the total cost for each car, we can decide which car is the better deal.

The total cost for each car is **purchase price + operating cost**.

We assume a constant usage and gas price for ten years, so the operating cost depends on the cost of driving the car for one year.

The operating cost is **10 x annual fuel cost**.

The annual fuel cost is **price per gallon x annual fuel consumed**.

The annual fuel consumed is **annual miles driven / fuel efficiency**. For example, if you drive the car for 15,000 miles and the fuel efficiency is 15 miles/gallon, the car consumes 1,000 gallons.

Step 3 Describe each subtask in pseudocode.

In your description, arrange the steps so that any intermediate values are computed before they are needed in other computations. For example, list the step

    total cost = purchase price + operating cost

after you have computed **operating cost**.

Here is the algorithm for deciding which car to buy.

    For each car, compute the total cost as follows:
        annual fuel consumed = annual miles driven / fuel efficiency
        annual fuel cost = price per gallon x annual fuel consumed
        operating cost = 10 x annual fuel cost
        total cost = purchase price + operating cost
    If total cost1 < total cost2

How To guides give step-by-step guidance for common programming tasks, emphasizing planning and testing. They answer the beginner's question, "Now what do I do?" and integrate key concepts into a problem-solving sequence.

Worked Examples apply the steps in the How To to a different example, illustrating how they can be used to plan, implement, and test a solution to another programming problem.

WORKED EXAMPLE 1.1

Writing an Algorithm for Tiling a Floor

This Worked Example shows how to develop an algorithm for laying tile in an alternating pattern of colors.

Example tables support beginners with multiple, concrete examples. These tables point out common errors and present another quick reference to the section's topic.

Table 1 Variable Declarations in Java	
Variable Name	Comment
`int cans = 6;`	Declares an integer variable and initializes it with 6.
`int total = cans + bottles;`	The initial value need not be a constant. (Of course, cans and bottles must have been previously declared.)
🚫 `bottles = 1;`	**Error:** The type is missing. This statement is not a declaration but an assignment of a new value to an existing variable—see Section 2.2.
🚫 `int bottles = "10";`	**Error:** You cannot initialize a number with a string.
`int bottles;`	Declares an integer variable without initializing it. This can be a cause for errors—see Common Error 2.1 on page 37.
`int cans, bottles;`	Declares two integer variables in a single statement. In this book, we will declare each variable in a separate statement.

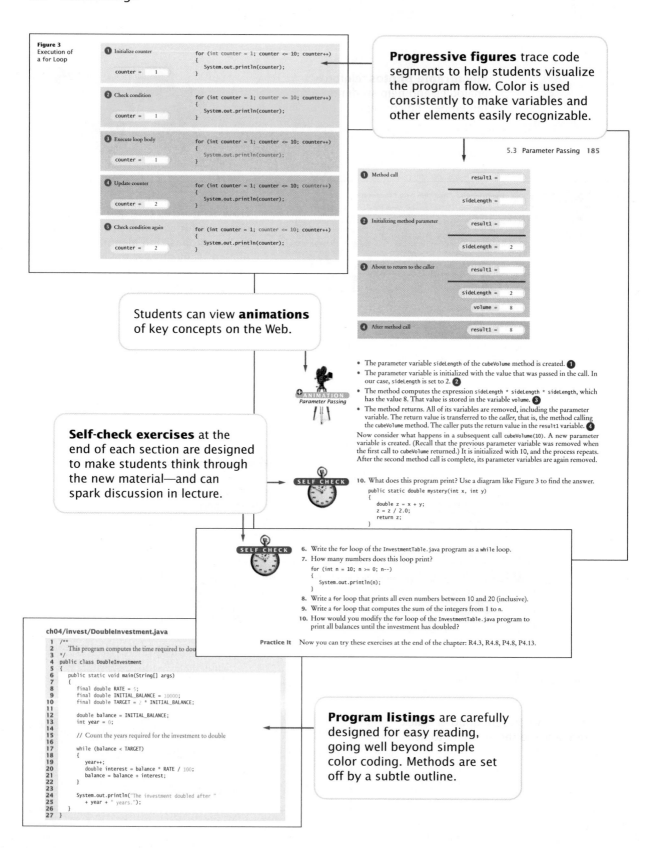

Figure 3
Execution of a for Loop

1 Initialize counter

```
for (int counter = 1; counter <= 10; counter++)
{
    System.out.println(counter);
}
```
counter = 1

2 Check condition

```
for (int counter = 1; counter <= 10; counter++)
{
    System.out.println(counter);
}
```
counter = 1

3 Execute loop body

```
for (int counter = 1; counter <= 10; counter++)
{
    System.out.println(counter);
}
```
counter = 1

4 Update counter

```
for (int counter = 1; counter <= 10; counter++)
{
    System.out.println(counter);
}
```
counter = 2

5 Check condition again

```
for (int counter = 1; counter <= 10; counter++)
{
    System.out.println(counter);
}
```
counter = 2

Progressive figures trace code segments to help students visualize the program flow. Color is used consistently to make variables and other elements easily recognizable.

5.3 Parameter Passing 185

1 Method call
result1 =
sideLength =

2 Initializing method parameter
result1 =
sideLength = 2

3 About to return to the caller
result1 =
sideLength = 2
volume = 8

4 After method call
result1 = 8

Students can view **animations** of key concepts on the Web.

ANIMATION
Parameter Passing

- The parameter variable sideLength of the cubeVolume method is created. **1**
- The parameter variable is initialized with the value that was passed in the call. In our case, sideLength is set to 2. **2**
- The method computes the expression sideLength * sideLength * sideLength, which has the value 8. That value is stored in the variable volume. **3**
- The method returns. All of its variables are removed, including the parameter variable. The return value is transferred to the *caller*, that is, the method calling the cubeVolume method. The caller puts the return value in the result1 variable. **4**

Now consider what happens in a subsequent call cubeVolume(10). A new parameter variable is created. (Recall that the previous parameter variable was removed when the first call to cubeVolume returned.) It is initialized with 10, and the process repeats. After the second method call is complete, its parameter variables are again removed.

Self-check exercises at the end of each section are designed to make students think through the new material—and can spark discussion in lecture.

SELF CHECK

10. What does this program print? Use a diagram like Figure 3 to find the answer.

```
public static double mystery(int x, int y)
{
    double z = x + y;
    z = z / 2.0;
    return z;
}
```

SELF CHECK

6. Write the for loop of the InvestmentTable.java program as a while loop.
7. How many numbers does this loop print?

```
for (int n = 10; n >= 0; n--)
{
    System.out.println(n);
}
```

8. Write a for loop that prints all even numbers between 10 and 20 (inclusive).
9. Write a for loop that computes the sum of the integers from 1 to n.
10. How would you modify the for loop of the InvestmentTable.java program to print all balances until the investment has doubled?

Practice It Now you can try these exercises at the end of the chapter: R4.3, R4.8, P4.8, P4.13.

ch04/invest/DoubleInvestment.java

```
1  /**
2     This program computes the time required to dou
3  */
4  public class DoubleInvestment
5  {
6     public static void main(String[] args)
7     {
8        final double RATE = 5;
9        final double INITIAL_BALANCE = 10000;
10       final double TARGET = 2 * INITIAL_BALANCE;
11
12       double balance = INITIAL_BALANCE;
13       int year = 0;
14
15       // Count the years required for the investment to double
16
17       while (balance < TARGET)
18       {
19          year++;
20          double interest = balance * RATE / 100;
21          balance = balance + interest;
22       }
23
24       System.out.println("The investment doubled after "
25          + year + " years.");
26    }
27 }
```

Program listings are carefully designed for easy reading, going well beyond simple color coding. Methods are set off by a subtle outline.

Common Errors describe the kinds of errors that students often make, with an explanation of why the errors occur, and what to do about them.

Common Error 6.4

Length and Size

Unfortunately, the Java syntax for determining the number of elements in an array, an array list, and a string is not at all consistent. It is a common error to confuse these. You just have to remember the correct syntax for every data type.

Data Type	Number of Elements
Array	a.length
Array list	a.size()
String	a.length()

Programming Tip 4.1

Programming Tips explain good programming practices, and encourage students to be more productive with tips and techniques such as hand-tracing.

Hand-Tracing Loops

In Programming Tip 3.5, you learned about the method of hand-tracing. This method is particularly effective for understanding how a loop works.

Consider this example. What value is displayed?

```
int n = 1729; ❶
int sum = 0;
while (n > 0) ❷
{
   int digit = n % 10; ❸❹❺❻
   sum = sum + digit;
   n = n / 10;
}
System.out.println(sum); ❼
```

1. There are three variables: n, sum, and digit. The first two variables are initialized with 1729 and 0 before the loop is entered.

n	sum	digit
1729	0	

2. Because n is positive, enter the loop.

3. The variable digit is set to 9 (the remainder of dividing 1729 by 10). The variable sum is

Special Topic 6.2

Special Topics present optional topics and provide additional explanation of others. New features of Java 7 are also covered in these notes.

A Sorting Algorithm

A *sorting algorithm* rearranges the elements of a sequence so that they are stored in sorted order. Here is a simple sorting algorithm, called **selection sort**. Consider sorting the following array data:

[0][1][2][3][4]
11 9 17 5 12

An obvious first step is to find the smallest element. In this case the smallest element is 5, stored in data[3]. You should move the 5 to the beginning of the array. Of course, there is already an element stored in data[0], namely 11. Therefore you cannot simply move data[3] into data[0] without moving the 11 somewhere else. You don't yet know where the 11 should end up, but you know for certain that it should not be in data[0]. Simply get it out of the way by *swapping it* with data[3].

[0][1][2][3][4]
5 9 17 11 12

Now the first element is in the correct place. In the foregoing figure, the darker color indicates the portion of the array that is already sorted.

Next take the minimum of the remaining entries data[1]...data[4]. That minimum value, 9, is already in the correct place. You don't need to do anything in this case, simply extend the sorted area by one to the right:

[0][1][2][3][4]
5 9 17 11 12

Repeat the process. The minimum value of the unsorted region is 11, which needs to be swapped with the first value of the unsorted region, 17.

[0][1][2][3][4]
5 9 11 17 12

Random Facts provide historical and social information on computing—for interest and to fulfill the "historical and social context" requirements of the ACM/IEEE curriculum guidelines.

Random Fact 4.1 **The First Bug**

According to legend, the first bug was found in the Mark II, a huge electromechanical computer at Harvard University. It really was caused by a bug—a moth was trapped in a relay switch.

Actually, from the note that the operator left in the log book next to the moth (see the figure), it appears as if the term "bug" had already been in active use at the time.

The pioneering computer scientist Maurice Wilkes wrote, "Somehow, at the Moore School and afterwards, one had always assumed there would be no particular difficulty in getting programs right. I can remember the exact instant in time at which it dawned on me that a great part of my future life would be spent finding mistakes in my own programs."

The First Bug

WileyPLUS

WileyPLUS is an online environment that supports students and instructors. This book's WileyPLUS course can complement the printed text or replace it altogether.

For Students

Different learning styles, different levels of proficiency, different levels of preparation—each student is unique. WileyPLUS empowers all students to take advantage of their individual strengths.

Integrated, multi-media resources—including audio and visual exhibits and demonstration problems—encourage active learning and provide multiple study paths to fit each student's learning preferences.

- Worked Examples apply the problem-solving steps in the book to another realistic example.
- Screencast Videos present the author explaining the steps he is taking and showing his work as he solves a programming problem.
- Animations of key concepts allow students to replay dynamic explanations that instructors usually provide on a whiteboard.

Self-assessments are linked to relevant portions of the text. Students can take control of their own learning and practice until they master the material.

- Practice quizzes can reveal areas where students need to focus.
- Guided lab exercises can be assigned for self-study or for use in the lab.
- "Code completion" questions enable students to practice programming skills by filling in small code snippets and getting immediate feedback.

For Instructors

WileyPLUS includes all of the instructor resources found on the companion site, and more.

WileyPLUS gives you tools for identifying those students who are falling behind, allowing you to intervene accordingly, without having to wait for them to come to office hours.

- Practice quizzes for pre-reading assessment, self-quizzing, or additional practice can be used as-is or modified for your course needs.
- Multi-step guided laboratory exercises can be used in lab or assigned for extra student practice.

WileyPLUS simplifies and automates student performance assessment, making assignments, and scoring student work.

- An extensive set of multiple-choice questions for quizzing and testing have been developed to focus on skills, not just terminology.
- "Code completion" questions can also be added to online quizzes.
- Solutions to all review and programming exercises are provided.

With WileyPLUS ...

Students can read the book online and take advantage of searching and cross-linking.

Instructors can assign drill-and-practice questions to check that students did their reading and grasp basic concepts.

Students can practice programming by filling in small code snippets and getting immediate feedback.

Students can play and replay dynamic explanations of concepts and program flow.

Students can watch and listen as the author solves a problem step-by-step.

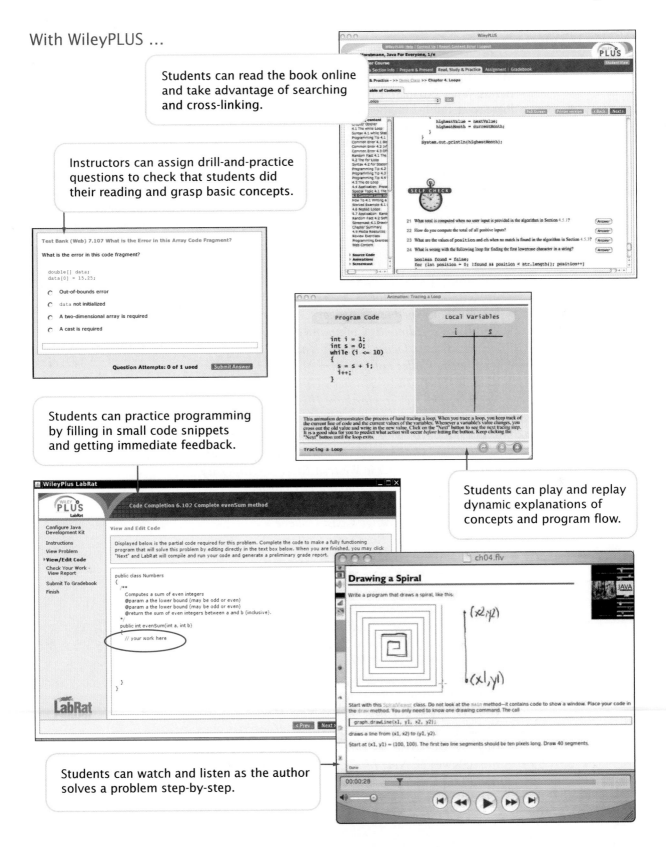

To order *Java for Everyone* with its WileyPLUS course for your students, use ISBN 978-0-470-43721-6.

Acknowledgments

Many thanks to Beth Golub, Lauren Sapira, Andre Legaspi, Don Fowley, Mike Berlin, Janet Foxman, Lisa Gee, and Bud Peters at John Wiley & Sons, and Vickie Piercey at Publishing Services for their help with this project. An especially deep acknowledgment and thanks goes to Cindy Johnson for her hard work, sound judgment, and amazing attention to detail.

I am grateful to Elizabeth Boese, Carolyn Schauble, Julius Dichter, Kathy Liszka, Tony Nguyen, Fred Richard, Donald Smith, and Richard Sharp for their work on the supplemental material.

Many thanks to the individuals who reviewed the manuscript for this edition, made valuable suggestions, and brought an embarrassingly large number of errors and omissions to my attention. They include:

Lynn Aaron, *SUNY Rockland Community College*
William C. Barge, *Trine University*
Bruce J. Barton, *Suffolk County Community College*
Eric Bishop, *Northland Pioneer College*
Paul Bladek, *Edmonds Community College*
Irene E. Bruno, *George Mason University*
Joe Burgin, *College of Southern Maryland*
Xuemin Chen, *Texas Southern University*
Geoffrey D. Decker, *Northern Illinois University*
Julius Dichter, *University of Bridgeport*
Tom Duffy, *Norwalk Community College*
Sander Eller, *California State Polytechnic University, Pomona*
Chris Fietkiewicz, *Case Western Reserve University*
Terrell Foty, *Portland Community College*
Ryan Garlick, *University of North Texas*
Stephen Gilbert, *Orange Coast College*
Peter van der Goes, *Rose State College*
Billie Goldstein, *Temple University*
Michael Gourley, *University of Central Oklahoma*
Grigoriy Grinberg, *Montgomery College*
Bruce Haft, *Glendale Community College*
Nancy Harris, *James Madison University*
Allan M. Hart, *Minnesota State University, Mankato*
Ric Heishman, *George Mason University*
Katherin Herbert, *Montclair State University*
Rodney Hoffman, *Occidental College*
Andree Jacobson, *University of New Mexico*
Christopher M. Johnson, *Guilford College*
Mugdha Khaladkar, *New Jersey Institute of Technology*
Morty Kwestel, *New Jersey Institute of Technology*
Hong Lin, *University of Houston, Downtown*
Cheng Luo, *Coppin State University*
Lydia Macaulay, *Tarrant County College*

John S. Mallozzi, *Iona College*
Deborah Mathews, *J. Sargeant Reynolds Community College*
Drew McDermott, *Yale University*
Michael L. Mick, *Purdue University, Calumet*
Jeanne Milostan, *University of California-Merced*
Tony Tuan Nguyen, *De Anza College*
James Papademas, *Oakton Community College*
James T. Pepe, *Bentley University*
Linda L. Preece, *Southern Illinois University*
Craig Reinhart, *California Lutheran University*
Chaman Lal Sabharwal, *Missouri University of Science & Technology*
Jeffrey Paul Scott, *Blackhawk Technical College*
Amon Seagull, *NOVA Southeastern University*
Victor Shtern, *Boston University*
Donald W. Smith, *Columbia College*
Peter Spoerri, *Fairfield University*
David R. Stampf, *Suffolk County Community College*
Peter Stanchev, *Kettering University*
Robert Strader, *Stephen F. Austin State University*
Monica Sweat, *Georgia Tech University*
Dave Sullivan, *Boston University*
Joseph Szurek, *University of Pittsburgh, Greensburg*
Russell Tessier, *University of Massachusetts, Amherst*
Megan Thomas, *California State University, Stanislaus*
Philip Ventura, *Broward College*
David R. Vineyard, *Kettering University*
Qi Wang, *Northwest Vista College*
Reginald White, *Black Hawk Community College*
Chen Ye, *University of Illinois, Chicago*

A special thank you to all of our class testers:

Michael Ondrasek and the students of Wright State University
Irene Bruno and the students of George Mason University
Cihan Varol and the students of Sam Houston University
David Vineyard and the students of Kettering University
Cindy Tanner and the students of West Virginia University
Andrew Juraszek and the students of J. Sargeant Reynolds Community College
Daisy Sang and the students of California State Polytechnic University, Pomona
Dawn McKinney and the students of University of South Alabama
Nadimpalli Mahadev and the students of Fitchburg State College
Robert Burton and the students of Brigham Young University
Nancy Harris and the students of James Madison University
Tim Weale, Paolo Bucci, and the students of Ohio State University

CONTENTS

✚   Available online only in WileyPLUS and at www.wiley.com/college/horstmann.

⊕ Available online in WileyPLUS and at www.wiley.com/college/horstmann.

ALPHABETICAL LIST OF SYNTAX BOXES

✚ Available online only in WileyPLUS and at www.wiley.com/college/horstmann.

Programming Tips	Special Topics	Random Facts

➕ Available online only in WileyPLUS and at www.wiley.com/college/horstmann.

➕ Available online only in WileyPLUS and at www.wiley.com/college/horstmann.

Programming Tips

Special Topics

Random Facts

➕ Available online only in WileyPLUS and at www.wiley.com/college/horstmann.

CHAPTER	Common Errors	How Tos and Worked Examples
11 Graphics and Event Handling (WEB ONLY) ➕	Modifying Parameter Types in the Implementing Method ➕ By Default, Components Have Zero Width and Height ➕ Forgetting to Attach a Listener ➕ Forgetting to Repaint ➕	Drawing Graphical Shapes ➕
12 Graphical User Interfaces (WEB ONLY) ➕		Laying Out a User Interface ➕ Implementing a Graphical User Interface (GUI) ➕
13 Recursion (WEB ONLY) ➕	Infinite Recursion ➕ Tracing Through Recursive Methods ➕	Thinking Recursively ➕ Finding Files ➕

➕ Available online only in WileyPLUS and at www.wiley.com/college/horstmann.

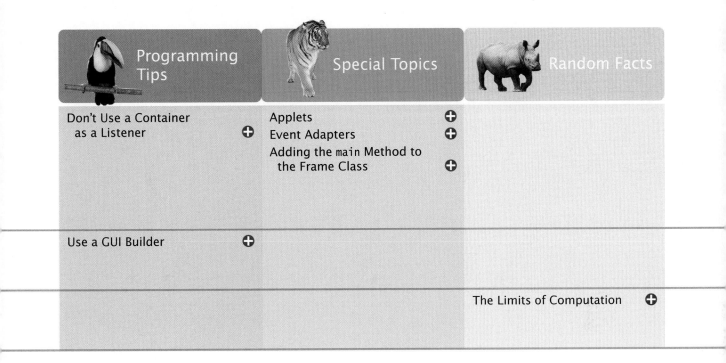

⊕ Available online only in WileyPLUS and at www.wiley.com/college/horstmann.

CHAPTER 1

INTRODUCTION

CHAPTER GOALS

To learn about computers
and programming

To compile and run your first Java program

To recognize compile-time and run-time errors

To describe an algorithm with pseudocode

CHAPTER CONTENTS

Just as you gather tools, study a project, and make a plan for tackling it, in this chapter you will gather up the basics you need to start learning to program. After a brief introduction to computer hardware, software, and programming in general, you will learn how to write and run your first Java program. You will also learn how to diagnose and fix programming errors, and how to use pseudocode to describe an algorithm—a step-by-step description of how to solve a problem—as you plan your computer programs.

1.1 Computer Programs

Computers execute very basic instructions in rapid succession.

You have probably used a computer for work or fun. Many people use computers for everyday tasks such as electronic banking or writing a term paper. Computers are good for such tasks. They can handle repetitive chores, such as totaling up numbers or placing words on a page, without getting bored or exhausted.

The flexibility of a computer is quite an amazing phenomenon. The same machine can balance your checkbook, print your term paper, and play a game. In contrast, other machines carry out a much narrower range of tasks; a car drives and a toaster toasts. Computers can carry out a wide range of tasks because they execute different programs, each of which directs the computer to work on a specific task.

A computer program is a sequence of instructions and decisions.

The computer itself is a machine that stores data (numbers, words, pictures), interacts with devices (the monitor, the sound system, the printer), and executes programs. A **computer program** tells a computer, in minute detail, the sequence of steps that are needed to fulfill a task. The physical computer and peripheral devices are collectively called the **hardware**. The programs the computer executes are called the **software**.

Today's computer programs are so sophisticated that it is hard to believe that they are composed of extremely primitive instructions. A typical instruction may be one of the following:

- Put a red dot at this screen position.
- Add up these two numbers.
- If this value is negative, continue the program at a certain instruction.

The computer user has the illusion of smooth interaction because a program contains a huge number of such instructions, and because the computer can execute them at great speed.

Programming is the act of designing and implementing computer programs.

The act of designing and implementing computer programs is called **programming**. In this book, you will learn how to program a computer—that is, how to direct the computer to execute tasks.

To write a computer game with motion and sound effects or a word processor that supports fancy fonts and pictures is a complex task that requires a team of many highly-skilled programmers. Your first programming efforts will be more mundane. The concepts and skills you learn in this book form an important foundation, and you should not be disappointed if your first programs do not rival the sophisticated software that is familiar to you. Actually, you will find that there is an immense thrill even in simple programming tasks. It is an amazing experience to see the computer precisely and quickly carry out a task that would take you hours of drudgery, to make small changes in a program that lead to immediate improvements, and to see the computer become an extension of your mental powers.

SELF CHECK

1. What is required to play music on a computer?
2. Why is a CD player less flexible than a computer?
3. What does a computer user need to know about programming in order to play a video game?

1.2 The Anatomy of a Computer

To understand the programming process, you need to have a rudimentary understanding of the building blocks that make up a computer. We will look at a personal computer. Larger computers have faster, larger, or more powerful components, but they have fundamentally the same design.

At the heart of the computer lies the **central processing unit (CPU)** (see Figure 1). The inside wiring of the CPU is enormously complicated. For example, the Intel Core processor (a popular CPU for personal computers at the time of this writing) is composed of several hundred million structural elements, called **transistors**.

> The central processing unit (CPU) performs program control and data processing.

The CPU performs program control and data processing. That is, the CPU locates and executes the program instructions; it carries out arithmetic operations such as addition, subtraction, multiplication, and division; it fetches data from external memory or devices and stores processed data back.

> Storage devices include memory and secondary storage.

The computer stores both data and programs. There are two kinds of storage. **Primary storage** is made from memory chips: electronic circuits that can store data, provided they are supplied with electric power. **Secondary storage**, usually a **hard disk** (see Figure 2), provides slower and less expensive storage that persists without electricity. A hard disk consists of rotating platters, which are coated with a magnetic material, and read/write heads, which can detect and change the magnetic flux on the platters.

Figure 1 Central Processing Unit

Figure 2 A Hard Disk

Programs and data are typically stored on the hard disk and loaded into memory when the program starts. The program then updates the data in memory and writes the modified data back to the hard disk.

To interact with a human user, a computer requires peripheral devices. The computer transmits information (called *output*) to the user through a display screen, speakers, and printers. The user can enter information (called *input*) for the computer by using a keyboard or a pointing device such as a mouse.

Some computers are self-contained units, whereas others are interconnected through **networks**. Through the network cabling, the computer can read data and programs from central storage locations or send data to other computers. To the

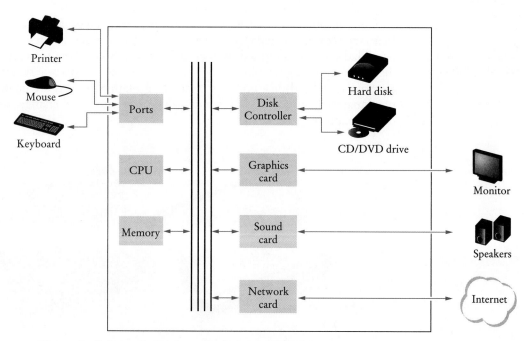

Figure 3 Schematic Design of a Personal Computer

user of a networked computer, it may not even be obvious which data reside on the computer itself and which are transmitted through the network.

Figure 3 gives a schematic overview of the architecture of a personal computer. Program instructions and data (such as text, numbers, audio, or video) are stored on the hard disk, on a compact disk (or DVD), or elsewhere on the network. When a program is started, it is brought into memory, where the CPU can read it. The CPU reads the program one instruction at a time. As directed by these instructions, the CPU reads data, modifies it, and writes it back to memory or the hard disk. Some program instructions will cause the CPU to place dots on the display screen or printer or to vibrate the speaker. As these actions happen many times over and at great speed, the human user will perceive images and sound. Some program instructions read user input from the keyboard or mouse. The program analyzes the nature of these inputs and then executes the next appropriate instruction.

SELF CHECK

4. Where is a program stored when it is not currently running?
5. Which part of the computer carries out arithmetic operations, such as addition and multiplication?

Random Fact 1.1 The ENIAC and the Dawn of Computing

The ENIAC (*e*lectronic *n*umerical *i*ntegrator *a*nd *c*omputer) was the first usable electronic computer. It was designed by J. Presper Eckert and John Mauchly at the University of Pennsylvania and was completed in 1946—two years before transistors were invented. The computer was housed in a large room and consisted of many cabinets containing about 18,000 vacuum tubes (see Figure 4). Vacuum tubes burned out at the rate of several tubes per day. An attendant with a shopping cart full of tubes constantly made the rounds and replaced defective ones. The computer was programmed by connecting wires on panels. Each wiring configuration would set up the computer for a particular problem. To have the computer work on a different problem, the wires had to be replugged.

Work on the ENIAC was supported by the U.S. Navy, which was interested in computations of ballistic tables that would give the trajectory of a projectile, depending on the wind resistance, initial velocity, and atmospheric conditions. To compute the trajectories, one must find the numerical solutions of certain differential equations; hence the name "numerical integrator". Before machines like the ENIAC were developed, humans did this kind of work, and until the 1950s the word "computer" referred to these people. The ENIAC was later used for peaceful purposes, such as the tabulation of U.S. Census data.

Figure 4 The ENIAC

1.3 The Java Programming Language

In order to write a computer program, you need to provide a sequence of instructions that the CPU can execute. A computer program consists of a large number of simple CPU instructions, and it is tedious and error-prone to specify them one by one. For that reason, **high-level programming languages** have been created. In a high-level language, you specify the actions that your program should carry out. A **compiler** translates the high-level instructions into the more detailed instructions required by the CPU. Many different programming languages have been designed for different purposes.

Java was originally designed for programming consumer devices, but it was first successfully used to write Internet applets.

In 1991, a group led by James Gosling and Patrick Naughton at Sun Microsystems designed a programming language, code-named "Green", for use in consumer devices, such as intelligent television "set-top" boxes. The language was designed to be simple, secure, and usable for many different processor types. No customer was ever found for this technology.

James Gosling

Gosling recounts that in 1994 the team realized, "We could write a really cool browser. It was one of the few things in the client/server mainstream that needed some of the weird things we'd done: architecture neutral, real-time, reliable, secure". Java was introduced to an enthusiastic crowd at the SunWorld exhibition in 1995, together with a browser that ran **applets**—Java code that can be located anywhere on the Internet. Figure 5 shows a typical example of an applet.

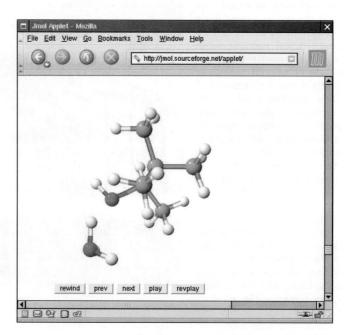

Figure 5
An Applet for Visualizing Molecules
Running in a Browser Window
(*http://jmol.sourceforge.net/applet/*)

Since then, Java has grown at a phenomenal rate. Programmers have embraced the language because it is simpler than its closest rival, C++. In addition, Java has a rich **library** that makes it possible to write portable programs that can bypass proprietary operating systems—a feature that was eagerly sought by those who wanted to be independent of those proprietary systems and was bitterly fought by their vendors. A "micro edition" and an "enterprise edition" of the Java library make Java programmers at home on hardware ranging from smart cards and cell phones to the largest Internet servers.

Because Java was designed for the Internet, it has two attributes that make it very suitable for beginners: safety and portability.

> Java was designed to be safe and portable, benefiting both Internet users and students.

The safety features of the Java language make it possible to run Java programs in a browser without fear that they might attack your computer. As an added benefit, these features also help you to learn the language faster. When you make an error that results in unsafe behavior, you receive an accurate error report.

> Java programs are distributed as instructions for a virtual machine, making them platform-independent.

The other benefit of Java is portability. The same Java program will run, without change, on Windows, UNIX, Linux, or Macintosh. In order to achieve portability, the Java compiler does not translate Java programs directly into CPU instructions. Instead, compiled Java programs contain instructions for the Java **virtual machine**, a program that simulates a real CPU. Portability is another benefit for the beginning student. You do not have to learn how to write programs for different platforms.

At this time, Java is firmly established as one of the most important languages for general-purpose programming as well as for computer science instruction. However, although Java is a good language for beginners, it is not perfect, for three reasons.

Because Java was not specifically designed for students, no thought was given to making it really simple to write basic programs. A certain amount of technical machinery is necessary in Java to write even the simplest programs. This is not a problem for professional programmers, but it can be a nuisance for beginning students. As you learn how to program in Java, there will be times when you will be asked to be satisfied with a preliminary explanation and wait for more complete detail in a later chapter.

Java has been revised and extended many times during its life—see Table 1. In this book, we assume that you have Java version 5 or later.

Table 1	Java Versions	
Version	Year	Important New Features
1.0	1996	
1.1	1997	Inner classes
1.2	1998	Swing, Collections framework
1.3	2000	Performance enhancements
1.4	2002	Assertions, XML support
5	2004	Generic classes, enhanced for loop, auto-boxing, enumerations, annotations
6	2006	Library improvements
7	2010	Small language changes and library improvements

Java has a very large library. Focus on learning those parts of the library that you need for your programming projects.

Finally, you cannot hope to learn all of Java in one course. The Java language itself is relatively simple, but Java contains a vast set of *library packages* that are required to write useful programs. There are packages for graphics, user interface design, cryptography, networking, sound, database storage, and many other purposes. Even expert Java programmers cannot hope to know the contents of all of the packages—they just use those that they need for particular projects.

Using this book, you should expect to learn a good deal about the Java language and about the most important packages. Keep in mind that the central goal of this book is not to make you memorize Java minutiae, but to teach you how to think about programming.

SELF CHECK

6. What are the two most important benefits of the Java language?
7. How long does it take to learn the entire Java library?

1.4 Becoming Familiar With Your Programming Environment

Set aside some time to become familiar with the programming environment that you will use for your class work.

Many students find that the tools they need as programmers are very different from the software with which they are familiar. You should spend some time making yourself familiar with your programming environment. Because computer systems vary widely, this book can only give an outline of the steps you need to follow. It is a good idea to participate in a hands-on lab, or to ask a knowledgeable friend to give you a tour.

Step 1   Start the Java development environment.

An editor is a program for entering and modifying text, such as a Java program.

Computer systems differ greatly in this regard. On many computers there is an **integrated development environment** in which you can write and test your programs. On other computers you first launch an **editor,** a program that functions like a word processor, in which you can enter your Java instructions; you then open a *console window* and type commands to execute your program. You need to find out how to get started with your environment.

Step 2   Write a simple program.

The traditional choice for the very first program in a new programming language is a program that displays a simple greeting: "Hello, World!". Let us follow that tradition. Here is the "Hello, World!" program in Java.

```java
public class HelloPrinter
{
   public static void main(String[] args)
   {
      System.out.println("Hello, World!");
   }
}
```

We will examine this program in the next section.

Figure 6
Running the
`HelloPrinter`
Program in an
Integrated
Development
Environment

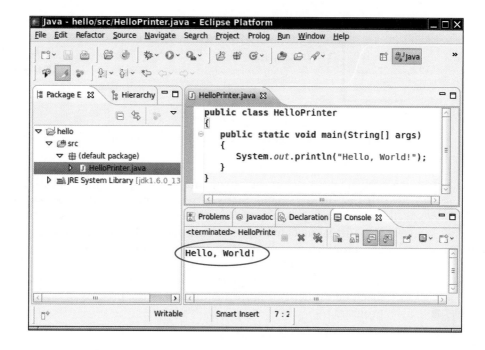

No matter which programming environment you use, you begin your activity by typing the program statements into an editor window.

Create a new file and call it `HelloPrinter.java`, using the steps that are appropriate for your environment. (If your environment requires that you supply a project name in addition to the file name, use the name `hello` for the project.) Enter the program instructions *exactly* as they are given above. Alternatively, locate an electronic copy in this book's companion code and paste it into your editor.

> Java is case sensitive. You must be careful about distinguishing between upper- and lowercase letters.

As you write this program, pay careful attention to the various symbols, and keep in mind that Java is **case sensitive**. You must enter upper- and lowercase letters exactly as they appear in the program listing. You cannot type `MAIN` or `PrintLn`. If you are not careful, you will run into problems—see Common Error 1.2 on page 16.

Step 3 Run the program.

The process for running a program depends greatly on your programming environment. You may have to click a button or enter some commands. When you run the test program, the message

```
Hello, World!
```

will appear somewhere on the screen (see Figures 6 and 7).

Figure 7
Running the
`HelloPrinter`
Program in a
Console Window

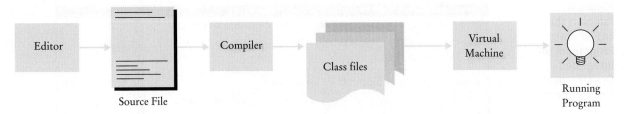

Figure 8 From Source Code to Running Program

ANIMATION
Compilation Process

The Java compiler translates source code into class files that contain instructions for the Java virtual machine.

In order to run your program, the Java compiler translates your **source code** (that is, the statements that you wrote) into *class files*. A class file contains instructions for the Java virtual machine. After the compiler has translated your program into virtual machine instructions, the virtual machine executes them. In some programming environments, the compiler and virtual machine are essentially invisible to the programmer—they are automatically executed whenever you ask to run a Java program. In other environments, you need to launch the compiler and virtual machine explicitly. Figure 8 summarizes the process of creating and running a Java program.

Step 4 Organize your work.

As a programmer, you write programs, try them out, and improve them. You store your programs in **files**. Files are stored in **folders** or **directories**. A folder can contain files as well as other folders, which themselves can contain more files and folders (see Figure 9). This hierarchy can be quite large, and you need not be concerned

Figure 9 A Folder Hierarchy

with all of its branches. However, you should create folders for organizing your work. It is a good idea to make a separate folder for your programming class. Inside that folder, make a separate folder for each program.

Some programming environments place your programs into a default location if you don't specify a folder yourself. In that case, you need to find out where those files are located.

Be sure that you understand where your files are located in the folder hierarchy. This information is essential when you submit files for grading, and for making backup copies (see Programming Tip 1.1).

SELF CHECK

8. Where is the `HelloPrinter.java` file stored on your computer?

9. What do you do to protect yourself from data loss when you work on programming projects?

Programming Tip 1.1

Backup Copies

You will spend many hours creating and improving Java programs. It is easy to delete a file by accident, and occasionally files are lost because of a computer malfunction. Retyping the contents of lost files is frustrating and time-consuming. It is therefore crucially important that you learn how to safeguard files and get in the habit of doing so *before* disaster strikes. Backing up files on a memory stick is an easy and convenient storage method for many people. Another increasingly popular form of backup is Internet file storage. Here are a few pointers to keep in mind.

Develop a strategy for keeping backup copies of your work before disaster strikes.

- *Back up often.* Backing up a file takes only a few seconds, and you will hate yourself if you have to spend many hours recreating work that you could have saved easily. I recommend that you back up your work once every thirty minutes.

- *Rotate backups.* Use more than one directory for backups, and rotate them. That is, first back up onto the first directory. Then back up onto the second directory. Then use the third, and then go back to the first. That way you always have three recent backups. If your recent changes made matters worse, you can then go back to the older version.

- *Pay attention to the backup direction.* Backing up involves copying files from one place to another. It is important that you do this right—that is, copy from your work location to the backup location. If you do it the wrong way, you will overwrite a newer file with an older version.

- *Check your backups once in a while.* Double-check that your backups are where you think they are. There is nothing more frustrating than to find out that the backups are not there when you need them.

- *Relax, then restore.* When you lose a file and need to restore it from a backup, you are likely to be in an unhappy, nervous state. Take a deep breath and think through the recovery process before you start. It is not uncommon for an agitated computer user to wipe out the last backup when trying to restore a damaged file.

1.5 Analyzing Your First Program

In this section, we will analyze the first Java program in detail. Here again is the source code:

ch01/hello/HelloPrinter.java

```
1   public class HelloPrinter
2   {
3      public static void main(String[] args)
4      {
5         System.out.println("Hello, World!");
6      }
7   }
```

The line,

```
public class HelloPrinter
```

indicates the declaration of a **class** called HelloPrinter.

> Classes are the fundamental building blocks of Java programs.

Every Java program consists of one or more classes. Classes are the fundamental building blocks of Java programs. You will have to wait until Chapter 7 for a full explanation of classes.

The word public denotes that the class is usable by the "public". You will later encounter private features.

In Java, every source file can contain at most one public class, and the name of the public class must match the name of the file containing the class. For example, the class HelloPrinter must be contained in a file HelloPrinter.java.

The construction

```
public static void main(String[] args)
{
   . . .
}
```

> Every Java application contains a class with a main method. When the application starts, the instructions in the main method are executed.

declares a **method** called main. A method contains a collection of programming instructions that describe how to carry out a particular task. Every Java application must have a main method. Most Java programs contain other methods besides main, and you will see in Chapter 5 how to write other methods.

The term static is explained in more detail in Chapter 7, and the meaning of String[] args is covered in Chapter 8. At this time, simply consider

> Each class contains declarations of methods. Each method contains a sequence of instructions.

```
public class ClassName
{
   public static void main(String[] args)
   {
      . . .
   }
}
```

as a part of the "plumbing" that is required to a Java program. Our first program has all instructions inside the main method of a class.

The main method contains one or more instructions called **statements**. Each statement ends in a semicolon (;). When a program runs, the statements in the main method are executed one by one.

Syntax 1.1 Java Program

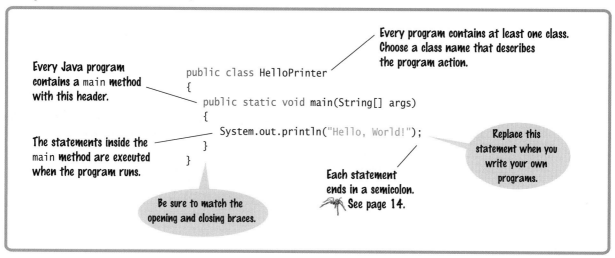

Every Java program contains a main **method** with this header.

Every program contains at least one class. Choose a class name that describes the program action.

The statements inside the main **method** are executed when the program runs.

```
public class HelloPrinter
{
   public static void main(String[] args)
   {
      System.out.println("Hello, World!");
   }
}
```

Replace this statement when you write your own programs.

Be sure to match the opening and closing braces.

Each statement ends in a semicolon. See page 14.

In our example program, the main method has a single statement:

```
System.out.println("Hello, World!");
```

This statement prints a line of text, namely "Hello, World!". In this statement, we *call* a method which, for reasons that we will not explain here, is specified by the rather long name System.out.println.

We do not have to implement this method—the programmers who wrote the Java library already did that for us. We simply want the method to perform its intended task, namely to print a value.

Whenever you call a method in Java, you need to specify

> A method is called by specifying the method and its parameters.

1. The method you want to use (in this case, System.out.println).
2. Any values the method needs to carry out its task (in this case, "Hello, World!"). The technical term for such a value is a **parameter**. Parameters are enclosed in parentheses. Multiple parameters are separated by commas.

A sequence of characters enclosed in quotation marks

```
"Hello, World!"
```

> A string is a sequence of characters enclosed in quotation marks.

is called a **string**. You must enclose the contents of the string inside quotation marks so that the compiler knows you literally mean "Hello, World!". There is a reason for this requirement. Suppose you need to print the word *main*. By enclosing it in quotation marks, "main", the compiler knows you mean the sequence of characters m a i n, not the method named main. The rule is simply that you must enclose all text strings in quotation marks, so that the compiler considers them plain text and does not try to interpret them as program instructions.

You can also print numerical values. For example, the statement

```
System.out.println(3 + 4);
```

displays the number 7.

The `System.out.println` method prints a string or a number and then starts a new line. For example, the sequence of statements

```
System.out.println("Hello");
System.out.println("World!");
```

prints two lines of text:

```
Hello
World!
```

There is a second method, `System.out.print`, that you can use to print an item without starting a new line. For example, the output of the two statements

```
System.out.print("00");
System.out.println(3 + 4);
```

is the single line

```
007
```

SELF CHECK

10. How do you modify the `HelloPrinter` program to greet you instead?

11. How would you modify the `HelloPrinter` program to print the words "Hello," and "World!" on two lines?

12. Would the program continue to work if you replaced line 5 with this statement?

```
System.out.println(Hello);
```

13. What does the following set of statements print?

```
System.out.print("My lucky number is");
System.out.println(3 + 4 + 5);
```

14. What do the following statements print?

```
System.out.println("Hello");
System.out.println("");
System.out.println("World");
```

Practice It Now you can try these exercises at the end of the chapter: R1.6, R1.7, P1.5, P1.7.

Omitting Semicolons

In Java every statement must end in a semicolon. Forgetting to type a semicolon is a common error. It confuses the compiler, because the compiler uses the semicolon to find where one statement ends and the next one starts. The compiler does not use line breaks or closing braces to recognize the end of statements. For example, the compiler considers

```
System.out.println("Hello")
System.out.println("World!");
```

a single statement, as if you had written

```
System.out.println("Hello") System.out.println("World!");
```

Then it doesn't understand that statement, because it does not expect the word `System` following the closing parenthesis after `"Hello"`. The remedy is simple. Scan every statement for a terminating semicolon, just as you would check that every English sentence ends in a period.

1.6 Errors

Experiment a little with the `HelloPrinter` program. What happens if you make a typing error such as

```
System.ou.println("Hello, World!");
System.out.println("Hello, Word!");
```

Programmers spend a fair amount of time fixing compile-time and run-time errors.

> A compile-time error is a violation of the programming language rules that is detected by the compiler.

In the first case, the compiler will complain. It will say that it has no clue what you mean by `ou`. The exact wording of the error message is dependent on your development environment, but it might be something like "Cannot find symbol ou". This is a **compile-time error**. Something is wrong according to the rules of the language and the compiler finds it. For this reason, compile-time errors are often called *syntax errors*. When the compiler finds one or more errors, it refuses to translate the program into Java virtual machine instructions, and as a consequence you have no program that you can run. You must fix the error and compile again. In fact, the compiler is quite picky, and it is common to go through several rounds of fixing compile-time errors before compilation succeeds for the first time.

If the compiler finds an error, it will not simply stop and give up. It will try to report as many errors as it can find, so you can fix them all at once.

Sometimes, an error throws the compiler off track. Suppose, for example, you forget the quotation marks around a string: `System.out.println(Hello, World!)`. The compiler will not complain about the missing quotation marks. Instead, it will report "Cannot find symbol Hello". Unfortunately, the compiler is not very smart and it does not realize that you meant to use a string. It is up to you to realize that you need to enclose strings in quotation marks.

The error in the second line is of a different kind. The program will compile and run, but its output will be wrong. It will print

```
Hello, Word!
```

> A run-time error causes a program to take an action that the programmer did not intend.

This is a **run-time error**. The program is syntactically correct and does something, but it doesn't do what it is supposed to do. Because run-time errors are caused by logical flaws in the program, they are often called *logic errors*.

This particular run-time error did not include an error message. It simply produced the wrong output. Some kinds of run-time errors are so severe that they generate an **exception**: an error message from the Java virtual machine. For example, if your program includes the statement

```
System.out.println(1/0);
```

you will get a run-time error message "Division by zero".

During program development, errors are unavoidable. Once a program is longer than a few lines, it would require superhuman concentration to enter it correctly without slipping up once. You will find yourself omitting semicolons or quotation marks more often than you would like, but the compiler will track down these problems for you.

Run-time errors are more troublesome. The compiler will not find them—in fact, the compiler will cheerfully translate any program as long as its syntax is correct—but the resulting program will do something wrong. It is the responsibility of the program author to test the program and find any run-time errors.

15. Suppose you omit the "" characters around `Hello, World!` from the `Hello-Printer.java` program. Is this a compile-time error or a run-time error?

16. Suppose you change `println` to `printline` in the `HelloPrinter.java` program. Is this a compile-time error or a run-time error?

17. Suppose you change `main` to `hello` in the `HelloPrinter.java` program. Is this a compile-time error or a run-time error?

18. When you used your computer, you may have experienced a program that "crashed" (quit spontaneously) or "hung" (failed to respond to your input). Is that behavior a compile-time error or a run-time error?

19. Why can't you test a program for run-time errors when it has compiler errors?

Practice It Now you can try these exercises at the end of the chapter: R1.8, R1.9, R1.10.

Common Error 1.2

Misspelling Words

If you accidentally misspell a word, then strange things may happen, and it may not always be completely obvious from the error messages what went wrong. Here is a good example of how simple spelling errors can cause trouble:

```java
public class HelloPrinter
{
    public static void Main(String[] args)
    {
        System.out.println("Hello, World!");
    }
}
```

This class declares a method called `Main`. The compiler will not consider this to be the same as the `main` method, because `Main` starts with an uppercase letter and the Java language is case sensitive. Upper- and lowercase letters are considered to be completely different from each other, and to the compiler `Main` is no better match for `main` than `rain`. The compiler will cheerfully compile your `Main` method, but when the Java virtual machine reads the compiled file, it will complain about the missing `main` method and refuse to run the program. Of course, the message "missing main method" should give you a clue where to look for the error.

If you get an error message that seems to indicate that the compiler or virtual machine is on the wrong track, it is a good idea to check for spelling and capitalization. If you misspell the name of a symbol (for example, `ou` instead of `out`), the compiler will produce a message such as "cannot find symbol ou". That error message is usually a good clue that you made a spelling error.

1.7 Algorithms

You will soon learn how to program calculations and decision making in Java. But before we look at the mechanics of implementing computations in the next chapter, let's consider how you can describe the steps that are necessary for finding the solution for a problem.

You may have run across advertisements that encourage you to pay for a computerized service that matches you up with a love partner. Think how this might work. You fill out a form and send it in. Others do the same. The data are processed by a computer program. Is it reasonable to assume that the computer can perform the task of finding the best match for you? Suppose your younger brother, not the computer, had all the forms on his desk. What instructions could you give him? You can't say, "Find the best-looking person who likes inline skating and browsing the Internet". There is no objective standard for good looks, and your brother's opinion (or that of a computer program analyzing the digitized photo) will likely be different from yours. If

Finding the perfect partner is not a problem that a computer can solve.

you can't give written instructions for someone to solve the problem, there is no way the computer can magically find the right solution. The computer can only do what you tell it to do. It just does it faster, without getting bored or exhausted.

For that reason, a computerized match-making service cannot guarantee to find the optimal match for you. Instead, you may be presented with a set of potential partners who share common interests with you. That is a task that a computer program can solve.

Now consider the following investment problem:

You put $10,000 into a bank account that earns 5 percent interest per year. How many years does it take for the account balance to be double the original?

Could you solve this problem by hand? Sure, you could. You figure out the balance as follows:

year	balance
0	10000
1	10000.00 x 1.05 = 10500.00
2	10500.00 x 1.05 = 11025.00
3	11025.00 x 1.05 = 11576.25
4	11576.25 x 1.05 = 12155.06

You keep going until the balance is at least $20,000. Then the last number in the year column is the answer.

Of course, carrying out this computation is intensely boring to you or your younger brother. But computers are very good at carrying out repetitive calculations quickly and flawlessly. What is important to the computer is a description of the steps for finding the solution. Each step must be clear and unambiguous, requiring no guesswork. Here is such a description:

Start with a year value of 0 and a balance of $10,000.

year	balance
0	10000

Repeat the following steps while the balance is less than $20,000.
    Add 1 to the year value.
    Multiply the balance value by 1.05 (a 5 percent increase).

year	balance
0	10000
1	10500
14	19799.32
⑮	20789.28

Report the final year value as the answer.

Pseudocode is an informal description of a sequence of steps for solving a problem.

Of course, these steps are not yet in a language that a computer can understand, but you will soon learn how to formulate them in Java. This informal description is called **pseudocode**.

There are no strict requirements for pseudocode because it is read by human readers, not a computer program. Here are the kinds of pseudocode statements that we will use in this book:

• Use statements such as the following to describe how a value is set or changed:

    total cost = purchase price + operating cost

    or

    Multiply the balance value by 1.05.

    or

    Remove the first and last character from the word.

• You can describe decisions and repetitions as follows:

    If total cost 1 < total cost 2
    While the balance is less than $20,000
    For each picture in the sequence

    Use indentation to indicate which statements should be selected or repeated:

    For each car
        operating cost = 10 x annual fuel cost
        total cost = purchase price + operating cost

    Here, the indentation indicates that both statements should be executed for each car.

• Indicate results with statements such as:

    Choose car 1.
    Report the final year value as the answer.

An algorithm for solving a problem is a sequence of steps that is unambiguous, executable, and terminating.

The exact wording is not important. What is important is that pseudocode describes a sequence of steps that is

• Unambiguous

• Executable

• Terminating

An algorithm is a recipe for finding a solution.

The step sequence is *unambiguous* when there are precise instructions for what to do at each step and where to go next. There is no room for guesswork or personal opinion. A step is *executable* when it can be carried out in practice. Had we said to use the actual interest rate that will be charged in years to come, and not a fixed rate of 5 percent per year, that step would not have been executable, because there is no way for anyone to know what that interest rate will be. A sequence of steps is *terminating* if it will eventually come to an end. In our example, it requires a bit of thought to see that the sequence will not go on forever: With every step, the balance goes up by at least $500, so eventually it must reach $20,000.

A sequence of steps that is unambiguous, executable, and terminating is called an **algorithm**. We have found an algorithm to solve our investment problem, and thus we can find the solution by programming a computer. The existence of an algorithm is an essential prerequisite for programming a task. You need to first discover and describe an algorithm for the task that you want to solve before you start programming (see Figure 10).

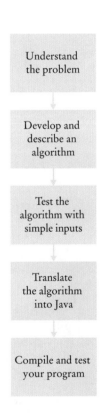

Understand the problem

Develop and describe an algorithm

Test the algorithm with simple inputs

Translate the algorithm into Java

Compile and test your program

Figure 10 The Software Development Process

SELF CHECK

20. Suppose the interest rate was 20 percent. How long would it take for the investment to double?

21. Suppose your cell phone carrier charges you $29.95 for up to 300 minutes of calls, and $0.45 for each additional minute, plus 12.5 percent taxes and fees. Give an algorithm to compute the monthly charge from a given number of minutes.

22. Consider the following pseudocode for finding the most attractive photo from a sequence of photos:

    Pick the first photo and call it "the best so far".
    For each photo in the sequence
        If it is more attractive than the "best so far"
            Discard "the best so far".
            Call this photo "the best so far".
    The photo called "the best so far" is the most attractive photo in the sequence.

    Is this an algorithm that will find the most attractive photo?

23. Suppose each photo in Self Check 22 had a price tag. Give an algorithm for finding the most expensive photo.

24. Suppose you have a random sequence of black and white marbles and want to rearrange it so that the black and white marbles are grouped together. Consider this algorithm:

    Repeat until sorted
        Locate the first black marble that is preceded by a white marble, and switch them.

    What does the algorithm do with the sequence ○●○●●? Spell out the steps until the algorithm stops.

25. Suppose you have a random sequence of colored marbles. Consider this pseudocode:

    Repeat until sorted
        Locate the first marble that is preceded by a marble of a different color, and switch them.

    Why is this not an algorithm?

Practice It   Now you can try these exercises at the end of the chapter: R1.14, R1.16, P1.4.

HOW TO 1.1

Describing an Algorithm with Pseudocode

This is the first of many "How To" sections in this book that give you step-by-step procedures for carrying out important tasks in developing computer programs.

Before you are ready to write a program in Java, you need to develop an algorithm—a method for arriving at a solution for a particular problem. Describe the algorithm in pseudocode: a sequence of precise steps formulated in English.

For example, consider this problem: You have the choice of buying two cars. One is more fuel efficient than the other, but also more expensive. You know the price and fuel efficiency (in miles per gallon, mpg) of both cars. You plan to keep the car for ten years. Assume a price of $4 per gallon of gas and usage of 15,000 miles per year. You will pay cash for the car and not worry about financing costs. Which car is the better deal?

Step 1   Determine the inputs and outputs.

In our sample problem, we have these inputs:

- purchase price1 and fuel efficiency1, the price and fuel efficiency (in mpg) of the first car
- purchase price2 and fuel efficiency2, the price and fuel efficiency of the second car

We simply want to know which car is the better buy. That is the desired output.

Step 2 Break down the problem into smaller tasks.

For each car, we need to know the total cost of driving it. Let's do this computation separately for each car. Once we have the total cost for each car, we can decide which car is the better deal.

The total cost for each car is **purchase price + operating cost**.

We assume a constant usage and gas price for ten years, so the operating cost depends on the cost of driving the car for one year.

The operating cost is **10 x annual fuel cost**.

The annual fuel cost is **price per gallon x annual fuel consumed**.

The annual fuel consumed is **annual miles driven / fuel efficiency**. For example, if you drive the car for 15,000 miles and the fuel efficiency is 15 miles/gallon, the car consumes 1,000 gallons.

Step 3 Describe each subtask in pseudocode.

In your description, arrange the steps so that any intermediate values are computed before they are needed in other computations. For example, list the step

total cost = purchase price + operating cost

after you have computed **operating cost**.

Here is the algorithm for deciding which car to buy.

```
For each car, compute the total cost as follows:
    annual fuel consumed = annual miles driven / fuel efficiency
    annual fuel cost = price per gallon x annual fuel consumed
    operating cost = 10 x annual fuel cost
    total cost = purchase price + operating cost
If total cost1 < total cost2
    Choose car1.
Else
    Choose car2.
```

Step 4 Test your pseudocode by working a problem.

We will use these sample values:

Car 1: $25,000, 50 miles/gallon
Car 2: $20,000, 30 miles/gallon

Here is the calculation for the cost of the first car.

```
annual fuel consumed = annual miles driven / fuel efficiency = 15000 / 50 = 300
annual fuel cost = price per gallon x annual fuel consumed = 4 x 300 = 1200
operating cost = 10 x annual fuel cost = 10 x 1200 = 12000
total cost = purchase price + operating cost = 25000 + 12000 = 37000
```

Similarly, the total cost for the second car is $40,000. Therefore, the output of the algorithm is to choose car 1.

WORKED EXAMPLE 1.1   **Writing an Algorithm for Tiling a Floor**

This Worked Example shows how to develop an algorithm for laying tile in an alternating pattern of colors.

➕ Available online in WileyPLUS and at www.wiley.com/college/horstmann.

SCREENCAST 1.1   **Compiling and Running a Program**

This Screencast Video shows how to compile and run a simple Java program.

CHAPTER SUMMARY

- Computers execute very basic instructions in rapid succession.
- A computer program is a sequence of instructions and decisions.
- Programming is the act of designing and implementing computer programs.

- The central processing unit (CPU) performs program control and data processing.
- Storage devices include memory and secondary storage.

- Java was originally designed for programming consumer devices, but it was first successfully used to write Internet applets.
- Java was designed to be safe and portable, benefiting both Internet users and students.
- Java programs are distributed as instructions for a virtual machine, making them platform-independent.
- Java has a very large library. Focus on learning those parts of the library that you need for your programming projects.

- Set aside some time to become familiar with the programming environment that you will use for your class work.
- An editor is a program for entering and modifying text, such as a Java program.
- Java is case sensitive. You must be careful about distinguishing between upper- and lowercase letters.
- The Java compiler translates source code into class files that contain instructions for the Java virtual machine.

- Develop a strategy for keeping backup copies of your work before disaster strikes.

✚ Available online in WileyPLUS and at www.wiley.com/college/horstmann.

- Classes are the fundamental building blocks of Java programs.
  - Every Java application contains a class with a main method. When the application starts, the instructions in the main method are executed.
  - Each class contains declarations of methods. Each method contains a sequence of instructions.
  - A method is called by specifying the method and its parameters.
  - A string is a sequence of characters enclosed in quotation marks.

- A compile-time error is a violation of the programming language rules that is detected by the compiler.
- A run-time error causes a program to take an action that the programmer did not intend.

- Pseudocode is an informal description of a sequence of steps for solving a problem.
- An algorithm for solving a problem is a sequence of steps that is unambiguous, executable, and terminating.

MEDIA RESOURCES

WILEY
PLUS
www.wiley.com/
college/
horstmann

- ***Worked Example*** Writing an Algorithm for Tiling a Floor
- Guided Lab Exercises
- ⊕ ***Animation*** Compilation Process
- ⊕ ***Screencast*** Compiling and Running a Program
- ⊕ Practice Quiz
- ⊕ Code Completion Exercises

REVIEW EXERCISES

★ **R1.1** Explain the difference between using a computer program and programming a computer.

★ **R1.2** Which parts of a computer can store program code? Which can store user data?

★ **R1.3** Which parts of a computer serve to give information to the user? Which parts take user input?

★★★ **R1.4** A toaster is a single-function device, but a computer can be programmed to carry out different tasks. Is your cell phone a single-function device, or is it a programmable computer? (Your answer will depend on your cell phone model.)

★★ **R1.5** On your own computer or on a lab computer, find the exact location (folder or directory name) of

a. The sample file HelloPrinter.java, which you wrote with the editor

b. The Java program launcher java.exe or java

c. The library file rt.jar that contains the run-time library

★★ **R1.6** What does this program print?

```java
public class Test
{
    public static void main(String[] args)
    {
        System.out.println("39 + 3");
        System.out.println(39 + 3);
    }
}
```

★★ **R1.7** What does this program print?

```java
public class Test
{
    public static void main(String[] args)
    {
        System.out.print("Hello");
        System.out.println("World");
    }
}
```

Pay close attention to spaces.

★★ **R1.8** What is the compile-time error in this program?

```java
public class Test
{
    public static void main(String[] args)
    {
        System.out.println("Hello", "World!");
    }
}
```

★★ **R1.9** Write three versions of the HelloPrinter.java program that have different compile-time errors. Write a version that has a run-time error.

★ **R1.10** How do you discover syntax errors? How do you discover logic errors?

★★ **R1.11** Write an algorithm to settle the following question: A bank account starts out with $10,000. Interest is compounded monthly at 6 percent per year (0.5 percent per month). Every month, $500 is withdrawn to meet college expenses. After how many years is the account depleted?

★★★ **R1.12** Consider the question in Exercise R1.11. Suppose the numbers ($10,000, 6 percent, $500) were user selectable. Are there values for which the algorithm you developed would not terminate? If so, change the algorithm to make sure it always terminates.

★★★ **R1.13** In order to estimate the cost of painting a house, a painter needs to know the surface area of the exterior. Develop an algorithm for computing that value. Your inputs are the width, length, and height of the house, the number of windows and doors, and their dimensions. (Assume the windows and doors have a uniform size.)

★★ **R1.14** You want to decide whether you should drive your car to work or take the train. You know the one-way distance from your home to your place of work, and the fuel efficiency of your car (in miles per gallon). You also know the one-way price of a train ticket. You assume the cost of gas at $4 per gallon, and car maintenance at 5 cents per mile. Write an algorithm to decide which commute is cheaper.

★★ **R1.15** You want to find out which fraction of your car's use is for commuting to work, and which is for personal use. You know the one-way distance from your home to your place of work. For a particular period, you recorded the beginning and ending mileage on the odometer and the number of work days. Write an algorithm to settle this question.

★ **R1.16** In the problem described in How To 1.1 on page 20, you made assumptions about the price of gas and the annual usage. Ideally, you would like to know which car is the better deal without making these assumptions. Why can't a computer program solve that problem?

★★★ **R1.17** The value of π can be computed according to the following formula:

$$\frac{\pi}{4} = 1 - \frac{1}{3} + \frac{1}{5} - \frac{1}{7} + \frac{1}{9} - \cdots$$

Write an algorithm to compute π. Because the formula is an infinite series and an algorithm must stop after a finite number of steps, you should stop when you have the result determined to six significant digits.

★★ **R1.18** Suppose you put your younger brother in charge of backing up your work. Write a set of detailed instructions for carrying out his task. Explain how often he should do it, and what files he needs to copy from which folder to which location. Explain how he should verify that the backup was carried out correctly.

PROGRAMMING EXERCISES

★ **P1.1** Write a program that prints a greeting of your choice, perhaps in a language other than English.

★★ **P1.2** Write a program that prints the sum of the first ten positive integers, $1 + 2 + \cdots + 10$.

★★ **P1.3** Write a program that prints the product of the first ten positive integers, $1 \times 2 \times \cdots \times 10$. (Use * to indicate multiplication in Java.)

★★ **P1.4** Write a program that prints the balance of an account after the first, second, and third year. The account has an initial balance of $1,000 and earns 5 percent interest per year.

★ **P1.5** Write a program that displays your name inside a box on the terminal screen, like this:

> Dave

Do your best to approximate lines with characters such as | - +.

★★★ **P1.6** Write a program that prints your name in large letters, such as

```
*   *    **    ****    ****    *   *
*   *   *  *   *   *   *   *   *   *
*****   *  *   ****    ****      * *
*   *  ******  *   *   *   *      *
*   *  *    *  *   *   *   *      *
```

★★ **P1.7** Write a program that prints a face similar to (but different from) the following:

```
      /////
    +"""""+
   (| o o |)
    |  ^  |
    | '-' |
    +-----+
```

★★ **P1.8** Write a program that prints a house that looks exactly like the following:

```
     +
    + +
   +   +
  +-----+
  | .-. |
  | | | |
  +-+-+-+
```

★★★ **P1.9** Write a program that prints an animal speaking a greeting, similar to (but different from) the following:

```
  /\_/\     -----
 ( ' ' )  / Hello \
 (  -  ) <  Junior |
  | | |   \ Coder!/
 (_|_)     -----
```

★ **P1.10** Write a program that prints three items, such as the names of your three best friends or favorite movies, on three separate lines.

★ **P1.11** Write a program that prints a poem of your choice. If you don't have a favorite poem, search the Internet for "Emily Dickinson" or "e e cummings".

★★ **P1.12** Write a program that prints an imitation of a Piet Mondrian painting. (Search the Internet if you are not familiar with his paintings.) Use character sequences such as @@@ or ::: to indicate different colors, and use - and | to form lines.

★★ **P1.13** Write a program that prints the United States flag, using * and = characters.

★★ **P1.14** Type in and run the following program:

```java
import javax.swing.JOptionPane;

public class DialogViewer
{
    public static void main(String[] args)
    {
        JOptionPane.showMessageDialog(null, "Hello, World!");
        System.exit(0);
    }
}
```

Then modify the program to show the message "Hello, *your name!*".

★★ **P1.15** Type in and run the following program:

```java
import javax.swing.JOptionPane;

public class DialogViewer
{
    public static void main(String[] args)
    {
        String name = JOptionPane.showInputDialog("What is your name?");
        System.out.println(name);
        System.exit(0);
    }
}
```

Then modify the program to print "Hello, *name!*", displaying the name that the user typed in.

★★★ **P1.16** Modify the program from Exercise P1.15 so that the dialog continues with the message "My name is Hal! What would you like me to do?" Discard the user's input and display a message such as

```
I'm sorry, Dave. I'm afraid I can't do that.
```

Replace Dave with the name that was provided by the user.

★★ **P1.17** Type in and run the following program:

```java
import java.net.URL;
import javax.swing.ImageIcon;
import javax.swing.JOptionPane;

public class Test
{
    public static void main(String[] args) throws Exception
    {
        URL imageLocation = new URL(
                "http://horstmann.com/java4everyone/duke.gif");
        JOptionPane.showMessageDialog(null, "Hello", "Title",
                JOptionPane.PLAIN_MESSAGE, new ImageIcon(imageLocation));
        System.exit(0);
    }
}
```

Then modify it to show a different greeting and image.

1. A program that reads the data on the CD and sends output to the speakers and the screen.
2. A CD player can do one thing—play music CDs. It cannot execute programs.
3. Nothing.
4. In secondary storage, typically a hard disk.
5. The central processing unit.
6. Safety and portability.
7. No one person can learn the entire library—it is too large.
8. The answer varies among systems. A typical answer might be `/home/dave/cs1/hello/HelloPrinter.java` or `c:\Users\Dave\Workspace\hello\HelloPrinter.java`
9. You back up your files and folders.
10. Change `World` to `Dave`, or whatever your name is:

    ```
    System.out.println("Hello, Dave!");
    ```

11. ```
    System.out.println("Hello,");
    System.out.println("World!");
    ```

12. No. The compiler would look for an item whose name is `Hello`. You need to enclose `Hello` in quotation marks: `System.out.println("Hello");`
13. The printout is `My lucky number is12`. It would be a good idea to add a space after the `is`.
14. `Hello`
    a blank line
    `World`
15. This is a compile-time error. The compiler will complain that it does not know the meanings of the words `Hello` and `World`.
16. This is a compile-time error. The compiler will complain that `System.out` does not have a method called `printline`.
17. This is a run-time error. It is perfectly legal to give the name `hello` to a method, so the compiler won't complain. But when the program is run, the virtual machine will look for a `main` method and won't find one.
18. It is a run-time error. After all, the program had been compiled in order for you to run it.
19. When a program has compiler errors, no class file is produced, and there is nothing to run.
20. 4 years:
    0 10,000
    1 12,000
    2 14,400
    3 17,280
    4 20,736
    ```

21. Is the number of minutes at most 300?

    a. If so, the answer is $29.95 \times 1.125 = 33.70$.

    b. If not,

        1. Compute the difference: (number of minutes) – 300.

        2. Multiply that difference by 0.45.

        3. Add $29.95.

        4. Multiply the total by 1.125. That is the answer.

22. No. The step **If it is more attractive than the "best so far"** is not executable because there is no objective way of deciding which of two photos is more attractive.

23. **Pick the first photo and call it "the most expensive so far".**
For each photo in the sequence
    If it is more expensive than "the most expensive so far"
        Discard "the most expensive so far".
        Call this photo "the most expensive so far".
The photo called "the most expensive so far" is the most expensive photo in the sequence.

24. The first black marble that is preceded by a white one is marked in blue:

○●○●●

Switching the two yields

●○○●●

The next black marble to be switched is

●○○●●

yielding

●○●○●

The next steps are

●●○○●

●●○●○

●●●○○

Now the sequence is sorted.

25. ○●○●●

The sequence doesn't terminate. Consider the input ○●○●○. The first two marbles keep getting switched.

FUNDAMENTAL DATA TYPES

To understand the properties and
  limitations of integers and
  floating-point numbers

To be able to declare and initialize variables and constants

To write arithmetic expressions and assignment statements

To create programs that read and process inputs, and display the results

To learn how to use the Java String type

CHAPTER CONTENTS

Numbers and character strings (such as the ones on this display board) are important data types in any Java program. In this chapter, you will learn how to work with numbers and text, and how to write simple programs that perform useful tasks with them.

2.1 Declaring Variables

When your program carries out computations, you will want to store values so that you can use them later. In a Java program, you use **variables** to store values. In this section, you will learn how to declare and use variables.

To illustrate the use of variables, we will develop a program that solves the following problem. Soft drinks are sold in cans and bottles. A store offers a six-pack of 12-ounce cans for the same price as a two-liter bottle. Which should you buy? (Twelve fluid ounces equal approximately 0.355 liters.)

In our program, we will declare variables for the number of cans per pack and for the volume of each can. Then we will compute the volume of a six-pack in liters and print out the answer.

What contains more soda? A six-pack of 12-ounce cans or a two-liter bottle?

2.1.1 Variable Declarations

The following statement declares a variable named cansPerPack:

```java
int cansPerPack = 6;
```

A variable is a storage location with a name.

A **variable** is a storage location in a computer program. Each variable has a name and holds a value.

A variable is similar to a parking space in a parking garage. The parking space has an identifier (such as "J 053"), and it can hold a vehicle. A variable has a name (such as cansPerPack), and it can hold a value (such as 6).

Like a variable in a computer program, a parking space has an identifier and a contents.

Syntax 2.1 Variable Declaration

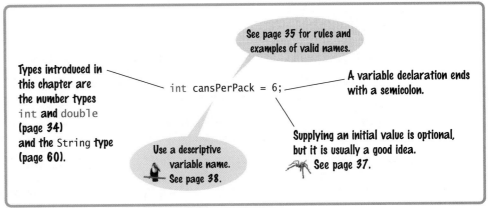

See page *35* for rules and examples of valid names.

Types introduced in this chapter are the number types `int` **and** `double` **(page 34)** and the `String` **type (page 60).**

```
int cansPerPack = 6;
```

A variable declaration ends with a semicolon.

Use a descriptive variable name. — See page *38*.

Supplying an initial value is optional, but it is usually a good idea. See page *37*.

When declaring a variable, you usually specify an initial value.

When declaring a variable, you usually want to **initialize** it. That is, you specify the value that should be stored in the variable. Consider again this variable declaration:

```
int cansPerPack = 6;
```

The variable `cansPerPack` is initialized with the value 6.

Like a parking space that is restricted to a certain type of vehicle (such as a compact car, motorcycle, or electric vehicle), a variable in Java stores data of a specific **type**. Java supports quite a few data types: numbers, text strings, files, dates, and many others. You must specify the type whenever you declare a variable (see Syntax 2.1).

When declaring a variable, you also specify the type of its values.

The `cansPerPack` variable is an **integer**, a whole number without a fractional part. In Java, this type is called `int`. (See the next section for more information about number types in Java.)

Note that the type comes before the variable name:

```
int cansPerPack = 6;
```

After you have declared and initialized a variable, you can use it. For example,

```
int cansPerPack = 6;
System.out.println(cansPerPack);
int cansPerCrate = 4 * cansPerPack;
```

Table 1 shows variations of variable declarations.

Each parking space is suitable for a particular type of vehicle, just as each variable holds a value of a particular type.

Table 1 Variable Declarations in Java

Variable Name	Comment
`int cans = 6;`	Declares an integer variable and initializes it with 6.
`int total = cans + bottles;`	The initial value need not be a constant. (Of course, `cans` and `bottles` must have been previously declared.)
🚫 `bottles = 1;`	**Error:** The type is missing. This statement is not a declaration but an assignment of a new value to an existing variable—see Section 2.2.
🚫 `int bottles = "10";`	**Error:** You cannot initialize a number with a string.
`int bottles;`	Declares an integer variable without initializing it. This can be a cause for errors—see Common Error 2.1 on page 37.
`int cans, bottles;`	Declares two integer variables in a single statement. In this book, we will declare each variable in a separate statement.

2.1.2 Number Types

> Use the `int` type for numbers that cannot have a fractional part.

In Java, there are several different types of numbers. You use the `int` type to denote a whole number without a fractional part. For example, there must be an integer number of cans in any pack of cans—you cannot have a fraction of a can.

When a fractional part is required (such as in the number 0.335), we use **floating-point numbers**. The most commonly used type for floating-point numbers in Java is called `double`. (If you want to know the reason, read Special Topic 2.1 on page 38.) Here is the declaration of a floating-point variable:

```
double canVolume = 0.335;
```

Table 2 Number Literals in Java

Number	Type	Comment
6	`int`	An integer has no fractional part.
–6	`int`	Integers can be negative.
0	`int`	Zero is an integer.
0.5	`double`	A number with a fractional part has type `double`.
1.0	`double`	An integer with a fractional part .0 has type `double`.
1E6	`double`	A number in exponential notation: 1×10^6 or 1000000. Numbers in exponential notation always have type `double`.
2.96E-2	`double`	Negative exponent: $2.96 \times 10^{-2} = 2.96 / 100 = 0.0296$
🚫 100,000		**Error:** Do not use a comma as a decimal separator.
🚫 3 1/2		**Error:** Do not use fractions; use decimal notation: 3.5

When a value such as 6 or 0.335 occurs in a Java program, it is called a number **literal**. Table 2 shows how to write integer and floating-point literals in Java.

2.1.3 Variable Names

When you declare a variable, you should pick a name that explains its purpose. For example, it is better to use a descriptive name, such as canVolume, than a terse name, such as cv.

In Java, there are a few simple rules for variable names:

1. Variable names must start with a letter or the underscore (_) character, and the remaining characters must be letters, numbers, or underscores. (Technically, the $ symbol is allowed as well, but you should not use it—it is intended for names that are automatically generated by tools.)

2. You cannot use other symbols such as ? or %. Spaces are not permitted inside names either. You can use uppercase letters to denote word boundaries, as in cansPerPack. This naming convention is called *camel case* because the uppercase letters in the middle of the name look like the humps of a camel.)

3. Variable names are **case sensitive**, that is, canVolume and canvolume are different names.

4. You cannot use **reserved words** such as double or class as names; these words are reserved exclusively for their special Java meanings. (See Appendix C for a listing of all reserved words in Java.)

5. It is a convention among Java programmers that variable names should start with a lowercase letter (such as canVolume) and class names should start with an uppercase letter (such as HelloPrinter). That way, it is easy to tell them apart.

Table 3 shows examples of legal and illegal variable names in Java.

Table 3 Variable Names in Java

Variable Name	Comment
canVolume1	Variable names consist of letters, numbers, and the underscore character.
x	In mathematics, you use short variable names such as *x* or *y*. This is legal in Java, but not very common, because it can make programs harder to understand (see Programming Tip 2.1 on page 38).
⚠ CanVolume	**Caution:** Variable names are case sensitive. This variable name is different from canVolume, and it violates the convention that variable names should start with a lowercase letter.
🚫 6pack	**Error:** Variable names cannot start with a number.
🚫 can volume	**Error:** Variable names cannot contain spaces.
🚫 double	**Error:** You cannot use a reserved word as a variable name.
🚫 ltr/fl.oz	**Error:** You cannot use symbols such as / or.

2.1.4 Comments

As your programs get more complex, you should add **comments**, explanations for human readers of your code. For example, here is a comment that explains the value used in a variable initialization:

```
double canVolume = 0.355; // Liters in a 12-ounce can
```

Use comments to add explanations for humans who read your code. The compiler ignores comments.

This comment explains the significance of the value 0.355 to a human reader. The compiler does not process comments at all. It ignores everything from a `//` delimiter to the end of the line.

It is a good practice to provide comments. This helps programmers who read your code understand your intent. In addition, you will find comments helpful when you review your own programs.

You use the `//` delimiter for short comments. If you have a longer comment, enclose it between `/*` and `*/` delimiters. The compiler ignores these delimiters and everything in between. For example,

```
/*
   There are approximately 0.335 liters in a 12-ounce can because one ounce
   equals 0.02957353 liter; see The International Systems of Units (SI) - Conversion
   Factors for General Use (NIST Special Publication 1038).
*/
```

Finally, start a comment that explains the purpose of a class with the `/**` delimiter instead of `/*`. Tools that analyze source files rely on that convention. For example,

```
/**
   This program computes the volume (in liters) of a six-pack of soda cans.
*/
```

We are now ready to finish our program. The program consists of the two variable declarations that we just discussed, followed by a statement to print their product. Because the result is larger than 2, we know that the six-pack contains more soda than the two-liter bottle.

ch02/volume1/Volume1.java

```java
 1  /**
 2     This program computes the volume (in liters) of a six-pack of soda cans.
 3  */
 4  public class Volume1
 5  {
 6     public static void main(String[] args)
 7     {
 8        int cansPerPack = 6;
 9        double canVolume = 0.355; // Liters in a 12-ounce can
10
11        System.out.print("A six-pack of 12-ounce cans contains ");
12        System.out.print(cansPerPack * canVolume);
13        System.out.println(" liters.");
14     }
15  }
```

Program Run

```
A six-pack of 12-ounce cans contains 2.13 liters.
```

Just as a television commentator explains the news, you use comments in your program to explain its behavior.

1. Declare a variable suitable for holding the number of bottles in a case.
2. What is wrong with the following variable declaration?

   ```
   int ounces per liter = 28.35
   ```
3. Declare and initialize two variables, `unitPrice` and `quantity`, to contain the unit price of a single bottle and the number of bottles purchased. Use reasonable initial values.
4. Use the variables declared in Self Check 3 to display the total purchase price.
5. Some drinks are sold in four-packs instead of six-packs. How would you change the `Volume1.java` program to compute the total volume?
6. What is wrong with this comment?

   ```
   double canVolume = 0.355; /* Liters in a 12-ounce can //
   ```
7. Suppose the type of the `cansPerPack` variable in `Volume1.java` was changed from `int` to `double`. What would be the effect on the program?

Using Undeclared or Uninitialized Variables

You must declare a variable before you use it for the first time. For example, the following sequence of statements would not be legal:

```
double canVolume = 12 * literPerOunce; // ERROR: literPerOunce is not yet declared
double literPerOunce = 0.0296;
```

In your program, the statements are compiled in order. When the compiler reaches the first statement, it does not know that `literPerOunce` will be declared in the next line, and it reports an error. The remedy is to reorder the declarations so that each variable is declared before it is used.

A related error is to leave a variable uninitialized:

```
int bottles;
int bottleVolume = bottles * 2; // ERROR: bottles is not yet initialized
```

The Java compiler will complain that you are using a variable that has not yet been given a value. The remedy is to assign a value to the variable before it is used.

Programming Tip 2.1

Choose Descriptive Variable Names

We could have saved ourselves a lot of typing by using shorter variable names, as in

```
double cv = 0.355;
```

Compare this declaration with the one that we actually used, though. Which one is easier to read? There is no comparison. Just reading `canVolume` is a lot less trouble than reading `cv` and then *figuring out* it must mean "can volume".

In practical programming, this is particularly important when programs are written by more than one person. It may be obvious to *you* that `cv` stands for can volume and not current velocity, but will it be obvious to the person who needs to update your code years later? For that matter, will you remember yourself what `cv` means when you look at the code three months from now?

Special Topic 2.1

Numeric Types in Java

In addition to the `int` and `double` types, Java has several other numeric types.

Java has two floating-point types. The `float` type uses half the storage of the `double` type that we use in this book, but it can only store about 7 decimal digits. (In the computer, numbers are represented in the binary number system, using digits 0 and 1.) Many years ago, when computers had far less memory than they have today, `float` was the standard type for floating-point computations, and programmers would indulge in the luxury of "double precision" only when they needed the additional digits. Today, the `float` type is rarely used.

Table 4	Java Number Types
Type	Description
int	The integer type, with range −2,147,483,648 (Integer.MIN_VALUE) . . . 2,147,483,647 (Integer.MAX_VALUE, about 2.14 billion)
byte	The type describing a byte consisting of 8 bits, with range −128 . . . 127
short	The short integer type, with range −32,768 . . . 32,767
long	The long integer type, with about 19 decimal digits
double	The double-precision floating-point type, with about 15 decimal digits and a range of about $\pm 10^{308}$
float	The single-precision floating-point type, with about 7 decimal digits and a range of about $\pm 10^{38}$
char	The character type, representing code units in the Unicode encoding scheme (see Section 2.6.6)

By the way, these numbers are called "floating-point" because of their internal representation in the computer. Consider numbers 29600, 2.96, and 0.0296. They can be represented in a very similar way: namely, as a sequence of the significant digits—296—and an indication of the position of the decimal point. When the values are multiplied or divided by 10, only the position of the decimal point changes; it "floats". Computers use base 2, not base 10, but the principle is the same.

In addition to the int type, Java has integer types byte, short, and long. Their ranges are shown in Table 4. (Their strange-looking limits are related to powers of 2, another consequence of the fact that computers use binary numbers.)

Common Error 2.2

Overflow

Because numbers are represented in the computer with a limited number of digits, they cannot represent arbitrary numbers.

The int type has a *limited range:* It can represent numbers up to a little more than two billion. For many applications, this is not a problem, but you cannot use an int to represent the world population.

If a computation yields a value that is outside the int range, the result *overflows*. No error is displayed. Instead, the result is truncated, yielding a useless value. For example,

```java
int oneThousand = 1000;
int oneMillion = 1000 * oneThousand;
int oneBillion = 1000 * oneMillion;
System.out.println(3 * oneBillion);
```

displays –1294967296.

In situations such as this, you can switch to double values. However, read Common Error 2.5 on page 54 for more information about a related issue: roundoff errors.

2.2 Variable Assignment

An assignment statement stores a new value in a variable, replacing the previously stored value.

You use an **assignment** statement to place a new value into a variable. Here is an example:

```java
cansPerPack = 8;
```

The left-hand side of an assignment statement consists of a variable. The value on the right-hand side is stored in the variable, overwriting its previous contents.

There is an important difference between a variable declaration and an assignment statement:

```java
int cansPerPack = 6; // Variable declaration
. . .
cansPerPack = 8; // Assignment statement
```

ANIMATION
Variable Initialization and Assignment

The first statement is the *declaration* of cansPerPack. It is an instruction to create a new variable of type int, to give it the name cansPerPack, and to initialize it with 6. The second statement is an *assignment statement:* an instruction to replace the contents of the *existing* variable cansPerPack with another value.

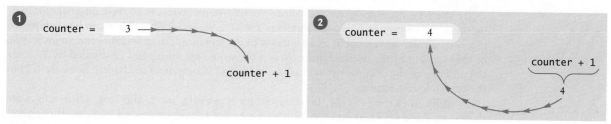

Figure 1 Incrementing a Variable

The assignment operator = does *not* denote mathematical equality.

The = sign doesn't mean that the left-hand side *is equal* to the right-hand side but that the right-hand side value is copied into the left-hand side variable. You should not confuse this *assignment operation* with the = used in algebra to denote *equality*. The assignment operator is an instruction to do something, namely place a value into a variable. The mathematical equality states the fact that two values are equal. For example, in Java, it is perfectly legal to write

```
counter = counter + 1;
```

It means to look up the value stored in the variable counter, add 1 to it, and store the result into counter. (See Figure 1.) The net effect of executing this statement is to increment counter by 1. For example, if counter was 3 before execution of the statement, it is set to 4 afterwards. Of course, in mathematics it would make no sense to write that counter = counter + 1; no value can equal itself plus 1.

The ++ operator adds 1 to a variable; the -- operator subtracts 1.

Changing a variable by adding or subtracting 1 is so common that there is a special shorthand for it, namely

```
counter++;
counter--;
```

Table 5	Modifying a Variable	
Statements	Contents of counter	Comments
counter = 1;	1	The previous content of the variable has been replaced.
counter = counter + 1;	2	Adds 1 to counter. Note that = is not mathematical equality.
counter++;	3	++ is a shorthand for adding 1 to a variable.
counter--;	2	-- is a shorthand for subtracting 1.
counter = in.nextInt();	The input value	Waits for the user to enter a value, and stores the value in the variable.
🚫 int counter = 4;		**Error:** This is not an assignment but an attempt to declare a second variable named counter.

Syntax 2.2 Assignment

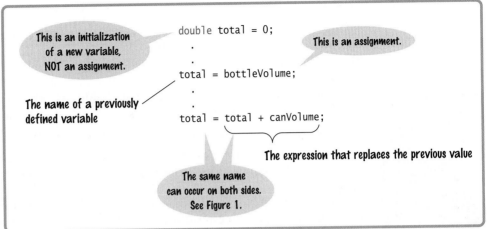

8. What is the value of mystery after this sequence of statements?

```
int mystery = 1;
mystery = 2 * mystery;
mystery++;
```

9. What is wrong with the following sequence of statements?

```
int mystery = 1;
mystery++;
int mystery = 2 * mystery;
```

10. How would you explain assignment using the parking space analogy?

11. What is the value of n after these statements?

```
n++; n--; n++;
```

12. Give two ways of adding 3 to the integer variable n.

Special Topic 2.2

Combining Assignment and Arithmetic

In Java, you can combine arithmetic and assignment. For example, the instruction

```
total += cans;
```

is a shortcut for

```
total = total + cans;
```

Similarly,

```
total *= 2;
```

is another way of writing

```
total = total * 2;
```

Many programmers find this a convenient shortcut. If you like it, go ahead and use it in your own code. For simplicity, we won't use it in this book, though.

2.3 Reading Input

In this section, you will see how to read user input. Consider for example the `Volume1.java` program on page 36. Rather than assuming that the price for the two-liter bottle and the six-pack of cans are identical, we can ask the program user for the prices.

When a program asks for user input, it should first print a message that tells the user which input is expected. Such a message is called a **prompt**.

```
System.out.print("Please enter the number of bottles: "); // Display prompt
```

Use the `print` method, not `println`, to display the prompt. You want the input to appear after the colon, not on the following line. Also remember to leave a space after the colon.

Because output is sent to `System.out`, you might think that you use `System.in` for input. Unfortunately, it isn't quite that simple. When Java was first designed, not much attention was given to reading keyboard input. It was assumed that all programmers would produce graphical user interfaces with text fields and menus. `System.in` was given a minimal set of features and must be combined with other classes to be useful.

A supermarket scanner reads bar codes. The Java Scanner reads numbers and text.

To read keyboard input, you obtain an *object* of a class called `Scanner`, using the following statement:

```
Scanner in = new Scanner(System.in);
```

You will learn more about objects and classes in Chapter 7. For now, simply include this statement whenever you want to read keyboard input.

When using the `Scanner` class, you need to carry out another step: import the class from its **package**. A package is a collection of classes with a related purpose. All classes in the Java library are contained in packages. The `System` class belongs to the package `java.lang`. The `Scanner` class belongs to the package `java.util`.

Java classes are grouped into packages. Use the import statement to use classes from packages.

Only the classes in the `java.lang` package are automatically available in your programs. To use the `Scanner` class from the `java.util` package, place the following declaration at the top of your program file:

```
import java.util.Scanner;
```

Syntax 2.3 Input Statement

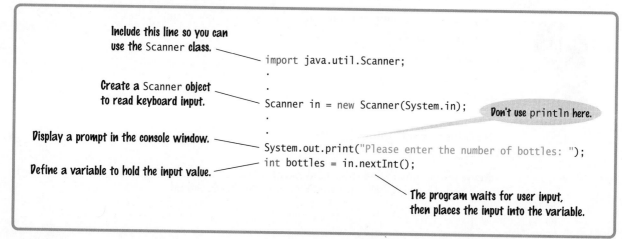

Include this line so you can use the Scanner class. — `import java.util.Scanner;`

Create a Scanner object to read keyboard input. — `Scanner in = new Scanner(System.in);`

Don't use `println` here.

Display a prompt in the console window. — `System.out.print("Please enter the number of bottles: ");`

Define a variable to hold the input value. — `int bottles = in.nextInt();`

The program waits for user input, then places the input into the variable.

Once you have a scanner, you use the `nextInt` method to read an integer value:

```
System.out.print("Please enter the number of bottles: ");
int bottles = in.nextInt();
```

Use the Scanner class to read keyboard input in a console window.

When the `nextInt` method is called, the program waits until the user types a number and hits the Enter key. After the user supplies the input, the number is placed into the `bottles` variable, and the program continues.

To read a floating-point number, use the `nextDouble` method instead:

```
System.out.print("Enter price: ");
double price = in.nextDouble();
```

SELF CHECK

13. Write statements to prompt for and read the user's age using a Scanner variable named `in`.

14. What is wrong with the following statement sequence?

```
System.out.print("Please enter the unit price: ");
double unitPrice = in.nextDouble();
int quantity = in.nextInt();
```

15. What is problematic about the following statement sequence?

```
System.out.print("Please enter the unit price: ");
double unitPrice = in.nextInt();
```

16. What is problematic about the following statement sequence?

```
System.out.print("Please enter the number of cans");
int cans = in.nextInt();
```

Programming Tip 2.2

Use the API Documentation

The classes and methods of the Java library are listed in the **API documentation**. The API is the "**application programming interface**". A programmer who uses the Java classes to put together a computer program (or *application*) is an *application programmer*. That's you. In contrast, the programmers who designed and implemented the library classes (such as Scanner) are *system programmers*.

> The API (Application Programming Interface) documentation lists the classes and methods of the Java library.

You can find the API documentation at `http://java.sun.com/javase/7/docs/api/`. The API documentation describes all classes in the Java library—there are thousands of them. Fortunately, only a few are of interest to the beginning programmer. To learn more about a class, click on its name in the left hand column. You can then find out the package to which the class belongs, and which methods it supports (see Figure 2). Click on the link of a method to get a detailed description.

Appendix D contains an abbreviated version of the API documentation.

Figure 2 The API Documentation of the Standard Java Library

2.4 Constants

> You cannot change the value of a variable that is declared as `final`.

When a variable is declared as `final`, it becomes a constant whose value can never change. Constants are commonly written using capital letters to distinguish them visually from regular variables:

```
final double BOTTLE_VOLUME = 2;
```

It is good programming style to use named constants in your program to explain the meanings of numeric values. For example, compare the statements

```
double volume = bottles * 2;
```

and

```
double volume = bottles * BOTTLE_VOLUME;
```

A programmer reading the first statement may not understand the significance of the number 2. The second statement, with a named constant, makes the computation much clearer.

The following program demonstrates the use of assignment statements, input operations, and constants. The program computes the total volume of a number of bottles and cans. First, we ask for the number of bottles and set `totalVolume` to the volume of the bottles. Then we ask for the number of cans and set `additionalVolume` to the volume of the cans. Finally, we add that volume to the total, using the following statement:

```
totalVolume = totalVolume + additionalVolume;
```

It means, "Compute the sum of `totalVolume` and `additionalVolume`, and place the result again into the variable `totalVolume`" (see Figure 3).

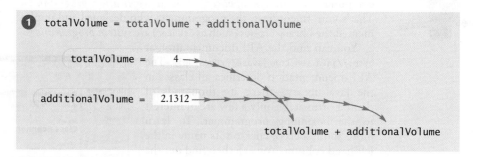

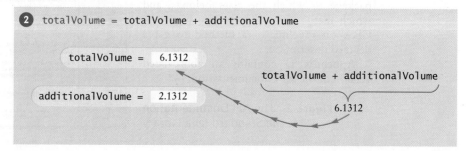

Figure 3
Updating the
Total Volume

ch02/volume2/Volume2.java

```java
1   import java.util.Scanner;
2
3   /**
4      This program prints the total volume of a number of bottles and cans.
5   */
6   public class Volume2
7   {
8      public static void main(String[] args)
9      {
10        final double BOTTLE_VOLUME = 2;
11        final double LITER_PER_OUNCE = 0.0296;
12        final double CAN_VOLUME = 12 * LITER_PER_OUNCE;
13
14        // Display prompt
15
16        System.out.print("Please enter the number of bottles: ");
17
18        // Read number of bottles
19
20        Scanner in = new Scanner(System.in);
21        int bottles = in.nextInt();
22
23        // Start the computation of the total volume
24
25        double totalVolume = bottles * BOTTLE_VOLUME;
26
27        // Read number of cans
28
29        System.out.print("Please enter the number of cans: ");
30        int cans = in.nextInt();
31
32        double additionalVolume = cans * CAN_VOLUME;
33
34        // Update the total volume
35
36        totalVolume = totalVolume + additionalVolume;
37
38        System.out.print("Total volume: ");
39        System.out.println(totalVolume);
40     }
41  }
```

Program Run

```
Please enter the number of bottles: 2
Please enter the number of cans: 6
Total volume: 6.1312
```

SELF CHECK

17. Why are the variables cans and bottles not declared as final?
18. Improve the following statement by introducing a constant:
    ```java
    double totalVolume = canVolume * 6;
    ```
19. What is wrong with the following statement sequence?
    ```java
    final double BOTTLE_VOLUME = 2;
    System.out.print("How many liters per bottle? ");
    BOTTLE_VOLUME = in.nextDouble();
    ```

Practice It   Now you can try these exercises at the end of the chapter: P2.3, P2.8, P2.12.

Programming Tip 2.3

Do Not Use Magic Numbers

A **magic number** is a numeric constant that appears in your code without explanation. For example,

```
totalVolume = bottles * 2;
```

Why 2? Are bottles twice as voluminous as cans? No, the reason is that every bottle contains 2 liters. Use a named constant to make the code self-documenting:

```
final double BOTTLE_VOLUME = 2;
totalVolume = bottles * BOTTLE_VOLUME;
```

There is another reason for using named constants. Suppose circumstances change, and the bottle volume is now 1.5 liters. If you used a named constant, you make a single change, and you are done. Otherwise, you have to look at every value of 2 in your program and ponder whether it meant a bottle volume, or something else. In a program that is more than a few pages long, that is incredibly tedious and error-prone.

Even the most reasonable cosmic constant is going to change one day. You think there are seven days per week? Your customers on Mars are going to be pretty unhappy about your silly prejudice. Make a constant

```
final int DAYS_PER_WEEK = 7;
```

2.5 Arithmetic

In the following sections, you will learn how to carry out arithmetic calculations in Java.

2.5.1 Arithmetic Operators

Java supports the same four basic arithmetic operations as a calculator—addition, subtraction, multiplication, and division—but it uses different symbols for multiplication and division.

You must write a * b to denote multiplication. Unlike in mathematics, you can not write a b, a · b, or a × b. Similarly, division is always indicated with a /, never a ÷ or a fraction bar.

For example, $\frac{a+b}{2}$ becomes (a + b) / 2.

The combination of variables, literals, operators, and/or method calls is called an **expression**. For example, (a + b) / 2 is an expression.

Parentheses are used just as in algebra: to indicate in which order the parts of the expression should be computed. For example, in the expression (a + b) / 2, the sum a + b is computed first, and then the sum is divided by 2. In contrast, in the expression

```
a + b / 2
```

only b is divided by 2, and then the sum of a and b / 2 is formed. As in regular algebraic notation, multiplication and division have a *higher precedence* than addition and subtraction. For example, in the expression a + b / 2, the / is carried out first, even though the + operation occurs further to the left.

If you mix integer and floating-point values in an arithmetic expression, the result is a floating-point value. For example, 7 + 4.0 is the floating-point value 11.0.

> Mixing integers and floating-point values in an arithmetic expression yields a floating-point value.

2.5.2 Integer Division and Remainder

Division works as you would expect, as long as at least one of the numbers involved is a floating-point number. That is,

```
7.0 / 4.0
7 / 4.0
7.0 / 4
```

> If both arguments of / are integers, the remainder is discarded.

all yield 1.75. However, if *both* numbers are integers, then the result of the division is always an integer, with the remainder discarded. That is,

```
7 / 4
```

evaluates to 1 because 7 divided by 4 is 1 with a remainder of 3 (which is discarded). This can be a source of subtle programming errors—see Common Error 2.3 on page 53.

If you are interested in the remainder only, use the % operator:

```
7 % 4
```

> The % operator computes the remainder of an integer division.

is 3, the remainder of the integer division of 7 by 4. The % symbol has no analog in algebra. It was chosen because it looks similar to /, and the remainder operation is related to division. The operator is called **modulus**. (Some people call it *modulo* or *mod*.) It has no relationship with the percent operation that you find on some calculators.

Here is a typical use for the integer / and % operations. Suppose you have an amount of pennies in a piggybank:

```
int pennies = 1729;
```

You want to determine the value in dollars and cents. You obtain the dollars through an integer division by 100.

```
int dollars = pennies / 100;   // Sets dollars to 17
```

Integer division and the % operator yield the dollar and cent values of a piggybank full of pennies.

The integer division discards the remainder. To obtain the remainder, use the % operator:

```
int cents = pennies % 100;   // Sets cents to 29
```

2.5.3 Powers and Roots

The Java library declares many mathematical functions, such as Math.sqrt (square root) and Math.pow (raising to a power).

In Java, there are no symbols for powers and roots. To compute them, you must call methods. To take the square root of a number, you use the Math.sqrt method. For example, $\sqrt{x}$ is written as Math.sqrt(x). To compute x^n, you write Math.pow(x, n).

In algebra, you use fractions, exponents, and roots to arrange expressions in a compact two-dimensional form. In Java, you have to write all expressions in a linear arrangement.

For example, the mathematical expression

$$b \times \left(1 + \frac{r}{100}\right)^n$$

becomes

```
b * Math.pow(1 + r / 100, n)
```

Figure 4 shows how to analyze such an expression. Table 6 shows additional mathematical methods.

Table 6	Other Mathematical Methods and Constants
Method	Description
Math.sin(x)	sine of x (x in radians)
Math.cos(x)	cosine of x
Math.tan(x)	tangent of x
Math.log10(x)	(decimal log) $\log_{10}(x)$, $x > 0$
Math.abs(x)	absolute value $|x|$

2.5.4 Converting Floating-Point Numbers to Integers

Occasionally, you have a value of type double that you need to convert to the type int. It is an error to assign a floating-point value to an integer:

```
double balance = total + tax;
int dollars = balance; // Error: Cannot assign double to int
```

The compiler disallows this assignment because it is potentially dangerous:

- The fractional part is lost.
- The magnitude may be too large. (The largest integer is about 2 billion, but a floating-point number can be much larger.)

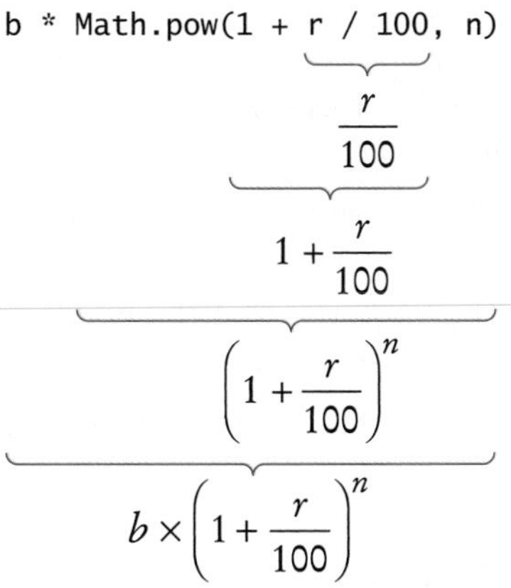

Figure 4
Analyzing an Expression

```
b * Math.pow(1 + r / 100, n)
```

$$\frac{r}{100}$$

$$1 + \frac{r}{100}$$

$$\left(1 + \frac{r}{100}\right)^n$$

$$b \times \left(1 + \frac{r}{100}\right)^n$$

You use a cast (*typeName*) to convert a value to a different type.

You must use the **cast** operator (int) to convert a convert floating-point value to an integer. Write the cast operator before the expression that you want to convert:

```
double balance = total + tax;
int dollars = (int) balance;
```

The cast (int) converts the floating-point value balance to an integer by discarding the fractional part. For example, if balance is 13.75, then dollars is set to 13.

When applying the cast operator to an arithmetic expression, you need to place the expression inside parentheses:

```
int dollars = (int) (total + tax);
```

Table 7 Arithmetic Expressions

Mathematical Expression	Java Expression	Comments
$\dfrac{x + y}{2}$	(x + y) / 2	The parentheses are required; x + y / 2 computes $x + \frac{y}{2}$.
$\dfrac{xy}{2}$	x * y / 2	Parentheses are not required; operators with the same precedence are evaluated left to right.
$\left(1 + \dfrac{r}{100}\right)^n$	Math.pow(1 + r / 100, n)	Use Math.pow(x, n) to compute x^n.
$\sqrt{a^2 + b^2}$	Math.sqrt(a * a + b * b)	a * a is simpler than Math.pow(a, 2).
$\dfrac{i + j + k}{3}$	(i + j + k) / 3.0	If i, j, and k are integers, using a denominator of 3.0 forces floating-point division.
π	Math.PI	Math.PI is a constant declared in the Math class.

Discarding the fractional part is not always appropriate. If you want to round a floating-point number to the nearest whole number, use the `Math.round` method. This method returns a `long` integer, because large floating-point numbers cannot be stored in an `int`.

```
long rounded = Math.round(balance);
```

If `balance` is 13.75, then `rounded` is set to 14.

If you know that the result can be stored in an `int` and does not require a `long`, you can use a cast:

```
int rounded = (int) Math.round(balance);
```

2.5.5 Formatted Output

When you print the result of a computation, you often want some control over its appearance. For example, when you print an amount in dollars and cents, you usually want it to be rounded to two significant digits. That is, you want the output to look like

```
Price per liter: 1.22
```

instead of

```
Price per liter: 1.21997
```

Use the `printf` method to specify how values should be formatted.

The following command displays the price with two digits after the decimal point:

```
System.out.printf("%.2f", price);
```

You can also specify a *field width*:

```
System.out.printf("%10.2f", price);
```

The price is printed using ten characters: six spaces followed by the four characters 1.22.

						1	.	2	2

The construct `%10.2f` is called a *format specifier:* it describes how a value should be formatted. There are quite a few format types—Table 8 shows the most important ones.

You use the `printf` method to line up your output in neat columns.

Table 8	Format Types	
Code	Type	Example
d	Decimal integer	123
f	Fixed floating-point	12.30
e	Exponential floating-point	1.23e+1
g	General floating-point (exponential notation is used for very large or very small values)	12.3
s	String	Tax:

Any characters that are not format specifiers are printed verbatim. For example, the command

```
System.out.printf("Price per liter:%10.2f", price);
```

prints

```
Price per liter:      1.22
```

You can use "flags" to modify a format. See Table 9 for the most common format flags. The flags immediately follow the % character. For example, the , flag indicates that you want to use decimal separators:

```
System.out.printf("%,10.2f", 12345);
```

prints

```
 12,345.00
```

You can print multiple values with a single call to the printf method. Consider this example:

```
System.out.printf("%-10s%10.2f", "Total:", total);
```

Table 9	Format Flags	
Flag	Meaning	Example
-	Left alignment	1.23 followed by spaces
0	Show leading zeroes	001.23
+	Show a plus sign for positive numbers	+1.23
(	Enclose negative numbers in parentheses	(1.23)
,	Show decimal separators	12,300
^	Convert letters to uppercase	1.23E+1

Here, we have two format specifiers.

- `%-10s` formats a left-justified string. The string `"Total:"` is padded with spaces so it becomes ten characters wide. The - indicates that the spaces are placed to the right.
- `%10.2f` formats a floating-point number, also in a field that is ten characters wide.

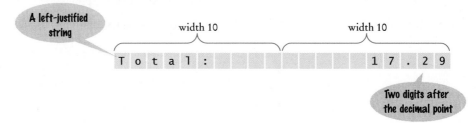

Our next example program will prompt for the price of a six-pack and then print out the price per liter. The program puts to work what you just learned about arithmetic and formatting.

ch02/volume3/Volume3.java

```
1   import java.util.Scanner;
2
3   /**
4      This program prints the price per liter for a six-pack of cans.
5   */
6
7   public class Volume3
8   {
9      public static void main(String[] args)
10     {
11        // Read price per pack
12
13        Scanner in = new Scanner(System.in);
14
15        System.out.print("Please enter the price for a six-pack: ");
16        double packPrice = in.nextDouble();
17
18        // Compute pack volume
19
20        final double LITER_PER_OUNCE = 0.0296;
21        final double CAN_VOLUME = 12 * LITER_PER_OUNCE;
22        final double PACK_VOLUME = 6 * CAN_VOLUME;
23
24        // Compute and print price per liter
25
26        double pricePerLiter = packPrice / PACK_VOLUME;
27
28        System.out.printf("Price per liter: %8.2f", pricePerLiter);
29        System.out.println();
30     }
31  }
```

Program Run

```
Please enter the price for a six-pack: 2.60
Price per liter:     1.22
```

20. A bank account earns interest of p percent per year. In Java, how do you compute the interest earned in one year? Assume variables `p` and `balance` of type `double` have already been declared.

21. In Java, how do you compute the side length of a square whose area is stored in the variable `area`?

22. The volume of a sphere is given by $V = \frac{4}{3}\pi r^3$.

If the radius is given by a variable `radius` of type `double`, write a Java expression for the volume.

23. What is the value of `1729 / 10` and `1729 % 10`?

24. Suppose a punch recipe calls for a given amount of orange soda, measured in ounces.

```
int amount = 32;
```

We can compute the number of 12-ounce cans needed, assuming that the amount doesn't evenly divide into 12:

```
int cansNeeded = amount / 12 + 1;
```

Use the `%` operator to determine how many ounces will be left over. For example, if 32 ounces are required, we need 3 cans and have 4 ounces left over.

25. What is the output of the following statement sequence?

```
int volume = 10;
System.out.printf("The volume is %5d", volume);
```

26. Using the `printf` method, print the values of the integer variables `bottles` and `cans` so that the output looks like this:

```
Bottles:       8
Cans:         24
```

The numbers to the right should line up. (You may assume that the numbers have at most 8 digits.)

Practice It Now you can try these exercises at the end of the chapter: R2.1, R2.3, P2.4, P2.11.

Unintended Integer Division

It is unfortunate that Java uses the same symbol, namely /, for both integer and floating-point division. These are really quite different operations. It is a common error to use integer division by accident. Consider this segment that computes the average of three integers.

```
System.out.print("Please enter your last three test scores: ");
int s1 = in.nextInt();
int s2 = in.nextInt()
int s3 = in.nextInt();
double average = (s1 + s2 + s3) / 3; // Error
System.out.printf("Your average score is %8.2f\n", average);
```

What could be wrong with that? Of course, the average of s1, s2, and s3 is

$$\frac{s1+s2+s3}{3}$$

Here, however, the / does not mean division in the mathematical sense. It denotes integer division because both s1 + s2 + s3 and 3 are integers. For example, if the scores add up to 14, the average is computed to be 4, the result of the integer division of 14 by 3. That integer 4 is then moved into the floating-point variable average. The remedy is to make the numerator or denominator into a floating-point number:

```
double total = s1 + s2 + s3;
double average = total / 3;
```

or

```
double average = (s1 + s2 + s3) / 3.0;
```

Common Error 2.4

Unbalanced Parentheses

Consider the expression

```
(-(b * b - 4 * a * c) / (2 * a)
```

What is wrong with it? Count the parentheses. There are three (and two). The parentheses are *unbalanced*. This kind of typing error is very common with complicated expressions. Now consider this expression.

```
-(b * b - (4 * a * c))) / 2 * a)
```

This expression has three (and three), but it still is not correct. In the middle of the expression,

```
-(b * b - (4 * a * c))) / 2 * a)
                     ↑
```

there are only two (but three), which is an error. In the middle of an expression, the count of (must be greater than or equal to the count of), and at the end of the expression the two counts must be the same.

Here is a simple trick to make the counting easier without using pencil and paper. It is difficult for the brain to keep two counts simultaneously. Keep only one count when scanning the expression. Start with 1 at the first opening parenthesis, add 1 whenever you see an opening parenthesis, and subtract one whenever you see a closing parenthesis. Say the numbers aloud as you scan the expression. If the count ever drops below zero, or is not zero at the end, the parentheses are unbalanced. For example, when scanning the previous expression, you would mutter

```
-(b * b - (4 * a * c ) ) ) / 2 * a)
 1         2           1 0 -1
```

and you would find the error.

Common Error 2.5

Roundoff Errors

Roundoff errors are a fact of life when calculating with floating-point numbers. You probably have encountered that phenomenon yourself with manual calculations. If you calculate 1/3 to two decimal places, you get 0.33. Multiplying again by 3, you obtain 0.99, not 1.00.

In the processor hardware, numbers are represented in the binary number system, using only digits 0 and 1. As with decimal numbers, you can get roundoff errors when binary digits are lost. They just may crop up at different places than you might expect. Here is an example.

```
public class RoundoffDemo
{
   public static void main(String[] args)
   {
```

```
        double price = 4.35;
        int cents = (int) (100 * price); // Should be 100 * 4.35 = 435
        System.out.println(cents); // Prints 434!
    }
}
```

Of course, one hundred times 4.35 is 435, but the program prints 434.

In the binary system, there is no exact representation for 4.35, just as there is no exact representation for 1/3 in the decimal system. The representation used by the computer is just a little less than 4.35, so 100 times that value is just a little less than 435. When a floating-point value is converted to an integer, the entire fractional part, which is almost 1, is thrown away, and the integer 434 is stored in cents. The remedy is to use the Math.round method:

```
int cents = (int) Math.round(100 * price);
```

Programming Tip 2.4

Spaces in Expressions

It is easier to read

```
x1 = (-b + Math.sqrt(b * b - 4 * a * c)) / (2 * a);
```

than

```
x1=(-b+Math.sqrt(b*b-4*a*c))/(2*a);
```

Simply put spaces around all operators + - * / % =. However, don't put a space after a *unary* minus: a – used to negate a single quantity, such as -b. That way, it can be easily distinguished from a *binary* minus, as in a - b.

It is customary not to put a space after a method name. That is, write Math.sqrt(x) and not Math.sqrt (x).

HOW TO 2.1

Carrying out Computations

Many programming problems require that you carry out arithmetic computations. This How To shows you how to turn a problem statement into pseudocode and, ultimately, a Java program.

For example, suppose you are asked to write a program that simulates a vending machine. A customer selects an item for purchase and inserts a bill into the vending machine. The vending machine dispenses the purchased item and gives change. We will assume that all item prices are multiples of 25 cents, and the machine gives all change in dollar coins and quarters. Your task is to compute how many coins of each type to return.

Step 1 Understand the problem: What are the inputs? What are the desired outputs?

In this problem, there are two inputs:

* The denomination of the bill that the customer inserts
* The price of the purchased item

There are two desired outputs:

* The number of dollar coins that the machine returns
* The number of quarters that the machine returns

A vending machine takes bills and gives change in coins.

Step 2 Work out examples by hand.

This is a very important step. If you can't compute a couple of solutions by hand, it's unlikely that you'll be able to write a program that automates the computation.

Let's assume that a customer purchased an item that cost $2.25 and inserted a $5 bill. The customer is due $2.75, or two dollar coins and three quarters.

That is easy for you to see, but how can a Java program come to the same conclusion? The key is to work in pennies, not dollars. The amount due the customer is 275 pennies. Dividing by 100 yields 2, the number of dollars. Dividing the remainder (75) by 25 yields 3, the number of quarters.

Step 3 Write pseudocode for computing the answers.

In the previous step, you worked out a specific instance of the problem. You now need to come up with a method that works in general.

Given an arbitrary item price and payment, how can you compute the coins due? First, compute the amount due in pennies:

amount due = 100 x bill value - item price in pennies

To get the dollars, divide by 100 and discard the remainder:

dollar coins = amount due / 100 (without remainder)

The remaining amount due can be computed in two ways. If you are familiar with the modulus operator, you can simply compute

amount due = amount due % 100

Alternatively, subtract the penny value of the dollar coins from the amount due:

amount due = amount due - 100 x dollar coins

To get the quarters due, divide by 25:

quarters = amount due / 25

Step 4 Declare the variables and constants that you need, and specify their types.

Here, we have five variables:

- `billValue`
- `itemPrice`
- `amountDue`
- `dollarCoins`
- `quarters`

Should we introduce constants to explain 100 and 25 as PENNIES_PER_DOLLAR and PENNIES_PER_QUARTER? Doing so will make it easier to convert the program to international markets, so we will take this step.

It is very important that amountDue and PENNIES_PER_DOLLAR are of type int because the computation of dollarCoins uses integer division. Similarly, the other variables are integers.

Step 5 Turn the pseudocode into Java statements.

If you did a thorough job with the pseudocode, this step should be easy. Of course, you have to know how to express mathematical operations (such as powers or integer division) in Java.

```java
amountDue = PENNIES_PER_DOLLAR * billValue - itemPrice;
dollarCoins = amountDue / PENNIES_PER_DOLLAR;
amountDue = amountDue % PENNIES_PER_DOLLAR;
quarters = amountDue / PENNIES_PER_QUARTER;
```

Step 6 Provide input and output.

Before starting the computation, we prompt the user for the bill value and item price:

```java
System.out.print("Enter bill value (1 = $1 bill, 5 = $5 bill, etc.): ");
billValue = in.nextInt();
System.out.print("Enter item price in pennies: ");
itemPrice = in.nextInt();
```

When the computation is finished, we display the result. For extra credit, we use the printf method to make sure that the output lines up neatly.

```java
System.out.printf("Dollar coins: %6d", dollarCoins);
System.out.printf("Quarters:     %6d", quarters);
```

Step 7 Provide a class with a main method.

Your computation needs to be placed into a class. Find an appropriate name for the class that describes the purpose of the computation. In our example, we will choose the name Vending-Machine.

Inside the class, supply a main method.

In the main method, you need to declare constants and variables (Step 4), carry out computations (Step 5), and provide input and output (Step 6). Clearly, you will want to first get the input, then do the computations, and finally show the output. Declare the constants at the beginning of the method, and declare each variable just before it is needed.

Here is the complete program, ch02/vending/VendingMachine.java:

```java
import java.util.Scanner;

/**
   This program simulates a vending machine that gives change.
*/
public class VendingMachine
{
   public static void main(String[] args)
   {
      Scanner in = new Scanner(System.in);

      final int PENNIES_PER_DOLLAR = 100;
      final int PENNIES_PER_QUARTER = 25;

      System.out.print("Enter bill value (1 = $1 bill, 5 = $5 bill, etc.): ");
      int billValue = in.nextInt();
      System.out.print("Enter item price in pennies: ");
      int itemPrice = in.nextInt();
```

```
// Compute change due

int amountDue = PENNIES_PER_DOLLAR * billValue - itemPrice;
int dollarCoins = amountDue / PENNIES_PER_DOLLAR;
amountDue = amountDue % PENNIES_PER_DOLLAR;
int quarters = amountDue / PENNIES_PER_QUARTER;

// Print change due

System.out.printf("Dollar coins: %6d", dollarCoins);
System.out.println();
System.out.printf("Quarters:      %6d\n", quarters);
System.out.println();
   }
}
```

Program Run

```
Enter bill value (1 = $1 bill, 5 = $5 bill, etc.): 5
Enter item price in pennies: 225
Dollar coins:     2
Quarters:         3
```

WORKED EXAMPLE 2.1 Computing the Cost of Stamps

This Worked Example uses arithmetic functions to simulate a stamp vending machine.

Random Fact 2.1 The Pentium Floating-Point Bug

In 1994, Intel Corporation released what was then its most powerful processor, the Pentium. Unlike previous generations of its processors, it had a very fast floating-point unit. Intel's goal was to compete aggressively with the makers of higher-end processors for engineering workstations. The Pentium was a huge success immediately.

In the summer of 1994, Dr. Thomas Nicely of Lynchburg College in Virginia ran an extensive set of computations to analyze the sums of reciprocals of certain sequences of prime numbers. The results were not always what his theory predicted, even after he took into account the inevitable roundoff errors. Then Dr. Nicely noted that the same program did produce the correct results when running on the slower 486 processor that preceded the Pentium in Intel's lineup. This should not have happened. The optimal roundoff behavior of floating-point calculations has been standardized by the Institute for Electrical and Electronic Engineers (IEEE) and Intel claimed to adhere to the IEEE standard in both the 486 and the Pentium processors.

Upon further checking, Dr. Nicely discovered that indeed there was a very small set of numbers for which the product of two numbers was computed differently on the two processors. For example,

$$4,195,835 - \left((4,195,835/3,145,727) \times 3,145,727\right)$$

is mathematically equal to 0, and it did compute as 0 on a 486 processor. On his Pentium processor the result was 256.

As it turned out, Intel had independently discovered the bug in its testing and had started to produce chips that fixed it. The bug was caused by an error in a table that was used to speed up the floating-point multiplication algorithm of the processor. Intel determined that the problem was exceedingly rare. They claimed that under normal use, a typical consumer would only notice the problem once every 27,000 years. Unfortunately for Intel, Dr. Nicely had not been a normal user.

2.6 Strings

Strings are sequences of characters.

Many programs process text, not numbers. Text consists of **characters**: letters, numbers, punctuation, spaces, and so on. A **string** is a sequence of characters. For example, the string "Harry" is a sequence of five characters.

2.6.1 The String Type

You can declare variables that hold strings.

```
String name = "Harry";
```

We distinguish between string variables (such as the variable name declared above) and string **literals** (character sequences enclosed in quotes, such as "Harry"). A string variable is simply a variable that can hold a string, just as an integer variable can hold an integer. A string literal denotes a particular string, just as a number literal (such as 2) denotes a particular number.

The length method yields the number of characters in a string.

The number of characters in a string is called the *length* of the string. For example, the length of "Harry" is 5. You can compute the length of a string with the length method.

```
int n = name.length();
```

A string of length 0 is called the *empty string*. It contains no characters and is written as "".

Now Intel had a real problem on its hands. It figured that the cost of replacing all Pentium processors that it had sold so far would cost a great deal of money. Intel already had more orders for the chip than it could produce, and it would be particularly galling to have to give out the scarce chips as free replacements instead of selling them. Intel's management decided to punt on the issue and initially offered to replace the processors only for those customers who could prove that their work required absolute precision in mathematical calculations. Naturally, that did not go over well with the hundreds of thousands of customers who had paid retail prices of $700 and more for a Pentium chip and did not want to live with the nagging feeling that perhaps, one day, their income tax program would produce a faulty return.

Ultimately, Intel caved in to public demand and replaced all defective chips, at a cost of about 475 million dollars.

This graph shows a set of numbers for which the original Pentium processor obtained the wrong quotient.

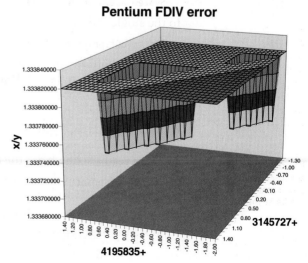

2.6.2 Concatenation

Use the + operator to *concatenate* strings; that is, to put them together to yield a longer string.

Given two strings, such as "Harry" and "Morgan", you can **concatenate** them to one long string. The result consists of all characters in the first string, followed by all characters in the second string. In Java, you use the + operator to concatenate two strings.

For example,

```
String fName = "Harry";
String lName = "Morgan";
String name = fName + lName;
```

results in the string

```
"HarryMorgan"
```

What if you'd like the first and last name separated by a space? No problem:

```
String name = fName + " " + lName;
```

This statement concatenates three strings: fName, the string literal " ", and lName. The result is

```
"Harry Morgan"
```

The + operator concatenates two strings, provided that one of the expressions, either to the left or the right of a + operator, is a string. The other one is automatically forced to become a string as well, and both strings are concatenated.

For example, consider this code:

```
String a = "Agent";
int n = 7;
String bond = a + n;
```

Whenever one of the arguments of the + operator is a string, the other argument is converted to a string.

Because a is a string, n is converted from the integer 7 to the string "7". Then the two strings "Agent" and "7" are concatenated to form the string "Agent7".

This concatenation is very useful for reducing the number of System.out.print instructions. For example, you can combine

```
System.out.print("The total is ");
System.out.println(total);
```

to the single call

```
System.out.println("The total is " + total);
```

The concatenation "The total is " + total computes a single string that consists of the string "The total is ", followed by the string equivalent of the number total.

2.6.3 String Input

Use the next or nextLine method of the Scanner class to read a string.

You can read a string from the console:

```
System.out.print("Please enter your name: ");
String name = in.next();
```

When a string is read with the next method, only one word is read. For example, suppose the user types

```
Harry Morgan
```

as the response to the prompt. This input consists of two words. The call `in.next()` yields the string `"Harry"`. You can use another call to `in.next()` to read the second word.

Alternatively, you can call the `nextLine` method. It returns a string consisting of all input until the user hits the Enter key. In our example, the call `in.nextLine()` would return the string `"Harry Morgan"`. You should use the `nextLine` method if you don't know how many words are contained in an input string.

2.6.4 Converting Strings to Numbers

Sometimes you have a string that contains a number, usually from user input. For example, suppose that the string variable `input` has the value `"19"`. To get the integer value 19, you use the `Integer.parseInt` method:

```
int count = Integer.parseInt(input);
    // count is the integer 19
```

To convert a string containing floating-point digits to its floating-point value, use the `Double.parseDouble` method. For example, suppose `input` is the string `"3.95"`.

```
double price = Double.parseDouble(input);
    // price is the floating-point number 3.95
```

> If a string contains the digits of a number, you use the `Integer.parseInt` or `Double.parseDouble` method to obtain the number value.

2.6.5 Escape Sequences

To include a quotation mark in a literal string, precede it with a backslash (\), like this:

```
"He said \"Hello\""
```

The backslash is not included in the string. It indicates that the quotation mark that follows should be a part of the string and not mark the end of the string. The sequence \" is called an **escape sequence**.

To include a backslash in a string, use the escape sequence \\, like this:

```
"C:\\Temp\\Secret.txt"
```

Another common escape sequence is \n, which denotes a **newline** character. Printing a newline character causes the start of a new line on the display. For example, the statement

```
System.out.print("*\n**\n***\n");
```

prints the characters

```
*
**
***
```

on three separate lines.

2.6.6 Strings and Characters

Strings are sequences of Unicode characters (see Random Fact 2.2 on page 66). In Java, a **character** is a value of the type char. Characters have numeric values. You can find the values of the characters that are used in Western European languages in Appendix B. For example, if you look up the value for the character 'H', you can see that is actually encoded as the number 72.

A string is a sequence of characters.

Character literals are delimited by single quotes, and you should not confuse them with strings.

- 'H' is a character, a value of type char.
- "H" is a string containing a single character, a value of type String.

The charAt method returns a char value from a string. The first string position is labeled 0, the second one 1, and so on.

H a r r y
0 1 2 3 4

String positions are counted starting with 0.

The position number of the last character (4 for the string "Harry") is always one less than the length of the string.

For example, the statement

```
String greeting = "Harry";
char start = greeting.charAt(0);
char last = greeting.charAt(4);
```

sets start to the value 'H' and last to the value 'y'.

2.6.7 Substrings

Once you have a string, you can extract substrings by using the substring method. The method call

```
str.substring(start, pastEnd)
```

returns a string that is made up of the characters in the string str, starting at position start, and containing all characters up to, but not including, the position pastEnd. Here is an example:

```
String greeting = "Hello!";
String sub = greeting.substring(0, 2); // sub is "He"
```

The substring operation makes a string that consists of two characters taken from the string greeting.

H e l l o !
0 1 2 3 4 5

Let's figure out how to extract the substring "lo". Count characters starting at 0, not 1. You find that l has position number 3. The first character that you don't want, !, is the character at position 5. Therefore, the appropriate substring command is

```
String sub2 = greeting.substring(3, 5);
```

It is curious that you must specify the position of the first character that you do want and then the first character that you don't want. There is one advantage to this setup. You can easily compute the length of the substring: It is pastEnd - start. For example, the string "lo" has length 5 − 3 = 2.

If you omit the second parameter of the substring method, then all characters from the starting position to the end of the string are copied. For example,

```
String tail = greeting.substring(2); // Copies all characters from position 2 on
```

sets tail to the string "llo!".

Here is a simple program that puts these concepts to work. The program asks for your name and that of your significant other. It then prints out your initials.

The operation first.substring(0, 1) makes a string consisting of one character, taken from the start of first. The program does the same for the second. Then it concatenates the resulting one-character strings with the string literal "&" to get a string of length 3, the initials string. (See Figure 5.)

Initials are formed from the first letter of each name.

Figure 5 Building the initials String

ch02/initials/Initials.java

```
1   import java.util.Scanner;
2
3   /**
4      This program prints a pair of initials.
5   */
6   public class Initials
7   {
8      public static void main(String[] args)
9      {
10        Scanner in = new Scanner(System.in);
11
```

```
12        // Get the names of the couple
13
14        System.out.print("Enter your first name: ");
15        String first = in.nextLine();
16        System.out.print("Enter your significant other's first name: ");
17        String second = in.nextLine();
18
19        // Compute and display the inscription
20
21        String initials = first.substring(0, 1)
22            + "&" + second.substring(0, 1);
23        System.out.println(initials);
24    }
25 }
```

Program Run

```
Enter your first name: Rodolfo
Enter your significant other's first name: Sally
R&S
```

Table 10 String Operations

Statement	Result	Comment
string str = "Ja"; str = str + "va";	str is set to "Java"	When applied to strings, + denotes concatenation.
String name = in.next(); (User input: Harry Morgan)	name contains "Harry"	The next method places the next word into the string variable.
String name = in.nextLine(); (User input: Harry Morgan)	name contains "Harry Morgan"	Use the nextLine method to read more than one word.
String greeting = "H & S"; int n = greeting.length();	n is set to 5	Each space counts as one character.
String str = "Sally"; char ch = str.charAt(1);	ch is set to 'a'	This is a char value, not a String. Note that the initial position is 0.
String str = "Sally"; String str2 = str.substring(1, 4);	str2 is set to "all"	Extracts the substring starting at position 1 and ending before position 4.
String str = "Sally"; String str2 = str.substring(1);	str2 is set to "ally"	If you omit the length, all characters from the position until the end are included.
String str = "Sally"; String str2 = str.substring(1, 2);	str2 is set to "a"	Extracts a substring of length 1; contrast with str.charAt(1).
String last = str.substring(str.length() - 1);	last is set to the string containing the last character in str	The last character has position str.length() - 1.

27. What is the length of the string `"Java Program"`?

28. Consider this string variable.

```
String str = "Java Program";
```

Give a call to the `substring` method that returns the substring `"gram"`.

29. Use string concatenation to turn the string variable `str` from Self Check 28 into `"Java Programming"`.

30. What does the following statement sequence print?

```
String str = "Harry";
int n = str.length();
String mystery = str.substring(0, 1) + str.substring(n - 1, n);
System.out.println(mystery);
```

31. Give an input statement to read a name of the form "John Q. Public".

Practice It Now you can try these exercises at the end of the chapter: R2.4, R2.7, P2.9, P2.16.

Instance Methods and Static Methods

In this chapter, you have learned how to read, process, and print numbers and strings. Many of these tasks involve various method calls. You may have noticed syntactical differences in these method calls. For example, to compute the square root of a number `num`, you call `Math.sqrt(num)`, but to compute the length of a string `str`, you call `str.length()`. This section explains the reasons behind these differences.

The Java language distinguishes between values of **primitive types** and **objects**. Numbers and characters, as well as the values `false` and `true` that you will see in Chapter 3, are primitive. All other values are objects. Examples of objects are

- a string such as `"Hello"`.
- a Scanner object obtained by calling `in = new Scanner(System.in)`.
- `System.in` and `System.out`.

In Java, each object belongs to a **class**. For example,

- All strings are objects of the `String` class.
- A scanner object belongs to the `Scanner` class.
- `System.out` is an object of the `PrintStream` class. (It is useful to know this so that you can look up the valid methods in the API documentation; see Programming Tip 2.2 on page 43.)

A class declares the methods that you can use with its objects. Here are examples of methods that are invoked on objects:

```
"Hello".substring(0, 1)
in.nextDouble()
System.out.println("Hello")
```

A method is invoked with the **dot notation**: the object is followed by the name of the method, and the method is followed by parameters enclosed in parentheses.

The method is invoked on this object.   This is the name of the method.   These parameters are inputs to the method.

```
System.out.println("Hello")
```

You cannot invoke methods on numbers. For example, the call 2.sqrt() would be an error.

In Java, classes can declare methods that are *not* invoked on objects. Such methods are called **static methods**. (The term "static" is a historical holdover from the C and C++ programming languages. It has nothing to do with the usual meaning of the word.) For example, the Math class declares a static method sqrt. You call it by giving the name of the class and method, then the name of the numeric input: Math.sqrt(2).

The name of the class   The name of the static method

Math.sqrt(2)

In contrast, a method that is invoked on an object is called an **instance method**. As a rule of thumb, you use static methods when you manipulate numbers. You use instance methods when you process strings or perform input/output. You will learn more about the distinction between static and instance methods in Chapter 7.

Random Fact 2.2 International Alphabets and Unicode

The English alphabet is pretty simple: upper- and lowercase *a* to *z*. Other European languages have accent marks and special characters. For example, German has three so-called *umlaut* characters, ä, ö, ü, and a *double-s* character ß. These are not optional frills; you couldn't write a page of German text without using these characters a few times. German keyboards have keys for these characters.

The German Keyboard Layout

Many countries don't use the Roman script at all. Russian, Greek, Hebrew, Arabic, and Thai letters, to name just a few, have completely different shapes. To complicate matters, Hebrew and Arabic are typed from right to left. Each of these alphabets has about as many characters as the English alphabet.

Hebrew, Arabic, and English

The Chinese languages as well as Japanese and Korean use Chinese characters. Each character represents an idea or thing. Words are made up of one or more of these ideographic characters. Over 70,000 ideographs are known.

Starting in 1988, a consortium of hardware and software manufacturers developed a uniform encoding scheme called **Unicode** that is capable of encoding text in essentially all written languages of the world. An early version of Unicode used 16 bits for each character. The Java char type corresponds to that encoding. Today Unicode has grown to a 21-bit code, with definitions for over 100,000 characters. There are even plans to add codes for extinct languages, such as Egyptian hieroglyphics. Unfortunately, that means that a Java char does not always correspond to a Unicode character. Some characters in languages such as Chinese or ancient Egyptian occupy two char values.

The Chinese Script

SCREENCAST 2.1   **Computing Distances on Earth**

In this Screencast Video, you will see how to write a program that computes the distance between any two points on Earth.

CHAPTER SUMMARY

- A variable is a storage location with a name.
- When declaring a variable, you usually specify an initial value.

- When declaring a variable, you also specify the type of its values.

- Use the int type for numbers that cannot have a fractional part.
- Use the double type for floating-point numbers.
- By convention, variable names should start with a lowercase letter.

- Use comments to add explanations for humans who read your code. The compiler ignores comments.

- An assignment statement stores a new value in a variable, replacing the previously stored value.
- The assignment operator = does *not* denote mathematical equality.
- The ++ operator adds 1 to a variable; the -- operator subtracts 1.

- Java classes are grouped into packages. Use the import statement to use classes from packages.
- Use the Scanner class to read keyboard input in a console window.

- The API (Application Programming Interface) documentation lists the classes and methods of the Java library.

- You cannot change the value of a variable that is declared as final.

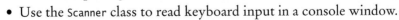

➕ Available online in WileyPLUS and at www.wiley.com/college/horstmann.

- Mixing integers and floating-point values in an arithmetic expression yields a floating-point value.
  - If both arguments of / are integers, the remainder is discarded.
  - The % operator computes the remainder of an integer division.
  - The Java library declares many mathematical functions, such as Math.sqrt (square root) and Math.pow (raising to a power).
  - You use a cast (*typeName*) to convert a value to a different type.
  - Use the printf method to specify how values should be formatted.

- Strings are sequences of characters.

- The length method yields the number of characters in a string.

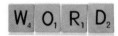

- Use the + operator to concatenate strings; that is, to put them together to yield a longer string.
- Whenever one of the arguments of the + operator is a string, the other argument is converted to a string.
- Use the next or nextLine method of the Scanner class to read a string.
- If a string contains the digits of a number, you use the Integer.parseInt or Double.parseDouble method to obtain the number value.
- String positions are counted starting with 0.

MEDIA RESOURCES

www.wiley.com/
college/
horstmann

- • **Worked Example** Computing the Cost of Stamps
- • Guided Lab Exercises
- ➕ **Animation** Variable Initialization and Assignment
- ➕ **Screencast** Computing Distances on Earth
- ➕ Practice Quiz
- ➕ Code Completion Exercises

REVIEW EXERCISES

★★ **R2.1** Write the following mathematical expressions in Java.

$$s = s_0 + v_0 t + \frac{1}{2} g t^2$$

$$G = 4\pi^2 \frac{a^3}{p^2(m_1 + m_2)}$$

$$FV = PV \cdot \left(1 + \frac{INT}{100}\right)^{YRS}$$

$$c = \sqrt{a^2 + b^2 - 2ab \cos\gamma}$$

★★ **R2.2** Write the following Java expressions in mathematical notation.

a. `dm = m * (Math.sqrt(1 + v / c) / Math.sqrt(1 - v / c) - 1);`
b. `volume = Math.PI * r * r * h;`
c. `volume = 4 * Math.PI * Math.pow(r, 3) / 3;`
d. `z = Math.sqrt(x * x + y * y);`

★★ **R2.3** What are the values of the following expressions? In each line, assume that

```
double x = 2.5;
double y = -1.5;
int m = 18;
int n = 4;
```

a. `x + n * y - (x + n) * y`
b. `m / n + m % n`
c. `5 * x - n / 5`
d. `1 - (1 - (1 - (1 - (1 - n))))`
e. `Math.sqrt(Math.sqrt(n))`

★★ **R2.4** What are the values of the following expressions? In each line, assume that

```
String s = "Hello";
String t = "World";
```

a. `s.length() + t.length()`
b. `s.substring(1, 2)`
c. `s.substring(s.length() / 2, s.length())`
d. `s + t`
e. `t + s`

★ **R2.5** Find at least five *compile-time* errors in the following program.

```
public class HasErrors
{
   public static void main();
   {
```

```
                    System.out.print(Please enter two numbers:)
                    x = in.readDouble;
                    y = in.readDouble;
                    System.out.printline("The sum is " + x + y);
                }
            }
```

★★ **R2.6** Find three *run-time* errors in the following program.

```
public class HasErrors
{
    public static void main(String[] args)
    {
        int x = 0;
        int y = 0;
        Scanner in = new Scanner("System.in");
        System.out.print("Please enter an integer:");
        x = in.readInt();
        System.out.print("Please enter another integer: ");
        x = in.readInt();
        System.out.println("The sum is " + x + y);
    }
}
```

★ **R2.7** Explain the difference between 2.0 and "2.0".

★ **R2.8** Explain what each of the following program segments computes:

   a. x = 2;
   　 y = x + x;
   b. s = "2";
   　 t = s + s;

★★ **R2.9** Write pseudocode for a program that reads a word and then prints the first character, the last character, and the characters in the middle. For example, if the input is Harry, the program prints H y arr.

★★ **R2.10** Write pseudocode for a program that reads a name (such as Harold James Morgan) and then prints a monogram consisting of the initial letters of the first, middle, and last name (such as HJM).

★★★ **R2.11** Write pseudocode for a program that computes the first and last digit of a number. For example, if the input is 23456, the program should print out 2 and 6. *Hint:* %, Math.log10.

★★ **R2.12** Modify the pseudocode for the program in How To 2.1 on page 55 so that the program gives change in quarters, dimes, and nickels. You can assume that the price is a multiple of 5 cents.

★★ **R2.13** The following pseudocode describes how to obtain the name of a day, given the day number (0 = Sunday, 1 = Monday, and so on.)

   Declare a string called names containing "SunMonTueWedThuFriSat".
   Compute the starting position as 3 x the day number.
   Extract the substring of names at the starting position with length 3.

   Check this pseudocode, using the day number 4. Draw a diagram of the string that is being computed, similar to Figure 5.

★★★ **R2.14** The following pseudocode describes how to swap two letters in a word.

> **We are given a string str and two positions i and j. (i comes before j)**
> **Set first to the substring from the start of the string to the last position before i.**
> **Set middle to the substring from positions i + 1 to j - 1.**
> **Set last to the substring from position j + 1 to the end of the string.**
> **Concatenate the following five strings: first, the string containing just the character at position j,**
> **middle, the string containing just the character at position i, and last.**

Check this pseudocode, using the string "Gateway" and positions 2 and 4. Draw a diagram of the string that is being computed, similar to Figure 5.

★★ **R2.15** How do you get the first character of a string? The last character? How do you remove the first character? The last character?

★★★ **R2.16** Write a program that prints the values

```
3 * 1000 * 1000 * 1000
3.0 * 1000 * 1000 * 1000
```

Explain the results.

★ **R2.17** This chapter contains a number of recommendations regarding variables and constants that make programs easier to read and maintain. Briefly summarize these recommendations.

PROGRAMMING EXERCISES

★ **P2.1** Write a program that reads a number and displays the square, cube, and fourth power. Use the Math.pow method only for the fourth power.

★★ **P2.2** Write a program that prompts the user for two integers and then prints
- The sum
- The difference
- The product
- The average
- The distance (absolute value of the difference)
- The maximum (the larger of the two)
- The minimum (the smaller of the two)

Hint: The max and min functions are declared in the Math class.

★★ **P2.3** Write a program that prompts the user for a measurement in meters and then converts it to miles, feet, and inches.

★ **P2.4** Write a program that prompts the user for a radius and then prints
- The area and circumference of a circle with that radius
- The volume and surface area of a sphere with that radius

★★ **P2.5** Write a program that asks the user for the lengths of the sides of a rectangle. Then print
- The area and perimeter of the rectangle
- The length of the diagonal (use the Pythagorean theorem)

★   P2.6   Improve the program discussed in How To 2.1 on page 55 to allow input of quarters in addition to bills.

★★★   P2.7   Write a program that helps a person decide whether to buy a hybrid car. Your program's inputs should be:

- The cost of a new car
- The estimated miles driven per year
- The estimated gas price
- The efficiency in miles per gallon
- The estimated resale value after 5 years

Compute the total cost of owning the car for 5 years. (For simplicity, we will not take the cost of financing into account.) Obtain realistic prices for a new and used hybrid and a comparable car from the Web. Run your program twice, using today's gas price and 15,000 miles per year. Include pseudocode and the program runs with your assignment.

★★   P2.8   The following pseudocode describes how a bookstore computes the price of an order from the total price and the number of the books that were ordered.

> Read the total book price and the number of books.
> Compute the tax (7.5% of the total book price).
> Compute the shipping charge ($2 per book).
> The price of the order is the sum of the total book price, the tax, and the shipping charge.
> Print the price of the order.

Translate this pseudocode into a Java program.

★★   P2.9   The following pseudocode describes how to turn a string containing a ten-digit phone number (such as "4155551212") into a more readable string with parentheses and dashes, like this: "(415) 555-1212".

> Take the substring consisting of the first three characters and surround it with "(" and ") ". This is the area code.
> Concatenate the area code, the substring consisting of the next three characters, a hyphen, and the substring consisting of the last four characters. This is the formatted number.

Translate this pseudocode into a Java program that reads a telephone number into a string variable, computes the formatted number, and prints it.

★★   P2.10   The following pseudocode describes how to extract the dollars and cents from a price given as a floating-point value. For example, a price 2.95 yields values 2 and 95 for the dollars and cents.

> Assign the price to an integer variable dollars.
> Multiply the difference price - dollars by 100 and add 0.5.
> Assign the result to an integer variable cents.

Translate this pseudocode into a Java program. Read a price and print the dollars and cents. Test your program with inputs 2.95 and 4.35.

★★ **P2.11** *Giving change.* Implement a program that directs a cashier how to give change. The program has two inputs: the amount due and the amount received from the customer. Display the dollars, quarters, dimes, nickels, and pennies that the customer should receive in return. In order to avoid roundoff errors, the program user should supply both amounts in pennies, for example 274 instead of 2.74.

★★ **P2.12** Write a program that asks the user to input

- The number of gallons of gas in the tank
- The fuel efficiency in miles per gallon
- The price of gas per gallon

Then print the cost per 100 miles and how far the car can go with the gas in the tank.

★ **P2.13** *File names and extensions.* Write a program that prompts the user for the drive letter (C), the path (\Windows\System), the file name (Readme), and the extension (txt). Then print the complete file name C:\Windows\System\Readme.txt. (If you use UNIX or a Macintosh, skip the drive name and use / instead of \ to separate directories.)

★ **P2.14** Enhance the output of Exercise P2.2 so that the numbers are properly aligned:

```
Sum:           45
Difference:    -5
Product:       500
Average:       22.50
Distance:       5
Maximum:       25
Minimum:       20
```

★★★ **P2.15** Write a program that reads a number between 1,000 and 999,999 from the user, where the user enters a comma in the input. Then print the number without a comma. Here is a sample dialog; the user input is in color:

```
Please enter an integer between 1,000 and 999,999: 23,456
23456
```

Hint: Read the input as a string. Measure the length of the string. Suppose it contains n characters. Then extract substrings consisting of the first $n - 4$ characters and the last three characters.

★ **P2.16** *Printing a grid.* Write a program that prints the following grid to play tic-tac-toe.

```
+--+--+--+
|  |  |  |
+--+--+--+
|  |  |  |
+--+--+--+
|  |  |  |
+--+--+--+
```

Of course, you could simply write seven statements of the form

```
System.out.println("+--+--+--+");
```

You should do it the smart way, though. Declare string variables to hold two kinds of patterns: a comb-shaped pattern and the bottom line. Print the comb three times and the bottom line once.

★★ **P2.17** Write a program that reads in an integer and breaks it into a sequence of individual digits. For example, the input 16384 is displayed as

```
1 6 3 8 4
```

You may assume that the input has no more than five digits and is not negative.

★★ **P2.18** Write a program that reads two times in military format (0900, 1730) and prints the number of hours and minutes between the two times. Here is a sample run. User input is in color.

```
Please enter the first time: 0900
Please enter the second time: 1730
8 hours 30 minutes
```

Extra credit if you can deal with the case where the first time is later than the second:

```
Please enter the first time: 1730
Please enter the second time: 0900
15 hours 30 minutes
```

★★★ **P2.19** *Writing large letters.* A large letter H can be produced like this:

```
*   *
*   *
*****
*   *
*   *
```

It can be declared as a string literal like this:

```
final string LETTER_H = "*   *\n*   *\n*****\n*   *\n*   *\n";
```

(The \n escape sequence denotes a "newline" character that causes subsequent characters to be printed on a new line.) Do the same for the letters E, L, and O. Then write the message

```
H
E
L
L
O
```

in large letters.

★★ **P2.20** Write a program that transforms numbers 1, 2, 3, …, 12 into the corresponding month names January, February, March, …, December. *Hint:* Make a very long string "January February March …", in which you add spaces such that each month name has *the same length*. Then use substring to extract the month you want.

ANSWERS TO SELF-CHECK QUESTIONS

1. One possible answer is

   ```
   int bottlesPerCase = 8;
   ```

   You may choose a different variable name or a different initialization value, but your variable should have type `int`.

2. There are three errors:
   - You cannot have spaces in variable names.
   - The variable type should be `double` because it holds a fractional value.
   - There is a semicolon missing at the end of the statement.

3. ```
   double unitPrice = 1.95;
   int quantity = 2;
   ```

4. ```
   System.out.print("Total price: "); System.out.println(unitPrice * quantity);
   ```

5. Change the declaration of `cansPerPack` to

   ```
   int cansPerPack = 4;
   ```

6. You need to use a `*/` delimiter to close a comment that begins with a `/*`:

   ```
   double canVolume = 0.355; /* Liters in a 12-ounce can */
   ```

7. The program would compile, and it would display the same result. However, a person reading the program might find it confusing that fractional cans are being considered.

8. The variable `mystery` is initialized to 1. The assignment statement changes `mystery` to 2. The increment statement changes it to 3.

9. The last statement is a variable declaration, but `mystery` has already been declared. Remedy: Drop the `int` in the last statement.

10. Assignment would occur when one car is replaced by another in the parking space.

11. One more than before the statements were executed.

12. ```
    n = n + 3;
    n++; n++; n++;
    ```

13. ```
    System.out.print("How old are you? ");
    int age = in.nextInt();
    ```

14. There is no prompt that alerts the program user to enter the quantity.

15. The second statement calls `nextInt`, not `nextDouble`. If the user were to enter a price such as 1.95, only the 1 would be placed into the variable.

16. There is no colon and space at the end of the prompt. A dialog would look like this:

    ```
    Please enter the number of cans6
    ```

17. They are not constants. Their values are modified by the input statements.

18. ```
    final int CANS_PER_PACK = 6;
    double totalVolume = canVolume * CANS_PER_PACK;
    ```

19. You cannot modify the value of a `final` variable.

20. ```
    double interest = balance * p / 100;
    ```

21. ```
    double sideLength = Math.sqrt(area);
    ```

22. ```
    4 * PI * Math.pow(radius, 3) / 3
    ```
    or `(4.0 / 3) * PI * Math.pow(radius, 3)`,
    but not `(4 / 3) * PI * Math.pow(radius, 3)`

23. 172 and 9

24. `int leftover = 12 - amount % 12;`

25. `The total volume is    10`

There are four spaces between is and 10. One space originates from the format string (the space between s and %), and three spaces are added before 10 to achieve a field width of 5.

26. Here is a simple solution.

```
System.out.printf("Bottles: %8d\n", bottles);
System.out.printf("Cans:    %8d\n", cans);
```

Note the spaces after Cans:. Alternatively, you can use format specifiers for the strings. You can even combine all output into a single statement:

```
System.out.printf("%-9s%8d\n%-9s%8d\n", "Bottles: ", bottles, "Cans:", cans);
```

27. The length is 12. The space counts as a character.

28. `str.substring(8, 12)` or `str.substring(8)`

29. `str = str + "ming";`

30. `Hy`

31. `name = in.nextLine();`

DECISIONS

One of the essential features of computer programs is their ability to make decisions. Like a train that changes tracks depending on how the switches are set, a program can take different actions depending on inputs and other circumstances.

In this chapter, you will learn how to program simple and complex decisions. You will apply what you learn to the task of checking user input.

3.1 The if Statement

The if statement allows a program to carry out different actions depending on the nature of the data to be processed.

The if statement is used to implement a decision (see Syntax 3.1). When a condition is fulfilled, one set of statements is executed. Otherwise, another set of statements is executed.

Here is an example using the if statement. In many countries, the number 13 is considered unlucky. Rather than offending superstitious tenants, building owners sometimes skip the thirteenth floor; floor 12 is immediately followed by floor 14. Of course, floor 13 is not usually left empty or, as some conspiracy theorists believe, filled with secret offices and research labs. It is simply called floor 14. The computer that controls the building elevators needs to compensate for this foible and adjust all floor numbers above 13.

Let's simulate this process in Java. We will ask the user to type in the desired floor number and then compute the actual floor. When the input is above 13, then we need to decrement the input to obtain the actual floor. For example, if the user provides an input of 20, the program determines the actual floor as 19. Otherwise, we simply use the supplied floor number.

This elevator panel "skips" the thirteenth floor. The floor is not actually missing—the computer that controls the elevator adjusts the floor numbers above 13.

```java
int actualFloor;

if (floor > 13)
{
   actualFloor = floor - 1;
}
else
{
   actualFloor = floor;
}
```

The flowchart in Figure 1 shows the branching behavior.

In our example, each branch of the if statement contains a single statement. You can include as many statements in each branch as you like. Sometimes, it happens

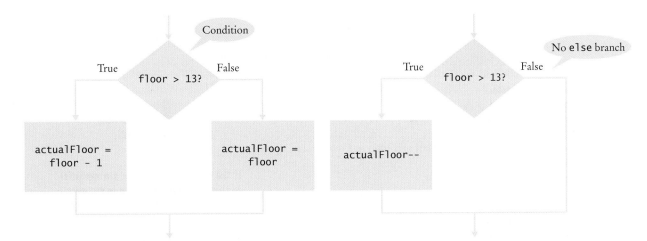

Figure 1
Flowchart for if Statement

Figure 2
Flowchart for if Statement with No else Branch

that there is nothing to do in the else branch of the statement. In that case, you can omit it entirely, such as in this example:

```
int actualFloor = floor;

if (floor > 13)
{
   actualFloor--;
} // No else needed
```

See Figure 2 for the flowchart.

The following program puts the if statement to work. This program asks for the desired floor and then prints out the actual floor.

An if *statement is like a fork in the road. Depending upon a decision, different parts of the program are executed.*

Syntax 3.1 if Statement

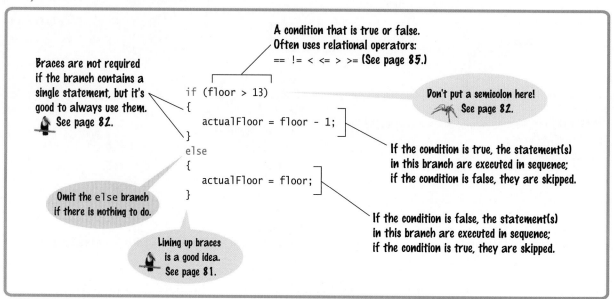

ch03/elevator/ElevatorSimulation.java

```
1   import java.util.Scanner;
2
3   /**
4      This program simulates an elevator panel that skips the 13th floor.
5   */
6   public class ElevatorSimulation
7   {
8      public static void main(String[] args)
9      {
10        Scanner in = new Scanner(System.in);
11        System.out.print("Floor: ");
12        int floor = in.nextInt();
13
14        // Adjust floor if necessary
15
16        int actualFloor;
17        if (floor > 13)
18        {
19           actualFloor = floor - 1;
20        }
21        else
22        {
23           actualFloor = floor;
24        }
25
26        System.out.println("The elevator will travel to the actual floor "
27           + actualFloor);
28     }
29  }
```

Program Run

```
Floor: 20
The elevator will travel to the actual floor 19
```

1. In some Asian countries, the number 14 is considered unlucky. Some building owners play it safe and skip *both* the thirteenth and the fourteenth floor. How would you modify the sample program to handle such a building?

2. Consider the following `if` statement to compute a discounted price:

```
if (originalPrice > 100)
{
    discountedPrice = originalPrice - 20;
}
else
{
    discountedPrice = originalPrice - 10;
}
```

   What is the discounted price if the original price is 95? 100? 105?

3. Compare this `if` statement with the one in Self Check 2:

```
if (originalPrice < 100)
{
    discountedPrice = originalPrice - 10;
}
else
{
    discountedPrice = originalPrice - 20;
}
```

   Do the two statements always compute the same value? If not, when do the values differ?

4. Consider the following statements to compute a discounted price:

```
discountedPrice = originalPrice;
if (originalPrice > 100)
{
    discountedPrice = originalPrice - 10;
}
```

   What is the discounted price if the original price is 95? 100? 105?

5. The variables `fuelAmount` and `fuelCapacity` hold the actual amount of fuel and the size of the fuel tank of a vehicle. If less than 10 percent is remaining in the tank, a status light should show a red color; otherwise it shows a green color. Simulate this process by printing out either "red" or "green".

Practice It   Now you can try these exercises at the end of the chapter: R3.3, R3.4, P3.15.

Brace Layout

The compiler doesn't care where you place braces. In this book, we follow the simple rule of making { and } line up.

```
if (floor > 13)
{
    floor--;
}
```

This style makes it easy to spot matching braces. Some programmers put the opening brace on the same line as the `if`:

```
if (floor > 13) {
    floor--;
}
```

This style makes it harder to match the braces, but it saves a line of code, allowing you to view more code on the screen without scrolling. There are passionate advocates of both styles.

It is important that you pick a layout style and stick with it consistently within a

Properly lining up your code makes your programs easier to read.

given programming project. Which style you choose may depend on your personal preference or a coding style guide that you need to follow.

Programming Tip 3.2

Always Use Braces

When the body of an `if` statement consists of a single statement, you need not use braces. For example, the following is legal:

```
if (floor > 13)
    floor--;
```

However, it is a good idea to always include the braces:

```
if (floor > 13)
{
    floor--;
}
```

The braces make your code easier to read. They also make it easier for you to maintain the code because you won't have to worry about adding braces when you add statements inside an `if` statement.

Common Error 3.1

A Semicolon After the `if` Condition

The following code fragment has an unfortunate error:

```
if (floor > 13) ; // ERROR
{
    floor--;
}
```

There should be no semicolon after the `if` condition. The compiler interprets this statement as follows: If `floor` is greater than 13, execute the statement that is denoted by a single semicolon, that is, the do-nothing statement. The statement enclosed in braces is no longer a part of the `if` statement. It is always executed. In other words, even if the value of `floor` is not above 13, it is decremented.

Programming Tip 3.3

Tabs

Block-structured code has the property that nested statements are indented by one or more levels:

```
public class ElevatorSimulation
{
   public static void main(String[] args)
   {
      int floor;
      . . .
      if (floor > 13)
      {
         floor--;
      }
      . . .
   }
   |   |   |   |
   0   1   2   3    Indentation level
}
```

How do you move the cursor from the leftmost column to the appropriate indentation level? A perfectly reasonable strategy is to hit the space bar a sufficient number of times. With most editors, you can use the Tab key instead. A tab moves the cursor to the next indentation level. Some editors even have an option to fill in the tabs automatically.

While the Tab *key* is nice, some editors use *tab characters* for alignment, which is not so nice. Tab characters can lead to problems when you send your file to another person or a printer. There is no universal agreement on the width of a tab character, and some software will ignore tab characters altogether. It

You use the Tab key to move the cursor to the next indentation level.

is therefore best to save your files with spaces instead of tabs. Most editors have a setting to automatically convert all tabs to spaces. Look at the documentation of your development environment to find out how to activate this useful setting.

Special Topic 3.1

The Conditional Operator

Java has a *conditional operator* of the form

   condition ? *value*$_1$: *value*$_2$

The value of that expression is either *value*$_1$ if the test passes or *value*$_2$ if it fails. For example, we can compute the actual floor number as

```
actualFloor = floor > 13 ? floor - 1 : floor;
```

which is equivalent to

```
if (floor > 13) { actualFloor = floor - 1; } else { actualFloor = floor; }
```

You can use the conditional operator anywhere that a value is expected, for example:

```
System.out.println("Actual floor: " + (floor > 13 ? floor - 1 : floor));
```

We don't use the conditional operator in this book, but it is a convenient construct that you will find in many Java programs.

Programming Tip 3.4

Avoid Duplication in Branches

Look to see whether you *duplicate code* in each branch. If so, move it out of the if statement. Here is an example of such duplication:

```
if (floor > 13)
{
   actualFloor = floor - 1;
   System.out.println("Actual floor: " + actualFloor);
}
else
{
   actualFloor = floor;
   System.out.println("Actual floor: " + actualFloor);
}
```

The output statement is exactly the same in both branches. This is not an error—the program will run correctly. However, you can simplify the program by moving the duplicated statement, like this:

```
if (floor > 13)
{
   actualFloor = floor - 1;
}
else
{
   actualFloor = floor;
}
System.out.println("Actual floor: " + actualFloor);
```

Removing duplication is particularly important when programs are maintained for a long time. When there are two sets of statements with the same effect, it can easily happen that a programmer modifies one set but not the other.

3.2 Comparing Numbers and Strings

Relational operators
(< <= > >= == !=)
are used to compare
numbers and strings.

Every if statement contains a condition. In many cases, the condition involves comparing two values. For example, in the previous examples we tested floor > 13. The comparison > is called a **relational operator**. Java has six relational operators (see Table 1).

As you can see, only two Java relational operators (> and <) look as you would expect from the mathematical notation. Computer keyboards do not have keys for ≥, ≤, or ≠, but the >=, <=, and != operators are easy to remember because they look similar. The == operator is initially confusing to most

In Java, you use a relational operator to check whether one value is greater than another.

Table 1 Relational Operators		
Java	Math Notation	Description
>	>	Greater than
>=	≥	Greater than or equal
<	<	Less than
<=	≤	Less than or equal
==	=	Equal
!=	≠	Not equal

newcomers to Java. In Java, = already has a meaning, namely assignment. The ==
operator denotes equality testing:

```
floor = 13; // Assign 13 to floor
if (floor == 13)   // Test whether floor equals 13
```

You must remember to use == inside tests and to use = outside tests.

Syntax 3.2   Comparisons

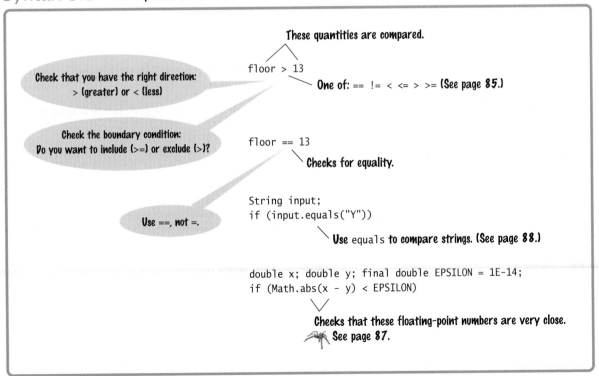

These quantities are compared.

floor > 13

Check that you have the right direction:
> (greater) or < (less)

One of: == != < <= > >= (See page 85.)

Check the boundary condition:
Do you want to include (>=) or exclude (>)?

floor == 13

Checks for equality.

Use ==, not =.

```
String input;
if (input.equals("Y"))
```

Use equals to compare strings. (See page 88.)

```
double x; double y; final double EPSILON = 1E-14;
if (Math.abs(x - y) < EPSILON)
```

Checks that these floating-point numbers are very close.
See page 87.

The relational operators in Table 1 have a lower precedence than the arithmetic operators. That means, you can write arithmetic expressions on either side of the relational operator without using parentheses. For example, in the expression

```
floor - 1 < 13
```

both sides (`floor - 1` and `13`) of the `<` operator are evaluated, and the results are compared. Appendix B shows a table of the Java operators and their precedence.

To test whether two strings are equal to each other, you must use the method called `equals`:

```
if (string1.equals(string2)) . . .
```

Do not use the == operator to compare strings. Use the equals method instead.

Do not use the `==` operator to compare strings. The comparison

```
if (string1 == string2) // Not useful
```

has an unrelated meaning. It tests whether the two strings are stored in the same location. You can have strings with identical contents stored in different locations, so this test never makes sense in actual programming; see Common Error 3.3 on page 88.

Table 2 summarizes how to compare values in Java.

Table 2 Relational Operator Examples

Expression	Value	Comment
`3 <= 4`	true	3 is less than 4; `<=` tests for "less than or equal".
🚫 `3 =< 4`	**Error**	The "less than or equal" operator is `<=`, not `=<`. The "less than" symbol comes first.
`3 > 4`	false	`>` is the opposite of `<=`.
`4 < 4`	false	The left-hand side must be strictly smaller than the right-hand side.
`4 <= 4`	true	Both sides are equal; `<=` tests for "less than or equal".
`3 == 5 - 2`	true	`==` tests for equality.
`3 != 5 - 1`	true	`!=` tests for inequality. It is true that 3 is not 5 – 1.
🚫 `3 = 6 / 2`	**Error**	Use `==` to test for equality.
`1.0 / 3.0 == 0.333333333`	false	Although the values are very close to one another, they are not exactly equal. See Common Error 3.2 on page 87.
🚫 `"10" > 5`	**Error**	You cannot compare a string to a number.
`"Tomato".substring(0, 3).equals("Tom")`	true	Always use the equals method to check whether two strings have the same contents.
`"Tomato".substring(0, 3) == ("Tom")`	false	Never use `==` to compare strings; it only checks whether the strings are stored in the same location. See Common Error 3.3 on page 88.

6. Which of the following conditions are true, provided a is 3 and b is 4?

   a. a + 1 <= b
   b. a + 1 >= b
   c. a + 1 != b

7. Give the opposite of the condition

```
floor > 13
```

8. What is the error in this statement?

```
if (scoreA = scoreB)
{
    System.out.println("Tie");
}
```

9. Supply a condition in this if statement to test whether the user entered a Y:

```
System.out.println("Enter Y to quit.");
String input = in.next();
if (. . .)
{
    System.out.println("Goodbye.");
    return;
}
```

10. How do you test that a string str is the empty string?

Practice It   Now you can try these exercises at the end of the chapter: R3.2, R3.5, P3.13.

Exact Comparison of Floating-Point Numbers

Floating-point numbers have only a limited precision, and calculations can introduce round-off errors. You must take these inevitable roundoffs into account when comparing floating-point numbers. For example, the following code multiplies the square root of 2 by itself. Ideally, we expect to get the answer 2:

```
double r = Math.sqrt(2.0);
if (r * r == 2.0)
{
    System.out.println("Math.sqrt(2.0) squared is 2.0");
}
else
{
    System.out.println("Math.sqrt(2.0) squared is not 2.0 but " + r * r);
}
```

This program displays

```
Math.sqrt(2.0) squared is not 2.0 but 2.00000000000000044
```

It does not make sense in most circumstances to compare floating-point numbers exactly. Instead, we should test whether they are *close enough*. That is, the magnitude of their difference should be less than some threshold. Mathematically, we would write that x and y are close enough if

$$|x - y| < \varepsilon$$

for a very small number, ε. ε is the Greek letter epsilon, a letter used to denote a very small quantity. It is common to set ε to 10^{-14} when comparing double numbers:

Take limited precision into account when comparing floating-point numbers.

```
final double EPSILON = 1E-14;
double r = Math.sqrt(2.0);
if (Math.abs(r * r - 2.0) < EPSILON)
{
    System.out.println("Math.sqrt(2.0) squared is approximately 2.0");
}
```

Using == to Compare Strings

If you write

```
if (nickname == "Rob")
```

then the test succeeds only if the variable `nickname` refers to the exact same location as the string literal `"Rob"`. The test will pass if a string variable was initialized with the same string literal:

```
String nickname = "Rob";
. . .
if (nickname == "Rob") // Test is true
```

However, if the string with the letters R o b has been assembled in some other way, then the test will fail:

```
String name = "Robert";
String nickname = name.substring(0, 3);
. . .
if (nickname == "Rob") // Test is false
```

In this case, the `substring` method produces a string in a different memory location. Even though both strings have the same contents, the comparison fails.

You must remember never to use == to compare strings. Always use `equals` to check whether two strings have the same contents.

Lexicographic Ordering of Strings

If two strings are not identical to each other, you still may want to know the relationship between them. The `compareTo` method compares strings in "lexicographic" order. This ordering is very similar to the way in which words are sorted in a dictionary. If

```
string1.compareTo(string2) < 0
```

then the string `string1` comes before the string `string2` in the dictionary. For example, this is the case if `string1` is `"Harry"`, and `string2` is `"Hello"`. If

```
string1.compareTo(string2) > 0
```

then `string1` comes after `string2` in dictionary order.
Finally, if

```
string1.compareTo(string2) == 0
```

then `string1` and `string2` are equal.

To see which of two terms comes first in the dictionary, consider the first letter in which they differ.

There are a few technical differences between the ordering in a dictionary and the lexicographic ordering in Java. In Java:

The compareTo method compares strings in lexicographic order.

- All uppercase letters come before the lowercase letters. For example, "Z" comes before "a".
- The space character comes before all printable characters.
- Numbers come before letters.
- For the ordering of punctuation marks, see Appendix A.

When comparing two strings, you compare the first letters of each word, then the second letters, and so on, until one of the strings ends or you find the first letter pair that doesn't match.

If one of the strings ends, the longer string is considered the "larger" one. For example, compare "car" with "cart". The first three letters match, and we reach the end of the first string. Therefore "car" comes before "cart" in lexicographic ordering.

When you reach a mismatch, the string containing the "larger" character is considered "larger". For example, let's compare "cat" with "cart". The first two letters match. Because t comes after r, the string "cat" comes after "cart" in the lexicographic ordering.

| c | a | r |

| c | a | r | t |

| c | a | t |

Letters match / r comes before t

Lexicographic Ordering

Implementing an if Statement

This How To walks you through the process of implementing an if statement. We will illustrate the steps with the following example problem:

The university bookstore has a Kilobyte Day sale every October 24, giving an 8 percent discount on all computer accessory purchases if the price is less than $128, and a 16 percent discount if the price is at least $128. Write a program that asks the cashier for the original price and then prints the discounted price.

Step 1 Decide upon the branching condition.

In our sample problem, the obvious choice for the condition is:

`original price < 128?`

That is just fine, and we will use that condition in our solution.

But you could equally well come up with a correct solution if you choose the opposite condition: Is the original price at least $128? You might choose this condition if you put yourself into the position of a shopper who wants to know when the bigger discount applies.

Sales discounts are often higher for expensive products. Use the if statement to implement such a decision.

Step 2 Give pseudocode for the work that needs to be done when the condition is true.

In this step, you list the action or actions that are taken in the "positive" branch. The details depend on your problem. You may want to print a message, compute values, or even exit the program.

In our example, we need to apply an 8 percent discount:

discounted price = 0.92 x original price

Step 3   Give pseudocode for the work (if any) that needs to be done when the condition is *not* true.

What do you want to do in the case that the condition of Step 1 is not satisfied? Sometimes, you want to do nothing at all. In that case, use an if statement without an else branch.

In our example, the condition tested whether the price was less than $128. If that condition is *not* true, the price is at least $128, so the higher discount of 16 percent applies to the sale:

discounted price = 0.84 x original price

Step 4   Double-check relational operators.

First, be sure that the test goes in the right *direction*. It is a common error to confuse > and <. Next, consider whether you should use the < operator or its close cousin, the <= operator.

What should happen if the original price is exactly $128? Reading the problem carefully, we find that the lower discount applies if the original price is *less than* $128, and the higher discount applies when it is *at least* $128. A price of $128 should therefore *not* fulfill our condition, and we must use <, not <=.

Step 5   Remove duplication.

Check which actions are common to both branches, and move them outside. (See Programming Tip 3.4 on page 84.)

In our example, we have two statements of the form

discounted price = ___ x original price

They only differ in the discount rate. It is best to just set the rate in the branches, and to do the computation afterwards:

If original price < 128
    discount rate = 0.92
Else
        discount rate = 0.84
discounted price = discount rate x original price

Step 6   Test both branches.

Formulate two test cases, one that fulfills the condition of the if statement, and one that does not. Ask yourself what should happen in each case. Then follow the pseudocode and act each of them out.

In our example, let us consider two scenarios for the original price: $100 and $200. We expect that the first price is discounted by $8, the second by $32.

When the original price is 100, then the condition 100 < 128 is true, and we get

discount rate = 0.92
discounted price = 0.92 x 100 = 92

When the original price is 200, then the condition 200 < 128 is false, and

discount rate = 0.84
discounted price = 0.84 x 200 = 168

In both cases, we get the expected answer.

Step 7   Assemble the if statement in Java.

Type the skeleton

```
if ()
{
```

```
   }
   else
   {
   }
```

and fill it in, as shown in Syntax 3.1 on page 80. Omit the `else` branch if it is not needed. In our example, the completed statement is

```
if (originalPrice < 128)
{
   discountRate = 0.92;
}
else
{
   discountRate = 0.84;
}
discountedPrice = discountRate * originalPrice;
```

WORKED EXAMPLE 3.1 **Extracting the Middle**

This Worked Example shows how to extract the middle character from a string, or the two middle characters if the length of the string is even.

c	r	a	t	e
0	1	2	3	4

Random Fact 3.1 The Denver Airport Luggage Handling System

Making decisions is an essential part of any computer program. Nowhere is this more obvious than in a computer system that helps sort luggage at an airport. After scanning the luggage identification codes, the system sorts the items and routes them to different conveyor belts. Human operators then place the items onto trucks. When the city of Denver built a huge airport to replace an outdated and congested facility, the luggage system contractor went a step further. The new system was designed to replace the human operators with robotic carts. Unfortunately, the system plainly did not work. It was plagued by mechanical problems, such as luggage falling onto the tracks and jamming carts. Equally frustrating were the software glitches. Carts would uselessly accumulate at some locations when they were needed elsewhere.

The airport had been scheduled for opening in 1993, but without a functioning luggage system, the opening was delayed for over a year while the contractor tried to fix the problems. The contractor never succeeded, and ultimately a manual system was installed. The delay cost the city and airlines close to a billion dollars, and the contractor, once the leading luggage systems vendor in the United States, went bankrupt.

Clearly, it is very risky to build a large system based on a technology that has never been tried on a smaller scale. As robots and the software that controls them get better over time, they will take on a larger share of luggage handling in the future. But it is likely that this will happen in an incremental fashion.

The Denver airport originally had a fully automatic system for moving luggage, replacing human operators with robotic carts. Unfortunately, the system never worked and was dismantled before the airport was opened.

3.3 Multiple Alternatives

Multiple if statements can be combined to evaluate complex decisions.

In Section 3.1, you saw how to program a two-way branch with an `if` statement. In many situations, there are more than two cases. In this section, you will see how to implement a decision with multiple alternatives.

For example, consider a program that displays the effect of an earthquake, as measured by the Richter scale (see Table 3).

The 1989 Loma Prieta earthquake that damaged the Bay Bridge in San Francisco and destroyed many buildings measured 7.1 on the Richter scale.

Table 3 Richter Scale	
Value	Effect
8	Most structures fall
7	Many buildings destroyed
6	Many buildings considerably damaged, some collapse
4.5	Damage to poorly constructed buildings

The Richter scale is a measurement of the strength of an earthquake. Every step in the scale, for example from 6.0 to 7.0, signifies a tenfold increase in the strength of the quake.

In this case, there are five branches: one each for the four descriptions of damage, and one for no destruction. Figure 3 shows the flowchart for this multiple-branch statement.

You use multiple `if` statements to implement multiple alternatives, like this:

+ ANIMATION
Multiple Alternatives

```
if (richter >= 8.0)
{
    System.out.println("Most structures fall");
}
else if (richter >= 7.0)
{
    System.out.println("Many buildings destroyed");
}
else if (richter >= 6.0)
{
    System.out.println("Many buildings considerably damaged, some collapse");
}
else if (richter >= 4.5)
{
    System.out.println("Damage to poorly constructed buildings");
}
else
{
    System.out.println("No destruction of buildings");
}
```

As soon as one of the four tests succeeds, the effect is displayed, and no further tests are attempted. If none of the four cases applies, the final `else` clause applies, and a

Figure 3
Multiple Alternatives

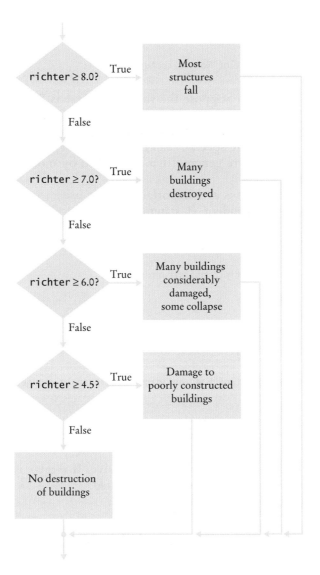

default message is printed. (See ch03/earthquake/EarthquakeStrength.java for the full program.)

Here you must sort the conditions and test against the largest cutoff first. Suppose we reverse the order of tests:

```java
if (richter >= 4.5) // Tests in wrong order
{
    System.out.println("Damage to poorly constructed buildings");
}
else if (richter >= 6.0)
{
    System.out.println("Many buildings considerably damaged, some collapse");
}
else if (richter >= 7.0)
{
    System.out.println("Many buildings destroyed");
```

```
   }
   else if (richter >= 8.0)
   {
       System.out.println("Most structures fall");
   }
```

This does not work. Suppose the value of `richter` is 7.1. That value is at least 4.5, matching the first case. The other tests will never be attempted.

The remedy is to test the more specific conditions first. Here, the condition `richter >= 8.0` is more specific than the condition `richter >= 7.0`, and the condition `richter >= 4.5` is more general (that is, fulfilled by more values) than either of the first two.

In this example, it is also important that we use an `if/else if/else` sequence, not just multiple independent `if` statements. Consider this sequence of independent tests.

When using multiple `if` statements, test general conditions after more specific conditions.

```
   if (richter >= 8.0) // Didn't use else
   {
       System.out.println("Most structures fall");
   }
   if (richter >= 7.0)
   {
       System.out.println("Many buildings destroyed");
   }
   if (richter >= 6.0)
   {
       System.out.println("Many buildings considerably damaged, some collapse");
   }
   if (richter >= 4.5)
   {
       System.out.println("Damage to poorly constructed buildings");
   }
```

Now the alternatives are no longer exclusive. If `richter` is 7.1, then the last *three* tests all match, and three messages are printed.

SELF CHECK

11. In a game program, the scores of players A and B are stored in variables `scoreA` and `scoreB`. Assuming that the player with the larger score wins, write an `if/else if/else` sequence that prints out `"A won"`, `"B won"`, or `"Game tied"`.

12. Write a conditional statement with three branches that sets s to 1 if x is positive, to −1 if x is negative, and to 0 if x is zero.

13. How could you achieve the task of Self Check 12 with only two branches?

14. Beginners sometimes write statements such as the following:

```
   if (price > 100)
   {
       discountedPrice = price - 20;
   }
   else if (price <= 100)
   {
       discountedPrice = price - 10;
   }
```

Explain how this code can be improved.

15. Suppose the user enters -1 into the `EarthquakeStrength.java` program. What is printed?

16. Suppose we want to have the `EarthquakeStrength.java` program check whether the user entered a negative number. What branch would you add to the `if` statement, and where?

Practice It Now you can try these exercises at the end of the chapter: R3.15, P3.1, P3.6.

Special Topic 3.3

The `switch` Statement

An `if/else if/else` sequence that compares a value against several alternatives can be implemented as a `switch` statement. For example,

```
int digit = . . .;
switch (digit)
{
   case 1: digitName = "one"; break;
   case 2: digitName = "two"; break;
   case 3: digitName = "three"; break;
   case 4: digitName = "four"; break;
   case 5: digitName = "five"; break;
   case 6: digitName = "six"; break;
   case 7: digitName = "seven"; break;
   case 8: digitName = "eight"; break;
   case 9: digitName = "nine"; break;
   default: digitName = ""; break;
}
```

This is a shortcut for

```
int digit = . . .;
if (digit == 1) { digitName = "one"; }
else if (digit == 2) { digitName = "two"; }
else if (digit == 3) { digitName = "three"; }
else if (digit == 4) { digitName = "four"; }
else if (digit == 5) { digitName = "five"; }
else if (digit == 6) { digitName = "six"; }
else if (digit == 7) { digitName = "seven"; }
else if (digit == 8) { digitName = "eight"; }
else if (digit == 9) { digitName = "nine"; }
else { digitName = ""; }
```

It isn't much of a shortcut, but it has one advantage—it is obvious that all branches test the *same* value, namely `digit`.

The `switch` statement can be applied only in narrow circumstances. The values in the case clauses must be constants. They can be integers or characters. As of Java 7, strings are permitted as well. You cannot use a `switch` statement to branch on floating-point values.

Every branch of the switch must be terminated by a break instruction. If the break is missing, execution *falls through* to the next branch, and so on, until a break or the end of the `switch` is reached. In practice, this fall-through behavior is

The `switch` statement lets you choose from a fixed set of alternatives.

rarely useful, but it is a common cause of errors. If you accidentally forget a break statement, your program compiles but executes unwanted code. Many programmers consider the `switch` statement somewhat dangerous and prefer the `if` statement.

We leave it to you to use the switch statement for your own code or not. At any rate, you need to have a reading knowledge of switch in case you find it in other programmers' code.

3.4 Nested Branches

It is often necessary to include an if statement inside another. Such an arrangement is called a *nested* set of statements. Here is a typical example.

In the United States, different tax rates are used depending on the taxpayer's marital status. There are different tax schedules for single and for married taxpayers. Married taxpayers add their income together and pay taxes on the total. Table 4 gives the tax rate computations, using a simplification of the schedules in effect for the 2008 tax year. A different tax rate applies to each "bracket". In this schedule, the income at the first bracket is taxed at 10 percent, and the income at the second bracket is taxed at 25 percent. The income limits for each bracket depend on the marital status.

Now compute the taxes due, given a filing status and an income figure. The key point is that there are two *levels* of decision making. First, you must branch on the marital status. Then, for each marital status, you must have another branch on income level.

The two-level decision process is reflected in two levels of if statements in the program at the end of this section. (See Figure 4 for a flowchart.) In theory, nesting can go deeper than two levels. A three-level decision process (first by state, then by filing status, then by income level) requires three nesting levels.

Computing income taxes requires multiple levels of decisions.

Table 4 Federal Tax Rate Schedule		
If your status is Single and if the taxable income is	the tax is	of the amount over
at most $32,000	10%	$0
over $32,000	$3,200 + 25%	$32,000
If your status is Married and if the taxable income is	the tax is	of the amount over
at most $64,000	10%	$0
over $64,000	$6,400 + 25%	$64,000

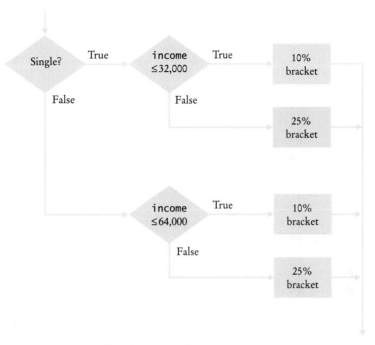

Figure 4 Income Tax Computation

ch03/tax/TaxCalculator.java

```
1   import java.util.Scanner;
2
3   /**
4      This program computes income taxes, using a simplified tax schedule.
5   */
6   public class TaxCalculator
7   {
8      public static void main(String[] args)
9      {
10        final double RATE1 = 0.10;
11        final double RATE2 = 0.25;
12        final double RATE1_SINGLE_LIMIT = 32000;
13        final double RATE1_MARRIED_LIMIT = 64000;
14
15        double tax1 = 0;
16        double tax2 = 0;
17
18        // Read income and marital status
19
20        Scanner in = new Scanner(System.in);
21        System.out.print("Please enter your income: ");
22        double income = in.nextDouble();
23
24        System.out.print("Please enter s for single, m for married: ");
25        String maritalStatus = in.next();
26
```

```
27          // Compute taxes due
28
29          if (maritalStatus.equals("s"))
30          {
31             if (income <= RATE1_SINGLE_LIMIT)
32             {
33                tax1 = RATE1 * income;
34             }
35             else
36             {
37                tax1 = RATE1 * RATE1_SINGLE_LIMIT;
38                tax2 = RATE2 * (income - RATE1_SINGLE_LIMIT);
39             }
40          }
41          else
42          {
43             if (income <= RATE1_MARRIED_LIMIT)
44             {
45                tax1 = RATE1 * income;
46             }
47             else
48             {
49                tax1 = RATE1 * RATE1_MARRIED_LIMIT;
50                tax2 = RATE2 * (income - RATE1_MARRIED_LIMIT);
51             }
52          }
53
54          double totalTax = tax1 + tax2;
55
56          System.out.println("The tax is $" + totalTax);
57       }
58 }
```

Program Run

```
Please enter your income: 80000
Please enter s for single, m for married: m
The tax is $10400
```

SELF CHECK

17. What is the amount of tax that a single taxpayer pays on an income of $32,000?

18. Would that amount change if the first nested if statement changed from

```
if (income <= RATE1_SINGLE_LIMIT)
```
to
```
if (income < RATE1_SINGLE_LIMIT)
```

19. Suppose Harry and Sally each make $40,000 per year. Would they save taxes if they married?

20. How would you modify the TaxCalculator.java program in order to check that the user entered a correct value for the marital status (i.e., s or m)?

21. Some people object to higher tax rates for higher incomes, claiming that you might end up with less money after taxes when you get a raise for working hard. What is the flaw in this argument?

Practice It   Now you can try these exercises at the end of the chapter: R3.7, R3.14, P3.12, P3.17.

Hand-Tracing

A very useful technique for understanding whether a program works correctly is called *hand-tracing*. You simulate the program's activity on a sheet of paper. You can use this method with pseudocode or Java code.

Get an index card, a cocktail napkin, or whatever sheet of paper is within reach. Make a column for each variable. Have the program code ready. Use a marker, such as a paper clip, to mark the current statement. In your mind, execute statements one at a time. Every time the value of a variable changes, cross out the old value and write the new value below the old one.

For example, let's trace the tax program with the data from the program run on page 97. In lines 15 and 16, tax1 and tax2 are initialized to 0.

Hand-tracing helps you understand whether a program works correctly.

```
 8  public static void main(String[] args)
 9  {
10     final double RATE1 = 0.10;
11     final double RATE2 = 0.25;
12     final double RATE1_SINGLE_LIMIT = 32000;
13     final double RATE1_MARRIED_LIMIT = 64000;
14
15     double tax1 = 0;
16     double tax2 = 0;
17
```

tax1	tax2	income	marital status
0	0		

In lines 22 and 25, income and maritalStatus are initialized by input statements.

```
20     Scanner in = new Scanner(System.in);
21     System.out.print("Please enter your income: ");
22     double income = in.nextDouble();
23
24     System.out.print("Please enter s for single, m for married: ");
25     String maritalStatus = in.next();
```

tax1	tax2	income	marital status
0	0	80000	m

Because maritalStatus is not "s", we move to the else branch of the outer if statement (line 41).

```
29     if (maritalStatus.equals("s"))
30     {
31        if (income <= RATE1_SINGLE_LIMIT)
32        {
33           tax1 = RATE1 * income;
34        }
35        else
36        {
37           tax1 = RATE1 * RATE1_SINGLE_LIMIT;
38           tax2 = RATE2 * (income - RATE1_SINGLE_LIMIT);
39        }
40     }
41     else
42     {
```

Because income is not <= 64000, we move to the else branch of the inner if statement (line 47).

```
43        if (income <= RATE1_MARRIED_LIMIT)
44        {
45           tax1 = RATE1 * income;
46        }
47        else
48        {
49           tax1 = RATE1 * RATE1_MARRIED_LIMIT;
50           tax2 = RATE2 * (income - RATE1_MARRIED_LIMIT);
51        }
```

The values of tax1 and tax2 are updated.

```
48      {
49          tax1 = RATE1 * RATE1_MARRIED_LIMIT;
50          tax2 = RATE2 * (income - RATE1_MARRIED_LIMIT);
51      }
52  }
53
```

tax1	tax2	income	marital status
0̸	0̸	80000	m
6400	4000		

Their sum totalTax is computed and printed. Then the program ends.

```
54      double totalTax = tax1 + tax2;
55
56      System.out.println("The tax is $" + totalTax);
57  }
```

tax1	tax2	income	marital status	total tax
0̸	0̸	80000	m	
6400	4000			10400

Because the program trace shows the expected output ($10,400), it successfully demonstrated that this test case works correctly.

Programming Tip 3.6

Prepare Test Cases Ahead of Time

Consider how to test the tax computation program. Of course, you cannot try out all possible inputs of filing status and income level. Even if you could, there would be no point in trying them all. If the program correctly computes one or two tax amounts in a given bracket, then we have a good reason to believe that all amounts will be correct.

You want to aim for complete *coverage* of all decision points. Here is a plan for obtaining a comprehensive set of test cases:

- There are two possibilities for the filing status and two tax brackets for each status, yielding four test cases.
- Test a handful of **boundary test cases**, such as an income that is at the boundary between two brackets, and a zero income.
- If you are responsible for error checking (which is discussed in Section 3.7), also test an invalid input, such as a negative income.

Make a list of the test cases and the expected outputs:

Test Case		Expected Output	Comment
30,000	s	3,000	10% bracket
72,000	s	13,200	3,200 + 25% of 40,000
50,000	m	5,000	10% bracket
104,000	m	16,400	6,400 + 25% of 40,000
32,000	s	3,200	boundary case
0		0	boundary case

It is always a good idea to design test cases *before* starting to code. Working through the test cases gives you a better understanding of the algorithm that you are about to implement.

Programming Tip 3.7

Make a Schedule and Make Time for Unexpected Problems

Commercial software is notorious for being delivered later than promised. For example, Microsoft originally promised that its Windows Vista operating system would be available late in 2003, then in 2005, then in March 2006; it finally was released in January 2007. Some of the early promises might not have been realistic. It was in Microsoft's interest to let prospective customers expect the imminent availability of the product. Had customers known the actual delivery date, they might have switched to a different product in the meantime. Undeniably, though, Microsoft had not anticipated the full complexity of the tasks it had set itself to solve.

Microsoft can delay the delivery of its product, but it is likely that you cannot. As a student or a programmer, you are expected to manage your time wisely and to finish your assignments on time. You can probably do simple programming exercises the night before the due date, but an assignment that looks twice as hard may well take four times as long, because more things can go wrong. You should therefore make a schedule whenever you start a programming project.

First, estimate realistically how much time it will take you to:

- Design the program logic.

- Develop test cases.

- Type the program in and fix syntax errors.

- Test and debug the program.

For example, for the income tax program I might estimate an hour for the design; 30 minutes for developing test cases; an hour for data entry and fixing syntax errors; and an hour for testing and debugging. That is a total of 3.5 hours. If I work two hours a day on this project, it will take me almost two days.

Then think of things that can go wrong. Your computer might break down. You might

Make a schedule for your programming work and build in time for problems.

be stumped by a problem with the computer system. (That is a particularly important concern for beginners. It is *very* common to lose a day over a trivial problem just because it takes time to track down a person who knows the magic command to overcome it.) As a rule of thumb, *double* the time of your estimate. That is, you should start four days, not two days, before the due date. If nothing went wrong, great; you have the program done two days early. When the inevitable problem occurs, you have a cushion of time that protects you from embarrassment and failure.

Common Error 3.4

The Dangling `else` Problem

When an `if` statement is nested inside another `if` statement, the following error may occur.

```
double shippingCharge = 5.00; // $5 inside continental U.S.
if (country.equals("USA"))
   if (state.equals("HI"))
      shippingCharge = 10.00; // Hawaii is more expensive
else // Pitfall!
   shippingCharge = 20.00; // As are foreign shipments
```

The indentation level seems to suggest that the `else` is grouped with the test `country.equals("USA")`. Unfortunately, that is not the case. The compiler ignores all indentation and matches the `else` with the preceding `if`. That is, the code is actually

```
double shippingCharge = 5.00; // $5 inside continental U.S.
if (country.equals("USA"))
   if (state.equals("HI"))
      shippingCharge = 10.00; // Hawaii is more expensive
   else // Pitfall!
      shippingCharge = 20.00; // As are foreign shipments
```

That isn't what you want. You want to group the `else` with the first `if`.

The ambiguous `else` is called a *dangling* `else`. You can avoid this pitfall if you *always use braces*, as recommended in Programming Tip 3.2 on page 82:

```
double shippingCharge = 5.00; // $5 inside continental U.S.
if (country.equals("USA"))
{
   if (state.equals("HI"))
   {
      shippingCharge = 10.00; // Hawaii is more expensive
   }
}
else
{
   shippingCharge = 20.00; // As are foreign shipments
}
```

3.5 Boolean Variables and Operators

The Boolean type `boolean` has two values, `false` and `true`.

A Boolean variable is also called a flag because it can be either up (true) or down (false).

Sometimes, you need to evaluate a logical condition in one part of a program and use it elsewhere. To store a condition that can be true or false, you use a *Boolean variable*. Boolean variables are named after the mathematician George Boole (1815–1864), a pioneer in the study of logic.

In Java, the `boolean` data type has exactly two values, denoted `false` and `true`. These values are not strings or integers; they are special values, just for Boolean variables. Here is a declaration of a Boolean variable:

```
boolean failed = true;
```

You can use the value later in your program to make a decision:

```
if (failed) // Only executed if failed has been set to true
{
   . . .
}
```

The `Character` class declares several useful methods that return a Boolean value (see Table 5).

BOOLE ORDERS LUNCH

NO, NO, YES, NO, NO, YES
YES, NO, NO, NO, YES...

Table 5 Character Testing Methods

Method	Examples of Accepted Characters
isDigit	0, 1, 2
isLetter	A, B, C, a, b, c
isUpperCase	A, B, C
isLowerCase	a, b, c
isWhiteSpace	space, newline, tab

For example, the call

```
Character.isDigit(ch)
```

returns true if ch is a digit ('0' . . . '9' or a digit in another writing system—see Random Fact 2.2), false otherwise.

> Java has two Boolean operators that combine conditions: && (*and*) and || (*or*).

When you make complex decisions, you often need to combine Boolean values. An operator that combines Boolean conditions is called a **Boolean operator**. In Java, the && operator (called *and*) yields true only when both conditions are true. The || operator (called *or*) yields the result true if at least one of the conditions is true.

Suppose you write a program that processes temperature values, and you want to test whether a given temperature corresponds to liquid water. (At sea level, water freezes at 0 degrees Celsius and boils at 100 degrees.) Water is liquid if the temperature is greater than zero *and* less than 100:

```
if (temp > 0 && temp < 100) { System.out.println("Liquid"); }
```

The condition of the test has two parts, joined by the && operator. Each part is a Boolean value that can be true or false. The combined expression is true if both individual expressions are true. If either one of the expressions is false, then the result is also false (see Figure 5).

The Boolean operators && and || have a lower precedence than the relational operators. For that reason, you can write relational expressions on either side of the Boolean operators without using parentheses. For example, in the expression

```
temp > 0 && temp < 100
```

A	B	A && B
true	true	true
true	false	false
false	true	false
false	false	false

A	B	A || B
true	true	true
true	false	true
false	true	true
false	false	false

A	!A
true	false
false	true

Figure 5 Boolean Truth Tables

At this geyser in Iceland, you can see ice, liquid water, and steam.

the expressions temp > 0 and temp < 100 are evaluated first. Then the && operator combines the results. Appendix B shows a table of the Java operators and their precedence.

Conversely, let's test whether water is not liquid at a given temperature. That is the case when the temperature is at most 0 *or* at least 100. Use the || (*or*) operator to combine the expressions:

```
if (temp <= 0 || temp >= 100) { System.out.println("Not liquid"); }
```

Figure 6 shows flowcharts for these examples.

Sometimes you need to *invert* a condition with the *not* logical operator. The ! operator takes a single condition and evaluates to true if that condition is false and to false if the condition is true. In this example, output occurs if the value of the Boolean variable frozen is false:

> To invert a condition, use the ! (*not*) operator.

```
if (!frozen) { System.out.println("Not frozen"); }
```

Table 6 illustrates additional examples of evaluating Boolean operators.

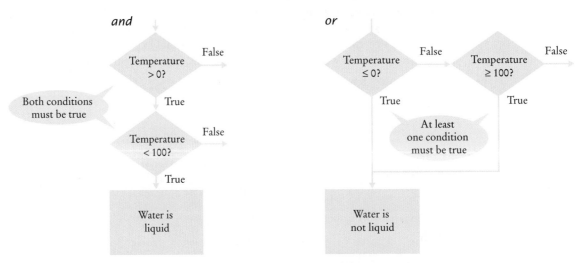

Figure 6 Flowcharts for *and* and *or* Combinations

Table 6 Boolean Operator Examples

Expression	Value	Comment
0 < 200 && 200 < 100	false	Only the first condition is true.
0 < 200 || 200 < 100	true	The first condition is true.
0 < 200 || 100 < 200	true	The || is not a test for "either-or". If both conditions are true, the result is true.
0 < x && x < 100 || x == -1	(0 < x && x < 100) || x == -1	The && operator has a higher precedence than the || operator (see Appendix B).
🚫 0 < x < 100	**Error**	**Error:** This expression does not test whether x is between 0 and 100. The expression 0 < x is a Boolean value. You cannot compare a Boolean value with the integer 100.
🚫 x && y > 0	**Error**	**Error:** This expression does not test whether x and y are positive. The left-hand side of && is an integer, x, and the right-hand side, y > 0, is a Boolean value. You cannot use && with an integer argument.
!(0 < 200)	false	0 < 200 is true, therefore its negation is false.
frozen == true	frozen	There is no need to compare a Boolean variable with true.
frozen == false	!frozen	It is clearer to use ! than to compare with false.

SELF CHECK

22. Suppose x and y are two integers. How do you test whether both of them are zero?
23. How do you test whether at least one of them is zero?
24. How do you test whether *exactly one of them* is zero?
25. What is the value of !!frozen?
26. What is the advantage of using the type boolean rather than strings "false"/"true" or integers 0/1?

Practice It   Now you can try these exercises at the end of the chapter: R3.21, P3.21, P3.23.

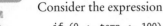

Common Error 3.5

Combining Multiple Relational Operators

Consider the expression

```
if (0 <= temp <= 100) // Error
```

This looks just like the mathematical test $0 \leq temp \leq 100$. But in Java, it is a compile-time error.

Let us dissect the condition. The first half, `0 <= temp`, is a test with an outcome `true` or `false`. The outcome of that test (`true` or `false`) is then compared against 100. This seems to make no sense. Is `true` larger than 100 or not? Can one compare truth values and numbers? In Java, you cannot. The Java compiler rejects this statement.

Instead, use `&&` to combine two separate tests:

```
if (0 <= temp && temp <= 100) . . .
```

Another common error, along the same lines, is to write

```
if (input == 1 || 2) . . . // Error
```

to test whether `input` is 1 or 2. Again, the Java compiler flags this construct as an error. You cannot apply the `||` operator to numbers. You need to write two Boolean expressions and join them with the `||` operator:

```
if (input == 1 || input == 2) . . .
```

Common Error 3.6

Confusing `&&` and `||` Conditions

It is a surprisingly common error to confuse *and* and *or* conditions. A value lies between 0 and 100 if it is at least 0 *and* at most 100. It lies outside that range if it is less than 0 *or* greater than 100. There is no golden rule; you just have to think carefully.

Often the *and* or *or* is clearly stated, and then it isn't too hard to implement it. But sometimes the wording isn't as explicit. It is quite common that the individual conditions are nicely set apart in a bulleted list, but with little indication of how they should be combined. Consider these instructions for filing a tax return. You can claim single filing status if any one of the following is true:

- You were never married.
- You were legally separated or divorced on the last day of the tax year.
- You were widowed, and did not remarry.

Since the test passes if *any one* of the conditions is true, you must combine the conditions with *or*. Elsewhere, the same instructions state that you may use the more advantageous status of married filing jointly if all five of the following conditions are true:

- Your spouse died less than two years ago and you did not remarry.
- You have a child whom you can claim as dependent.
- That child lived in your home for all of the tax year.
- You paid over half the cost of keeping up your home for this child.
- You filed a joint return with your spouse the year he or she died.

Because *all* of the conditions must be true for the test to pass, you must combine them with an *and*.

Special Topic 3.4

Lazy Evaluation of Boolean Operators

The && and || operators are computed using **lazy evaluation**. In other words, logical expressions are evaluated from left to right, and evaluation stops as soon as the truth value is determined. When an && is evaluated and the first condition is false, the second condition is not evaluated, because it does not matter what the outcome of the second test is.

For example, consider the expression

```
quantity > 0 && price / quantity < 10
```

Suppose the value of quantity is zero. Then the test quantity > 0 fails, and the second test is not attempted. That is just as well, because it is illegal to divide by zero.

Similarly, when the first condition of an || expression is true, then the remainder is not evaluated because the result must be true.

> The && and || operators are computed *lazily*: As soon as the truth value is determined, no further conditions are evaluated.

Lazy evaluation stops as soon as the result is known.

Special Topic 3.5

De Morgan's Law

Humans generally have a hard time comprehending logical conditions with *not* operators applied to *and/or* expressions. De Morgan's Law, named after the logician Augustus De Morgan (1806–1871), can be used to simplify these Boolean expressions.

Suppose we want to charge a higher shipping rate if we don't ship within the continental United States.

```
if (!(country.equals("USA") && !state.equals("AK") && !state.equals("HI")))
{
    shippingCharge = 20.00;
}
```

This test is a little bit complicated, and you have to think carefully through the logic. When it is *not* true that the country is USA *and* the state is not Alaska *and* the state is not Hawaii, then charge $20.00. Huh? It is not true that some people won't be confused by this code.

The computer doesn't care, but it takes human programmers to write and maintain the code. Therefore, it is useful to know how to simplify such a condition.

De Morgan's Law has two forms: one for the negation of an *and* expression and one for the negation of an *or* expression:

> De Morgan's law tells you how to negate && and || conditions.

!(A && B)   is the same as   !A || !B
!(A || B)   is the same as   !A && !B

Pay particular attention to the fact that the *and* and *or* operators are *reversed* by moving the *not* inward. For example, the negation of "the state is Alaska *or* it is Hawaii",

```
!(state.equals("AK") || state.equals("HI"))
```

is "the state is not Alaska *and* it is not Hawaii":

```
!state.equals("AK") && !state.equals("HI")
```

Now apply the law to our shipping charge computation:

```
!(country.equals("USA")
    && !state.equals("AK")
    && !state.equals("HI"))
```

is equivalent to

```
!country.equals("USA")
    || !!state.equals("AK")
    || !!state.equals("HI"))
```

Since two ! cancel each other out, the result is simpler test

```
!country.equals("USA")
    || state.equals("AK")
    || state.equals("HI")
```

In other words, higher shipping charges apply when the destination is outside the United States or to Alaska or Hawaii.

To simplify conditions with negations of *and* or *or* expressions, it is usually a good idea to apply De Morgan's Law to move the negations to the innermost level.

3.6 Application: Input Validation

Like a quality control worker, you want to make sure that user input is correct before processing it.

An important application for the if statement is *input validation*. Whenever your program accepts user input, you need to make sure that the user-supplied values are valid before you use them in your computations.

Consider our elevator program. Assume that the elevator panel has buttons labeled 1 through 20 (but not 13). The following are illegal inputs:

- The number 13
- Zero or a negative number
- A number larger than 20
- An input that is not a sequence of digits, such as the string five

In each of these cases, we will want to give an error message and exit the program.

It is simple to guard against an input of 13:

```
if (floor == 13)
{
    System.out.println("Error: There is no thirteenth floor.");
}
```

Here is how you ensure that the user doesn't enter a number outside the valid range:

```
if (floor <= 0 || floor > 20)
{
    System.out.println("Error: The floor must be between 1 and 20.");
}
```

However, dealing with an input that is not a valid integer is a more serious problem. When the statement

```
floor = in.nextInt();
```

is executed, and the user types in an input that is not an integer (such as five), then the integer variable floor is not set. Instead, a run-time exception occurs and the program is terminated. To avoid this problem, you should first call the hasNextInt method which checks whether the next input is an integer. If that method returns true, you can safely call nextInt. Otherwise, print an error message and exit the program.

```java
if (in.hasNextInt())
{
   int floor = in.nextInt();
   Process the input value
}
else
{
   System.out.println("Error: Not an integer.");
}
```

Here is the complete elevator program with input validation.

ch03/elevator2/ElevatorSimulation2.java

```java
1   import java.util.Scanner;
2
3   /**
4      This program simulates an elevator panel that skips the 13th floor, checking for
5      input errors.
6   */
7   public class ElevatorSimulation2
8   {
9      public static void main(String[] args)
10     {
11        Scanner in = new Scanner(System.in);
12        System.out.print("Floor: ");
13        if (!in.hasNextInt())
14        {
15           // Now we know that the user entered an integer
16
17           int floor = in.nextInt();
18
19           if (floor == 13)
20           {
21              System.out.println("Error: There is no thirteenth floor.");
22           }
23           else if (floor <= 0 || floor > 20)
24           {
25              System.out.println("Error: The floor must be between 1 and 20.");
26           }
27           else
28           {
29              // Now we know that the input is valid
30
31              int actualFloor = floor;
32              if (floor > 13)
33              {
34                 actualFloor = floor - 1;
```

```
35              }
36
37              System.out.println("The elevator will travel to the actual floor "
38                  + actualFloor);
39          }
40      }
41      else
42      {
43          System.out.println("Error: Not an integer.");
44      }
45   }
46 }
```

Program Run

```
Floor: 13
Error: There is no thirteenth floor.
```

27. Consider the ElevatorSimulation2 program. What output do you get when the input is

a. 100

b. −1

c. 20

d. thirteen

Random Fact 3.2 **Artificial Intelligence**

When one uses a sophisticated computer program such as a tax preparation package, one is bound to attribute some intelligence to the computer. The computer asks sensible questions and makes computations that we find a mental challenge. After all, if doing one's taxes were easy, we wouldn't need a computer to do it for us.

As programmers, however, we know that all this apparent intelligence is an illusion. Human programmers have carefully "coached" the software in all possible scenarios, and it simply replays the actions and decisions that were programmed into it.

Would it be possible to write computer programs that are genuinely intelligent in some sense? From the earliest days of computing, there was a sense that the human brain might be nothing but an immense computer, and that it might well be feasible to program computers to imitate some processes of human thought. Serious research into *artificial intelligence* began in the mid-1950s, and the first twenty years brought some impressive successes. Programs that play chess—surely an activity that appears to require remarkable intellectual powers—have become so good that they now routinely beat all but the best human players. As far back as 1975, an *expert-system* program called Mycin gained fame for being better in diagnosing meningitis in patients than the average physician.

However, there were serious setbacks as well. From 1982 to 1992, the Japanese government embarked on a massive research project, funded at over 40 billion Japanese yen. It was known as the *Fifth-Generation Project*. Its goal was to develop new hardware and software to greatly improve the performance of expert system software. At its outset, the project created fear in other countries that the Japanese computer industry was about to become the undisputed leader in the field. However, the end results were disappointing and did little to bring artificial intelligence applications to market.

From the very outset, one of the stated goals of the artificial intelligence community was to produce software that could translate text from one language to another, for example from English to Russian. That undertaking proved to be enormously complicated. Human language appears to be much more subtle and interwoven with the human experience than had originally been thought. Even the grammar-checking tools that come with word-processing programs today are more of a gimmick than a useful tool, and analyzing grammar is just the first step in translating sentences.

The CYC (from en*cyc*lopedia) project, started by Douglas Lenat in 1984, tries to codify the implicit assumptions that underlie human speech and writing. The team members

28. Your task is to rewrite lines 19–26 of the `ElevatorSimulation2` program so that there is a single `if` statement with a complex condition:

```
if (. . .)
{
    System.out.println("Error: Invalid floor number");
    return;
}
```

What is the condition?

29. In the Sherlock Holmes story "The Adventure of the Sussex Vampire", the inimitable detective uttered these words: "Matilda Briggs was not the name of a young woman, Watson, … It was a ship which is associated with the giant rat of Sumatra, a story for which the world is not yet prepared." Over a hundred years later, researchers found giant rats in Western New Guinea, another part of Indonesia.

Suppose you are charged with writing a program that processes rat weights. It contains the statements

```
System.out.print("Enter weight in kg: ");
double weight = in.nextDouble();
```

What input checks should you supply?

When processing inputs, you want to reject values that are too large. But how large is too large? These giant rats, found in Western New Guinea, are about five times the size of a city rat.

started out analyzing news articles and asked themselves what unmentioned facts are necessary to actually understand the sentences. For example, consider the sentence "Last fall she enrolled in Michigan State". The reader automatically realizes that "fall" is not related to falling down in this context, but refers to the season. While there is a state of Michigan, here Michigan State denotes the university. A priori, a computer program has none of this knowledge. The goal of the CYC project is to extract and store the requisite facts—that is, (1) people enroll in universities; (2) Michigan is a state; (3) many states have universities named X State University, often abbreviated as X State; (4) most people enroll in a university in the fall. By 1995, the project had codified about 100,000 common-sense concepts and about a million facts of knowledge relating them. Even this massive amount of data has not proven sufficient for useful applications.

In recent years, artificial intelligence technology has seen substantial advances. One of the most astounding examples is the outcome of a series of "grand challenges" for autonomous vehicles posed by the Defense Advanced Research Projects Agency (DARPA). Competitors were invited to submit a computer-controlled vehicle that had to complete an obstacle course without a human driver or remote control. The first event, in 2004, was a disappointment, with none of the entrants finishing the route. In 2005, five vehicles completed a grueling 212 km course in the Mojave desert. Stanford's Stanley came in first, with an average speed of 30 km/h. In 2007, DARPA moved the competition to an "urban" environment, an abandoned air force base. Vehicles had to be able to interact with each other, following

Winner of the 2007 DARPA Urban Challenge

California traffic laws. As Stanford's Sebastian Thrun explained, "In the last Grand Challenge, it didn't really matter whether an obstacle was a rock or a bush, because either way you'd just drive around it. The current challenge is to move from just sensing the environment to understanding it."

30. Consider the following test program:

```java
public class Test
{
    public static void main(String[] args)
    {
        Scanner in = new Scanner(System.in);
        System.out.print("Enter an integer: ");
        int m = in.nextInt();
        System.out.print("Enter another integer: ");
        int n = in.nextInt();
        System.out.println(m + " " + n);
    }
}
```

Run this program and supply inputs 2 and three at the prompts. What happens?
Why?

Practice It   Now you can try these exercises at the end of the chapter: R3.1, R3.24, P3.25.

SCREENCAST 3.1   **The Genetic Code**

Watch this Screencast Video to see how to build a "decoder ring" for
the genetic code.

CHAPTER SUMMARY

- The `if` statement allows a program to carry out different actions
  depending on the nature of the data to be processed.

- Relational operators (`<` `<=` `>` `>=` `==` `!=`) are used to compare numbers and strings.
- Do not use the `==` operator to compare strings. Use the `equals` method instead.

- The `compareTo` method compares strings in lexicographic order.

- Multiple `if` statements can be combined to evaluate complex decisions.
  - When using multiple `if` statements, test general conditions after more specific conditions.

- The Boolean type `boolean` has two values, `false` and `true`.
  - Java has two Boolean operators that combine conditions: `&&` (*and*) and `||` (*or*).
  - To invert a condition, use the `!` (*not*) operator.
  - The `&&` and `||` operators are computed *lazily:* As soon as the truth value is determined, no further conditions are evaluated.
  - De Morgan's law tells you how to negate `&&` and `||` conditions.

- Call the `hasNextInt` or `hasNextDouble` method to ensure that the next input is a number.

MEDIA RESOURCES

www.wiley.com/
college/
horstmann

- **Worked Example** Extracting the Middle
- Guided Lab Exercises
- ⊕ **Animation** Multiple Alternatives
- ⊕ **Animation** Nested Branches
- ⊕ **Screencast** The Genetic Code
- ⊕ Practice Quiz
- ⊕ Code Completion Exercises

REVIEW EXERCISES

★★   **R3.1** Find the errors in the following `if` statements.

a. `if x > 0 then System.out.print(x);`

b. `if (1 + x > Math.pow(x, Math.sqrt(2)) { y = y + x; }`

c. `if (x = 1) { y++; }`

d.
```
x = in.nextInt();
if (in.hasNextInt())
{
   sum = sum + x;
}
else
{
   System.out.println("Bad input for x");
}
```

★ **R3.2** What do these code fragments print?

a.
```java
int n = 1;
int m = -1;
if (n < -m) { System.out.print(n); }
else { System.out.print(m); }
```

b.
```java
int n = 1;
int m = -1;
if (-n >= m) { System.out.print(n); }
else { System.out.print(m); }
```

c.
```java
double x = 0;
double y = 1;
if (Math.abs(x - y) < 1) { System.out.print(x); }
else { System.out.print(y); }
```

d.
```java
double x = Math.sqrt(2);
double y = 2;
if (x * x == y) { System.out.print(x); }
else { System.out.print(y); }
```

★★ **R3.3** Suppose x and y are variables of type `double`. Write a code fragment that sets y to x if x is positive and to 0 otherwise.

★★ **R3.4** Suppose x and y are variables of type `double`. Write a code fragment that sets y to the absolute value of x without calling the `Math.abs` function. Use an `if` statement.

★★ **R3.5** Explain why it is more difficult to compare floating-point numbers than integers. Write Java code to test whether an integer n equals 10 and whether a floating-point number x is approximately equal to 10.

★ **R3.6** Why is it more difficult to compare floating-point numbers than integers? It is easy to confuse the = and == operators. Write a test program containing a statement

```java
if (floor = 13)
```

What error message do you get? Write another test program containing the statement

```java
count == 0;
```

What does your compiler do when you compile the program?

★★ **R3.7** Each square on a chess board can be described by a letter and number, such as g5 in this example:

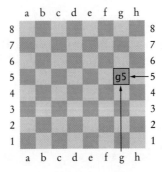

The following pseudocode describes an algorithm that determines whether a square with a given letter and number is dark (black) or light (white).

```
If the letter is an a, c, e, or g
    If the number is odd
        color = "black"
    Else
        color = "white"
Else
    If the number is even
        color = "black"
    Else
        color = "white"
```

Using the procedure in Programming Tip 3.5 on page 99, trace this pseudocode with input g5.

★★ **R3.8** Give a set of four test cases for the algorithm of Exercise R3.7 that covers all branches.

★★ **R3.9** In a scheduling program, we want to check whether two appointments overlap. For simplicity, appointments start at a full hour, and we use military time (with hours 0–24). The following pseudocode describes an algorithm that determines whether the appointment with start time **start1** and end time **end1** overlaps with the appointment with start time **start2** and end time **end2**.

```
If start1 > start2
    s = start1
Else
    s = start2
If end1 < end2
    e = end1
Else
    e = end2
If s < e
    The appointments overlap.
Else
    The appointments don't overlap.
```

Trace this algorithm with an appointment from 10–12 and one from 11–13, then with an appointment from 10–11 and one from 12–13.

★★ **R3.10** Write pseudocode for a program that prompts the user for a month and day and prints out whether it is one of the following four holidays:

- New Year's Day (January 1)
- Independence Day (July 4)
- Veterans Day (November 11)
- Christmas Day (December 25)

★★ **R3.11** Write pseudocode for a program that assigns letter grades for a quiz, according to the following table:

Score	Grade
90–100	A
80–89	B
70–79	C
60–69	D
< 60	F

★★ **R3.12** Explain how the lexicographic ordering of strings in Java differs from the ordering of words in a dictionary or telephone book. *Hint:* Consider strings such as IBM, wiley.com, Century 21, and While-U-Wait.

★★ **R3.13** Of the following pairs of strings, which comes first in lexicographic order?
    a. "Tom", "Jerry"
    b. "Tom", "Tomato"
    c. "church", "Churchill"
    d. "car manufacturer", "carburetor"
    e. "Harry", "hairy"
    f. "Java", " Car"
    g. "Tom", "Tom"
    h. "Car", "Carl"
    i. "car", "bar"

★ **R3.14** Explain the difference between an if/else if/else sequence and nested if statements. Give an example of each.

★★ **R3.15** Give an example of an if/else if/else sequence where the order of the tests does not matter. Give an example where the order of the tests matters.

★★ **R3.16** Give a set of test cases for the tax program in Exercise P3.18. Manually compute the expected results.

★★ **R3.17** Make up another Java code example that shows the dangling else problem, using the following statement: A student with a GPA of at least 1.5, but less than 2, is on probation. With less than 1.5, the student is failing.

★★★ **R3.18** Complete the following truth table by finding the truth values of the Boolean expressions for all combinations of the Boolean inputs p, q, and r.

p	q	r	(p && q) || !r	!(p && (q || !r))
false	false	false		
false	false	true		
false	true	false		
. . .				
5 more combinations				
. . .				

★★★ **R3.19** True or false? *A* && *B* is the same as *B* && *A* for any Boolean conditions *A* and *B*.

★ **R3.20** The "advanced search" feature of many search engines allows you to use Boolean operators for complex queries, such as "(cats OR dogs) AND NOT pets". Contrast these search operators with the Boolean operators in Java.

★★ **R3.21** Suppose the value of b is false and the value of x is 0. What is the value of each of the following expressions?

      a. b && x == 0
      b. b || x == 0
      c. !b && x == 0
      d. !b || x == 0
      e. b && x != 0
      f. b || x != 0
      g. !b && x != 0
      h. !b || x != 0

★★ **R3.22** Simplify the following expressions. Here, b is a variable of type boolean.

      a. b == true
      b. b == false
      c. b != true
      d. b != false

★★★ **R3.23** Simplify the following statements. Here, b is a variable of type boolean and n is a variable of type int.

      a. if (n == 0) { b = true; } else { b = false; }
        (*Hint:* What is the value of n == 0?)
      b. if (n == 0) { b = false; } else { b = true; }
      c. b = false; if (n > 1) { if (n < 2) { b = true; } }
      d. if (n < 1) { b = true; } else { b = n > 2; }

★ **R3.24** What is wrong with the following program?

```
System.out.print("Enter the number of quarters: ");
int quarters = in.nextInt();
if (in.hasNextInt())
{
   total = total + quarters * 0.25;
   System.out.println("Total: " + total);
}
else
{
   System.out.println("Input error.");
}
```

PROGRAMMING EXERCISES

★ **P3.1** Write a program that reads a temperature value and the letter C for Celsius or F for Fahrenheit. Print whether water is liquid, solid, or gaseous at the given temperature at sea level.

★ **P3.2** The boiling point of water drops by about one degree centigrade for every 300 meters (or 1,000 feet) of altitude. Improve the program of Exercise P3.1 to allow the user to supply the altitude in meters or feet.

★★ **P3.3** Write a program that translates a letter grade into a number grade. Letter grades are A, B, C, D, and F, possibly followed by + or −. Their numeric values are 4, 3, 2, 1, and 0. There is no F+ or F−. A + increases the numeric value by 0.3, a − decreases it by 0.3. However, an A+ has value 4.0.

```
Enter a letter grade: B-
The numeric value is 2.7.
```

★★ **P3.4** Write a program that translates a number between 0 and 4 into the closest letter grade. For example, the number 2.8 (which might have been the average of several grades) would be converted to B−. Break ties in favor of the better grade; for example 2.85 should be a B.

★★ **P3.5** Write a program that takes user input describing a playing card in the following shorthand notation:

A	Ace
2 ... 10	Card values
J	Jack
Q	Queen
K	King
D	Diamonds
H	Hearts
S	Spades
C	Clubs

Your program should print the full description of the card. For example,

```
Enter the card notation: QS
Queen of Spades
```

★ **P3.6** Write a program that prompts the user for a wavelength value and prints a description of the corresponding part of the electromagnetic spectrum, as given in Table 7.

Table 7	Electromagnetic Spectrum	
Type	Wavelength (m)	Frequency (Hz)
Radio Waves	$> 10^{-1}$	$< 3 \times 10^9$
Microwaves	10^{-3} to 10^{-1}	3×10^9 to 3×10^{11}
Infrared	7×10^{-7} to 10^{-3}	3×10^{11} to 4×10^{14}
Visible light	4×10^{-7} to 7×10^{-7}	4×10^{14} to 7.5×10^{14}
Ultraviolet	10^{-8} to 4×10^{-7}	7.5×10^{14} to 3×10^{16}
X-rays	10^{-11} to 10^{-8}	3×10^{16} to 3×10^{19}
Gamma rays	$< 10^{-11}$	$> 3 \times 10^{19}$

★ **P3.7** Repeat Exercise P3.6, modifying the program so that it prompts for the frequency instead.

★★   **P3.8**   Repeat Exercise P3.6, modifying the program so that it first asks the user whether the input will be a wavelength or a frequency.

★★   **P3.9**   Write a program that reads in three floating-point numbers and prints the largest of the three inputs. For example:

```
Please enter three numbers: 4 9 2.5
The largest number is 9.
```

★★   **P3.10**   Write a program that reads in three strings and sorts them lexicographically.

```
Enter three strings: Charlie Able Baker
Able
Baker
Charlie
```

★★   **P3.11**   When two points in time are compared, each given as hours (in military time, ranging from 0 and 23) and minutes, the following pseudocode determines which comes first.

```
If hour1 < hour2
    time1 comes first.
Else if hour1 and hour2 are the same
    If minute1 < minute2
        time1 comes first.
    Else if minute1 and minute2 are the same
        time1 and time2 are the same.
    Else
        time2 comes first.
Else
    time2 comes first.
```

Write a program that prompts the user for two points in time and prints the time that comes first, then the other time.

★★   **P3.12**   The following algorithm yields the season (Spring, Summer, Fall, or Winter) for a given month and day.

```
If month is 1, 2, or 3, season = "Winter"
Else if month is 4, 5, or 6, season = "Spring"
Else if month is 7, 8, or 9, season = "Summer"
Else if month is 10, 11, or 12, season = "Fall"
If month is divisible by 3 and day >= 21
    If season is "Winter", season = "Spring"
    Else if season is "Spring", season = "Summer"
    Else if season is "Summer", season = "Fall"
    Else season = "Winter"
```

Write a program that prompts the user for a month and day and then prints the season, as determined by this algorithm.

★★   **P3.13**   Write a program that reads in two floating-point numbers and tests whether they are the same up to two decimal places. Here are two sample runs.

```
Enter two floating-point numbers: 2.0 1.99998
They are the same up to two decimal places.
Enter two floating-point numbers: 2.0 1.98999
They are different.
```

★★★ **P3.14** Write a program to simulate a bank transaction. There are two bank accounts: checking and savings. First, ask for the initial balances of the bank accounts; reject negative balances. Then ask for the transactions; options are deposit, withdrawal, and transfer. Then ask for the account; options are checking and savings. Then ask for the amount; reject transactions that overdraw an account. At the end, print the balances of both accounts.

★★ **P3.15** Write a program that reads in the name and salary of an employee. Here the salary will denote an *hourly* wage, such as $9.25. Then ask how many hours the employee worked in the past week. Be sure to accept fractional hours. Compute the pay. Any overtime work (over 40 hours per week) is paid at 150 percent of the regular wage. Print a paycheck for the employee.

★★★ **P3.16** Write a program that prompts for the day and month of the user's birthday and then prints a horoscope. Make up fortunes for programmers, like this:

```
Please enter your birthday (month and day): 6 16
Gemini are experts at figuring out the behavior of complicated programs.
You feel where bugs are coming from and then stay one step ahead. Tonight,
your style wins approval from a tough critic.
```

Each fortune should contain the name of the astrological sign. (You will find the names and date ranges of the signs at a distressingly large number of sites on the Internet.)

★★ **P3.17** The original U.S. income tax of 1913 was quite simple. The tax was

- 1 percent on the first $50,000.
- 2 percent on the amount over $50,000 up to $75,000.
- 3 percent on the amount over $75,000 up to $100,000.
- 4 percent on the amount over $100,000 up to $250,000.
- 5 percent on the amount over $250,000 up to $500,000.
- 6 percent on the amount over $500,000.

There was no separate schedule for single or married taxpayers. Write a program that computes the income tax according to this schedule.

★★★ **P3.18** Write a program that computes taxes for the following schedule.

If your status is Single and if the taxable income is over	but not over	the tax is	of the amount over
$0	$8,000	10%	$0
$8,000	$32,000	$800 + 15%	$8,000
$32,000		$4,400 + 25%	$32,000
If your status is Married and if the taxable income is over	but not over	the tax is	of the amount over
$0	$16,000	10%	$0
$16,000	$64,000	$1,600 + 15%	$16,000
$64,000		$8,800 + 25%	$64,000

★★★ **P3.19** The `TaxCalculator.java` program uses a simplified version of the 2008 U.S. income tax schedule. Look up the tax brackets and rates for the current year, for both single and married filers, and implement a program that computes the actual income tax.

★★★ **P3.20** *Unit conversion.* Write a unit conversion program that asks the users from which unit they want to convert (fl. oz, gal, oz, lb, in, ft, mi) and to which unit they want to convert (ml, l, g, kg, mm, cm, m, km). Reject incompatible conversions (such as gal → km). Ask for the value to be converted, then display the result:

```
Convert from? gal
Convert to? ml
Value? 2.5
2.5 gal = 9462.5 ml
```

★ **P3.21** Write a program that prompts the user to provide a single character from the alphabet. Print `Vowel` or `Consonant`, depending on the user input. If the user input is not a letter (between a and z or A and Z), or is a string of length > 1, print an error message.

★★★ **P3.22** *Roman numbers.* Write a program that converts a positive integer into the Roman number system. The Roman number system has digits

I	1
V	5
X	10
L	50
C	100
D	500
M	1,000

Numbers are formed according to the following rules. (1) Only numbers up to 3,999 are represented. (2) As in the decimal system, the thousands, hundreds, tens, and ones are expressed separately. (3) The numbers 1 to 9 are expressed as

I	1
II	2
III	3
IV	4
V	5
VI	6
VII	7
VIII	8
IX	9

As you can see, an I preceding a V or X is subtracted from the value, and you can never have more than three I's in a row. (4) Tens and hundreds are done the same way, except that the letters X, L, C and C, D, M are used instead of I, V, X, respectively.

Your program should take an input, such as 1978, and convert it to Roman numerals, MCMLXXVIII.

★★ **P3.23** Write a program that asks the user to enter a month (1 for January, 2 for February, and so on) and then prints the number of days in the month. For February, print "28 or 29 days".

```
Enter a month: 5
30 days
```

Do not use a separate if/else branch for each month. Use Boolean operators.

★★★ **P3.24** A year with 366 days is called a leap year. Leap years are necessary to keep the calendar synchronized with the sun because the earth revolves around the sun once every 365.25 days. Actually, that figure is not entirely precise, and for all dates after 1582 the *Gregorian correction* applies. Usually years that are divisible by 4 are leap years, for example 1996. However, years that are divisible by 100 (for example, 1900) are not leap years, but years that are divisible by 400 are leap years (for example, 2000). Write a program that asks the user for a year and computes whether that year is a leap year. Use a single if statement and Boolean operators.

★ **P3.25** Add error handling to Exercise P3.2. If the user does not enter a number when expected, or provides an invalid unit for the altitude, print an error message and end the program.

ANSWERS TO SELF-CHECK QUESTIONS

1. Change the if statement to

   ```
   if (floor > 14)
   {
       actualFloor = floor - 2;
   }
   ```

2. 85. 90. 85.

3. The only difference is if originalPrice is 100. The statement in Self Check 2 sets discountedPrice to 90; this one sets it to 80.

4. 95. 100. 95.

5. ```
   if (fuelAmount < 0.10 * fuelCapacity)
   {
       System.out.println("red");
   }
   else
   {
       System.out.println("green");
   }
   ```

6. (a) and (b) are both true, (c) is false.

7. floor <= 13

8. The values should be compared with ==, not =.

9. input.equals("Y")

10. str.equals("") or str.length() == 0

11. ```
    if (scoreA > scoreB) { System.out.println("A won"); }
    else if (scoreA < scoreB) { System.out.println("B won"); }
    else { System.out.println("Game tied"); }
    ```

12. ```
    if (x > 0) { s = 1; }
    else if (x < 0) { s = -1; }
    else { s = 0; }
    ```

13. You could first set s to one of the three values:

    ```
    s = 0;
    if (x > 0) { s = 1; }
    else if (x < 0) { s = -1; }
    ```

14. The if (price <= 100) can be omitted (leaving just else), making it clear that the else branch is the sole alternative.

15. No destruction of buildings.

16. Add a branch

    ```
    else if (richter < 0) { System.out.println("Error: Negative input"); }
    ```

    before the final else.

17. 3200.

18. No. Then the computation is $0.10 \times 32000 + 0.25 \times (32000 - 32000)$.

19. No. Their individual tax is $5,200 each, and if they married, they would pay $10,400. Actually, taxpayers in higher tax brackets (which our program does not model) may pay higher taxes when they marry, a phenomenon known as the *marriage penalty*.
    ```

20. Change else in line 41 to else if (maritalStatus.equals("m")), and add another branch after line 51:

    ```
    else { System.out.println("Error: marital status should be s or m."); }
    ```

21. The higher tax rate is only applied on the income in the higher bracket. Suppose you are single and make $31,900. Should you try to get a $200 raise? Absolutely: you get to keep 90 percent of the first $100 and 75 percent of the next $100.

22. x == 0 && y == 0

23. x == 0 || y == 0

24. (x == 0 && y != 0) || (y == 0 && x != 0)

25. The same as the value of frozen.

26. You are guaranteed that there are no other values. With strings or integers, you would need to check that no values such as "maybe" or –1 enter your calculations.

27. (a) Error: The floor must be between 1 and 20. (b) Error: The floor must be between 1 and 20. (c) 19 (d) Error: Not an integer.

28. floor == 13 || floor <= 0 || floor > 20

29. Check for in.hasNextDouble(), to make sure a researcher didn't supply an input such as oh my. Check for weight <= 0, because any rat must surely have a positive weight. We don't know how giant a rat could be, but the New Guinea rats weighed no more than 2 kg. A regular house rat (*rattus rattus*) weighs up to 0.2 kg, so we'll say that any weight > 10 kg was surely an input error, perhaps confusing grams and kilograms. Thus, the checks are

    ```
    if (!in.hasNextDouble())
    {
       System.out.print("Error: Not a number");
       return;
    }
    double weight = in.nextDouble();
    if (weight < 0)
    {
       System.out.println("Error: Weight cannot be negative.");
       return;
    }
    if (weight > 10)
    {
       System.out.println("Error: Weight > 10 kg.");
       return;
    }
    ```

30. The second input fails, and the program terminates without printing anything.

CHAPTER 4

LOOPS

CHAPTER GOALS

To learn about while, for, and do loops

To become familiar with common
loop algorithms

To understand nested loops

To implement programs that read and process data sets

To use a computer for simulations

CHAPTER CONTENTS

In a loop, a part of a program is repeated over and over, until a specific goal is reached. Loops are important for calculations that require repeated steps and for processing input consisting of many data items. In this chapter, you will learn about loop statements in Java, as well as techniques for writing programs that simulate activities in the real world.

4.1 The while Loop

In this section, you will learn about *loop statements* that repeatedly execute instructions until a goal has been reached.

Recall the investment problem from Chapter 1. You put $10,000 into a bank account that earns 5 percent interest per year. How many years does it take for the account balance to be double the original investment?

In Chapter 1 we developed the following algorithm for this problem:

Because the interest earned also earns interest, a bank balance grows exponentially.

Start with a year value of 0 and a balance of $10,000.

year	balance
0	$10,000

Repeat the following steps while the balance is less than $20,000.
   Add 1 to the year value.
   Multiply the balance value by 1.05 (a 5 percent increase).
Report the final year value as the answer.

You now know how to declare and update the variables in Java. What you don't yet know is how to carry out "Repeat steps while the balance is less than $20,000".

In a particle accelerator, subatomic particles repeatedly traverse a loop-shaped tunnel until they gain the speed required for physical experiments. Similarly, in computer science, statements in a loop are executed until a goal is achieved.

Figure 1   Flowchart of a while Loop

A loop executes instructions repeatedly while a condition is true.

In Java, the while statement implements such a repetition (see Syntax 4.1). The code

```java
while (condition)
{
    statements
}
```

keeps executing the statements while the condition is true. In our case, we want to increment the year counter and add interest while the balance is less than the target balance of $20,000:

```java
while (balance < TARGET)
{
    year++;
    double interest = balance * RATE / 100;
    balance = balance + interest;
}
```

A while statement is an example of a **loop**. If you draw a flowchart, the flow of execution loops again to the point where the condition is tested (see Figure 1).

+ ANIMATION
Tracing a Loop

Syntax 4.1   while Statement

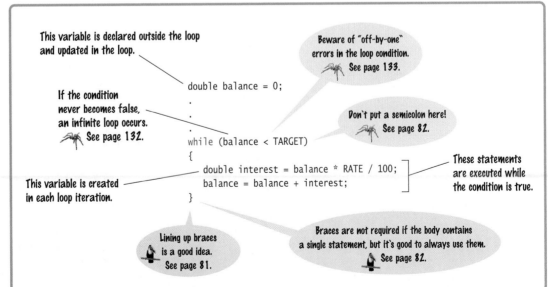

This variable is declared outside the loop and updated in the loop.

Beware of "off-by-one" errors in the loop condition.
See page 133.

If the condition never becomes false, an infinite loop occurs.
See page 132.

```java
double balance = 0;
.
.
.
while (balance < TARGET)
{
    double interest = balance * RATE / 100;
    balance = balance + interest;
}
```

Don't put a semicolon here!
See page 82.

These statements are executed while the condition is true.

This variable is created in each loop iteration.

Lining up braces is a good idea.
See page 81.

Braces are not required if the body contains a single statement, but it's good to always use them.
See page 82.

When you declare a variable *inside* the loop body, the variable is created for each iteration of the loop and removed after the end of each iteration. For example, consider the interest variable in this loop:

```
while (balance < TARGET)
{
    year++;
    double interest = balance * RATE / 100;
    balance = balance + interest;
} // interest no longer declared here
```

A new interest **variable** is created in each iteration.

In contrast, the balance and years variables were declared *outside* the loop body. That way, the same variable is used for all iterations of the loop.

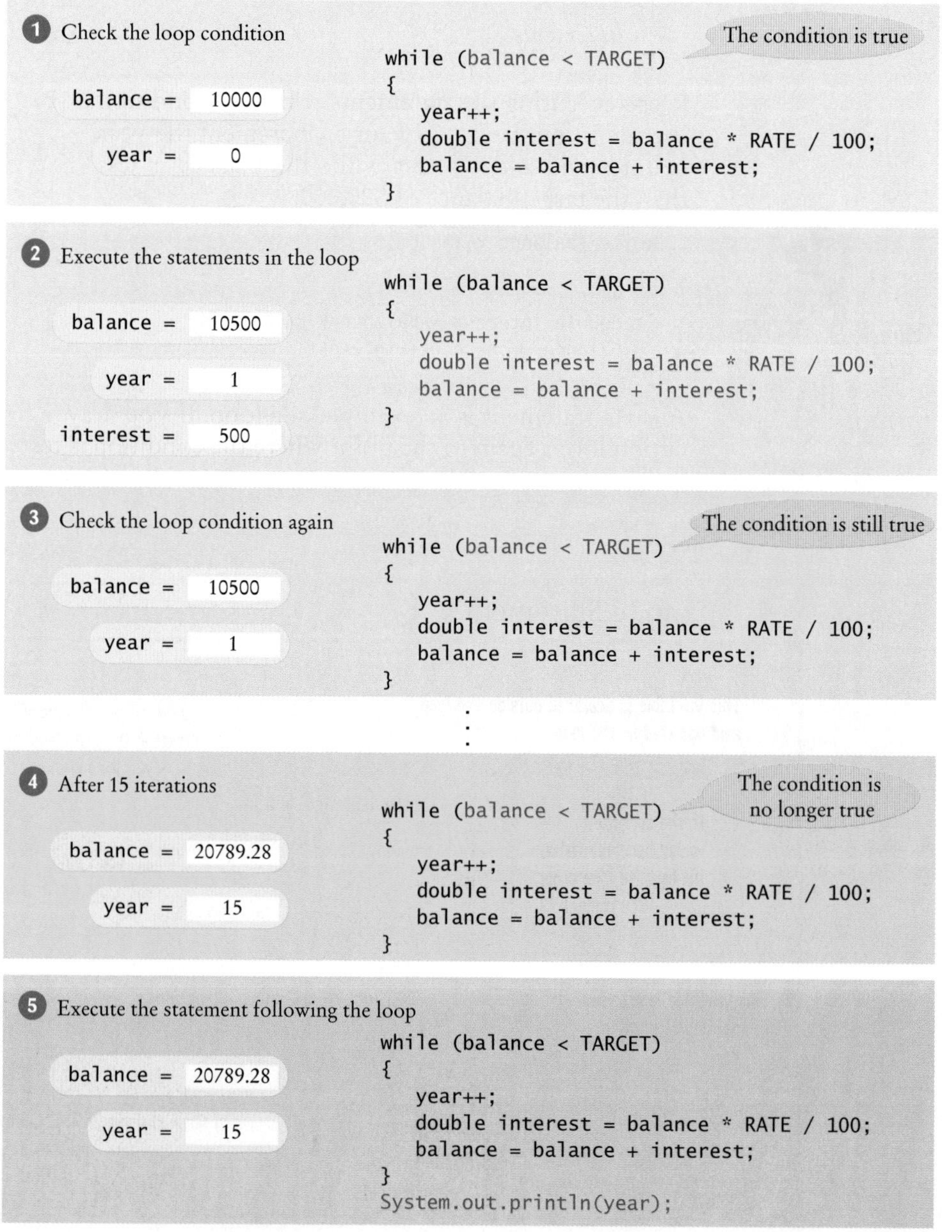

Figure 2
Execution of the
DoubleInvestment
Loop

1 Check the loop condition

The condition is true

```
balance =    10000

year =    0
```

```
while (balance < TARGET)
{
    year++;
    double interest = balance * RATE / 100;
    balance = balance + interest;
}
```

2 Execute the statements in the loop

```
balance =    10500

year =    1

interest =    500
```

```
while (balance < TARGET)
{
    year++;
    double interest = balance * RATE / 100;
    balance = balance + interest;
}
```

3 Check the loop condition again

The condition is still true

```
balance =    10500

year =    1
```

```
while (balance < TARGET)
{
    year++;
    double interest = balance * RATE / 100;
    balance = balance + interest;
}
```

⋮

4 After 15 iterations

The condition is no longer true

```
balance =    20789.28

year =    15
```

```
while (balance < TARGET)
{
    year++;
    double interest = balance * RATE / 100;
    balance = balance + interest;
}
```

5 Execute the statement following the loop

```
balance =    20789.28

year =    15
```

```
while (balance < TARGET)
{
    year++;
    double interest = balance * RATE / 100;
    balance = balance + interest;
}
System.out.println(year);
```

Here is the program that solves the investment problem. Figure 2 illustrates the program's execution.

ch04/invest/DoubleInvestment.java

```java
1   /**
2      This program computes the time required to double an investment.
3   */
4   public class DoubleInvestment
5   {
6      public static void main(String[] args)
7      {
8         final double RATE = 5;
9         final double INITIAL_BALANCE = 10000;
10        final double TARGET = 2 * INITIAL_BALANCE;
11
12        double balance = INITIAL_BALANCE;
13        int year = 0;
14
15        // Count the years required for the investment to double
16
17        while (balance < TARGET)
18        {
19           year++;
20           double interest = balance * RATE / 100;
21           balance = balance + interest;
22        }
23
24        System.out.println("The investment doubled after "
25           + year + " years.");
26     }
27  }
```

Program Run

```
The investment doubled after 15 years.
```

SELF CHECK

1. How many years does it take for the investment to triple? Modify the program and run it.

2. If the interest rate is 10 percent per year, how many years does it take for the investment to double? Modify the program and run it.

3. Modify the program so that the balance after each year is printed. How did you do that?

4. Suppose we change the program so that the condition of the while loop is

   `while (balance <= TARGET)`

   What is the effect on the program? Why?

5. What does the following loop print?

   ```java
   int n = 1;
   while (n < 100)
   {
      n = 2 * n;
      System.out.println(n + " ");
   }
   ```

Practice It   Now you can try these exercises at the end of the chapter: R4.2, R4.4, P4.14.

Table 1 while Loop Examples		
Loop	Output	Explanation

`i = 0; sum = 0;`
`while (sum < 10)`
`{`
`    i++; sum = sum + i;`
`    Print i and sum;`
`}`
	1 1
	2 3
	3 6
	4 10
		When sum is 10, the loop condition is false, and the loop ends.

`i = 0; sum = 0;`
`while (sum < 10)`
`{`
`    i++; sum = sum - i;`
`    Print i and sum;`
`}`
	1 -1
	2 -3
	3 -6
	4 -10
	. . .
		Because sum never reaches 10, this is an "infinite loop" (see Common Error 4.2 on page 132).

`i = 0; sum = 0;`
`while (sum < 0)`
`{`
`    i++; sum = sum - i;`
`    Print i and sum;`
`}`
	(No output)	The statement sum < 0 is false when the condition is first checked, and the loop is never executed.

`i = 0; sum = 0;`
`while (sum >= 10)`
`{`
`    i++; sum = sum + i;`
`    Print i and sum;`
`}`
	(No output)	The programmer probably thought, "Stop when the sum is at least 10." However, the loop condition controls when the loop is executed, not when it ends (see Common Error 4.1 on page 132).

`i = 0; sum = 0;`
`while (sum < 10) ;`
`{`
`    i++; sum = sum + i;`
`    Print i and sum;`
`}`
	(No output, program does not terminate)	Note the semicolon before the {. This loop has an empty body. It runs forever, checking whether sum < 0 and doing nothing in the body.

Programming Tip 4.1

Hand-Tracing Loops

In Programming Tip 3.5, you learned about the method of hand-tracing. This method is particularly effective for understanding how a loop works.

Consider this example. What value is displayed?

```
int n = 1729;  ①
int sum = 0;
while (n > 0)  ②
{
    int digit = n % 10;  ③ ④ ⑤ ⑥
    sum = sum + digit;
    n = n / 10;
}
System.out.println(sum);  ⑦
```

1. There are three variables: n, sum, and digit. The first two variables are initialized with 1729 and 0 before the loop is entered.

n	sum	digit
1729	0	

2. Because n is positive, enter the loop.

3. The variable digit is set to 9 (the remainder of dividing 1729 by 10). The variable sum is set to 0 + 9 = 9. Finally, n becomes 172. (Recall that the remainder in the division 1729 / 10 is discarded because both arguments are integers.). Cross out the old values and write the new ones under the old ones.

n	sum	digit
~~1729~~	~~0~~	
172	9	9

4. Because n > 0, we repeat the loop. Now digit becomes 2, sum is set to 9 + 2 = 11, and n is set to 17.

n	sum	digit
~~1729~~	~~0~~	
~~172~~	~~9~~	~~9~~
17	11	2

5. Because n is still not zero, we repeat the loop, setting digit to 7, sum to 11 + 7 = 18, and n to 1.

n	sum	digit
~~1729~~	~~0~~	
~~172~~	~~9~~	~~9~~
~~17~~	~~11~~	~~2~~
1	18	7

6. We enter the loop one last time. Now digit is set to 1, sum to 19, and n becomes zero.

n	sum	digit
~~1729~~	~~0~~	
~~172~~	~~9~~	~~9~~
~~17~~	~~11~~	~~2~~
~~1~~	~~18~~	~~7~~
0	19	1

7. The condition n > 0 is now false, and we continue with the output statement after the loop. The value that is output is 19.

Of course, you can get the same answer by just running the code. The hope is that by hand-tracing, you gain an *insight*. Consider again what happens in each iteration:

- We extract the last digit of n.
- We add that digit to sum.
- We strip the digit off n.

In other words, the loop forms the sum of the digits in n. You now know what the loop does for any value of n, not just the one in the example.

Why would anyone want to form the sum of the digits? Operations of this kind are useful for checking the validity of credit card numbers and other forms of ID numbers—see Exercise P4.2.

Don't Think "Are We There Yet?"

When doing something repetitive, most of us want to know when we are done. For example, you may think, "I want to get at least $20,000," and set the loop condition to

```
balance >= TARGET
```

But the while loop thinks the opposite: How long am I allowed to keep going? The correct loop condition is

```
while (balance < TARGET)
```

In other words: "Keep at it while the balance is less than the target."

When writing a loop condition, don't ask, "Are we there yet?" The condition determines how long the loop will keep going.

Infinite Loops

A very annoying loop error is an *infinite loop:* a loop that runs forever and can be stopped only by killing the program or restarting the computer. If there are output statements in the program, then reams and reams of output flash by on the screen. Otherwise, the program just sits there and *hangs*, seeming to do nothing. On some systems, you can kill a hanging program by hitting Ctrl + C. On others, you can close the window in which the program runs.

A common reason for infinite loops is forgetting to update the variable that controls the loop:

```
year = 1;
while (year <= 20)
{
   double interest = balance * RATE / 100;
   balance = balance + interest;
}
```

Here the programmer forgot to add a year++ command in the loop. As a result, the year always stays at 1, and the loop never comes to an end.

Another common reason for an infinite loop is accidentally incrementing a counter that should be decremented (or vice versa). Consider this example:

```
year = 20;
while (year > 0)
{
   double interest = balance * RATE / 100;
   balance = balance + interest;
   year++;
}
```

The year variable really should have been decremented, not incremented. This is a common error because incrementing counters is so much more common than decrementing that your fingers may type the ++ on autopilot. As a consequence, year is always larger than 0, and the loop never ends. (Actually, year may eventually exceed the largest representable positive integer and *wrap around* to a negative number. Then the loop ends—of course, with a completely wrong result.)

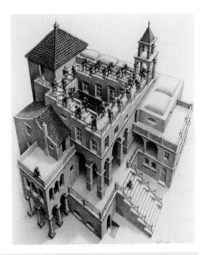

In this famous engraving by M.C. Escher, the hooded figures traverse an infinite loop, a loop that never ends.

Common Error 4.3

Off-by-One Errors

Consider our computation of the number of years that are required to double an investment:

```
int year = 0;
while (balance < TARGET)
{
   year++;
   balance = balance * (1 + RATE / 100);
```

```
   }
   System.out.println("The investment doubled after "
      + year + " years.");
```

Should year start at 0 or at 1? Should you test for `balance < TARGET` or for `balance <= TARGET`? It is easy to be *off by one* in these expressions.

Some people try to solve **off-by-one errors** by randomly inserting +1 or -1 until the program seems to work—a terrible strategy. It can take a long time to compile and test all the various possibilities. Expending a small amount of mental effort is a real time saver.

Fortunately, off-by-one errors are easy to avoid, simply by thinking through a couple of test cases and using the information from the test cases to come up with a rationale for your decisions.

> An off-by-one error is a common error when programming loops. Think through simple test cases to avoid this type of error.

Should year start at 0 or at 1? Look at a scenario with simple values: an initial balance of $100 and an interest rate of 50 percent. After year 1, the balance is $150, and after year 2 it is $225, or over $200. So the investment doubled after 2 years. The loop executed two times, incrementing year each time. Hence year must start at 0, not at 1.

year	balance
0	$100
1	$150
2	$225

In other words, the `balance` variable denotes the balance after the end of the year. At the outset, the `balance` variable contains the balance after year 0 and not after year 1.

Next, should you use a < or <= comparison in the test? This is harder to figure out, because it is rare for the balance to be exactly twice the initial balance. There is one case when this happens, namely when the interest is 100 percent. The loop executes once. Now year is 1, and balance is exactly equal to `2 * INITIAL_BALANCE`. Has the investment doubled after one year? It has. Therefore, the loop should not execute again. If the test condition is `balance < TARGET`, the loop stops, as it should. If the test condition had been `balance <= TARGET`, the loop would have executed once more.

In other words, you keep adding interest while the balance *has not yet doubled*.

Random Fact 4.1 The First Bug

According to legend, the first bug was found in the Mark II, a huge electromechanical computer at Harvard University. It really was caused by a bug—a moth was trapped in a relay switch.

Actually, from the note that the operator left in the log book next to the moth (see the figure), it appears as if the term "bug" had already been in active use at the time.

The pioneering computer scientist Maurice Wilkes wrote, "Somehow, at the Moore School and afterwards, one had always assumed there would be no particular difficulty in getting programs right. I can remember the exact instant in time at which it dawned on me that a great part of my future life would be spent finding mistakes in my own programs."

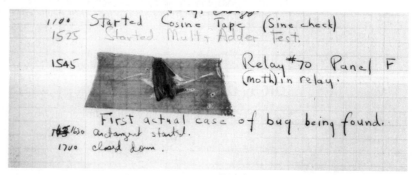

The First Bug

4.2 The for Loop

The for loop is used when a value runs from a starting point to an ending point with a constant increment or decrement.

It often happens that you want to execute a sequence of statements a given number of times. You can use a while loop that is controlled by a counter, as in the following example:

```java
int counter = 1; // Initialize the counter
while (counter <= 10) // Check the counter
{
    System.out.println(counter);
    counter++; // Update the counter
}
```

Because this loop type is so common, there is a special form for it, called the for loop (see Syntax 4.2).

```java
for (int counter = 1; counter <= 10; counter++)
{
    System.out.println(counter);
}
```

Some people call this loop *count-controlled*. In contrast, the while loop of the preceding section can be called an *event-controlled* loop because it executes until an event occurs; namely that the balance reaches the target. Another commonly used term for a count-controlled loop is *definite*. You know from the outset that the loop body will be executed a definite number of times; ten times in our example. In contrast, you do not know how many iterations it takes to accumulate a target balance. Such a loop is called *indefinite*.

You can visualize the for loop as an orderly sequence of steps.

Syntax 4.2   for Statement

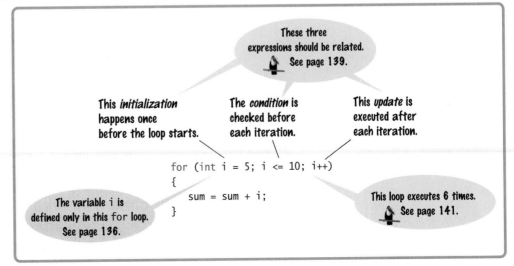

These three expressions should be related. See page 139.

This *initialization* happens once before the loop starts.

The *condition* is checked before each iteration.

This *update* is executed after each iteration.

```java
for (int i = 5; i <= 10; i++)
{
    sum = sum + i;
}
```

The variable i is defined only in this for loop. See page 136.

This loop executes 6 times. See page 141.

ANIMATION
The for Loop

The for loop neatly groups the initialization, condition, and update expressions together. However, it is important to realize that these expressions are *not* executed together (see Figure 3).

- The initialization is executed once, before the loop is entered. **1**
- The condition is checked before each iteration. **2** **5**
- The update is executed after each iteration. **4**

A for loop can count down instead of up:

```
for (int counter = 10; counter >= 0; counter--) . . .
```

The increment or decrement need not be in steps of 1:

```
for (int counter = 0; counter <= 10; counter = counter + 2) . . .
```

See Table 2 for additional variations.

So far, we have always declared the counter variable in the loop initialization:

```
for (int counter = 1; counter <= 10; counter++)
{
   . . .
}
// counter no longer declared here
```

Such a variable is declared for all iterations of the loop, but you cannot use it after the loop. If you declare the counter variable before the loop, you can continue to use it after the loop:

```
int counter;
for (counter = 1; counter <= 10; counter++)
{
   . . .
}
// counter still declared here
```

Table 2   for Loop Examples

Loop	Values of i	Comment
`for (i = 0; i <= 5; i++)`	0 1 2 3 4 5	Note that the loop is executed 6 times. (See Programming Tip 4.4 on page 141.)
`for (i = 5; i >= 0; i--)`	5 4 3 2 1 0	Use i-- for decreasing values.
`for (i = 0; i < 9; i = i + 2)`	0 2 4 6 8	Use i = i + 2 for a step size of 2.
`for (i = 0; i != 9; i = i + 2)`	0 2 4 6 8 10 12 14 ... (infinite loop)	You can use < or <= instead of != to avoid this problem.
`for (i = 1; i <= 20; i = i * 2)`	1 2 4 8 16	You can specify any rule for modifying i, such as doubling it in every step.
`for (i = 0; i < str.length(); i++)`	0 1 2 ... until the last valid index of the string str	In the loop body, use the expression str.charAt(i) to get the ith character.

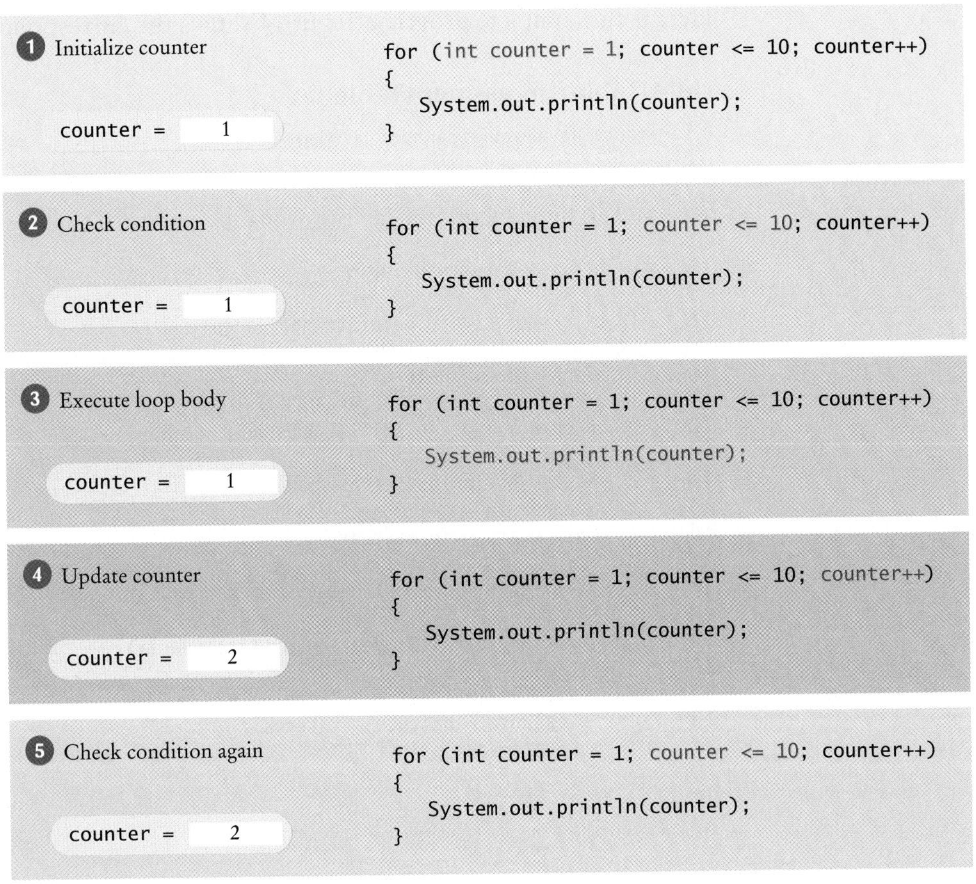

Figure 3
Execution of
a for Loop

1 Initialize counter

```
for (int counter = 1; counter <= 10; counter++)
{
    System.out.println(counter);
}
```

counter =   1

2 Check condition

```
for (int counter = 1; counter <= 10; counter++)
{
    System.out.println(counter);
}
```

counter =   1

3 Execute loop body

```
for (int counter = 1; counter <= 10; counter++)
{
    System.out.println(counter);
}
```

counter =   1

4 Update counter

```
for (int counter = 1; counter <= 10; counter++)
{
    System.out.println(counter);
}
```

counter =   2

5 Check condition again

```
for (int counter = 1; counter <= 10; counter++)
{
    System.out.println(counter);
}
```

counter =   2

Here is a typical use of the for loop. We want to print the balance of our savings account over a period of years, as shown in this table:

Year	Balance
1	10500.00
2	11025.00
3	11576.25
4	12155.06
5	12762.82

The for loop pattern applies because the variable year starts at 1 and then moves in constant increments until it reaches the target:

```
for (int year = 1; year <= nyears; year++)
{
    Update balance.
    Print year and balance.
}
```

Here is the complete program. Figure 4 shows the corresponding flowchart.

ch04/table/InvestmentTable.java

```java
1   import java.util.Scanner;
2
3   /**
4      This program prints a table showing the growth of an investment.
5   */
6   public class InvestmentTable
7   {
8      public static void main(String[] args)
9      {
10        final double RATE = 5;
11        final double INITIAL_BALANCE = 10000;
12        double balance = INITIAL_BALANCE;
13
14        System.out.print("Enter number of years: ");
15        Scanner in = new Scanner(System.in);
16        int nyears = in.nextInt();
17
18        // Print the table of balances for each year
19
20        for (int year = 1; year <= nyears; year++)
21        {
22           double interest = balance * RATE / 100;
23           balance = balance + interest;
24           System.out.printf("%4d %10.2f\n", year, balance);
25        }
26     }
27  }
```

Program Run

```
Enter number of years: 10
    1   10500.00
    2   11025.00
    3   11576.25
    4   12155.06
    5   12762.82
    6   13400.96
    7   14071.00
    8   14774.55
    9   15513.28
   10   16288.95
```

Another common use of the for loop is to traverse all characters of a string:

```java
for (int i = 0; i < str.length(); i++)
{
   char ch = str.charAt(i);
   Process ch
}
```

Note that the counter variable i starts at 0, and the loop is terminated when i reaches the length of the string. For example, if str has length 5, i takes on the values 0, 1, 2, 3, and 4. These are the valid positions in the string.

Figure 4
Flowchart of a for Loop

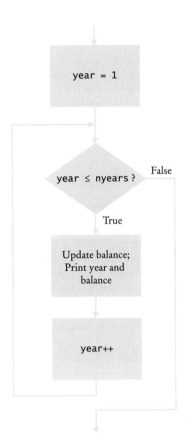

SELF CHECK

6. Write the for loop of the InvestmentTable.java program as a while loop.

7. How many numbers does this loop print?

```
for (int n = 10; n >= 0; n--)
{
    System.out.println(n);
}
```

8. Write a for loop that prints all even numbers between 10 and 20 (inclusive).

9. Write a for loop that computes the sum of the integers from 1 to n.

10. How would you modify the for loop of the InvestmentTable.java program to print all balances until the investment has doubled?

Practice It Now you can try these exercises at the end of the chapter: R4.3, R4.8, P4.8, P4.13.

Programming Tip 4.2

Use for **Loops for Their Intended Purpose Only**

A for loop is an *idiom* for a loop of a particular form. A value runs from the start to the end, with a constant increment or decrement.

The compiler won't check whether the initialization, condition, and update expressions are related. For example, the following loop is legal:

```
// Confusing—unrelated expressions
for (System.out.print("Inputs: "); in.hasNextDouble(); sum = sum + x)
{
```

```
    x = in.nextDouble();
}
```

However, programmers reading such a for loop will be confused because it does not match their expectations. Use a while loop for iterations that do not follow the for idiom.

You should also be careful not to update the loop counter in the body of a for loop. Consider the following example:

```
for (int counter = 1; counter <= 100; counter++)
{
    if (counter % 10 == 0) // Skip values that are divisible by 10
    {
        counter++; // Bad style—you should not update the counter in a for loop
    }
    System.out.println(counter);
}
```

Updating the counter inside a for loop is confusing because the counter is updated *again* at the end of the loop iteration. In some loop iterations, counter is incremented once, in others twice. This goes against the intuition of a programmer who sees a for loop.

If you find yourself in this situation, you can either change from a for loop to a while loop, or implement the "skipping" behavior in another way. For example:

```
for (int counter = 1; counter <= 100; counter++)
{
    if (counter % 10 != 0) // Skip values that are divisible by 10
    {
        System.out.println(counter);
    }
}
```

Programming Tip 4.3

Choose Loop Bounds That Match Your Task

Suppose you want to print line numbers that go from 1 to 10. Of course, you will want to use a loop

```
for (int i = 1; i <= 10; i++)
```

The values for i are bounded by the relation $1 \leq i \leq 10$. Because there are $\leq$ on both bounds, the bounds are called **symmetric**.

When traversing the characters in a string, it is more natural to use the bounds

```
for (int i = 0; i < str.length(); i++)
```

In this loop, i traverses all valid positions in the string. You can access the ith character as str.charAt(i). The values for i are bounded by $0 \leq i < str.length()$, with a $\leq$ to the left and a $<$ to the right. That is appropriate, because str.length() is not a valid position. Such bounds are called **asymmetric**.

In this case, it is not a good idea to use symmetric bounds:

```
for (int i = 0; i <= str.length() - 1; i++) // Use < instead
```

The asymmetric form is easier to understand.

Count Iterations

Finding the correct lower and upper bounds for an iteration can be confusing. Should you start at 0 or at 1? Should you use <= b or < b as a termination condition?

Counting the number of iterations is a very useful device for better understanding a loop. Counting is easier for loops with asymmetric bounds. The loop

```
for (int i = a; i < b; i++)
```

is executed b - a times. For example, the loop traversing the characters in a string,

```
for (int i = 0; i < str.length(); i++)
```

runs str.length() times. That makes perfect sense, since there are str.length() characters in a string.

The loop with symmetric bounds,

```
for (int i = a; i <= b; i++)
```

is executed b - a + 1 times. That "+1" is the source of many programming errors.

For example,

```
for (int i = 0; i <= 10; i++)
```

runs 11 times. Maybe that is what you want; if not, start at 1 or use < 10.

One way to visualize this "+1" error is by looking at a fence. Each section has one fence post to the left, and there is a final post on the right of the last section. Forgetting to count the last value is often called a "fence post error".

How many posts do you need for a fence with four sections? It is easy to be "off by one" with problems such as this one.

4.3 The do Loop

The do loop is appropriate when the loop body must be executed at least once.

Sometimes you want to execute the body of a loop at least once and perform the loop test after the body is executed. The do loop serves that purpose:

```
do
{
    statements
}
while (condition);
```

The body of the do loop is executed first, then the condition is tested.

Figure 5
Flowchart of a do Loop

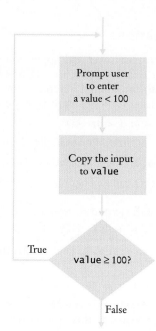

Some people call such a loop a *post-test loop* because the condition is tested after completing the loop body. In contrast, while and for loops are *pre-test loops*. In those loop types, the condition is tested before entering the loop body.

A typical example for a do loop is input validation. Suppose you ask a user to enter a value < 100. If the user didn't pay attention and entered a larger value, you ask again, until the value is correct. Of course, you cannot test the value until the user has entered it. This is a perfect fit for the do loop (see Figure 5):

```java
int value;
do
{
   System.out.print("Enter an integer < 100: ");
   value = in.nextInt();
}
while (value >= 100);
```

SELF CHECK

11. Suppose that we want to check for inputs that are at least 0 and at most 100. Modify the do loop for this check.

12. Rewrite the input check do loop using a while loop. What is the disadvantage of your solution?

13. Suppose Java didn't have a do loop. Could you rewrite any do loop as a while loop?

14. Write a do loop that reads integers and computes their sum. Stop when reading the value 0.

15. Write a do loop that reads integers and computes their sum. Stop when reading the same value twice in a row. For example, if the input is 1 2 3 4 4, then the sum is 14 and the loop stops.

Practice It Now you can try these exercises at the end of the chapter: R4.7, R4.13, R4.14.

4.4 Application: Processing Sentinel Values

In this section, you will learn how to write loops that read and process a sequence of input values.

A sentinel value denotes the end of a data set, but it is not part of the data.

Whenever you read a sequence of inputs, you need to have some method of indicating the end of the sequence. Sometimes you are lucky and no input value can be zero. Then you can prompt the user to keep entering numbers, or 0 to finish the sequence. If zero is allowed but negative numbers are not, you can use –1 to indicate termination.

Such a value, which is not an actual input, but serves as a signal for termination, is called a **sentinel**.

Let's put this technique to work in a program that computes the average of a set of salary values. In our sample program, we will use –1 as a sentinel. An employee would surely not work for a negative salary, but there may be volunteers who work for free.

Inside the loop, we read an input. If the input is not –1, we process it. In order to compute the average, we need the total sum of all salaries, and the number of inputs.

```
salary = in.nextDouble();
if (salary != -1)
{
   sum = sum + salary;
   count++;
}
```

We stay in the loop while the sentinel value is not detected.

```
while (salary != -1)
{
   . . .
}
```

There is just one problem: When the loop is entered for the first time, no data value has been read. We must make sure to initialize salary with some value other than the sentinel:

```
double salary = 0; // Any value other than -1 will do
```

In the military, a sentinel guards a border or passage. In computer science, a sentinel value denotes the border between a data set and unrelated input.

After the loop has finished, we compute and print the average. Here is the complete program.

ch04/sentinel/SentinelDemo.java

```
1   import java.util.Scanner;
2
3   /**
4      This program prints the average of salary values that are terminated with a sentinel.
5   */
6   public class SentinelDemo
7   {
8      public static void main(String[] args)
9      {
10        double sum = 0;
11        int count = 0;
12        double salary = 0;
13        System.out.print("Enter salaries, -1 to finish: ");
14        Scanner in = new Scanner(System.in);
15
16        // Process data until the sentinel is entered
17
18        while (salary != -1)
19        {
20           salary = in.nextDouble();
21           if (salary != -1)
22           {
23              sum = sum + salary;
24              count++;
25           }
26        }
27
28        // Compute and print the average
29
30        if (count > 0)
31        {
32           double average = sum / count;
33           System.out.println("Average salary: " + average);
34        }
35        else
36        {
37           System.out.println("No data");
38        }
39     }
40  }
```

Program Run

```
Enter salaries, -1 to finish: 10 10 40 -1
Average salary: 20
```

Some programmers don't like the "trick" of initializing the input variable with a value other than the sentinel. Another approach is to use a Boolean variable:

```
System.out.print("Enter salaries, -1 to finish: ");
boolean done = false;
while (!done)
{
```

You can use a
Boolean variable to
control a loop. Set
the variable before
entering the loop,
then set it to the
opposite to leave
the loop.

```
      value = in.nextDouble();
      if (value == -1)
      {
         done = true;
      }
      else
      {
         Process value.
      }
   }
```

Special Topic 4.1 on page 146 shows an alternative mechanism for leaving such a loop.

Now consider the case in which any number (positive, negative, or zero) can be an acceptable input. In such a situation, you must use a sentinel that is not a number (such as the letter Q). As you have seen in Section 3.6, the condition

```
in.hasNextDouble()
```

is false if the next input is not a floating-point number. Therefore, you can read and process a set of inputs with the following loop:

```
System.out.print("Enter values, Q to quit: ");
while (in.hasNextDouble())
{
   value = in.nextDouble();
   Process value.
}
```

SELF CHECK

16. What does the SentinelDemo.java program print when the user immediately types −1 when prompted for a value?

17. Why does the SentinelDemo.java program have *two* checks of the form

```
salary != -1
```

18. What would happen if the declaration of the salary variable in SentinelDemo.java was changed to

```
double salary = -1;
```

19. In the last example of this section, we prompt the user "Enter values, Q to quit." What happens when the user enters a different letter?

20. What is wrong with the following loop for reading a sequence of values?

```
System.out.print("Enter values, Q to quit: ");
do
{
   double value = in.nextDouble();
   sum = sum + value;
   count++;
}
while (in.hasNextDouble())
```

Practice It   Now you can try these exercises at the end of the chapter: R4.11, P4.3, P4.4.

Special Topic 4.1

The Loop-and-a-Half Problem and the break Statement

Consider again this loop for processing inputs until a sentinel value has been reached:

```java
boolean done = false;
while (!done)
{
   double value = in.nextDouble();
   if (value == -1)
   {
      done = true;
   }
   else
   {
      Process value.
   }
}
```

The actual test for loop termination is in the middle of the loop, not at the top. This is called a **loop and a half** because one must go halfway into the loop before knowing whether one needs to terminate.

As an alternative, you can use the break reserved word.

```java
while (true)
{
   double value = in.nextDouble();
   if (value == -1) { break; }
   Process value.
}
```

The break statement breaks out of the enclosing loop, independent of the loop condition. When the break statement is encountered, the loop is terminated, and the statement following the loop is executed.

In the loop-and-a-half case, break statements can be beneficial. But it is difficult to lay down clear rules as to when they are safe and when they should be avoided. We do not use the break statement in this book.

4.5 Common Loop Algorithms

In the following sections, we discuss some of the most common algorithms that are implemented as loops. You can use them as starting points for your loop designs.

4.5.1 Sum and Average Value

Computing the sum of a number of inputs is a very common task. Keep a *running total:* a variable to which you add each input value. Of course, the total should be initialized with 0.

```java
double total = 0;
while (in.hasNextDouble())
{
   double input = in.nextDouble();
   total = total + input;
}
```

Note that the `total` variable is declared outside the loop. We want the loop to update a single variable. The `input` variable is declared inside the loop. A separate variable is created for each input and removed at the end of each loop iteration.

To compute an average, count how many values you have, and divide by the count. Be sure to check that the count is not zero.

```java
double total = 0;
int count = 0;
while (in.hasNextDouble())
{
   double input = in.nextDouble();
   total = total + input;
   count++;
}
double average = 0;
if (count > 0) { average = total / count; }
```

4.5.2 Counting Matches

You often want to know how many values fulfill a particular condition. For example, you may want to count how many uppercase letters are in a string. Keep a *counter*, a variable that is initialized with 0 and incremented whenever there is a match.

```java
int upperCaseLetters = 0;
for (int i = 0; i < str.length(); i++)
{
   char ch = str.charAt(i);
   if (Character.isUpperCase(ch))
   {
      upperCaseLetters++;
   }
}
```

For example, if `str` is the string `"Hello, World!"`, `upperCaseLetters` is incremented twice (when `i` is 0 and 7).

This loop can also be used for scanning inputs. The following loop reads text, a word at a time, and counts the number of words with at most three letters:

```java
int shortWords = 0;
while (in.hasNext())
{
   String input = in.next();
   if (in.length() <= 3)
   {
      shortWords++;
   }
}
```

In a loop that counts matches, a counter is incremented whenever a match is found.

4.5.3 Finding the First Match

When you count the values that fulfill a condition, you need to look at all values. However, if your task is to find a match, then you can stop as soon as the condition is fulfilled.

Here is a loop that finds the first lowercase letter in a string. Because we do not visit all elements in the string, a while loop is a better choice than a for loop:

```
boolean found = false;
char ch = '?';
int position = 0;
while (!found && position < str.length())
{
   ch = str.charAt(position);
   if (Character.isLowerCase(ch)) { found = true; }
   else { position++; }
}
```

If a match was found, then found is true, ch is the first matching character, and position is the index of the first match. If the loop did not find a match, then found remains false after the end of the loop.

In the preceding example, we searched a string for a character that matches a condition. You can apply the same process to user input. Suppose you are asking a user to enter a positive value < 100. Keep asking until the user provides a correct input:

```
boolean valid = false;
double input = 0;
while (!valid)
{
   System.out.print("Please enter a positive value < 100: ");
   input = in.nextDouble();
   if (0 < input && input < 100) { valid = true; }
   else { System.out.println("Invalid input."); }
}
```

Note that the variable input is declared *outside* the while loop because you will want to use the input after the loop has finished. If it had been declared inside the loop body, you would not be able to use it outside the loop.

When searching, you look at items until a match is found.

4.5.4 Maximum and Minimum

To compute the largest value in a sequence, keep a variable that stores the largest element that you have encountered, and update it when you find a larger one.

```
double largest = in.nextDouble();
while (in.hasNextDouble())
{
    double input = in.nextDouble();
    if (input > largest)
    {
        largest = input;
    }
}
```

This algorithm requires that there is at least one input.

To compute the smallest value, simply reverse the comparison:

```
double smallest = in.nextDouble();
while (in.hasNextDouble())
{
    double input = in.nextDouble();
    if (input < smallest)
    {
        smallest = input;
    }
}
```

To find the height of the tallest bus rider, remember the largest value so far, and update it whenever you see a taller one.

4.5.5 Comparing Adjacent Values

When processing a sequence of values in a loop, you sometimes need to compare a value with the value that just preceded it. For example, suppose you want to check whether a sequence of inputs contains adjacent duplicates such as 1 7 2 9 9 4 9.

Now you face a challenge. Consider the typical loop for reading a value:

```
double input;
while (in.hasNextDouble())
{
```

```
    input = in.nextDouble();
    . . .
}
```

How can you compare the current input with the preceding one? At any time, `input` contains the current input, overwriting the previous one.

The answer is to store the previous input, like this:

When comparing adjacent values, store the previous value in a variable.

```
double input = 0;
while (in.hasNextDouble())
{
    double previous = input;
    input = in.nextDouble();
    if (input == previous)
    {
        System.out.println("Duplicate input");
    }
}
```

One problem remains. When the loop is entered for the first time, `input` has not yet been set. You can solve this problem with an initial input operation outside the loop:

```
double input = in.nextDouble();
while (in.hasNextDouble())
{
    double previous = input;
    input = in.nextDouble();
    if (input == previous)
    {
        System.out.println("Duplicate input");
    }
}
```

SELF CHECK

21. What total is computed when no user input is provided in the algorithm in Section 4.5.1?

22. How do you compute the total of all positive inputs?

23. What are the values of `position` and `ch` when no match is found in the algorithm in Section 4.5.3?

24. What is wrong with the following loop for finding the position of the first lowercase character in a string?

```
boolean found = false;
for (int position = 0; !found && position < str.length(); position++)
{
    char ch = str.charAt(position);
    if (Character.isLowerCase(ch)) { found = true; }
}
```

25. How do you find the position of the *last* lowercase character in a string?

26. What happens with the algorithm in Section 4.5.5 when no input is provided at all? How can you overcome that problem?

Practice It   Now you can try these exercises at the end of the chapter: P4.5, P4.9, P4.10.

HOW TO 4.1

Writing a Loop

This How To walks you through the process of implementing a loop statement. We will illustrate the steps with the following example problem:

Read twelve temperature values (one for each month), and display the number of the month with the highest temperature. For example, according to http://worldclimate.com, the average maximum temperatures for Death Valley are (in order by month):

18.2 22.6 26.4 31.1 36.6 42.2
45.7 44.5 40.2 33.1 24.2 17.6

In this case, the month with the highest temperature (45.7 degrees Celsius) is July, and the program should display 7.

Step 1 Decide what work must be done *inside* the loop.

Every loop needs to do some kind of repetitive work, such as

- Reading another item.
- Updating a value (such as a bank balance or total).
- Incrementing a counter.

If you can't figure out what needs to go inside the loop, start by writing down the steps that you would take if you solved the problem by hand. For example, with the temperature reading problem, you might write

> **Read first value.**
> **Read second value.**
> **If second value is higher than the first, set highest temperature to that value, highest month to 2.**
> **Read next value.**
> **If value is higher than the first and second, set highest temperature to that value, highest month to 3.**
> **Read next value.**
> **If value is higher than the highest temperature seen so far, set highest temperature to that value,**
>   **highest month to 4.**
>   . . .

Now look at these steps and reduce them to a set of *uniform* actions that can be placed into the loop body. The first action is easy:

> **Read next value.**

The next action is trickier. In our description, we used tests "higher than the first", "higher than the first and second", "higher than the highest temperature seen so far". We need to settle on one test that works for all iterations. The last formulation is the most general.

Similarly, we must find a general way of setting the highest month. We need a variable that stores the current month, running from 1 to 12. Then we can formulate the second loop action:

> **If value is higher than the highest temperature, set highest temperature to that value,**
>   **highest month to current month.**

Altogether our loop is

> **Repeat**
>   **Read next value.**
>   **If value is higher than the highest temperature,**
>   **set highest temperature to that value,**
>   **highest month to current month.**
>   **Increment current month.**

Step 2   Specify the loop condition.

What goal do you want to reach in your loop? Typical examples are
- Has a counter reached its final value?
- Have you read the last input value?
- Has a value reached a given threshold?

In our example, we simply want the current month to reach 12.

Step 3   Determine the loop type.

We distinguish between two major loop types. A *definite* or *count-controlled* loop is executed a definite number of times. In an *indefinite* or *event-controlled* loop, the number of iterations is not known in advance—the loop is executed until some event happens. A typical example of the latter is a loop that reads data until a sentinel is encountered.

Count-controlled loops can be implemented as for statements. For other loops, consider the loop condition. Do you need to complete one iteration of the loop body before you can tell when to terminate the loop? In that case, you should choose a do loop. Otherwise, use a while loop.

Sometimes, the condition for terminating a loop changes in the middle of the loop body. In that case, you can use a Boolean variable that specifies when you are ready to leave the loop. Follow this pattern:

```
boolean done = false;
while (!done)
{
    Do some work.
    If all work has been completed
    {
        done = true;
    }
    else
    {
        Do more work.
    }
}
```

Such a variable is called a **flag**.

In summary,
- If you know in advance how many times a loop is repeated, use a for loop.
- If the loop body must be executed at least once, use a do loop.
- Otherwise, use a while loop.

In our example, we read 12 temperature values. Therefore, we choose a for loop.

Step 4   Set up variables for entering the loop for the first time.

List all variables that are used and updated in the loop, and determine how to initialize them. Commonly, counters are initialized with 0 or 1, totals with 0.

In our example, the variables are

```
current month
highest value
highest month
```

We need to be careful how we set up the highest temperature value. We can't simply set it to 0. After all, our program needs to work with temperature values from Antarctica, all of which may be negative.

A good option is to set the highest temperature value to the first input value. Of course, then we need to remember to read in only 11 more values, with the current month starting at 2.

We also need to initialize the highest month with 1. After all, in an Australian city, we may never find a month that is warmer than January.

Step 5 Process the result after the loop has finished.

In many cases, the desired result is simply a variable that was updated in the loop body. For example, in our temperature program, the result is the highest month. Sometimes, the loop computes values that contribute to the final result. For example, suppose you are asked to average the temperatures. Then the loop should compute the sum, not the average. After the loop has completed, you are ready to compute the average: divide the sum by the number of inputs.

Here is our complete loop.

> Read first value; store as highest value.
> highest month = 1
> For current month from 2 to 12
>   Read next value.
>   If value is higher than the highest value
>   Set highest value to that value.
>   Set highest month to current month.

Step 6 Trace the loop with typical examples.

Hand trace your loop code, as described in Programming Tip 4.1 on page 130. Choose example values that are not too complex—executing the loop 3–5 times is enough to check for the most common errors. Pay special attention when entering the loop for the first and last time.

Sometimes, you want to make a slight modification to make tracing feasible. For example, when hand-tracing the investment doubling problem, use an interest rate of 20 percent rather than 5 percent. When hand-tracing the temperature loop, use 4 data values, not 12.

Let's say the data are 22.6 36.6 44.5 24.2. Here is the walkthrough:

current month	current value	highest month	highest value
		~~1~~	~~22.6~~
~~2~~	36.6	~~2~~	~~36.6~~
~~3~~	44.5	3	44.5
4	24.2		

The trace demonstrates that **highest month** and **highest value** are properly set.

Step 7 Implement the loop in Java.

Here's the loop for our example. Exercise P4.1 asks you to complete the program.

```java
double highestValue;
highestValue = in.nextDouble();
int highestMonth = 1;
for (int currentMonth = 2; currentMonth <= 12; currentMonth++)
{
   double nextValue = in.nextDouble();
   if (nextValue > highestValue)
   {
      highestValue = nextValue;
      highestMonth = currentMonth;
   }
}
System.out.println(highestMonth);
```

WORKED EXAMPLE 4.1 **Credit Card Processing**

This Worked Example uses a loop to remove spaces from a credit card number.

4.6 Nested Loops

> When the body of a loop contains another loop, the loops are nested. A typical use of nested loops is printing a table with rows and columns.

In Section 3.4, you saw how to nest two `if` statements. Similarly, complex iterations sometimes require a **nested loop**: a loop inside another loop statement. When processing tables, nested loops occur naturally. An outer loop iterates over all rows of the table. An inner loop deals with the columns in the current row.

In this section you will see how to print a table. For simplicity, we will simply print the powers of x, x^n, as in the table at right.

Here is the pseudocode for printing the table.

x^1	x^2	x^3	x^4
1	1	1	1
2	4	8	16
3	9	27	81
...	...	...	...
10	100	1000	10000

```
Print table header.
For x from 1 to 10
    Print table row.
    Print new line.
```

How do you print a table row? You need to print a value for each exponent. This requires a second loop.

```
For n from 1 to 4
    Print x^n.
```

This loop must be placed inside the preceding loop. We say that the inner loop is *nested* inside the outer loop.

There are 10 rows in the outer loop. For each x, the program prints four columns in the inner loop (see Figure 6). Thus, a total of $10 \times 4 = 40$ values are printed.

Following is the complete program. Note that we also use loops to print the table header. However, those loops are not nested.

The hour and minute displays in a digital clock are an example of nested loops. The hours loop 12 times, and for each hour, the minutes loop 60 times.

Figure 6
Flowchart of a Nested Loop

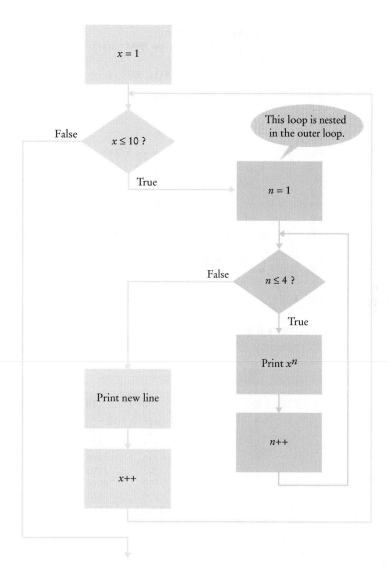

ch04/table2/PowerTable.java

```
1   /**
2       This program prints a table of powers of x.
3   */
4   public class PowerTable
5   {
6       public static void main(String[] args)
7       {
8           final int NMAX = 4;
9           final double XMAX = 10;
10
11          // Print table header
12
13          for (int n = 1; n <= NMAX; n++)
14          {
15              System.out.printf("%10d", n);
16          }
```

```
17      System.out.println();
18      for (int n = 1; n <= NMAX; n++)
19      {
20         System.out.printf("%10s", "x ");
21      }
22      System.out.println();
23
24      // Print table body
25
26      for (double x = 1; x <= XMAX; x++)
27      {
28         // Print table row
29
30         for (int n = 1; n <= NMAX; n++)
31         {
32            System.out.printf("%10.0f", Math.pow(x, n));
33         }
34         System.out.println();
35      }
36   }
37 }
```

Program Run

1	2	3	4
x	x	x	x
1	1	1	1
2	4	8	16
3	9	27	81
4	16	64	256
5	25	125	625
6	36	216	1296
7	49	343	2401
8	64	512	4096
9	81	729	6561
10	100	1000	10000

SELF CHECK

27. Why is there a statement `System.out.println();` in the outer loop but not in the inner loop?

28. How would you change the program so that all powers from x^0 to x^5 are displayed?

29. If you make the change in Self Check 28, how many values are displayed?

30. What do the following nested loops display?

```
for (int i = 0; i < 3; i++)
{
   for (int j = 0; j < 4; j++)
   {
      System.out.print((i + j) + " ");
   }
   System.out.println();
}
```

31. Write nested loops that make the following pattern of brackets:

[] [] [] []
[] [] [] []
[] [] [] []

Practice It Now you can try these exercises at the end of the chapter: R4.19, P4.19, P4.21.

Table 3 Nested Loop Examples		
Nested Loops	Output	Explanation
| ```
for (i = 1; i <= 3; i++)
{
    for (j = 1; j <= 4; j++) { Print "*" }
    System.out.println();
}
``` | ```
****
****
****
``` | Prints 3 rows of 4 asterisks each. |
| ```
for (i = 1; i <= 4; i++)
{
    for (j = 1; j <= 3; j++) { Print "*" }
    System.out.println();
}
``` | ```
***
***
***
***
``` | Prints 4 rows of 3 asterisks each. |
| ```
for (i = 1; i <= 4; i++)
{
    for (j = 1; j <= i; j++) { Print "*" }
    System.out.println();
}
``` | ```
*
**
***
****
``` | Prints 4 rows of lengths 1, 2, 3, and 4. |
| ```
for (i = 1; i <= 3; i++)
{
    for (j = 1; j <= 5; j++)
    {
        if (j % 2 == 0) { Print "*" }
        else { Print "-" }
    }
    System.out.println();
}
``` | ```
-*-*-
-*-*-
-*-*-
``` | Prints asterisks in even columns, dashes in odd columns. |
| ```
for (i = 1; i <= 3; i++)
{
    for (j = 1; j <= 5; j++)
    {
        if ((i + j) % 2 == 0) { Print "*" }
        else { Print " " }
    }
    System.out.println();
}
``` | ```
* * *
 * *
* * *
``` | Prints a checkerboard pattern. |

4.7 Application: Random Numbers and Simulations

In a simulation, you use the computer to simulate an activity. You can introduce randomness by calling the random number generator.

A *simulation program* uses the computer to simulate an activity in the real world (or an imaginary one). Simulations are commonly used for predicting climate change, analyzing traffic, picking stocks, and many other applications in science and business. In many simulations, one or more loops are used to modify the state of a system and observe the changes. You will see examples in the following sections.

4.7.1 Generating Random Numbers

Many events in the real world are difficult to predict with absolute precision, yet we can sometimes know the average behavior quite well. For example, a store may know from experience that a customer arrives every five minutes. Of course, that is an average—customers don't arrive in five minute intervals. To accurately model customer traffic, you want to take that random fluctuation into account. Now, how can you run such a simulation in the computer?

The Java library has a *random number generator*, which produces numbers that appear to be completely random. Calling `Math.random()` yields a random floating-point number that is ≥ 0 and < 1. Call `Math.random()` again, and you get a different number.

The following program calls `Math.random()` ten times.

ch04/random/RandomDemo.java

```
1   /**
2      This program prints ten random numbers between 0 and 1.
3   */
4   public class RandomDemo
5   {
6      public static void main(String[] args)
7      {
8         for (int i = 1; i <= 10; i++)
9         {
10           double r = Math.random();
11           System.out.println(r);
12        }
13     }
14  }
```

Program Run

```
0.2992436267816825
0.43860176045313537
0.7365753471168408
0.6880250194282326
0.1608272403783395
0.5362876579988844
0.3098705906424375
0.6602909916554179
0.1927951611482942
0.8632330736331089
```

Actually, the numbers are not completely random. They are drawn from sequences of numbers that don't repeat for a long time. These sequences are actually computed from fairly simple formulas; they just behave like random numbers. For that reason, they are often called **pseudorandom** numbers.

4.7.2 Simulating Die Tosses

In actual applications, you need to transform the output from the random number generator into different ranges. For example, to simulate the throw of a die, you need random integers between 1 and 6.

Here is the general recipe for computing random integers between two bounds a and b. As you know from Programming Tip 4.4 on page 141, there are b - a + 1 values between a and b, including the bounds themselves. First compute `(int) (Math.random() * (b - a + 1))` to obtain a random integer between 0 and b - a, then add a, yielding a random value between a and b:

```
int r = (int) (Math.random() * (b - a + 1)) + a;
```

Here is a program that simulates the throw of a pair of dice:

ch04/dice/Dice.java

```
1   /**
2       This program simulates tosses of a pair of dice.
3   */
4   public class Dice
5   {
6      public static void main(String[] args)
7      {
8         for (int i = 1; i <= 10; i++)
9         {
10           // Generate two random numbers between 1 and 6
11
12           int d1 = (int) (Math.random() * 6) + 1;
13           int d2 = (int) (Math.random() * 6) + 1;
14           System.out.println(d1 + " " + d2);
15        }
16        System.out.println();
17     }
18  }
```

Program Run

```
5 1
2 1
1 2
5 1
1 2
6 4
4 4
6 1
6 3
5 2
```

4.7.3 The Monte Carlo Method

The Monte Carlo method is an ingenious method for finding approximate solutions to problems that cannot be precisely solved. (The method is named after the famous casino in Monte Carlo.) Here is a typical example. It is difficult to compute the number π, but you can approximate it quite well with the following simulation.

Simulate shooting a dart into a square surrounding a circle of radius 1. That is easy: generate random x and y coordinates between −1 and 1.

If the generated point lies inside the circle, we count it as a *hit*. That is the case when $x^2 + y^2 \leq 1$. Because our shots are entirely random, we expect that the ratio of *hits / tries* is approximately equal to the ratio of the areas of the circle and the square, that is, $\pi / 4$. Therefore, our estimate for π is $4 \times$ *hits / tries*. This method yields an estimate for π, using nothing but simple arithmetic.

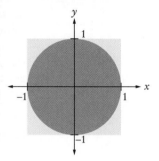

To generate a random value between −1 and 1, you compute:

```
double r = Math.random(); // 0 ≤ r < 1
double x = -1 + 2 * r; // –1 ≤ x < 1
```

As r ranges from 0 (inclusive) to 1 (exclusive), x ranges from $-1 + 2 \times 0 = -1$ (inclusive) to $-1 + 2 \times 1 = 1$ (exclusive). In our application, it does not matter that x never reaches 1. The points that fulfill the equation $x = 1$ lie on a line with area 0.

Here is the program that carries out the simulation.

Random Fact 4.2 Software Piracy

As you read this, you have written a few computer programs, and you have experienced firsthand how much effort it takes to write even the humblest of programs. Writing a real software product, such as a financial application or a computer game, takes a lot of time and money. Few people, and fewer companies, are going to spend that kind of time and money if they don't have a reasonable chance to make more money from their effort. (Actually, some companies give away their software in the hope that users will upgrade to more elaborate paid versions. Other companies give away the software that enables users to read and use files but sell the software needed to create those files. Finally, there are individuals who donate their time, out of enthusiasm, and produce programs that you can copy freely.)

When selling software, a company must rely on the honesty of its customers. It is an easy matter for an unscrupulous person to make copies of computer programs without paying for them. In most countries that is illegal. Most governments provide legal protection, such as copyright laws and patents, to encourage the development of new products. Countries that tolerate widespread piracy have found that they have an ample cheap supply of foreign software, but no local manufacturers willing to design good software for their own citizens, such as word processors in the local script or financial programs adapted to the local tax laws.

When a mass market for software first appeared, vendors were enraged by the money they lost through piracy. They tried to fight back by various schemes to ensure that only the legitimate owner could use the software. Some manufacturers used *key disks:* disks with special patterns of holes burned in by a laser, which couldn't be copied. Others used *dongles:* devices

ch04/circle/MonteCarlo.java

```java
1   /**
2       This program computes an estimate of pi by simulating dart throws onto a square.
3   */
4   public class MonteCarlo
5   {
6      public static void main(String[] args)
7      {
8         final int TRIES = 10000;
9
10        int hits = 0;
11        for (int i = 1; i <= TRIES; i++)
12        {
13           // Generate two random numbers between -1 and 1
14
15           double r = Math.random();
16           double x = -1 + 2 * r; // Between -1 and 1
17           r = Math.random();
18           double y = -1 + 2 * r;
19
20           // Check whether the point lies in the unit circle
21
22           if (x * x + y * y <= 1) { hits++; }
23        }
24
25        /*
26           The ratio hits / tries is approximately the same as the ratio
27           circle area / square area = pi / 4
28        */
29
30        double piEstimate = 4.0 * hits / TRIES;
31        System.out.println("Estimate for pi: " + piEstimate);
32     }
33  }
```

Program Run

```
Estimate for pi: 3.1504
```

that are attached to a printer port. Legitimate users hated these measures. They paid for the software, but they had to suffer through the inconvenience of inserting a key disk every time they started the software or having multiple dongles stick out from their computer. In the United States, market pressures forced most vendors to give up on these copy protection schemes, but they are still commonplace in other parts of the world.

Because it is so easy and inexpensive to pirate software, and the chance of being found out is minimal, you have to make a moral choice for yourself. If a package that you would really like to have is too expensive for your budget, do you steal it, or do you stay honest and get by with a more affordable product?

Of course, piracy is not limited to software. The same issues arise for other digital products as well. You may have had the opportunity to obtain copies of songs or movies without payment. Or you may have been frustrated by a copy protection device on your music player that made it difficult for you to listen to songs that you paid for. Admittedly, it can be difficult to have a lot of sympathy for a musical ensemble whose publisher charges a lot of money for what seems

to have been very little effort on their part, at least when compared to the effort that goes into designing and implementing a software package. Nevertheless, it seems only fair that artists and authors receive some compensation for their efforts. How to pay artists, authors, and programmers fairly, without burdening honest customers, is an unsolved problem at the time of this writing, and many computer scientists are engaged in research in this area.

SELF CHECK

32. How do you simulate a coin toss with the `Math.random()` method?

33. How do you simulate the picking of a random playing card?

34. Why does the loop body in `Dice.java` call `Math.random()` twice?

35. In many games, you throw a pair of dice to get a value between 2 and 12. What is wrong with this simulated throw of a pair of dice?

```java
int sum = (int) (Math.random() * 11) + 2;
```

36. How do you generate a random floating-point number ≥ 0 and < 100?

Practice It Now you can try these exercises at the end of the chapter: R4.20, P4.7, P4.25.

SCREENCAST 4.1 **Drawing a Spiral**

 In this Screencast Video, you will see how to develop a program that draws a spiral.

CHAPTER SUMMARY

- A loop executes instructions repeatedly while a condition is true.

- An off-by-one error is a common error when programming loops. Think through simple test cases to avoid this type of error.

- The `for` loop is used when a value runs from a starting point to an ending point with a constant increment or decrement.

  - The `do` loop is appropriate when the loop body must be executed at least once.

- A sentinel value denotes the end of a data set, but it is not part of the data.

  - You can use a Boolean variable to control a loop. Set the variable to `true` before entering the loop, then set it to `false` to leave the loop.

➕ Available online in WileyPLUS and at www.wiley.com/college/horstmann.

- When the body of a loop contains another loop, the loops are nested. A typical use of nested loops is printing a table with rows and columns.

- In a simulation, you use the computer to simulate an activity. You can introduce randomness by calling the random number generator.

MEDIA RESOURCES

www.wiley.com/
college/
horstmann

- **_Worked Example_** Credit Card Processing
- **Guided Lab Exercises**
- ⊕ **_Animation_** Tracing a Loop
- ⊕ **_Animation_** The for Loop
- ⊕ **_Screencast_** Drawing a Spiral
- ⊕ **Practice Quiz**
- ⊕ **Code Completion Exercises**

REVIEW EXERCISES

★★ **R4.1** Write a loop that computes

  a. The sum of all even numbers between 2 and 100 (inclusive).

  b. The sum of all squares between 1 and 100 (inclusive).

  c. The sum of all odd numbers between a and b (inclusive).

  d. The sum of all odd digits of n. (For example, if n is 32677, the sum would be $3 + 7 + 7 = 17$.)

★ **R4.2** Provide trace tables for these loops.

```
a. int i = 0; int j = 10; int n = 0;
   while (i < j) { i++; j--; n++; }
b. int i = 0; int j = 0; int n = 0;
   while (i < 10) { i++; n = n + i + j; j++; }
c. int i = 10; int j = 0; int n = 0;
   while (i > 0) { i--; j++; n = n + i - j; }
d. int i = 0; int j = 10; int n = 0;
   while (i != j) { i = i + 2; j = j - 2; n++; }
```

★ **R4.3** What do these loops print?

```
a. for (int i = 1; i < 10; i++) { System.out.print(i + " "); }
b. for (int i = 1; i < 10; i += 2) { System.out.print(i + " "); }
c. for (int i = 10; i > 1; i--) { System.out.print(i + " "); }
d. for (int i = 0; i < 10; i++) { System.out.print(i + " "); }
e. for (int i = 1; i < 10; i = i * 2) { System.out.print(i + " "); }
f. for (int i = 1; i < 10; i++) { if (i % 2 == 0) { System.out.print(i + " "); } }
```

★ **R4.4** What is an infinite loop? On your computer, how can you terminate a program that executes an infinite loop?

★★ **R4.5** What is an "off-by-one" error? Give an example from your own programming experience.

★ **R4.6** What is a sentinel value? Give a simple rule when it is appropriate to use a numeric sentinel value.

★ **R4.7** Which loop statements does Java support? Give simple rules for when to use each loop type.

★ **R4.8** How many iterations do the following loops carry out? Assume that i is not changed in the loop body.

> **a.** for (int i = 1; i <= 10; i++) . . .
> **b.** for (int i = 0; i < 10; i++) . . .
> **c.** for (int i = 10; i > 0; i--) . . .
> **d.** for (int i = -10; i <= 10; i++) . . .
> **e.** for (int i = 10; i >= 0; i++) . . .
> **f.** for (int i = -10; i <= 10; i = i + 2) . . .
> **g.** for (int i = -10; i <= 10; i = i + 3) . . .

★★ **R4.9** Write pseudocode for a program that prints a calendar such as the following:

```
Su  M  T  W Th  F Sa
             1  2  3  4
 5  6  7  8  9 10 11
12 13 14 15 16 17 18
19 20 21 22 23 24 25
26 27 28 29 30 31
```

★ **R4.10** Write pseudocode for a program that prints a Celsius/Fahrenheit conversion table such as the following:

```
Celsius | Fahrenheit
--------+-----------
      0 |         32
     10 |         50
     20 |         68
    . . .        . . .
    100 |        212
```

★★ **R4.11** Write pseudocode for a program that reads a sequence of student records and prints the total score for each student. Each record has the student's first and last name, followed by a sequence of test scores and a sentinel of –1. The sequence is terminated by the word END. Here is a sample sequence:

```
Harry Morgan 94 71 86 95 -1
Sally Lin 99 98 100 95 90 -1
END
```

Provide a trace table for this sample input.

★ **R4.12** Rewrite the following for loop into a while loop.

```
int s = 0;
for (int i = 1; i <= 10; i++)
{
```

```
        s = s + i;
    }
```

★ **R4.13** Rewrite the following do/while loop into a while loop.

```
int n = in.nextInt();
double x = 0;
double s;
do
{
    s = 1.0 / (1 + n * n);
    n++;
    x = x + s;
}
while (s > 0.01);
```

★ **R4.14** Provide trace tables of the following loops.

a.
```
int s = 1;
int n = 1;
while (s < 10) { s = s + n; }
n++;
```

b.
```
int s = 1;
for (int n = 1; n < 5; n++) { s = s + n; }
```

c.
```
int s = 1;
int n = 1;
do
{
    s = s + n;
    n++;
}
while (s < 10 * n);
```

★ **R4.15** What do the following loops print? Work out the answer by tracing the code, not by using the computer.

a.
```
int s = 1;
for (int n = 1; n <= 5; n++)
{
    s = s + n;
    System.out.print(s + " ");
}
```

b.
```
int s = 1;
for (int n = 1; s <= 10; System.out.print(s + " "))
{
    n = n + 2;
    s = s + n;
}
```

c.
```
int s = 1;
int n;
for (n = 1; n <= 5; n++)
{
    s = s + n;
    n++;
}
System.out.print(s + " " + n);
```

★ **R4.16** What do the following program segments print? Find the answers by tracing the code, not by using the computer.

a.
```java
int n = 1;
for (int i = 2; i < 5; i++) { n = n + i; }
System.out.print(n + " ");
```

b.
```java
int i;
double n = 1 / 2;
for (i = 2; i <= 5; i++) { n = n + 1.0 / i; }
System.out.print(i + " ");
```

c.
```java
double x = 1;
double y = 1;
int i = 0;
do
{
   y = y / 2;
   x = x + y;
   i++;
}
while (x < 1.8);
System.out.print(i + " ");
```

d.
```java
double x = 1;
double y = 1;
int i = 0;
while (y >= 1.5)
{
   x = x / 2;
   y = x + y;
   i++;
}
System.out.print(i + " ");
```

★★ **R4.17** Give an example of a for loop where symmetric bounds are more natural. Give an example of a for loop where asymmetric bounds are more natural.

★ **R4.18** What are nested loops? Give an example where a nested loop is typically used.

★★ **R4.19** The nested loops

```java
for (int i = 1; i <= height; i++)
{
   for (int j = 1; j <= width; j++) { System.out.print("*"); }
   System.out.println();
}
```

display a rectangle of a given width and height, such as

```
****
****
****
```

Write a *single* for loop that displays the same rectangle.

★★ **R4.20** Suppose you design an educational game to teach children how to read a clock. How do you generate random values for the hours and minutes?

★★★ **R4.21** In a travel simulation, Harry will visit one of his friends that are located in three states. He has ten friends in California, three in Nevada, and two in Utah. How do you produce a random number between 1 and 3, denoting the destination state, with a probability that is proportional to the number of friends in each state?

PROGRAMMING EXERCISES

★★   **P4.1** Complete the program in How To 4.1 on page 151. Your program should read twelve temperature values and print the month with the highest temperature.

★★★   **P4.2** *Credit Card Number Check.* The last digit of a credit card number is the *check digit*, which protects against transcription errors such as an error in a single digit or switching two digits. The following method is used to verify actual credit card numbers but, for simplicity, we will describe it for numbers with 8 digits instead of 16:

- Starting from the rightmost digit, form the sum of every other digit. For example, if the credit card number is 4358 9795, then you form the sum 5 + 7 + 8 + 3 = 23.
- Double each of the digits that were not included in the preceding step. Add all digits of the resulting numbers. For example, with the number given above, doubling the digits, starting with the next-to-last one, yields 18 18 10 8. Adding all digits in these values yields 1 + 8 + 1 + 8 + 1 + 0 + 8 = 27.
- Add the sums of the two preceding steps. If the last digit of the result is 0, the number is valid. In our case, 23 + 27 = 50, so the number is valid.

Write a program that implements this algorithm. The user should supply an 8-digit number, and you should print out whether the number is valid or not. If it is not valid, you should print the value of the check digit that would make it valid.

★★   **P4.3** *Currency conversion.* Write a program that first asks the user to type today's price for one dollar in Japanese yen, then reads U.S. dollar values and converts each to yen. Use 0 as a sentinel.

CHINA	CNY	7.3169	6.0910
EURO	EUR	0.6644	0.6100
JAPAN	JPY	109.00	102.00
SINGAPORE	SGD	1.3712	1.2630
HONG KONG	HKD	7.0043	6.4072
NEW ZEALAND	NZD	1.1646	1.0675
MYSIA	MYR	3.2536	2.7818

★★   **P4.4** Write a program that first asks the user to type in today's price of one dollar in Japanese yen, then reads U.S. dollar values and converts each to Japanese yen. Use 0 as the sentinel value to denote the end of dollar inputs. Then the program reads a sequence of yen amounts and converts them to dollars. The second sequence is terminated by another zero value.

★★   **P4.5** Write a program that reads a set of floating-point values. Ask the user to enter the values, then print

- the average of the values.
- the smallest of the values.
- the largest of the values.
- the range, that is the difference between the smallest and largest.

Of course, you may only prompt for the values once.

★ **P4.6** Translate the following pseudocode for finding the minimum value from a set of inputs into a Java program.

> Set a Boolean variable "first" to true.
> While another value has been read successfully
>   If first is true
>   Set the minimum to the value.
>   Set first to false.
>   Else if the value is less than the minimum
>   Set the minimum to the value.
> Print the minimum.

★★★ **P4.7** Translate the following pseudocode for randomly permuting the characters in a string into a Java program.

> Read a word.
> Repeat word.length() times
>   Pick a random position i in the word, but not the last position
>   Pick a random position j > i in the word.
>   Swap the letters at positions j and i.
> Print the word.

To swap the letters, construct substrings as follows:

```
first    i    middle    j    last
```

Then replace the string with

```
first + word.charAt(j) + middle + word.charAt(i) + last
```

★ **P4.8** Write a program that reads a word and prints each character of the word on a separate line. For example, if the user provides the input "Harry", the program prints

```
H
a
r
r
y
```

★★ **P4.9** Write a program that reads a word and prints the word in reverse. For example, if the user provides the input "Harry", the program prints

```
yrraH
```

★ **P4.10** Write a program that reads a word and prints the number of vowels in the word. For this exercise, assume that a e i o u y are vowels. For example, if the user provides the input "Harry", the program prints 2 vowels.

★★★ **P4.11** Write a program that reads a word and prints the number of syllables in the word. For this exercise, assume that syllables are determined as follows: Each sequence of vowels a e i o u y, except for the last e in a word, is a syllable. However, if that algorithm yields a count of 0, change it to 1. For example,

Word	Syllables
Harry	2
hairy	2
hare	1
the	1

★★★ **P4.12** Write a program that reads a word and prints all substrings, sorted by length. For example, if the user provides the input "rum", the program prints

```
r
u
m
ru
um
rum
```

★ **P4.13** Write a program that prints all powers of 2 from 2^0 up to 2^{20}.

★★ **P4.14** Write a program that reads a number and prints all of its *binary digits:* Print the remainder number % 2, then replace the number with number / 2. Keep going until the number is 0. For example, if the user provides the input 13, the output should be

```
1
0
1
1
```

★★ **P4.15** *Mean and standard deviation.* Write a program that reads a set of floating-point data values. Choose an appropriate mechanism for prompting for the end of the data set. When all values have been read, print out the count of the values, the average, and the standard deviation. The average of a data set $\{x_1, \ldots, x_n\}$ is $\bar{x} = \sum x_i / n$, where $\sum x_i = x_1 + \ldots + x_n$ is the sum of the input values. The standard deviation is

$$s = \sqrt{\frac{\sum (x_i - \bar{x})^2}{n - 1}}$$

However, this formula is not suitable for the task. By the time the program has computed $\bar{x}$, the individual x_i are long gone. Until you know how to save these values, use the numerically less stable formula

$$s = \sqrt{\frac{\sum x_i^2 - \frac{1}{n}\left(\sum x_i\right)^2}{n - 1}}$$

You can compute this quantity by keeping track of the count, the sum, and the sum of squares as you process the input values.

★★ **P4.16** The *Fibonacci numbers* are defined by the sequence

$$f_1 = 1$$
$$f_2 = 1$$
$$f_n = f_{n-1} + f_{n-2}$$

Reformulate that as

Fibonacci numbers describe the growth of a rabbit population.

```
fold1 = 1;
fold2 = 1;
fnew = fold1 + fold2;
```

After that, discard fold2, which is no longer needed, and set fold2 to fold1 and fold1 to fnew. Repeat an appropriate number of times.

Implement a program that prompts the user for an integer n and prints the nth Fibonacci number, using the above algorithm.

★★★ **P4.17** *Factoring of integers.* Write a program that asks the user for an integer and then prints out all its factors. For example, when the user enters 150, the program should print

```
2
3
5
5
```

★★★ **P4.18** *Prime numbers.* Write a program that prompts the user for an integer and then prints out all prime numbers up to that integer. For example, when the user enters 20, the program should print

```
2
3
5
7
11
13
17
19
```

Recall that a number is a prime number if it is not divisible by any number except 1 and itself.

★ **P4.19** Write a program that prints a multiplication table, like this:

```
1    2    3    4    5    6    7    8    9   10
2    4    6    8   10   12   14   16   18   20
3    6    9   12   15   18   21   24   27   30
     .  .  .
10   20   30   40   50   60   70   80   90  100
```

★★ **P4.20** Write a program that reads an integer and displays, using asterisks, a filled and hollow square, placed next to each other. For example if the side length is 5, the program should display

```
***** *****
***** *   *
***** *   *
***** *   *
***** *****
```

★★ **P4.21** Write a program that reads an integer and displays, using asterisks, a filled diamond of the given side length. For example, if the side length is 4, the program should display

```
   *
  ***
 *****
*******
 *****
  ***
   *
```

★★★ **P4.22** *Projectile flight.* Suppose a cannonball is propelled straight into the air with a starting velocity v_0. Any calculus book will state that the position of the ball after t seconds is $s(t) = -\frac{1}{2}gt^2 + v_0 t$, where $g = 9.81 \text{ m/sec}^2$ is the gravitational force of the earth. No calculus book ever mentions why someone would want to carry out such an obviously dangerous experiment, so we will do it in the safety of the computer.

In fact, we will confirm the theorem from calculus by a simulation. In our simulation, we will consider how the ball moves in very short time intervals Δt. In a short time interval the velocity v is nearly constant, and we can compute the distance the ball moves as $\Delta s = v\Delta t$. In our program, we will simply set

```
final double DELTA_T = 0.01;
```

and update the position by

```
s = s + v * DELTA_T;
```

The velocity changes constantly—in fact, it is reduced by the gravitational force of the earth. In a short time interval, $\Delta v = -g\Delta t$, we must keep the velocity updated as

```
v = v - g * DELTA_T;
```

In the next iteration the new velocity is used to update the distance.

Now run the simulation until the cannonball falls back to the earth. Get the initial velocity as an input (100 m/sec is a good value). Update the position and velocity 100 times per second, but print out the position only every full second. Also print out the values from the exact formula $s(t) = -\frac{1}{2}gt^2 + v_0 t$ for comparison.

What is the benefit of this kind of simulation when an exact formula is available? Well, the formula from the calculus book is *not* exact. Actually, the gravitational force diminishes the farther the cannonball is away from the surface of the earth. This complicates the algebra sufficiently that it is not possible to give an exact formula for the actual motion, but the computer simulation can simply be extended to apply a variable gravitational force. For cannonballs, the calculus-book formula is actually good enough, but computers are necessary to compute accurate trajectories for higher-flying objects such as ballistic missiles.

★★★   **P4.23**   *The game of Nim.* This is a well-known game with a number of variants. The following variant has an interesting winning strategy. Two players alternately take marbles from a pile. In each move, a player chooses how many marbles to take. The player must take at least one but at most half of the marbles. Then the other player takes a turn. The player who takes the last marble loses.

You will write a program in which the computer plays against a human opponent. Generate a random integer between 10 and 100 to denote the initial size of the pile. Generate a random integer between 0 and 1 to decide whether the computer or the human takes the first turn. Generate a random integer between 0 and 1 to decide whether the computer plays *smart* or *stupid*. In stupid mode the computer simply takes a random legal value (between 1 and *n*/2) from the pile whenever it has a turn. In smart mode the computer takes off enough marbles to make the size of the pile a power of two minus 1—that is, 3, 7, 15, 31, or 63. That is always a legal move, except when the size of the pile is currently one less than a power of two. In that case, the computer makes a random legal move.

You will note that the computer cannot be beaten in smart mode when it has the first move, unless the pile size happens to be 15, 31, or 63. Of course, a human player who has the first turn and knows the winning strategy can win against the computer.

★★ **P4.24** *The Drunkard's Walk.* A drunkard in a grid of streets randomly picks one of four directions and stumbles to the next intersection, then again randomly picks one of four directions, and so on. You might think that on average the drunkard doesn't move very far because the choices cancel each other out, but that is actually not the case.

Represent locations as integer pairs (*x*, *y*). Implement the drunkard's walk over 100 intersections, starting at (0, 0), and print the ending location.

★★ **P4.25** *The Monty Hall Paradox.* Marilyn vos Savant described the following problem (loosely based on a game show hosted by Monty Hall) in a popular magazine: "Suppose you're on a game show, and you're given the choice of three doors: Behind one door is a car; behind the others, goats. You pick a door, say No. 1, and the host, who knows what's behind the doors, opens another door, say No. 3, which has a goat. He then says to you, "Do you want to pick door No. 2?" Is it to your advantage to switch your choice?"

Ms. vos Savant proved that it is to your advantage, but many of her readers, including some mathematics professors, disagreed, arguing that the probability would not change because another door was opened.

Your task is to simulate this game show. In each iteration, randomly pick a door number between 1 and 3 for placing the car. Randomly have the player pick a door. Randomly have the game show host pick a door having a goat (but not the door that the player picked). Now increment a counter for strategy 1 if the player wins by switching to the host's choice, and increment a counter for strategy 2 if the player wins by sticking with the original choice. Run 1,000 iterations and print both counters.

★★ **P4.26** *The Buffon Needle Experiment.* The following experiment was devised by Comte Georges-Louis Leclerc de Buffon (1707–1788), a French naturalist. A needle of length 1 inch is dropped onto paper that is ruled with lines 2 inches apart. If the needle drops onto a line, we count it as a *hit*. (See Figure 7.) Buffon conjectured that the quotient *tries*/*hits* approximates π.

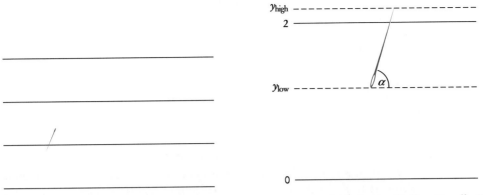

Figure 7   The Buffon Needle Experiment   **Figure 8**   A Hit in the Buffon Needle Experiment

For the Buffon needle experiment, you must generate two random numbers: one to describe the starting position and one to describe the angle of the needle with the *x*-axis. Then you need to test whether the needle touches a grid line.

Generate the *lower* point of the needle. Its *x*-coordinate is irrelevant, and you may assume its *y*-coordinate y_{low} to be any random number between 0 and 2. The angle α between the needle and the *x*-axis can be any value between 0 degrees and 180 degrees (π radians). The upper end of the needle has *y*-coordinate

$$y_{high} = y_{low} + \sin\alpha$$

The needle is a hit if y_{high} is at least 2, as shown in Figure 7. Stop after 10,000 tries and print the quotient *tries/hits*.

ANSWERS TO SELF-CHECK QUESTIONS

1. 23 years.
2. 7 years.
3. Add a statement

   `System.out.println(balance);`

   as the last statement in the `while` loop.
4. The program prints the same output. This is because the balance after 14 years is slightly below $20,000, and after 15 years, it is slightly above $20,000.
5. `2 4 8 16 32 64 128`

   Note that the value 128 is printed even though it is larger than 100.

6. ```
   int year = 1;
   while (year <= nyears)
   {
      balance = balance * (1 + RATE / 100);
      System.out.printf("%4d %10.2f\n", year, balance);
      year++;
   }
   ```
   ```

7. 11 numbers: 10 9 8 7 6 5 4 3 2 1 0

8.
```java
for (int i = 10; i <= 20; i = i + 2)
{
    System.out.println(i);
}
```

9.
```java
int sum = 0;
for (int i = 1; i <= n; i++)
{
    sum = sum + i;
}
```

10.
```java
for (int year = 1; balance <= 2 * INITIAL_BALANCE; year++)
```
However, it is best not to use a for loop in this case because the loop condition does not relate to the year variable. A while loop would be a better choice.

11.
```java
do
{
    System.out.println("Enter a value between 0 and 100: ");
    value = in.nextDouble();
}
while (value < 0 || value > 100);
```

12.
```java
int value = 100;
while (value >= 100)
{
    System.out.println("Enter a value < 100: ");
    value = in.nextDouble();
}
```
Here, the variable value had to be initialized with an artificial value to ensure that the loop is entered at least once.

13. Yes. The do loop
```java
do { body } while (condition);
```
is equivalent to this while loop:
```java
boolean first = true;
while (first || condition) { body; first = false; }
```

14.
```java
int x;
int sum = 0;
do
{
    x = in.nextInt();
    sum = sum + x;
}
while (x != 0);
```

15.
```java
int x = 0;
int previous;
do
{
    previous = x;
    x = in.nextInt();
    sum = sum + x;
}
while (previous != x);
```

16. No data

17. The first check ends the loop after the sentinel has been read. The second check ensures that the sentinel is not processed as an input value.

18. The `while` loop would never be entered. The user would never be prompted for input. Because count stays 0, the program would then print `"No data"`.

19. The `nextDouble` method also returns `false`. A more accurate prompt would have been: "Enter values, a key other than a digit to quit." But that might be more confusing to the program user who would need now ponder which key to choose.

20. If the user doesn't provide any numeric input, the first call to `in.nextDouble()` will fail.

21. The total is zero.

22.
```
double total = 0;
while (in.hasNextDouble())
{
    double input = in.nextDouble();
    if (input > 0) { total = total + input; }
}
```

23. `position i` is `str.length()` and `ch` is unchanged from its initial value, `'?'`. Note that `ch` must be initialized with some value—otherwise the compiler will complain about a possibly uninitialized variable.

24. The loop will stop when a match is found, but you cannot access the match because neither `position` nor `ch` are defined outside the loop.

25. Start the loop at the end of string:
```
boolean found = false;
char ch;
int i = str.length() - 1;
while (!found && i >= 0)
{
    ch = str.charAt(i);
    if (Character.isLowerCase(ch)) { found = true; }
    else { i--; }
}
```

26. The initial call to `in.nextDouble()` fails, terminating the program. One solution is to do all input in the loop and introduce a Boolean variable that checks whether the loop is entered for the first time.
```
double input = 0;
boolean first = true;
while (in.hasNextDouble())
{
    double previous = input;
    input = in.nextDouble();
    if (first) { first = false; }
    else if (input == previous) { System.out.println("Duplicate input"); }
}
```

27. All values in the inner loop should be displayed on the same line.

28. Change lines 13, 18, and 30 to `for (int n = 0; n <= NMAX; n++)`. Change `NMAX` to 5.

29. 60: The outer loop is executed 10 times, and the inner loop 6 times.

30. 0123
1234
2345

31.
```
for (int i = 1; i <= 3; i++)
{
    for (int j = 1; j <= 4; j++)
    {
        System.out.print("[]");
    }
    System.out.println();
}
```

32. Compute `(int) (Math.random() * 2)`, and use 0 for heads, 1 for tails, or the other way around.

33. Compute `(int) (Math.random() * 4)` and associate the numbers 0 . . . 3 with the four suits. Then compute `(int) (Math.random() * 13)` and associate the numbers 0 . . . 12 with Jack, Ace, 2 . . . 10, Queen, and King

34. We need to call it once for each die. If we printed the same value twice, the die tosses would not be independent.

35. The call will produce a value between 2 and 12, but all values have the same probability. When throwing a pair of dice, the number 7 is six times as likely as the number 2. The correct formula is

```
int sum = (int) (Math.random() * 6) + (int) (Math.random() * 6) + 2;
```

36. `Math.random() * 100.0`

CHAPTER 5

METHODS

A method packages a computation consisting of multiple steps into a form that can be easily understood and reused. (The person in the image to the left is in the middle of executing the method "make two cups of espresso".) In this chapter, you will learn how to design and implement your own methods. Using the process of stepwise refinement, you will be able to break up complex tasks into sets of cooperating methods.

5.1 Methods as Black Boxes

A method is a named sequence of instructions.

A **method** is a sequence of instructions with a name. You have already encountered several methods. For example, the method named pow, which was introduced in Chapter 2, contains instructions to compute a power x^y. Moreover, every Java program has a method called main.

You *call* a method in order to execute its instructions. For example, consider the following program fragment:

```java
public static void main(String[] args)
{
    double z = Math.pow(2, 3);
    . . .
}
```

By using the expression Math.pow(2, 3), main *calls* the Math.pow method, asking it to compute 2^3. The main method is temporarily suspended. The instructions of the Math.pow method execute and compute the result. The Math.pow method *returns* its result back to main, and the main method resumes execution (see Figure 1).

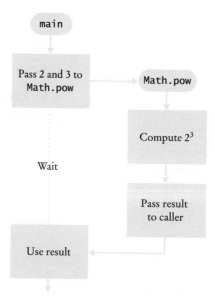

Figure 1 Execution Flow During a Method Call

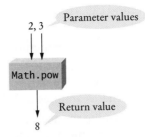

Figure 2 The Math.pow Method as a Black Box

When another method calls the Math.pow method, it provides "inputs", such as the values 2 and 3 in the call Math.pow(2, 3). In order to avoid confusion with inputs that are provided by a human user, these values are called **parameter values**. The "output" that the pow method computes is called the **return value**.

Methods can receive multiple parameters, but they return only one value. It is also possible to have methods with no parameters. An example is the Math.random method that requires no parameter to produce a random number.

The return value of a method is returned to the calling method, where it is processed according to the statement containing the method call. For example, suppose your program contains a statement

```
double z = Math.pow(2, 3);
```

When the Math.pow method returns its result, the return value is stored in the variable z.

Do not confuse returning a value with producing program output. If you want the return value to be printed, you need to add a statement such as System.out.print(z).

At this point, you may wonder how the Math.pow method performs its job. For example, how does Math.pow compute that 2^3 is 8? By multiplying $2 \times 2 \times 2$? With logarithms? Fortunately, as a user of the method, you *don't need to know* how the method is implemented. You just need to know the *specification* of the method: If you provide parameter values x and y, the method returns x^y. Engineers use the term *black box* for a device with a given specification but unknown implementation. You can think of Math.pow as a black box, as shown in Figure 2.

When you design your own methods, you will want to make them appear as black boxes to other programmers. Those programmers want to use your methods without knowing what goes on inside. Even if you are the only person working on a program, making each method into a black box pays off: there are fewer details that you need to keep in mind.

Parameter values are supplied when a method is called. The return value is the result that the method computes.

Even though a thermostat is usually white, you can think of it as a black box. The input is the desired temperature, and the output is a signal to the heater or air conditioner.

1. Consider the method call `Math.pow(3, 2)`. What are the parameter and return values?

2. What is the return value of the method call `Math.pow(Math.pow(2, 2), 2)`?

3. The `Math.ceil` method in the Java standard library is described as follows: The method receives a single parameter value *a* of type `double` and returns the smallest `double` value ≥ *a* that is an integer. What is the return value of `Math.ceil(2.3)`?

4. It is possible to determine the answer to Self Check 3 without knowing how the `Math.ceil` method is implemented. Use an engineering term to describe this aspect of the `Math.ceil` method.

Practice It   Now you can try these exercises at the end of the chapter: R5.3, R5.6.

5.2 Implementing Methods

In this section, you will learn how to implement a method from a given specification. We will use a very simple example: a method to compute the volume of a cube with a given side length.

The `cubeVolume` *method uses a given side length to compute the volume of a cube.*

> When declaring a method, you provide a name for the method, a name and type for each parameter, and a type for the result.

When writing this method, you need to

- Pick a name for the method (`cubeVolume`).
- Give a type and a name for each parameter variable (`double sideLength`).
- Specify the type of the return value (`double`).
- Add the `public static` modifiers. We will discuss the meanings of these modifiers in Chapter 7. For now, you should simply add them to your methods.

Put all this information together to form the first line of the method's declaration:

```
public static double cubeVolume(double sideLength)
```

Next, specify the *body* of the method. The body contains the variable declarations and statements that are executed when the method is called.

The volume of a cube of side length *s* is $s \times s \times s$. However, for greater clarity, our parameter variable has been called `sideLength`, not *s*, so we need to compute `sideLength * sideLength * sideLength`.

We will store this value in a variable called `volume`:

```
double volume = sideLength * sideLength * sideLength;
```

In order to return the result of the method, use the `return` statement:

```
return volume;
```

The return *statement gives the method's result to the caller.*

The body of a method is enclosed in braces. Here is the complete method:

```java
public static double cubeVolume(double sideLength)
{
   double volume = sideLength * sideLength * sideLength;
   return volume;
}
```

Let's put this method to use. We'll supply a main method that calls the cubeVolume method twice.

```java
public static void main(String[] args)
{
   double result1 = cubeVolume(2);
   double result2 = cubeVolume(10);
   System.out.println("A cube with side length 2 has volume " + result1);
   System.out.println("A cube with side length 10 has volume " + result2);
}
```

When the method is called with different parameter values, the method returns different results. Consider the call cubeVolume(2). The parameter value 2 corresponds to the sideLength parameter variable. Therefore, in this call, sideLength is 2. The method computes sideLength * sideLength * sideLength, or 2 * 2 * 2. When the method is called with a different parameter value, say 10, then the method computes 10 * 10 * 10.

Syntax 5.1   Method Declaration

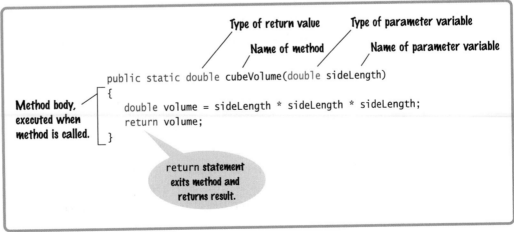

Now we combine both methods into a test program. Note that both methods are contained in the same class. Note the comment that describes the behavior of the method. (Programming Tip 5.1 on page 183 describes the format of the comment.)

ch05/cube/Cubes.java

```java
1   /**
2       This program computes the volumes of two cubes.
3   */
4   public class Cubes
5   {
6       public static void main(String[] args)
7       {
8           double result1 = cubeVolume(2);
9           double result2 = cubeVolume(10);
10          System.out.println("A cube with side length 2 has volume " + result1);
11          System.out.println("A cube with side length 10 has volume " + result2);
12      }
13
14      /**
15          Computes the volume of a cube.
16          @param sideLength the side length of the cube
17          @return the volume
18      */
19      public static double cubeVolume(double sideLength)
20      {
21          double volume = sideLength * sideLength * sideLength;
22          return volume;
23      }
24  }
```

Program Run

```
A cube with side length 2 has volume 8
A cube with side length 10 has volume 1000
```

SELF CHECK

5. What is the value of cubeVolume(3)?

6. What is the value of cubeVolume(cubeVolume(2))?

7. Provide an alternate implementation of the body of the cubeVolume method by calling the pow method.

8. Declare a method squareArea that computes the area of a square of a given side length.

9. Consider this method:

```java
public static int mystery(int x, int y)
{
    double result = (x + y) / (y - x);
    return result;
}
```

What is the result of the call mystery(2, 3)?

Practice It   Now you can try these exercises at the end of the chapter: R5.1, R5.2, P5.1, P5.2.

Method Comments

Whenever you write a method, you should *comment* its behavior. Comments are for human readers, not compilers. The Java language provides a standard layout for method comments, called the **javadoc** convention, as shown here:

```
/**
    Computes the volume of a cube.
    @param sideLength the side length of the cube
    @return the volume
*/
public static double cubeVolume(double sideLength)
{
    double volume = sideLength * sideLength * sideLength;
    return volume;
}
```

> Method comments explain the purpose of the method, the meaning of the parameters and return value, as well as any special requirements.

Comments are enclosed in /** and */ delimiters. The first line of the comment describes the purpose of the method. Each @param clause describes a parameter variable and the @return clause describes the return value.

Note that the method comment does not document the implementation (*how* the method carries out its work) but rather the design (*what* the method does). The comment allows other programmers to use the method as a "black box".

Turn Repeated Code Into a Method

When you write nearly identical code multiple times, you should probably introduce a method. Consider these statements:

```
int hours;
do
{
    System.out.print("Enter a value between 1 and 12: ");
    hours = in.nextInt();
}
while (hours < 1 || hours > 12);

int minutes;
do
{
    System.out.print("Enter a value between 0 and 59: ");
    minutes = in.nextInt();
}
while (minutes < 0 || minutes > 59);
```

Here, we read two variables, making sure that each of them is within a certain range. It is easy to extract the common behavior into a method:

```
/**
    Prompts a user to enter a value in a given range until the user
    provides a valid input.
    @param low the low end of the range
    @param high the high end of the range
    @return the value provided by the user
*/
public static int readValueBetween(int low, int high)
{
```

```
                    int input;
                    do
                    {
                       System.out.print("Enter a value between " + low + " and " + high + ": ");
                       Scanner in = new Scanner(System.in);
                       input = in.nextInt();
                    }
                    while (input < low || input > high);
                    return input;
                 }
```

Then use this method twice:

```
    int hours = readValueBetween(1, 12);
    int minutes = readValueBetween(0, 59);
```

Note how the code has become much easier to understand.

When carrying out the same task multiple times, use a method.

5.3 Parameter Passing

Parameter variables hold the parameter values supplied in the method call.

In this section, we examine the mechanism of parameter passing more closely. When a method is called, a variable is created for each parameter. This variable is called a **parameter variable**. (Another commonly used term is **formal parameter**.) In the method call, a value is supplied for each parameter, called the **parameter value**. (Other commonly used terms for this value are **actual parameter** and **argument**.) Each parameter variable is initialized with the corresponding parameter value.

Consider the method call illustrated in Figure 3:

```
    double result1 = cubeVolume(2);
```

A recipe for a fruit pie may say to use any kind of fruit. Here, "fruit" is an example of a parameter variable.

Figure 3
Parameter Passing

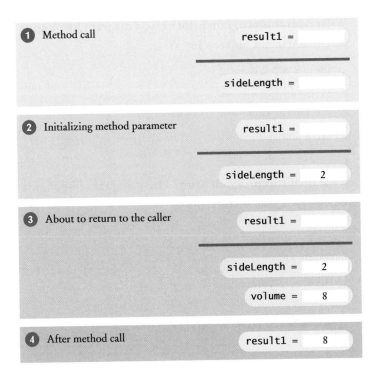

The detailed steps:

- The parameter variable sideLength of the cubeVolume method is created. ①
- The parameter variable is initialized with the value that was passed in the call. In our case, sideLength is set to 2. ②
- The method computes the expression sideLength * sideLength * sideLength, which has the value 8. That value is stored in the variable volume. ③
- The method returns. All of its variables are removed, including the parameter variable. The return value is transferred to the *caller*, that is, the method calling the cubeVolume method. The caller puts the return value in the result1 variable. ④

ANIMATION
Parameter Passing

Now consider what happens in a subsequent call, cubeVolume(10). A new parameter variable is created. (Recall that the previous parameter variable was removed when the first call to cubeVolume returned.) It is initialized with 10, and the process repeats. After the second method call is complete, its parameter variables are again removed.

SELF CHECK

10. What does this program print? Use a diagram like Figure 3 to find the answer.

```java
public static double mystery(int x, int y)
{
   double z = x + y;
   z = z / 2.0;
   return z;
}
public static void main(String[] args)
{
   int a = 5;
   int b = 7;
   System.out.println(mystery(a, b));
}
```

11. What does this program print? Use a diagram like Figure 3 to find the answer.

```java
public static int mystery(int x)
{
   int y = x * x;
   return y;
}
public static void main(String[] args)
{
   int a = 4;
   System.out.println(mystery(a + 1));
}
```

12. What does this program print? Use a diagram like Figure 3 to find the answer.

```java
public static int mystery(int n)
{
   n++;
   n++;
   return n;
}
public static void main(String[] args)
{
   int a = 5;
   System.out.println(mystery(a));
}
```

Practice It Now you can try these exercises at the end of the chapter: R5.5, R5.13, P5.5.

Programming Tip 5.3

Do Not Modify Parameter Variables

In Java, a parameter variable is just like any other variable. You can modify the values of the parameter variables in the body of a method. For example,

```java
public static int totalCents(int dollars, int cents)
{
   cents = dollars * 100 + cents; // Modifies parameter variable
   return cents;
}
```

However, many programmers find this practice confusing (see Common Error 5.1). To avoid the confusion, simply introduce a separate variable:

```java
public static int totalCents(int dollars, int cents)
{
   int result = dollars * 100 + cents;
   return result;
}
```

Common Error 5.1

Trying to Modify Parameters

The following method contains a common error: trying to modify a variable that was passed to it.

```java
public static int addTax(double price, double rate)
{
   double tax = price * rate / 100;
   price = price + tax; // Has no effect outside the method
   return tax;
```

```
    }
```
Now consider this call:
```
double total = 10;
addTax(total, 7.5); // Does not modify total
```
When the method is called, price is set to 10. Then price is changed to 10.75. When the method returns, all of its parameter variables are removed. Any values that have been assigned to them are simply forgotten. Note that total is *not* changed. In Java, a method can never change a variable of the calling method.

5.4 Return Values

> The return statement terminates a method call and yields the method result.

You use the return statement to specify the result of a method. In the preceding example, each return statement returned a constant or a variable. However, the return statement can return the value of any expression. Instead of saving the return value in a variable and returning the variable, it is often possible to eliminate the variable and return a more complex expression:

```
public static double cubeVolume(double sideLength)
{
    return sideLength * sideLength * sideLength;
}
```

When the return statement is processed, the method exits *immediately*. Some programmers find this behavior convenient for handling exceptional cases at the beginning of the method:

```
public static double cubeVolume(double sideLength)
{
    if (sideLength < 0) { return 0; }
    // Handle the regular case
    . . .
}
```

If the method is called with a negative value for sideLength, then the method returns 0 and the remainder of the method is not executed. (See Figure 4.)

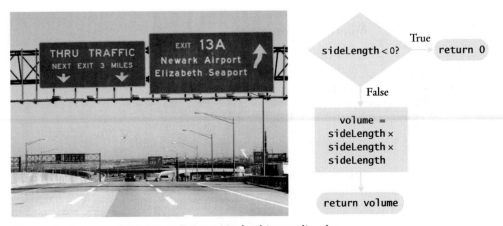

Figure 4 A return Statement Exits a Method Immediately

Every branch of a method needs to return a value. Consider the following incorrect method:

```java
public static double cubeVolume(double sideLength)
{
   if (sideLength >= 0)
   {
      return sideLength * sideLength * sideLength;
   } // Error—no return value if sideLength < 0
}
```

The compiler reports this as an error. A correct implementation is:

```java
public static double cubeVolume(double sideLength)
{
   if (sideLength >= 0)
   {
      return sideLength * sideLength * sideLength;
   }
   else
   {
      return 0;
   }
}
```

SELF CHECK

13. Suppose we change the body of the cubeVolume method to

```java
if (sideLength <= 0) { return 0; }
return sideLength * sideLength * sideLength;
```

How does this method differ from the one described in this section?

14. What does this method do?

```java
public static boolean mystery (int n)
{
   if (n % 2 == 0) { return true };
   else { return false; }
}
```

15. Implement the mystery method of Self Check 14 with a single return statement.

Practice It   Now you can try these exercises at the end of the chapter: R5.12, P5.12.

Common Error 5.2

Missing Return Value

It is a compile-time error if some branches of a method return a value and others do not. Consider this example:

```java
public static int sign(double x)
{
   if (x < 0) { return -1; }
   if (x > 0) { return 1; }
   // Error: missing return value if x equals 0
}
```

This method computes the sign of a number: –1 for negative numbers and +1 for positive numbers. If the parameter value is zero, however, no value is returned. The remedy is to add a statement return 0; to the end of the method.

HOW TO 5.1   Implementing a Method

A method is a computation that can be used multiple times with different parameter values, either in the same program or in different programs. Whenever a computation is needed more than once, turn it into a method.

To illustrate this process, suppose that you are helping archaeologists who research Egyptian pyramids. You have taken on the task of writing a method that determines the volume of a pyramid, given its height and base length.

Step 1   Describe what the method should do.

Provide a simple English description, such as "Compute the volume of a pyramid whose base is a square."

> Turn computations that can be reused into methods.

Step 2   Determine the method's "inputs".

Make a list of *all* the parameters that can vary. It is common for beginners to implement methods that are overly specific. For example, you may know that the great pyramid of Giza, the largest of the Egyptian pyramids, has a height of 146 meters and a base length of 230 meters. You should *not* use these numbers in your calculation, even if the original problem only asked about the great pyramid. It is just as easy—and far more useful—to write a method that computes the volume of *any* pyramid.

In our case, the parameters are the pyramid's height and base length. At this point, we have enough information to document the method:

```
/**
    Computes the volume of a pyramid whose base is a square.
    @param height the height of the pyramid
    @param baseLength the length of one side of the pyramid's base
    @return the volume of the pyramid
*/
```

Step 3   Determine the types of the parameters and the return value.

The height and base length can both be floating-point numbers. Therefore, we will choose the type double for both parameter variables. The computed volume is also a floating-point number, yielding a return type of double. Therefore, the method will be declared as

```
public static double pyramidVolume(double height, double baseLength)
```

Step 4   Write pseudocode for obtaining the desired result.

In most cases, a method needs to carry out several steps to find the desired answer. You may need to use mathematical formulas, branches, or loops. Express your method in pseudocode.

An Internet search yields the fact that the volume of a pyramid is computed as

volume = 1/3 x height x base area

Since the base is a square, we have

base area = base length x base length

Using these two equations, we can compute the volume from the parameter values.

Step 5   Implement the method body.

In our example, the method body is quite simple. Note the use of the return statement to return the result.

```java
public static double pyramidVolume(double height, double baseLength)
{
   double baseArea = baseLength * baseLength;
   return height * baseArea / 3;
}
```

Step 6 Test your method.

After implementing a method, you should test it in isolation. Such a test is called a **unit test**. Work out test cases by hand, and make sure that the method produces the correct results. For example, for a pyramid with height 9 and base length 10, we expect the area to be 1/3 × 9 × 100 = 300. If the height is 0, we expect an area of 0.

```java
public static void main(String[] args)
{
   System.out.println("Volume: " + pyramidVolume(9, 10));
   System.out.println("Expected: 300");
   System.out.println("Volume: " + pyramidVolume(0, 10));
   System.out.println("Expected: 0");
}
```

The output confirms that the method worked as expected:

```
Volume: 300
Expected: 300
Volume: 0
Expected: 0
```

WORKED EXAMPLE 5.1   **Generating Random Passwords**

This Worked Example creates a method that generates passwords of a given length with at least one digit and one special character.

5.5 Methods Without Return Values

Use a return type of void to indicate that a method does not return a value.

Sometimes, you need to carry out a sequence of instructions that does not yield a value. If that instruction sequence occurs multiple times, you will want to package it into a method. In Java, you use the return type void to indicate the absence of a return value.

Here is a typical example. Your task is to print a string in a box, like this:

```
-------
!Hello!
-------
```

A void method returns no value, but it can produce output.

➕ Available online in WileyPLUS and at www.wiley.com/college/horstmann.

However, different strings can be substituted for Hello. A method for this task can be declared as follows:

```
public static void boxString(String str)
```

Now you develop the body of the method in the usual way, by formulating a general method for solving the task.

> Print a line that contains the - character n + 2 times, where n is the length of the string.
> Print a line containing the string, surrounded with a ! to the left and right.
> Print another line containing the - character n + 2 times.

Here is the method implementation:

```
/**
    Prints a string in a box.
    @param str the string to print
*/
public static void boxString(String str)
{
   int n = str.length();
   for (int i = 0; i < n + 2; i++) { System.out.print("-"); }
   System.out.println();
   System.out.println("!" + str + "!");
   for (int i = 0; i < n + 2; i++) { System.out.print("-"); }
   System.out.println();
}
```

Note that this method doesn't compute any value. It performs some actions and then returns to the caller. (See the sample program ch05/box/Boxes.java.)

Because there is no return value, you cannot use boxString in an expression. You can call

```
boxString("Hello");
```

but not

```
result = boxString("Hello"); // Error: boxString doesn't return a result.
```

If you want to return from a void method before reaching the end, you use a return statement without a value. For example,

```
public static void boxString(String str)
{
   int n = str.length();
   if (n == 0)
   {
      return; // Return immediately
   }
   . . .
}
```

SELF CHECK

16. How do you generate the following printout, using the boxString method?

```
-------
!Hello!
-------
-------
!World!
-------
```

17. What is wrong with the following statement?

```
System.out.print(boxString("Hello"));
```

18. Implement a method shout that prints a line consisting of a string followed by three exclamation marks. For example, shout("Hello") should print Hello!!!. The method should not return a value.

19. How would you modify the boxString method to leave a space around the string that is being boxed, like this:

```
---------
! Hello !
---------
```

20. The boxString method contains the code for printing a line of - characters twice. Place that code into a separate method printLine, and use that method to simplify boxString. What is the code of both methods?

Practice It   Now you can try these exercises at the end of the chapter: R5.4, P5.15.

5.6 Stepwise Refinement

> Use the process of stepwise refinement to decompose complex tasks into simpler ones.

One of the most powerful strategies for problem solving is the process of **stepwise refinement**. To solve a difficult task, break it down into simpler tasks. Then keep breaking down the simpler tasks into even simpler ones, until you are left with tasks that you know how to solve.

A production process is broken down into sequences of assembly steps.

Now apply this process to a problem of everyday life. You get up in the morning and simply must **get coffee**. How do you get coffee? You see whether you can get someone else, such as your mother or mate, to bring you some. If that fails, you must **make coffee**. How do you make coffee? If there is instant coffee available, you can **make instant coffee**. How do you make instant coffee? Simply **boil water** and mix the boiling water with the instant coffee. How do you boil water? If there is a microwave, then you fill a cup with water, place it in the microwave and heat it for three minutes. Otherwise, you fill a kettle with water and heat it on the stove until the water comes to a boil. On the other hand, if you don't have instant coffee, you must **brew coffee**. How do you brew coffee? You add water to the coffee maker, put in a filter, **grind coffee**, put the coffee in the filter, and turn the coffee maker on. How do you grind coffee? You add coffee beans to the coffee grinder and push the button for 60 seconds.

Figure 5 shows a flowchart view of the coffee-making solution. Refinements are shown as expanding boxes. In Java, you implement a refinement as a method. For example, a method brewCoffee would call grindCoffee, and it would be called from a method makeCoffee.

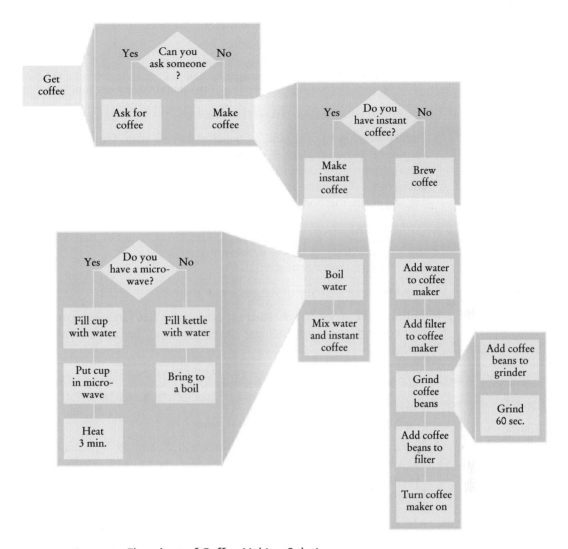

Figure 5 Flowchart of Coffee-Making Solution

Let us apply the process of stepwise refinement to a programming problem. When printing a check, it is customary to write the check amount both as a number ("$274.15") and as a text string ("two hundred seventy four dollars and 15 cents"). Doing so reduces the recipient's temptation to add a few digits in front of the amount. For a human, this isn't particularly difficult, but how can a computer do this? There is no built-in method that turns 274 into "two hundred seventy four". We need to program this method.

Here is the description of the method we want to write:

```
/**
    Turns a number into its English name.
    @param number a positive integer < 1,000
    @return the name of number (e.g., "two hundred seventy four")
*/
public static String intName(int number)
```

Before starting to program, we need to have a plan. Consider a simple case. If the number is between 1 and 9, we need to compute "one" ... "nine". In fact, we need the same computation *again* for the hundreds (two hundred). Any time you need something more than once, it is a good idea to turn that into a method. Rather than writing the entire method, write only the comment:

```
/**
    Turns a digit into its English name.
    @param digit an integer between 1 and 9
    @return the name of digit ("one" ... "nine")
*/
public static String digitName(int digit)
```

Numbers between 10 and 19 are special cases. Let's have a separate method teenName that converts them into strings "eleven", "twelve", "thirteen", and so on:

```
/**
    Turns a number between 10 and 19 into its English name.
    @param number an integer between 10 and 19
    @return the name of the number ("ten" ... "nineteen")
*/
public static String teenName(int number)
```

Next, suppose that the number is between 20 and 99. The name of such a number has two parts, such as "seventy four". We need a way of producing the first part, "twenty", "thirty", and so on. Again, we will put that computation into a separate method:

```
/**
    Gives the name of the tens part of a number between 20 and 99.
    @param number an integer between 20 and 99
    @return the name of the tens part of the number ("twenty" ... "ninety")
*/
public static String tensName(int number)
```

Now let us write the pseudocode for the intName method. If the number is between 100 and 999, then we show a digit and the word "hundred" (such as "two hundred"). We then remove the hundreds, for example reducing 274 to 74. Next, suppose the remaining part is at least 20 and at most 99. If the number is evenly divisible by 10, we use tensName, and we are done. Otherwise, we print the tens with tensName (such as "seventy") and remove the tens, reducing 74 to 4. In a separate branch, we deal with numbers that are at between 10 and 19. Finally, we print any remaining single digit (such as "four").

```
part = number (The part that still needs to be converted)
name = "" (The name of the number)
If part >= 100
    name = digitName(part / 100) + " hundred"
    Remove hundreds from part.
```

```
If part >= 20
    Append tensName(part) to name.
    Remove tens from part.
Else if part >= 10
    Append teenName(part) to name.
    part = 0

If (part > 0)
    Append digitName(part) to name.
```

ANIMATION
Tracing a Method

Translating the pseudocode into Java is straightforward. The result is shown in the source listing at the end of this section.

Note how we rely on helper methods to do much of the detail work. Using the process of stepwise refinement, we now need to consider these helper methods.

Let's start with the digitName method. This method is so simple to implement that pseudocode is not really required. Simply use an if statement with nine branches:

```java
public static String digitName(int digit)
{
    if (digit == 1) { return "one" };
    if (digit == 2) { return "two" };
    . . .
}
```

The teenName and tensName methods are similar.

This concludes the process of stepwise refinement. Here is the complete program.

ch05/intname/IntegerName.java

```java
 1  import java.util.Scanner;
 2
 3  /**
 4      This program turns an integer into its English name.
 5  */
 6  public class IntegerName
 7  {
 8     public static void main(String[] args)
 9     {
10        Scanner in = new Scanner(System.in);
11        System.out.print("Please enter a positive integer < 1000: ");
12        int input = in.nextInt();
13        System.out.println(intName(input));
14     }
15
16     /**
17         Turns a number into its English name.
18         @param number a positive integer < 1,000
19         @return the name of the number (e.g. "two hundred seventy four")
20     */
21     public static String intName(int number)
22     {
23        int part = number; // The part that still needs to be converted
24        String name = ""; // The name of the number
25
26        if (part >= 100)
27        {
28           name = digitName(part / 100) + " hundred";
29           part = part % 100;
```

```
30          }
31
32          if (part >= 20)
33          {
34             name = name + " " + tensName(part);
35             part = part % 10;
36          }
37          else if (part >= 10)
38          {
39             name = name + " " + teenName(part);
40             part = 0;
41          }
42
43          if (part > 0)
44          {
45             name = name + " " + digitName(part);
46          }
47
48          return name;
49       }
50
51    /**
52       Turns a digit into its English name.
53       @param digit an integer between 1 and 9
54       @return the name of digit ("one" . . . "nine")
55    */
56    public static String digitName(int digit)
57    {
58       if (digit == 1) { return "one"; }
59       if (digit == 2) { return "two"; }
60       if (digit == 3) { return "three"; }
61       if (digit == 4) { return "four"; }
62       if (digit == 5) { return "five"; }
63       if (digit == 6) { return "six"; }
64       if (digit == 7) { return "seven"; }
65       if (digit == 8) { return "eight"; }
66       if (digit == 9) { return "nine"; }
67       return "";
68    }
69
70    /**
71       Turns a number between 10 and 19 into its English name.
72       @param number an integer between 10 and 19
73       @return the name of the given number ("ten" . . . "nineteen")
74    */
75    public static String teenName(int number)
76    {
77       if (number == 10) { return "ten"; }
78       if (number == 11) { return "eleven"; }
79       if (number == 12) { return "twelve"; }
80       if (number == 13) { return "thirteen"; }
81       if (number == 14) { return "fourteen"; }
82       if (number == 15) { return "fifteen"; }
83       if (number == 16) { return "sixteen"; }
84       if (number == 17) { return "seventeen"; }
85       if (number == 18) { return "eighteen"; }
86       if (number == 19) { return "nineteen"; }
87       return "";
88    }
```

```
89
90      /**
91          Gives the name of the tens part of a number between 20 and 99.
92          @param number an integer between 20 and 99
93          @return the name of the tens part of the number ("twenty" . . . "ninety")
94      */
95      public static String tensName(int number)
96      {
97          if (number >= 90) { return "ninety"; }
98          if (number >= 80) { return "eighty"; }
99          if (number >= 70) { return "seventy"; }
100         if (number >= 60) { return "sixty"; }
101         if (number >= 50) { return "fifty"; }
102         if (number >= 40) { return "forty"; }
103         if (number >= 30) { return "thirty"; }
104         if (number >= 20) { return "twenty"; }
105         return "";
106     }
107 }
```

Program Run

```
Please enter a positive integer < 1000: 729
seven hundred twenty nine
```

SELF CHECK

21. Explain how you can improve the `intName` method so that it can handle parameter values up to 9999.

22. Why does line 40 set `part = 0`?

23. What happens when you call `intName(0)`? How can you change the `intName` method to handle this case correctly?

24. Trace the method call `intName(72)`, as described in Programming Tip 5.5.

25. Use the process of stepwise refinement to break down the task of printing the following table into simpler tasks.

```
+-----+-----------+
|  i  | i * i * i |
+-----+-----------+
|  1  |         1 |
|  2  |         8 |
    . . .        . . .
| 20  |      8000 |
+-----+-----------+
```

Practice It   Now you can try these exercises at the end of the chapter: R5.11, P5.8, P5.11.

Programming Tip 5.4   **Keep Methods Short**

There is a certain cost for writing a method. You need to design, code, and test the method. The method needs to be documented. You need to spend some effort to make the method reusable rather than tied to a specific context. To avoid this cost, it is always tempting just to stuff more and more code in one place rather than going through the trouble of breaking up the code into separate methods. It is quite common to see inexperienced programmers produce methods that are several hundred lines long.

As a rule of thumb, a method that is so long that its code will not fit on a single screen in your development environment should probably be broken up.

Tracing Methods

When you design a complex method, it is a good idea to carry out a manual walkthrough before entrusting your program to the computer.

Consider a method call that you want to study, such as intName(416). Make a table with the names and values of the parameter variables, like this:

number	
416	

Then write the names and initial values of the method variables.

number	part	name
416	416	""

We enter the test part >= 100. part / 100 is 4 and part % 100 is 16. digitName(4) is easily seen to be "four". (Had digitName been complicated, you would have started another sheet of paper to figure out that method call. It is quite common to accumulate several sheets in this way.)

Now name has changed to name + " " + digitName(part / 100) + " hundred", that is "four hundred", and part has changed to part % 100, or 16.

number	part	name
416	~~416~~	~~""~~
	16	"four hundred"

Now you enter the branch part >= 10. teensName(16) is sixteen, so the variables now have the values

number	part	name
416	~~416~~	~~""~~
	~~16~~	~~"four hundred"~~
	0	"four hundred sixteen"

Now it becomes clear why you need to set part to 0. Otherwise, you would enter the next branch and the result would be "four hundred sixteen six". Tracing the code is an effective way to understand the subtle aspects of a method.

Programming Tip 5.6

Stubs

When writing a larger program, it is not always feasible to implement and test all methods at once. You often need to test a method that calls another, but the other method hasn't yet been implemented. Then you can temporarily replace the missing method with a **stub**. A stub is a method that returns a simple value that is sufficient for testing another method. Here are examples of stub methods.

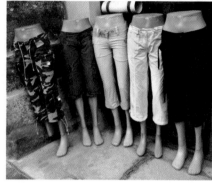

Stubs are incomplete methods that can be used for testing.

```
/**
    Turns a digit into its English name.
    @param digit an integer between 1 and 9
    @return the name of digit ("one" ... "nine")
*/
public static String digitName(int digit)
{
    return "mumble";
}


/**
    Gives the name of the tens part of a number between 20 and 99.
    @param number an integer between 20 and 99
    @return the tens name of the number ("twenty" ... "ninety")
*/
public static String tensName(int number)
{
    return "mumblety";
}
```

If you combine these stubs with the intName method and test it with a parameter value of 274, you will get a result of "mumble hundred mumblety mumble", which indicates that the basic logic of the intName method is working correctly.

WORKED EXAMPLE 5.2   **Calculating a Course Grade**

This Worked Example uses stepwise refinement to solve the problem of converting a set of letter grades into an average grade for a course.

⊕ Available online in WileyPLUS and at www.wiley.com/college/horstmann.

5.7 Variable Scope

As your programs get larger and contain more variables, you may encounter problems where you cannot access a variable that is defined in a different part of your program, or where two variable definitions conflict with each other. In order to resolve these problems, you need to be familiar with the concept of *variable scope*. The **scope** of a variable is the part of the program in which you can access it. For example, the scope of a method's parameter variable is the entire method. In the following code segment, the scope of the parameter sideLength is the entire cubeVolume method but not the main method.

> The scope of a variable is the part of the program in which it is visible.

```java
public static void main(String[] args)
{
    System.out.println(cubeVolume(10));
}

public static double cubeVolume(double sideLength)
{
    return sideLength * sideLength * sideLength;
}
```

A variable that is defined within a method is called a **local variable**. The scope of a local variable ranges from its declaration until the end of the block or for statement in which it is declared. For example, in the code segment below, the scope of the square variable is highlighted.

```java
public static void main(String[] args)
{
    int sum = 0;
    for (int i = 1; i <= 10; i++)
    {
        int square = i * i;
        sum = sum + square;
    }
    System.out.println(sum);
}
```

Note that a variable declared in a for statement only extends to the end of the for statement.

```java
public static void main(String[] args)
{
    int sum = 0;
    for (int i = 1; i <= 10; i++)
    {
        sum = sum + i * i;
    }
    System.out.println(sum);
}
```

Here is an example of a scope problem. The following code will not compile.

```java
public static void main(String[] args)
{
    double sideLength = 10;
    int result = cubeVolume();
    System.out.println(result);
```

```
   }

   public static double cubeVolume()
   {
      return sideLength * sideLength * sideLength; // ERROR
   }
```

Note the scope of the variable sideLength. The cubeVolume method attempts to read the variable, but it cannot—its scope does not extend outside the main method. The remedy is, of course, to pass it as a parameter.

It is possible to use the same variable name more than once in a program. Consider the result variables in the following example:

```
public static void main(String[] args)
{
   int result = square(3) + square(4);
   System.out.println(result);
}

public static int square(int n)
{
   int result = n * n;
   return result;
}
```

> Two local or parameter variables can have the same name, provided that their scopes do not overlap.

Each result variable is declared in a separate method, and their scopes do not overlap.

You can even have two variables with the same name in the same method, provided that their scopes do not overlap:

```
public static void main(String[] args)
{
   int sum = 0;
   for (int i = 1; i <= 10; i++)
   {
      sum = sum + i;
   }

   for (int i = 1; i <= 10; i++)
   {
      sum = sum + i * i;
   }
   System.out.println(sum);
}
```

In the same way that there can be a street named "Main Street" in different cities, a Java program can have multiple variables with the same name.

It is not legal to declare two variables with the same name in the same method in such a way that their scopes overlap. For example, the following is not legal:

```java
public static int sumOfSquares(int n)
{
   int sum = 0;
   for (int i = 1; i <= n; i++)
   {
      int n = i * i; // ERROR
      sum = sum + n;
   }
   return sum;
}
```

The scope of the local variable n is contained within the scope of the parameter variable n. In this case, you need to rename one of the variables.

SELF CHECK

Consider this sample program.

```java
1   public class Sample
2   {
3      public static void main(String[] args)
4      {
5         int x = 4;
6         x = mystery(x + 1);
7         System.out.println(s);
8      }
9
10     public static int mystery(int x)
11     {
12        int s = 0;
13        for (int i = 0; i < x; x++)
14        {
15           int x = i + 1;
16           s = s + x;
17        }
18        return s;
19     }
20  }
```

26. Which lines are in the scope of the variable i declared in line 13?

27. Which lines are in the scope of the parameter variable x declared in line 10?

28. The program declares two local variables with the same name whose scopes don't overlap. What are they?

29. There is a scope error in the mystery method. How do you fix it?

30. There is a scope error in the main method. What is it, and how do you fix it?

Practice It   Now you can try these exercises at the end of the chapter: R5.8, R5.9.

5.8 Recursive Methods (Optional)

A recursive method is a method that calls itself. This is not as unusual as it sounds at first. Suppose you face the arduous task of cleaning up an entire house. You may well say to yourself, "I'll pick a room and clean it, and then I'll clean the other rooms." In other words, the cleanup task calls itself, but with a simpler input. Eventually, all the rooms will be cleaned.

In Java, a recursive method uses the same principle. Here is a typical example. We want to print triangle patterns like this:

```
[]
[][]
[][][]
[][][][]
```

Cleaning up a house can be solved recursively: Clean one room, then clean up the rest.

Specifically, our task is to provide a method

```
public static void printTriangle(int sideLength)
```

The triangle given above is printed by calling `printTriangle(4)`. To see how recursion helps, consider how a triangle with side length 4 can be obtained from a triangle with side length 3.

```
[]
[][]
[][][]
[][][][]
```

Print the triangle with side length 3.
Print a line with four [].

More generally, here are the Java instructions for an arbitrary side length:

```java
public static void printTriangle(int sideLength)
{
    printTriangle(sideLength - 1);
    for (int i = 0; i < sideLength; i++)
    {
        System.out.print("[]");
    }
    System.out.println();
}
```

There is just one problem with this idea. When the side length is 1, we don't want to call `printTriangle(0)`, `printTriangle(-1)`, and so on. The solution is simply to treat this as a special case, and not to print anything when `sideLength` is less than 1.

```java
public static void printTriangle(int sideLength)
{
    if (sideLength < 1) { return; }
    printTriangle(sideLength - 1);
    for (int i = 0; i < sideLength; i++)
    {
        System.out.print("[]");
    }
    System.out.println();
}
```

A recursive computation solves a problem by using the solution of the same problem with simpler inputs.

Look at the printTriangle method one more time and notice how utterly reasonable it is. If the side length is 0, nothing needs to be printed. The next part is just as reasonable. Print the smaller triangle *and don't think about why that works*. Then print a row of []. Clearly, the result is a triangle of the desired size.

There are two key requirements to make sure that the recursion is successful:

- Every recursive call must simplify the task in some way.
- There must be special cases to handle the simplest tasks directly.

For a recursion to terminate, there must be special cases for the simplest inputs.

The printTriangle method calls itself again with smaller and smaller side lengths. Eventually the side length must reach 0, and the method stops calling itself.

Here is what happens when we print a triangle with side length 4.

- The call printTriangle(4) calls printTriangle(3).
  - The call printTriangle(3) calls printTriangle(2).
    - The call printTriangle(2) calls printTriangle(1).
      - The call printTriangle(1) calls printTriangle(0).
        - The call printTriangle(0) returns, doing nothing.
      - The call printTriangle(1) prints [].
    - The call printTriangle(2) prints [][].
  - The call printTriangle(3) prints [][][].
- The call printTriangle(4) prints [][][][].

ANIMATION
Tracing a Recursion

The call pattern of a recursive method looks complicated, and the key to the successful design of a recursive method is *not to think about it*.

Recursion is not really necessary to print triangle shapes. You can use nested loops, like this:

```
public static void printTriangle(int sideLength)
{
   for (int i = 0; i < sideLength; i++)
   {
      for (int j = 0; j < i; j++)
      {
         System.out.print("[]");
      }
      System.out.println();
   }
}
```

However, this pair of loops is a bit tricky. Many people find the recursive solution simpler to understand. (See ch05/triangle/TrianglePrinter.java in your source code.)

This set of Russian dolls looks similar to the call pattern of a recursive method.

SELF CHECK

31. Consider this slight modification of the `printTriangle` method:

```java
public static void printTriangle(int sideLength)
{
    if (sideLength < 1) { return; }
    for (int i = 0; i < sideLength; i++)
    {
        System.out.print("[]");
    }
    System.out.println();
    printTriangle(sideLength - 1);
}
```

What is the result of `printTriangle(4)`?

32. Consider this recursive method:

```java
public static int mystery(int n)
{
    if (n <= 0) { return 0; }
    return n + mystery(n - 1);
}
```

What is `mystery(4)`?

33. Consider this recursive method:

```java
public static int mystery(int n)
{
    if (n <= 0) { return 0; }
    return mystery(n / 2) + 1;
}
```

What is `mystery(20)`?

34. Write a recursive method for printing n box shapes [] in a row.

35. The `intName` method in Section 5.6 accepted parameter values < 1,000. Using a recursive call, extend its range to 999,999. For example an input of 12,345 should return "twelve thousand three hundred forty five".

Practice It   Now you can try these exercises at the end of the chapter: R5.15, P5.19, P5.21.

HOW TO 5.2   ### Thinking Recursively

To solve a problem recursively requires a different mindset than to solve it by programming loops. In fact, it helps if you are, or pretend to be, a bit lazy and let others do most of the work for you. If you need to solve a complex problem, pretend that "someone else" will do most of the heavy lifting and solve the problem for all simpler inputs. Then you only need to figure out how you can turn the solutions with simpler inputs into a solution for the whole problem.

To illustrate the recursive thinking process, consider the problem of How To 4.1, to compute the sum of the digits of a number. We want to design a method `digitSum` that computes the sum of the digits of an integer n.

For example, `digitSum(1729)` = 1 + 7 + 2 + 9 = 19

Step 1   Break the input into parts that can themselves be inputs to the problem.

In your mind, focus on a particular input or set of inputs for the task that you want to solve, and think how you can simplify the inputs. Look for simplifications that can be solved by the same task, and whose solutions are related to the original task.

In the digit sum problem, consider how we can simplify an input such as n = 1729. Would it help to subtract 1? After all, digitSum(1729) = digitSum(1728) + 1. But consider n = 1000. There seems to be no obvious relationship between digitSum(1000) and digitSum(999).

A much more promising idea is to remove the last digit, that is, compute n / 10 = 172. The digit sum of 172 is directly related to the digit sum of 1729.

> The key to finding a recursive solution is reducing the input to a simpler input for the same problem.

Step 2 Combine solutions with simpler inputs into a solution of the original problem.

In your mind, consider the solutions for the simpler inputs that you have discovered in Step 1. Don't worry *how* those solutions are obtained. Simply have faith that the solutions are readily available. Just say to yourself: These are simpler inputs, so someone else will solve the problem for me.

In the case of the digit sum task, ask yourself how you can obtain digitSum(1729) if you know digitSum(172). You simply add the last digit (9), and you are done. How do you get the last digit? As the remainder n % 10. The value digitSum(n) can therefore be obtained as

> When designing a recursive solution, do not worry about multiple nested calls. Simply focus on reducing a problem to a slightly simpler one.

digitSum(n / 10) + n % 10

Don't worry how digitSum(n / 10) is computed. The input is smaller, and therefore it works.

Random Fact 5.1 The Explosive Growth of Personal Computers

In 1971, Marcian E. "Ted" Hoff, an engineer at Intel Corporation, was working on a chip for a manufacturer of electronic calculators. He realized that it would be a better idea to develop a *general-purpose* chip that could be *programmed* to interface with the keys and display of a calculator, rather than to do yet another custom design. Thus, the *microprocessor* was born. At the time, its primary application was as a controller for calculators, washing machines, and the like. It took years for the computer industry to notice that a genuine central processing unit was now available as a single chip.

Hobbyists were the first to catch on. In 1974 the first computer *kit,* the Altair 8800, was available from MITS Electronics for about $350. The kit consisted of the microprocessor, a circuit board, a very small amount of memory, toggle switches, and a row of display lights. Purchasers had to solder and assemble it, then program it in machine language through the toggle switches. It was not a big hit.

The first big hit was the Apple II. It was a real computer with a keyboard, a monitor, and a floppy disk drive. When it was first released, users had a $3,000 machine that could play Space Invaders, run a primitive bookkeeping program, or let users program it in BASIC. The original Apple II did not even support lowercase letters, making it worthless for word processing. The breakthrough came in 1979 with a new spreadsheet program, VisiCalc. In a spreadsheet, you enter financial data and their relationships into a grid of rows and columns (see the figure at right). Then you modify some of the data and watch in real time how the others change. For example, you can see how changing the mix of widgets in a manufacturing plant might affect estimated costs and profits. Middle managers in companies, who understood computers and were fed up with having to wait for hours or days to get their data runs back from the computing center, snapped up VisiCalc and the computer that was needed to run it. For them, the computer was a spreadsheet machine.

The next big hit was the IBM Personal Computer, ever after known as the PC. It was the first widely available personal computer that used Intel's 16-bit processor, the 8086, whose successors are still being used in personal computers today. The success of the PC was based not on any engineering breakthroughs but on the fact that it was easy to *clone*. IBM published the computer's specifications in order to encourage third parties to develop plug-in cards. Perhaps IBM did not foresee that functionally equivalent versions of their computer could be recreated by others, but a variety of PC clone vendors emerged, and ultimately IBM stopped selling personal computers.

IBM never produced an *operating system* for its PCs—that is, the software that organizes the interaction between the user and the computer, starts application programs, and manages disk storage and other resources. Instead, IBM offered customers the option of three separate operating systems. Most customers couldn't care less about the operating system.

Step 3   Find solutions to the simplest inputs.

A recursive computation keeps simplifying its inputs. To make sure that the recursion comes to a stop, you must deal with the simplest inputs separately. Come up with special solutions for them. That is usually very easy.

Look at the simplest inputs for the digitSum problem:

* A number with a single digit
* 0

A number with a single digit is its own digit sum, so you can stop the recursion when n < 10, and return n in that case. Or, you can be even lazier. If n has a single digit, then digitSum(n / 10) + n % 10 equals digitSum(0) + n. You can simply terminate the recursion when n is zero.

Step 4   Implement the solution by combining the simple cases and the reduction step.

Now you are ready to implement the solution. Make separate cases for the simple inputs that you considered in Step 3. If the input isn't one of the simplest cases, then implement the logic you discovered in Step 2.

Here is the complete digitSum method:

```java
public static int digitSum(int n)
{
    if (n == 0) { return 0; } // Special case for terminating the recursion
    return digitSum(n / 10) + n % 10; // General case
}
```

They chose the system that was able to launch most of the few applications that existed at the time. It happened to be DOS (Disk Operating System) by Microsoft. Microsoft licensed the same operating system to other hardware vendors and encouraged software companies to write DOS applications.

A huge number of useful application programs for PC-compatible machines was the result.

PC applications were certainly useful, but they were not easy to learn. Every vendor developed a different *user interface:* the collection of keystrokes, menu options, and settings that a user needed to master to use a software package effectively. Data exchange between applications was difficult, because each program used a different data format. The Apple Macintosh changed all that in 1984. The designers of the Macintosh had the vision to supply an intuitive user interface with the computer and to force software developers to adhere to it. It took Microsoft and PC-compatible manufacturers years to catch up.

Most personal computers are used for accessing information from online sources, entertainment, word processing, and home finance. Some analysts predict that the personal computer will merge with the television set and cable network into an entertainment and information appliance.

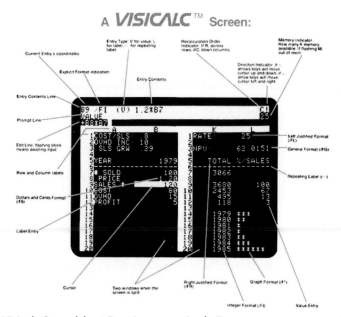

The Visicalc Spreadsheet Running on an Apple II

CHAPTER SUMMARY

- A method is a named sequence of instructions.
- Parameter values are supplied when a method is called. The return value is the result that the method computes.

- When declaring a method, you provide a name for the method, a name and type for each parameter, and a type for the result.
- Method comments explain the purpose of the method, the meaning of the parameters and return value, as well as any special requirements.

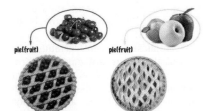

- Parameter variables hold the parameter values supplied in the method call.

- The return statement terminates a method call and yields the method result.
- Turn computations that can be reused into methods.

- Use a return type of void to indicate that a method does not return a value.

- Use the process of stepwise refinement to decompose complex tasks into simpler ones.

⊕ Available online in WileyPLUS and at www.wiley.com/college/horstmann.

- The scope of a variable is the part of the program in which it is visible.
- Two local or parameter variables can have the same name, provided that their scopes do not overlap.

- A recursive computation solves a problem by using the solution of the same problem with simpler inputs.
    - For a recursion to terminate, there must be special cases for the simplest inputs.
    - The key to finding a recursive solution is reducing the input to a simpler input for the same problem.
    - When designing a recursive solution, do not worry about multiple nested calls. Simply focus on reducing a problem to a slightly simpler one.

MEDIA RESOURCES

www.wiley.com/
college/
horstmann

- **Worked Example** Generating Random Passwords
- **Worked Example** Calculating a Course Grade
- Guided Lab Exercises
- ⊕ **Animation** Parameter Passing
- ⊕ **Animation** Tracing a Method
- ⊕ **Animation** Tracing a Recursion
- ⊕ **Screencast** Fully Justified Text
- ⊕ Practice Quiz
- ⊕ Code Completion Exercises

REVIEW EXERCISES

★ **R5.1** In which sequence are the lines of the program `Cubes.java` on page 182 executed, starting with the first line of `main`?

★ **R5.2** Write method headers for methods with the following descriptions:

   a. Computing the larger of two integers

   b. Computing the smallest of three floating-point numbers

   c. Checking whether an integer is a prime number, returning `true` if it is and `false` otherwise

   d. Checking whether a string is contained inside another string

   e. Computing the balance of an account with a given initial balance, an annual interest rate, and a number of years of earning interest

   f. Printing the balance of an account with a given initial balance and an annual interest rate over a given number of years

   g. Printing the calendar for a given month and year

   h. Computing the weekday for a given day, month, and year (as a string such as `"Monday"`)

   i. Generating a random integer between 1 and n

★ **R5.3** Give examples of the following methods from the Java library.

    a. A method with a double parameter and a `double` return value

    b. A method with two `double` parameters and a `double` return value

    c. A method with a `String` parameter and a `double` return value

    d. A method with no parameter and a `double` return value

★ **R5.4** True or false?

    a. A method has exactly one `return` statement.

    b. A method has at least one `return` statement.

    c. A method has at most one return value.

    d. A method with return value void never has a return statement.

    e. When executing a `return` statement, the method exits immediately.

    f. A method with return value void must print a result.

    g. A method without parameters always returns the same value.

★★ **R5.5** Consider these methods:

```java
public static double f(double x) { return g(x) + Math.sqrt(h(x)); }
public static double g(double x) { return 4 * h(x); }
public static double h(double x) { return x * x + k(x) - 1; }
public static double k(double x) { return 2 * (x + 1); }
```

Without actually compiling and running a program, determine the results of the following method calls.

    a. `double x1 = f(2);`

    b. `double x2 = g(h(2));`

    c. `double x3 = k(g(2) + h(2));`

    d. `double x4 = f(0) + f(1) + f(2);`

    e. `double x5 = f(-1) + g(-1) + h(-1) + k(-1);`

★ **R5.6** What is the difference between a parameter value and a return value? How many parameter values can a method call have? How many return values?

★★ **R5.7** Write pseudocode for a method that translates a telephone number with letters in it (such as 1-800-FLOWERS) into the actual phone number. Use the standard letters on a phone pad.

★★ **R5.8** Describe the scope error in the following program and explain how to fix it.

```
public class Conversation
{
   public static void main(String[] args)
   {
      Scanner in = new Scanner(System.in);
      System.out.print("What is your name? ");
      String input = in.nextLine();
      System.out.println("Hello, " + input);
      System.out.print("How old are you? ");
      int input = in.nextInt();
      input++;
      System.out.println("Next year, you will be " + input);
   }
}
```

★★   **R5.9** For each of the variables in the following program, indicate the scope. Then determine what the program prints, without actually running the program.

```
 1  public class Sample
 2  {
 3     public static void main(String[] args)
 4     {
 5        int i = 10;
 6        int b = g(i);
 7        System.out.println(b + i);
 8     }
 9
10     public static int f(int i)
11     {
12        int n = 0;
13        while (n * n <= i) { n++; }
14        return n - 1;
15     }
16
17     public static int g(int a)
18     {
19        int b = 0;
20        for (int n = 0; n < a; n++)
21        {
22           int i = f(n);
23           b = b + i;
24        }
25        return b;
26     }
27  }
```

★   **R5.10** Use the process of stepwise refinement to describe the process of making scrambled eggs. Discuss what you do if you do not find eggs in the refrigerator.

★   **R5.11** Perform a walkthrough of the intName method with the following parameter values:

a. 5

b. 12

c. 21

d. 301

e. 324

f. 0

g. -2

★★ **R5.12** Consider the following method:

```java
public static int f(int a)
{
   if (a < 0) { return -1; }
   int n = a;
   while (n > 0)
   {
      if (n % 2 == 0) // n is even
      {
         n = n / 2;
      }
      else if (n == 1) { return 1; }
      else { n = 3 * n + 1; }
   }
   return 0;
}
```

Perform traces of the computations f(-1), f(0), f(1), f(2), f(10), and f(100).

★★★ **R5.13** Consider the following method that is intended to swap the values of two integers:

```java
public static void falseSwap(int a, int b)
{
   int temp = a;
   a = b;
   b = temp;
}

public static void main(String[] args)
{
   int x = 3;
   int y = 4;
   falseSwap(x, y);
   System.out.println(x + " " + y);
}
```

Why doesn't the falseSwap method swap the contents of x and y?

★★★ **R5.14** Give pseudocode for a recursive method for printing all substrings of a given string. For example, the substrings of the string "rum" are "rum" itself, "ru", "um", "r", "u", "m", and the empty string. You may assume that all letters of the string are different.

★★★ **R5.15** Give pseudocode for a recursive method that sorts all letters in a string. For example, the string "goodbye" would be sorted into "bdegooy".

PROGRAMMING EXERCISES

★★ **P5.1** Write a method that computes the balance of a bank account with a given initial balance and interest rate, after a given number of years. Assume interest is compounded yearly.

★ **P5.2** Write a method

```java
public static String repeat(String str, int n)
```

that returns the string str repeated n times. For example, repeat("ho", 3) returns "hohoho".

★★ **P5.3** Write a method

```
public static int countVowels(String str)
```

that returns a count of all vowels in the string str. Vowels are the letters a, e, i, o, and u, and their uppercase variants.

★★ **P5.4** Write a method

```
public static int countWords(String str)
```

that returns a count of all words in the string str. Words are separated by spaces. For example, countWords("Mary had a little lamb") should return 5.

★★ **P5.5** It is a well-known phenomenon that most people are easily able to read a text whose words have two characters flipped, provided the first and last letter of each word are not changed. For example:

> I dn'ot gvie a dman for a man taht can olny sepll a wrod one way. (Mrak Taiwn)

Write a method String scramble(String word) that constructs a scrambled version of a given word, randomly flipping two characters other than the first and last one. Then write a program that reads words and prints the scrambled words.

★ **P5.6** Write methods

```
public static double sphereVolume(double r)

public static double sphereSurface(double r)

public static double cylinderVolume(double r, double h)

public static double cylinderSurface(double r, double h)

public static double coneVolume(double r, double h)

public static double coneSurface(double r, double h)
```

that compute the volume and surface area of a sphere with radius r, a cylinder with a circular base with radius r and height h, and a cone with a circular base with radius r and height h. Then write a program that prompts the user for the values of r and h, calls the six methods, and prints the results.

★★ **P5.7** Write a method

```
public static double readDouble(String prompt)
```

that displays the prompt string, followed by a space, reads a floating-point number in, and returns it. Here is a typical usage:

```
salary = readDouble("Please enter your salary:");
percentageRaise = readDouble("What percentage raise would you like?");
```

★★ **P5.8** Enhance the intName method so that it works correctly for values < 1,000,000,000.

★★ **P5.9** Enhance the intName method so that it works correctly for negative values and zero. *Caution:* Make sure the improved method doesn't print 20 as "twenty zero".

★★★ **P5.10** For some values (for example, 20), the intName method returns a string with a leading space (" twenty"). Repair that blemish and ensure that spaces are inserted only when necessary. *Hint:* There are two ways of accomplishing this. Either ensure that leading spaces are never inserted, or remove leading spaces from the result before returning it.

★★ **P5.11** Write a program that prints a paycheck. Ask the program user for the name of the employee, the hourly rate, and the number of hours worked. If the number of hours exceeds 40, the employee is paid "time and a half", that is, 150 percent of the hourly rate on the hours exceeding 40. Your check should look similar to that in the figure below. Use fictitious names for the payer and the bank. Be sure to use stepwise refinement and break your solution into several methods. Use the intName method to print the dollar amount of the check.

| (WJ)**WILEY** | John Wiley & Sons, Inc.
111 River Street
Hoboken, NJ 07030-5774 | Publishers' Bank Minnesota
2000 Prince Blvd
Jonesville, MN 55400 | CHECK
NUMBER | 063331 | $\frac{74\text{-}39}{311}$ 567390 |

		Date	Amount
PAY	4659484	04/29/10	$*******274.15

TWO HUNDRED SEVENTY FOUR AND 15 / 100 **
TO THE ORDER OF:

JOHN DOE
1009 Franklin Blvd
Sunnyvale, CA 95014

⑆478108240⑈ 200620375⑈ 1301⑆

★★ **P5.12** *Leap years.* Write a method

```
public static boolean isLeapYear(int year)
```

that tests whether a year is a leap year: that is, a year with 366 days. Exercise P3.24 describes how to test whether a year is a leap year. In this exercise, use multiple if statements and return statements to return the result as soon as you know it.

★★ **P5.13** Write a program that converts a Roman number such as MCMLXXVIII to its decimal number representation. *Hint:* First write a method that yields the numeric value of each of the letters. Then use the following algorithm:

```
total = 0
While the roman number string is not empty
    If value(first character) is at least value(second character), or the string has length 1
        Add value(first character) to total.
        Remove the character.
    Else
        Add the difference value(second character) - value(first character) to total.
        Remove both characters.
```

★★ **P5.14** In Exercise P3.22 you were asked to write a program to convert a number to its representation in Roman numerals. At the time, you did not know how to factor out common code, and as a consequence the resulting program was rather long. Rewrite that program by implementing and using the following method:

```
public static String romanDigit(int n, String one, String five, String ten)
```

That method translates one digit, using the strings specified for the one, five, and ten values. You would call the method as follows:

```
romanOnes = romanDigit(n % 10, "I", "V", "X");
n = n / 10;
romanTens = romanDigit(n % 10, "X", "L", "C");
. . .
```

★★★ **P5.15** *Postal bar codes.* For faster sorting of letters, the United States Postal Service encourages companies that send large volumes of mail to use a bar code denoting the zip code (see Figure 6).

The encoding scheme for a five-digit zip code is shown in Figure 7. There are full-height frame bars on each side. The five encoded digits are followed by a check digit, which is computed as follows: Add up all digits, and choose the check digit to make the sum a multiple of 10. For example, the zip code 95014 has a sum of 19, so the check digit is 1 to make the sum equal to 20.

Each digit of the zip code, and the check digit, is encoded according to the table at right, where | denotes a full bar and : a half bar:

1	: : : | |
2	: : | : |
3	: : | | :
4	: | : : |
5	: | : | :
6	: | | : :
7	| : : : |
8	| : : | :
9	| : | : :
0	| | : : :

Write a program that asks the user for a zip code and prints the bar code. Use : for half bars, | for full bars. For example, 95014 becomes

||:|:::|:|:|||::::::||:|::|:::|||

Provide these methods:

```
void printDigit(int d)
void printBarCode(int zipCode)
```

★★★ **P5.16** Write a program that reads in a bar code (with : denoting half bars and | denoting full bars) and prints out the zip code it represents. Make use of the fact that the digit for a 5-character bar code segment can be computed as follows:

Let $b_i = 1$ if the ith character of the segment is a full bar, 0 otherwise. Then the digit value is $d = b_0 \times 7 + b_1 \times 4 + b_2 \times 2 + b_3$. However, if that formula yields 11, then d is zero.

For example, the value of :||:: is $0 \times 7 + 1 \times 4 + 1 \times 2 + 0 = 6$.

Print an error message if the bar code is not correct. Check for the presence of the frame bars, and make sure that there are five segments, each of which contains two full and three half bars.

★★★★★★★★★★★★★★★ ECRLOT ★★ CO57

CODE C671RTS2
JOHN DOE   CO57
1009 FRANKLIN BLVD
SUNNYVALE   CA 95014 – 5143

IlIluulIlIlIlIlIlIlllllulIlIlIlIlIluulIlIlIlIlllIlIlullIlIlIl

Figure 6 A Postal Bar Code

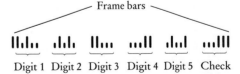

Digit 1 Digit 2 Digit 3 Digit 4 Digit 5 Check Digit

Figure 7 Encoding for Five-Digit Bar Codes

★ **P5.17** Write a program that prints instructions to get coffee, asking the user for input whenever a decision needs to be made. Decompose each task into a method, for example:

```
public static void brewCoffee()
{
```

```
System.out.println("Add water to the coffee maker.");
System.out.println("Put a filter in the coffee maker.");
grindCoffee();
System.out.println("Put the coffee in the filter.");
. . .
}
```

★★ **P5.18** Write a recursive method

```
public static String reverse(String str)
```

that computes the reverse of a string. For example, reverse("flow") should return "wolf". *Hint:* Reverse the substring starting at the second character, then add the first character at the end. For example, to reverse "flow", first reverse "low" to "wol", then add the "f" at the end.

★★ **P5.19** Write a recursive method

```
public static boolean isPalindrome(String str)
```

that returns true if str is a palindrome, that is, a word that is the same when reversed. Examples of palindrome are "deed", "rotor", or "aibohphobia". *Hint:* A word is a palindrome if the first and last letters match and the remainder is also a palindrome.

★★ **P5.20** Use recursion to implement a method boolean find(String str, String match) that tests whether match is contained in str:

```
boolean b = find("Mississippi", "sip"); // Sets b to true
```

Hint: If str starts with match, then you are done. If not, consider the string that you obtain by removing the first character.

★ **P5.21** Use recursion to determine the number of digits in a number n. *Hint:* If n is < 10, it has one digit. Otherwise, it has one more digit than n / 10.

★ **P5.22** Use recursion to compute a^n, where n is a positive integer. *Hint:* If n is 1, then $a^n = a$. If n is even, then $a^n = (a^{n/2})^2$. Otherwise, $a^n = a \times a^{n-1}$.

ANSWERS TO SELF-CHECK QUESTIONS

1. The parameter values are 3 and 2. The return value is 9.
2. The inner call to pow returns $2^2 = 4$. Therefore, the outer call returns $4^2 = 16$.
3. 3.0
4. Users of the method can treat it as a *black box*.
5. 27
6. $8 \times 8 \times 8 = 512$
7. ```
double volume = Math.pow(sideLength, 3);
return volume;
```
8. ```
public static double squareArea(double sideLength)
{
    double area = sideLength * sideLength;
    return area;
}
```
9. (2 + 3) / (3 - 2) = 5

10. When the method is called, x is set to 5, y is set to 7, and z becomes 12.0. Then z is changed to 6.0, and that value is returned and printed.

11. When the method is called, x is set to 5. Then y is set to 25, and that value is returned and printed.

12. When the method is called, n is set to 5. Then n is incremented twice, setting it to 7. That value is returned and printed.

13. It acts the same way: If sideLength is 0, it returns 0 directly instead of computing $0 \times 0 \times 0$.

14. It returns true if n is even; false if n is odd.

15. ```
public static boolean mystery(int n)
{
    return n % 2 == 0;
}
```

16. ```
boxString("Hello");
boxString("World");
```

17. The boxString method does not return a value. Therefore, you cannot use it in a call to the print method.

18. ```
public static void shout(String str)
{
    System.out.println(str ++ "!!!");
}
```

19. ```
public static void boxString(String str)
{
    int n = str.length();
    for (int i = 0; i < n + 4; i++) { System.out.print("-"); }
    System.out.println();
    System.out.println("! " + str + " !");
    for (int i = 0; i < n + 4; i++) { System.out.print("-"); }
    System.out.println()
}
```

20. ```
public static void printLine(int count)
{
    for (int i = 0; i < count; i++) { System.out.print("-"); }
    System.out.println();
}
public static void boxString(String str)
{
    int n = str.length();
    printLine(n + 2);
    System.out.println("!" + str + "!");
    printLine(n + 2);
}
```

21. Change line 28 to

    ```
    name = name + digitName(part / 100) + " hundred";
    ```

    In line 25, add the statement

    ```
    if (part >= 1000)
    {
        name = digitName(part / 1000) + "thousand ";
        part = part % 1000;
    }
    ```

    In line 18, change 1000 to 10000 in the comment.
    ```

22. In the case of "teens", we already have the last digit as part of the name.

23. Nothing is printed. One way of dealing with this case is to add the following statement before line 23.

```
if (number == 0) { return "zero"; }
```

24. Here is the approximate trace:

Note that the string starts with a blank space. Exercise P5.10 asks you to eliminate it.

25. Here is one possible solution. Break up the task **print table** into **print header** and **print body**. The **print header** task calls **print separator**, prints the header cells, and calls **print separator** again. The **print body** task repeatedly calls **print row** and then calls **print separator**.

26. Lines 14–17.

27. Lines 11–19.

28. The variables x defined in lines 5 and 15.

29. Rename the local variable x that is declared in line 15, or rename the parameter variable x that is declared in line 10.

30. The main method accesses the local variable s of the mystery method. Assuming that the main method intended to print the last value of s before the method returned, it should simply print the return value that is stored in its local variable x.

31. [][][][]
[][][]
[][]
[]

32. $4 + 3 + 2 + 1 + 0 = 10$

33. mystery(10) + 1 = mystery(5) + 2 = mystery(2) + 3 = mystery(1) + 4 = mystery(0) + 5 = 5

34. The idea is to print one [], then print n - 1 of them.

```
public static void printBoxes(int n)
{
   if (n == 0) { return; }
   System.out.print("[]");
   printBoxes(n - 1);
}
```

35. Simply add the following to the beginning of the method:

```
if (part >= 1000)
{
   return intName(part / 1000) + " thousand " + intName(part % 1000);
}
```

CHAPTER GOALS

To become familiar with using arrays and array lists to collect values

To use the enhanced for loop for traversing arrays and array lists

To learn about common algorithms for processing arrays and array lists

To learn how to use two-dimensional arrays

CHAPTER CONTENTS

In many programs, you need to collect large numbers of values. In Java, you use the array and array list constructs for this purpose. Arrays have a more concise syntax, whereas array lists can automatically grow to any desired size. In this chapter, you will learn about arrays, array lists, and common algorithms for processing them.

6.1 Arrays

We start this chapter by introducing the array data type. Arrays are the fundamental mechanism in Java for collecting multiple values. In the following sections, you will learn how to declare arrays and how to access array elements.

6.1.1 Declaring and Using Arrays

Suppose you write a program that reads a sequence of values and prints out the sequence, marking the largest value, like this:

```
32
54
67.5
29
35
80
115 <= largest value
44.5
100
65
```

You do not know which value to mark as the largest one until you have seen them all. After all, the last value might be the largest one. Therefore, the program must first store all values before it can print them.

Could you simply store each value in a separate variable? If you know that there are ten inputs, then you could store the data in ten variables data1, data2, data3, ..., data10. However, such a sequence of variables is not very practical to use. You would have to write quite a bit of code ten times, once for each of the variables. In Java, an **array** is a much better choice for storing a sequence of values of the same type.

Here we create an array that can hold ten values of type double:

```
new double[10]
```

The number of elements (here, 10) is called the *length* of the array.

The new operator constructs the array. You will want to store the array in a variable so that you can access it later.

The type of an array variable is the type of the element to be stored, followed by []. In this example, the type is double[], because the element type is double.

Here is the declaration of an array variable of type double[]:

```
double[] data;
```
1

An array collects a sequence of values of the same type.

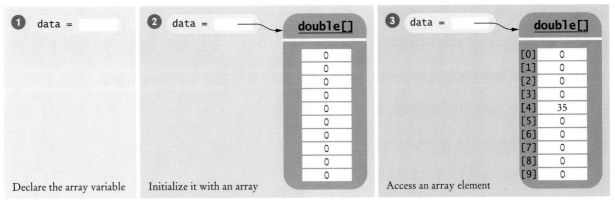

Figure 1 An Array of Size 10

When you declare an array variable, it is not yet initialized (see Figure 1). You need to initialize the variable with the array:

```
double[] data = new double[10]; ②
```

Now data is initialized with an array of 10 numbers. By default, each number in the array is 0.

When you declare an array, you can specify the initial values. For example,

```
double[] moreData = { 32, 54, 67.5, 29, 35, 80, 115, 44.5, 100, 65 };
```

When you supply initial values, you don't use the new operator. The compiler determines the length of the array by counting the initial values.

To access a value in the data array, you specify which "slot" you want to use. That is done with the [] operator:

> **Individual elements in an array data are accessed by an integer index i, using the notation data[i].**

```
data[4] = 35; ③
```

Now the number 4 slot of data is filled with 35 (see Figure 1). This "slot number" is called an *index*. Each slot in an array is called an *element*.

Because data is an array of double values, each element data[i] can be used like any variable of type double. For example, you can display the contents of the element with index 4 with the following command:

> **An array element can be used like any variable.**

```
System.out.println(data[4]);
```

Syntax 6.1 Arrays

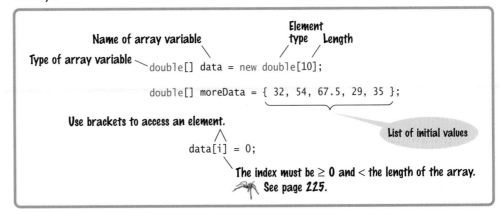

Before continuing, we must take care of an important detail of Java arrays. If you look carefully at Figure 1, you will find that the *fifth* element was filled with data when we changed data[4]. In Java, the elements of arrays are numbered *starting at 0*. That is, the legal elements for the data array are

Like a mailbox that is identified by a box number, an array element is identified by an index.

data[0], the first element

data[1], the second element

data[2], the third element

data[3], the fourth element

data[4], the fifth element

. . .

data[9], the tenth element

In other words, the declaration

```
int[] data = new int[10]
```

creates an array with ten elements whose index values range from 0 to 9.

You have to be careful about index values. Trying to access an element that does not exist in the array is a serious error. For example, if data has ten elements, you are not allowed to access data[20]. Attempting to access an element whose index is not within the valid index range is called a **bounds error**. The compiler does not catch this type of error. When a bounds error occurs at run time, it causes a run-time exception.

Here is a very common bounds error:

```
double[] data = new double[10];
data[10] = value;
```

> An array index must be at least zero and less than the size of the array.

> A bounds error, which occurs if you supply an invalid array index, can cause your program to terminate.

There is no data[10] in an array with ten elements—the legal index values range from 0 to 9.

To avoid bounds errors, you will want to know how many elements are in an array. The expression data.length yields the length of the data array. Note that there are no parentheses following length.

The following code ensures that you only access the array when the index variable i is within the legal bounds:

> Use the expression *array*.length to find the number of elements in an array.

```
if (0 <= i && i < data.length) { data[i] = value; }
```

Arrays suffer from a significant limitation: *their length is fixed*. If you start out with an array of 10 elements and later decide that you need to add additional elements, then you need to make a new array and copy all values of the existing array into the new array. We will discuss this process in detail in Section 6.3.8.

To visit all elements of an array, use a variable for the index. Suppose data has ten elements and the integer variable i takes values 0, 1, 2, and so on, up to 9. Then the expression data[i] yields each element in turn. For example, this loop displays all elements.

```
for (int i = 0; i < 10; i++)
{
   System.out.println(data[i]);
}
```

Table 1 Declaring Arrays

`int[] numbers = new int[10];`	An array of ten integers. All elements are initialized with zero.
`final int LENGTH = 10;` `int[] numbers = new int[LENGTH];`	It is a good idea to use a named constant instead of a "magic number".
`int length = in.nextInt();` `double[] data = new double[length];`	The length need not be a constant.
`int[] squares = { 0, 1, 4, 9, 16 };`	An array of five integers, with initial values.
`String[] friends = { "Emily", "Bob", "Cindy" };`	An array of three strings.
🚫 `double[] data = new int[10]`	**Error:** You cannot initialize a `double[]` variable with an array of type `int[]`.

Note that in the loop condition the index is *less than* 10 because there is no element corresponding to `data[10]`.

6.1.2 Array References

If you look closely at Figure 1, you will note that the variable data does not store any numbers. Instead, the array is stored elsewhere and the data variable holds a *reference* to the array. (The reference denotes the location of the array in memory.) When you access the values in an array, you need not be concerned about the fact that Java uses array references. This only becomes important when copying array references.

When you copy an array variable into another, both variables refer to the same array (see Figure 2).

> An array variable specifies the location of an array. Copying the reference yields a second reference to the same array.

```
int[] scores = { 10, 9, 7, 4, 5 };
int[] values = scores; // Copying array reference
```

You can modify the array through either of the variables:

```
scores[3] = 10;
System.out.println(values[3]); // Prints 10
```

Section 6.3.8 shows how you can make a copy of the *contents* of the array.

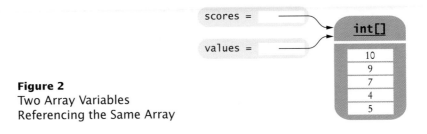

Figure 2
Two Array Variables
Referencing the Same Array

6.1.3 Partially Filled Arrays

With a partially filled array, you need to remember how many elements are filled.

An array cannot change size at run time. This is a problem when you don't know in advance how many elements you need. In that situation, you must come up with a good guess on the maximum number of elements that you need to store. For example, we may decide that we sometimes want to store more than ten values, but never more than 100:

```
final int LENGTH = 100;
double[] data = new double[LENGTH];
```

In a typical program run, only a part of the array will be occupied by actual elements. We call such an array a *partially filled array*. You must keep a *companion variable* that counts how many elements are actually used. In Figure 3 we call the companion variable currentSize.

The following loop collects data and fills up the data array.

```
int currentSize = 0;
Scanner in = new Scanner(System.in);
while (in.hasNextDouble())
{
    if (currentSize < data.length)
    {
        data[currentSize] = in.nextDouble();
        currentSize++;
    }
}
```

With a partially filled array, keep a companion variable for the current size.

At the end of this loop, currentSize contains the actual number of elements in the array. Note that you have to stop accepting inputs if the currentSize companion variable reaches the array length.

To process the gathered array elements, you again use the companion variable, not the array length. This loop prints the partially filled array:

```
for (int i = 0; i < currentSize; i++)
{
    System.out.println(data[i]);
}
```

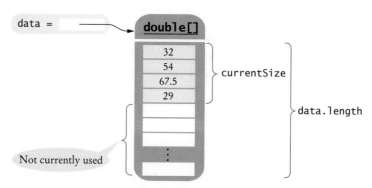

Figure 3 A Partially Filled Array

SELF CHECK

1. Declare an array of integers containing the first five prime numbers.

2. Assume the array primes has been initialized as described in Self Check 1. What does it contain after executing the following loop?

```
for (int i = 0; i < 2; i++)
{
    primes[4 - i] = primes[i];
}
```

3. Assume the array primes has been initialized as described in Self Check 1. What does it contain after executing the following loop?

```
for (int i = 0; i < 5; i++)
{
    primes[i]++;
}
```

4. Given the declaration

```
double[] data = new double[10];
```

write statements to put the value 10 into the elements of the array data with the lowest and the highest valid index.

5. Declare an array called words that can hold ten values of type String.

6. Declare an array containing two strings, "Yes", and "No".

7. Can you produce the output on page 220 without storing the input values in an array, by using an algorithm similar to the algorithm for finding the maximum in Section 4.5.4?

Practice It Now you can try these exercises at the end of the chapter: R6.1, R6.2, R6.6, P6.1.

Common Error 6.1

Bounds Errors

Perhaps the most common error in using arrays is accessing a nonexistent element.

```
double[] data = new double[10];
data[10] = 5.4;
    // Error—data has 10 elements with index values 0 to 9
```

If your program accesses an array through an out-of-bounds index, there is no compiler error message. Instead, the program will generate an exception at run time.

Common Error 6.2

Uninitialized Arrays

A common error is to allocate an array variable, but not an actual array.

```
double[] data;
data[0] = 29.95; // Error—data not initialized
```

The Java compiler will catch this error. The remedy is to initialize the variable with an array:

```
double[] data = new double[10];
```

Use Arrays for Sequences of Related Values

Arrays are intended for storing sequences of values with the same meaning. For example, an array of test scores makes perfect sense:

```
int[] scores = new int[NUMBER_OF_SCORES];
```

But an array

```
int[] personalData = new int[3];
```

that holds a person's age, bank balance, and shoe size in positions 0, 1, and 2 is bad design. It would be tedious for the programmer to remember which of these data values is stored in which array location. In this situation, it is far better to use three separate variables.

Random Fact 6.1 An Early Internet Worm

In November 1988, Robert Morris, a student at Cornell University, launched a so-called virus program that infected about 6,000 computers connected to the Internet across the United States. Tens of thousands of computer users were unable to read their e-mail or otherwise use their computers. All major universities and many high-tech companies were affected. (The Internet was much smaller then than it is now.)

The particular kind of virus used in this attack is called a worm. The virus program crawled from one computer on the Internet to the next. The worm would attempt to connect to finger, a program in the UNIX operating system for finding information on a user who has an account on a particular computer on the network. Like many programs in UNIX, finger was written in the C language. In order to store the user name, the finger program allocated an array of 512 characters, under the assumption that nobody would ever provide such a long input. Unfortunately, C does not check that an array index is less than the length of the array. If you write into an array using an index that is too large, you simply overwrite memory locations that belong to some other objects. In some versions of the finger program, the programmer had been lazy and had not checked whether the array holding the input characters was large enough to hold the input. So the worm

program purposefully filled the 512-character array with 536 bytes. The excess 24 bytes would overwrite a return address, which the attacker knew was stored just after the line buffer. When that method was finished, it didn't return to its caller but to code supplied by the worm (see the figure, A "Buffer Overrun" Attack). That code ran under the same superuser privileges as finger, allowing the worm to gain entry into the remote system. Had the programmer who wrote finger been more conscientious, this particular attack would not be possible.

In Java, as in C, all programmers must be very careful not to overrun array boundaries. However, in Java, this error causes a run-time exception, and it never corrupts memory outside the array. This is one of the safety features of Java.

One may well speculate what would possess the virus author to spend many weeks to plan the antisocial act of breaking into thousands of computers and disabling them. It appears that the break-in was fully intended by the author, but the disabling of the computers was a bug, caused by continuous reinfection. Morris was sentenced to 3 years probation, 400 hours of community service, and a $10,000 fine.

In recent years, computer attacks have intensified and the motives have become more sinister. Instead of dis-

abling computers, viruses often steal financial data or use the attacked computers for sending spam e-mail. Sadly, many of these attacks continue to be possible because of poorly written programs that are susceptible to buffer overrun errors.

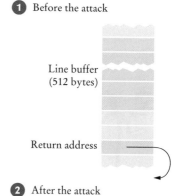

❶ Before the attack

Line buffer
(512 bytes)

Return address

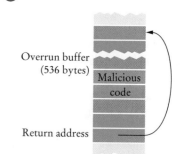

❷ After the attack

Overrun buffer
(536 bytes)

Malicious code

Return address

A "Buffer Overrun" Attack

6.2 The Enhanced for Loop

Often, you need to visit all elements of an array. The *enhanced* for *loop* makes this process particularly easy to program.

Here is how you use the enhanced for loop to total up all data values in an array data.

```
double[] data = . . .;
double sum = 0;
for (double element : data)
{
    sum = sum + element;
}
```

The loop body is executed for each element in the array data. At the beginning of each loop iteration, the next element is assigned to the variable element. Then the loop body is executed. You should read this loop as "for each element in data".

This loop is equivalent to the following for loop and an explicit index variable:

```
for (int i = 0; i < data.length; i++)
{
    double element = data[i];
    sum = sum + element;
}
```

Note an important difference between the "for each" loop and the ordinary for loop. In the "for each" loop, the *element variable* is assigned values data[0], data[1], and so on. In the ordinary for loop, the *index variable* i is assigned values 0, 1, and so on.

Keep in mind that the "for each" loop has a very specific purpose: getting the elements of a collection, from the beginning to the end. It is not suitable for all array algorithms. In particular, the "for each" loop does not allow you to modify the contents of an array. The following loop does not fill an array with zeroes:

```
for (double element : data)
{
    element = 0; // ERROR: this assignment does not modify array elements
}
```

The enhanced for loop is a convenient mechanism for traversing all elements in a collection.

Syntax 6.2 The "for each" Loop

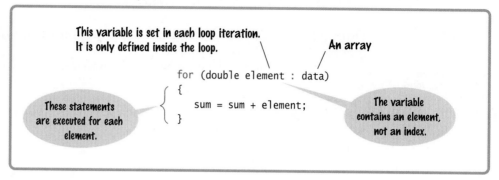

When the loop is executed, the variable `element` is set to `data[0]`. Then `element` is set to 0, then to `data[1]`, then to 0, and so on. The `data` array is not modified. The remedy is simple: Use an ordinary for loop:

```
for (int i = 0; i < data.length; i++)
{
    data[i] = 0; // OK
}
```

8. What does this "for each" loop do?

```
int counter = 0;
for (double value : data)
{
    if (value == 0) { counter++; }
}
```

9. Write a "for each" loop that prints all elements in the array `data`.

10. Write a "for each" loop that multiplies all elements in a `double[]` array named `factors`, accumulating the result in a variable named `product`.

11. Why is the "for each" loop not an appropriate shortcut for the following ordinary for loop?

```
for (int i = 0; i < data.length; i++) { data[i] = i * i; }
```

Practice It Now you can try these exercises at the end of the chapter: R6.7, R6.8, R6.9.

6.3 Common Array Algorithms

In the following sections, we discuss some of the most common algorithms for working with arrays. If you use a partially filled array, remember to replace `data.length` with the companion variable that represents the current size of the array.

6.3.1 Filling

This loop fills an array with squares (0, 1, 4, 9, 16, ...). Note that the element with index 0 contains 0^2, the element with index 1 contains 1^2, and so on.

```
for (int i = 0; i < data.length; i++)
{
   data[i] = i * i;
}
```

6.3.2 Sum and Average Value

You have already encountered this algorithm in Section 4.5.1. When the values are located in an array, the code looks much simpler:

```
double total = 0;
for (double element : data)
{
   total = total + element;
}
double average = 0;
if (data.length > 0) { average = total / data.length; }
```

6.3.3 Maximum and Minimum

Use the algorithm from Section 4.5.4 that keeps a variable for the largest element already encountered. Here is the implementation of that algorithm for an array:

```
double largest = data[0];
for (int i = 1; i < data.length; i++)
{
   if (data[i] > largest)
   {
      largest = data[i];
   }
}
```

Note that the loop starts at 1 because we initialize largest with data[0].

To compute the smallest value, reverse the comparison.

These algorithms require that the array contain at least one element.

6.3.4 Element Separators

To print five elements, you need four separators.

When you display the elements of an array, you usually want to separate them, often with commas or vertical lines, like this:

32 | 54 | 67.5 | 29 | 35

Note that there is one fewer separator than there are numbers. Print the separator before each element in the sequence *except the initial one* (with index 0) like this:

```
for (int i = 0; i < data.length; i++)
{
   if (i > 0)
   {
      System.out.print(" | ");
   }
   System.out.print(data[i]);
}
```

If you want comma separators, you can use the `Arrays.toString` method. The expression

```
Arrays.toString(data)
```

returns a string describing the contents of the array data in the form

```
[32, 54, 67.5, 29, 35]
```

The elements are surrounded by a pair of brackets and separated by commas. This can be convenient for debugging:

```
System.out.println("data=" + Arrays.toString(data));
```

6.3.5 Linear Search

To search for a specific element, visit the elements and stop when you encounter the match.

A linear search inspects elements in sequence until a match is found.

You often need to search for the position of a specific element in an array so that you can replace or remove it. Visit all elements until you have found a match or you have come to the end of the array. Here we search for the position of the first element in an array that is equal to 100.

```
int searchedValue = 100;
int pos = 0;
boolean found = false;
while (pos < data.length && !found)
{
    if (data[pos] == searchedValue)
    {
        found = true;
    }
    else
    {
        pos++;
    }
}
if (found) { System.out.println("Found at position: " + pos); }
else { System.out.println("Not found"); }
```

This algorithm is called **linear search** or *sequential search* because you inspect the elements in sequence. If the array is sorted, you can use the more efficient **binary search** algorithm—see Special Topic 6.3 on page 238.

6.3.6 Removing an Element

ANIMATION
Removing from an Array

Suppose you want to remove the element with index pos from the array data. First off, you need to keep a companion variable for tracking the number of valid values in the array, as explained in Section 6.1.3.

If the elements in the array are not in any particular order, simply overwrite the element to be removed with the *last* element of the array, then decrement the variable tracking the size of the array. (See Figure 4.)

```
data[pos] = data[currentSize - 1];
currentSize--;
```

The situation is more complex if the order of the elements matters. Then you must move all elements following the element to be removed to a lower index, and then decrement the variable holding the size of the array. (See Figure 5.)

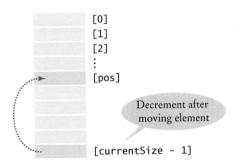

Figure 4
Removing an Element in an Unordered Array

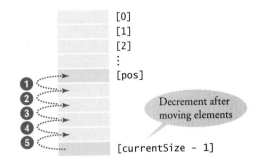

Figure 5
Removing an Element in an Ordered Array

```
for (int i = pos; i < currentSize - 1; i++)
{
    data[i] = data[i + 1];
}
currentSize--;
```

6.3.7 Inserting an Element

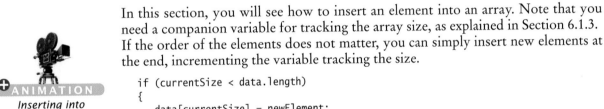

*Inserting into
an Array*

In this section, you will see how to insert an element into an array. Note that you need a companion variable for tracking the array size, as explained in Section 6.1.3. If the order of the elements does not matter, you can simply insert new elements at the end, incrementing the variable tracking the size.

```
if (currentSize < data.length)
{
    data[currentSize] = newElement;
    currentSize++;
}
```

It is more work to insert an element at a particular position in the middle of an array. First, move all elements after the insertion location to a higher index. Then insert the new element (see Figure 7).

Note the order of the movement: When you remove an element, you first move the next element to a lower index, then the one after that, until you finally get to the

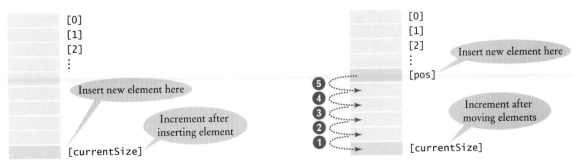

Figure 6
Inserting an Element in an Unordered Array

Figure 7
Inserting an Element in an Ordered Array

end of the array. When you insert an element, you start at the end of the array, move that element to a higher index, then move the one before that, and so on until you finally get to the insertion location.

```
if (currentSize < data.length)
{
    for (int i = currentSize; i > pos; i--)
    {
        data[i] = data[i - 1];
    }
    data[pos] = newElement;
    currentSize++;
}
```

6.3.8 Copying Arrays

Array variables do not themselves hold array elements. They hold a reference to the actual array. If you copy the reference, you get another reference to the same array (see Figure 8):

```
double[] data = new double[6];
. . .  // Fill array
double[] prices = data;  ❶
```

Use the Arrays.copyOf method to copy the elements of an array into a new array.

If you want to make a true copy of an array, as shown in Figure 8, call the Arrays.copyOf method.

```
double[] prices = Arrays.copyOf(data, data.length);  ❷
```

The call Arrays.copyOf(data, n) allocates an array of length n, copies the first n elements of data (or the entire data array if n > data.length) into that array, and returns it.

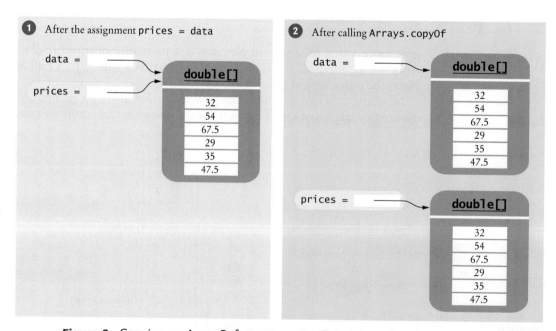

Figure 8 Copying an Array Reference versus Copying an Array

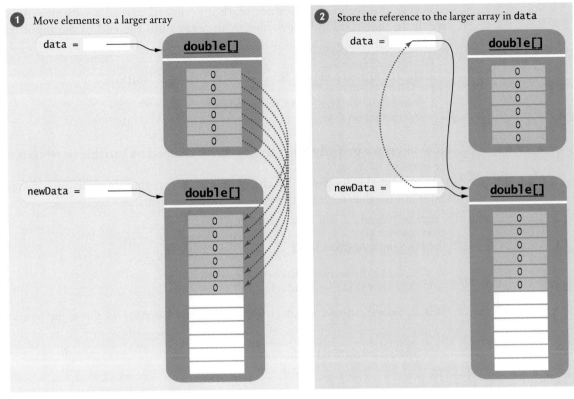

Figure 9 Growing an Array

Another use for Arrays.copyOf is to grow an array that has run out of space. The following statements have the effect of doubling the length of an array (see Figure 9):

```java
double[] newData = Arrays.copyOf(data, 2 * data.length); ➊
data = newData; ➋
```

The copyOf method was added in Java 6. If you use Java 5, replace

```java
double[] newData = Arrays.copyOf(data, n)
```

with

```java
double[] newData = new double[n];
for (int i = 0; i < n && i < data.length; i++) { newData[i] = data[i]; }
```

6.3.9 Reading Input

If you know how many input values the user will supply, it is simple to place them into an array:

```java
double[] inputs = new double[NUMBER_OF_INPUTS];
for (i = 0; i < inputs.length; i++)
{
   inputs[i] = in.nextDouble();
}
```

However, this technique does not work if you need to read a sequence of arbitrary length. In that case, add the values to an array until the end of the input has been reached.

```java
int currentSize = 0;
while (in.hasNextDouble() && currentSize < inputs.length)
{
    inputs[currentSize] = in.nextDouble();
    currentSize++;
}
```

Now `inputs` is a partially filled array, and the companion variable `currentSize` is set to the number of input values.

However, this loop silently throws away inputs that don't fit into the array. A better approach is to grow the array to hold all inputs.

```java
double[] inputs = new double[INITIAL_SIZE];
int currentSize = 0;
while (in.hasNextDouble())
{
    // Grow the array if it has been completely filled
    if (currentSize >= inputs.length)
    {
        inputs = Arrays.copyOf(inputs, 2 * inputs.length); // Grow the inputs array
    }

    inputs[currentSize] = in.nextDouble();
    currentSize++;
}
```

When you are done, you can discard any excess (unfilled) elements:

```java
inputs = Arrays.copyOf(inputs, currentSize);
```

The following program puts these algorithms to work, solving the task that we set ourselves at the beginning of this chapter: to mark the largest value in an input sequence.

ch06/largest/LargestInArray.java

```java
1   import java.util.Scanner;
2
3   /**
4       This program reads a sequence of values and prints them, marking the largest value.
5   */
6   public class LargestInArray
7   {
8       public static void main(String[] args)
9       {
10          final int LENGTH = 100;
11          double[] data = new double[LENGTH];
12          int currentSize = 0;
13
14          // Read inputs
15
16          System.out.println("Please enter values, Q to quit:");
17          Scanner in = new Scanner(System.in);
18          while (in.hasNextDouble() && currentSize < data.length)
19          {
20              data[currentSize] = in.nextDouble();
21              currentSize++;
```

```
22        }
23
24        // Find the largest value
25
26        double largest = data[0];
27        for (int i = 1; i < currentSize; i++)
28        {
29           if (data[i] > largest)
30           {
31              largest = data[i];
32           }
33        }
34
35        // Print all values, marking the largest
36
37        for (int i = 0; i < currentSize; i++)
38        {
39           System.out.print(data[i]);
40           if (data[i] == largest)
41           {
42              System.out.print(" <== largest value");
43           }
44           System.out.println();
45        }
46     }
47  }
```

Program Run

```
Please enter values, Q to quit:
35 80 115 44.5 Q
35
80
115 <== largest value
44.5
```

SELF CHECK

12. Given these inputs, what is the output of the LargestInArray program?

20 10 20 Q

13. Write a loop that counts how many elements in an array are equal to zero.

14. Consider the algorithm to find the largest element in an array. Why don't we initialize largest and i with zero, like this?

```
double largest = 0;
for (int i = 0; i < data.length; i++)
{
   if (data[i] > largest)
   {
      largest = data[i];
   }
}
```

15. When printing separators, we skipped the separator before the initial element. Rewrite the loop so that the separator is printed *after* each element, except for the last element.

16. What is wrong with these statements for printing an array with separators?

```
System.out.print(data[0]);
for (int i = 1; i < data.length; i++)
{
    System.out.print(", " + data[i]);
}
```

17. When finding the position of a match, we used a `while` loop, not a `for` loop. What is wrong with using this loop instead?

```
for (pos = 0; pos < data.length && !found; pos++)
{
    if (data[pos] > 100)
    {
        found = true;
    }
}
```

18. When inserting an element into an array, we moved the elements with larger index values, starting at the end of the array. Why is it wrong to start at the insertion location, like this?

```
for (int i = pos; i < currentSize - 1; i++)
{
    data[i + 1] = data[i];
}
```

Practice It Now you can try these exercises at the end of the chapter: R6.13, R6.16, P6.4, P6.10.

Underestimating the Size of a Data Set

Programmers commonly underestimate the amount of input data that a user will pour into an unsuspecting program. Suppose you write a program to search for text in a file. You store each line in a string, and keep an array of strings. How big do you make the array? Surely nobody is going to challenge your program with an input that is more than 100 lines. Really? It is very easy to feed in the entire text of *Alice in Wonderland* or *War and Peace* (which are available on the Internet). All of a sudden, your program has to deal with tens or hundreds of thousands of lines. You either need to allow for large inputs or politely reject the excess input.

Special Topic 6.1

Sorting with the Java Library

You often want to sort the elements of an array. Special Topic 6.2 shows you a sorting algorithm that is relatively simple but not very efficient. Efficient sorting algorithms are significantly more complex. Fortunately, the Java library provides an efficient sort method.

To sort an array data, call

```
Arrays.sort(data);
```

If the array is partially filled, call

```
Arrays.sort(data, 0, currentSize);
```

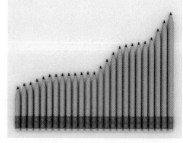

A Sorting Algorithm

A *sorting algorithm* rearranges the elements of a sequence so that they are stored in sorted order. Here is a simple sorting algorithm, called **selection sort**. Consider sorting the following array data:

```
[0][1][2][3][4]
11  9 17  5 12
```

An obvious first step is to find the smallest element. In this case the smallest element is 5, stored in data[3]. You should move the 5 to the beginning of the array. Of course, there is already an element stored in data[0], namely 11. Therefore you cannot simply move data[3] into data[0] without moving the 11 somewhere else. You don't yet know where the 11 should end up, but you know for certain that it should not be in data[0]. Simply get it out of the way by *swapping it* with data[3].

```
[0][1][2][3][4]
 5  9 17 11 12
```

Now the first element is in the correct place. In the foregoing figure, the darker color indicates the portion of the array that is already sorted.

Next take the minimum of the remaining entries data[1]...data[4]. That minimum value, 9, is already in the correct place. You don't need to do anything in this case, simply extend the sorted area by one to the right:

```
[0][1][2][3][4]
 5  9 17 11 12
```

Repeat the process. The minimum value of the unsorted region is 11, which needs to be swapped with the first value of the unsorted region, 17.

```
[0][1][2][3][4]
 5  9 11 17 12
```

Now the unsorted region is only two elements long; keep to the same successful strategy. The minimum element is 12. Swap it with the first value, 17.

```
[0][1][2][3][4]
 5  9 11 12 17
```

That leaves you with an unprocessed region of length 1, but of course a region of length 1 is always sorted. You are done.

Here is the Java code:

```java
for (int unsorted = 0; unsorted < data.length - 1; unsorted++)
{
    // Find the position of the minimum
    int minPos = unsorted;
    for (int i = unsorted + 1; i < data.length; i++)
    {
        if (data[i] < data[minPos]) { minPos = i; }
    }
    // Swap the minimum into the sorted area
    if (minPos != unsorted)
    {
```

```
            double temp = data[minPos];
            data[minPos] = data[unsorted];
            data[unsorted] = temp;
         }
      }
```

This algorithm is simple to understand, but unfortunately it is not very efficient. Computer scientists have studied sorting algorithms extensively and discovered significantly better algorithms. The sort methods of the Java library implement efficient algorithms—see Special Topic 6.1 on page 236.

Special Topic 6.3

Binary Search

When an array is sorted, there is a much faster search algorithm than the linear search of Section 6.3.5.

Consider the following sorted array data.

```
[0][1][2][3][4][5][6][7]
 1  5  8  9 12 17 20 32
```

We would like to see whether the value 15 is in the array. Let's narrow our search by finding whether the value is in the first or second half of the array. The last point in the first half of the data set, data[3], is 9, which is smaller than the value we are looking for. Hence, we should look in the second half of the array for a match, that is, in the sequence:

```
[0][1][2][3][4][5][6][7]
 1  5  8  9 12 17 20 32
```

Now the last value of the first half of this sequence is 17; hence, the value must be located in the sequence:

```
[0][1][2][3][4][5][6][7]
 1  5  8  9 12 17 20 32
```

The last value of the first half of this very short sequence is 12, which is smaller than the value that we are searching, so we must look in the second half:

```
[0][1][2][3][4][5][6][7]
 1  5  8  9 12 17 20 32
```

We still don't have a match because $15 \neq 17$, and we cannot divide the subsequence further. If we wanted to insert 15 into the sequence, we would need to insert it just before data[5].

This search process is called a **binary search**, because we cut the size of the search in half in each step. That cutting in half works only because we know that the sequence of values is sorted. Here is an implementation in Java.

```java
boolean found = false;
int low = 0;
int high = data.length - 1;
int pos = 0;
while (low <= high && !found)
{
   pos = (low + high) / 2; // Midpoint of the subsequence
   if (data[pos] == searchedValue) { found = true; }
   else if (data[pos] < searchedValue) { low = pos + 1; } // Look in second half
   else { high = pos - 1; } // Look in first half
```

```
    }
    if (found) { System.out.println("Found at position " + pos); }
    else { System.out.println("Not found. Insert before position " + pos); }
```

6.4 Using Arrays with Methods

In this section, we will explore how to write methods that process arrays.

Arrays can occur as method parameters and return values.

You can use arrays as method parameters in exactly the same way as any other values. For example, the following method computes the sum of an array of floating-point numbers:

```java
public static double sum(double[] data)
{
    double total = 0;
    for (double element : data)
    {
        total = total + element;
    }
    return total;
}
```

This method visits the array elements, but it does not modify them. It is also possible to modify the elements of an array. The following method multiplies all values of an array by a given factor.

```java
public static void multiply(double[] data, double factor)
{
    for (int i = 0; i < data.length; i++)
    {
        data[i] = data[i] * factor;
    }
}
```

Figure 10 traces the method call

```java
multiply(values, 10);
```

Note these steps:

- The parameter variables data and factor are created. **❶**
- The parameter variables are initialized with the values that are passed in the call. In our case, data is set to values and factor is set to 10. Note that values and data are references to the *same* array. **❷**

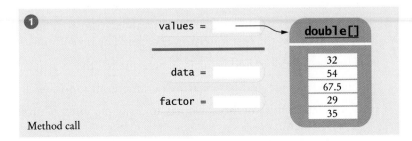

Figure 10
Trace of Call to
multiply Method

Figure 10
Trace of Call to
multiply Method
(continued)

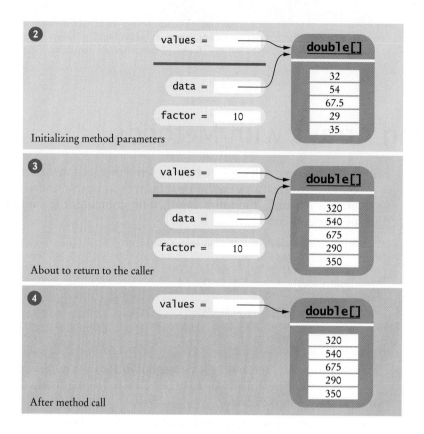

- The method multiplies all array elements by 10. ❸
- The method returns. Its parameter variables are removed. However, values still refers to the array with the modified values. ❹

A method can return an array. Simply build up the result in the method and return it. In this example, the squares method returns an array of squares from 0^2 up to $(n-1)^2$:

```java
public static int[] squares(int n)
{
   int[] result = new int[n];
   for (int i = 0; i < n; i++)
   {
      result[i] = i * i;
   }
   return result;
}
```

The following example program reads values from standard input, multiplies them by 10, and prints the result in reverse order. The program uses three methods:

- The readInputs method returns an array, using the algorithm of Section 6.3.9.
- The multiply method has an array parameter. It modifies the array elements.
- The printReversed method also has an array parameter, but it does not modify the array elements.

ch06/reverse/Reverse.java

```java
1  import java.util.Scanner;
2
3  /**
4     This program reads, scales and reverses a sequence of numbers.
5  */
6  public class Reverse
7  {
8     public static void main(String[] args)
9     {
10       double[] values = readInputs(5);
11       multiply(values, 10);
12       printReversed(values);
13    }
14
15    /**
16       Reads a sequence of floating-point numbers.
17       @param numberOfInputs the number of inputs to read
18       @return an array containing the input values
19    */
20    public static double[] readInputs(int numberOfInputs)
21    {
22       System.out.println("Enter " + numberOfInputs + " numbers: ");
23       Scanner in = new Scanner(System.in);
24       double[] inputs = new double[numberOfInputs];
25       for (int i = 0; i < inputs.length; i++)
26       {
27          inputs[i] = in.nextDouble();
28       }
29       return inputs;
30    }
31
32    /**
33       Multiplies all elements of an array by a factor.
34       @param data an array
35       @param factor the value with which element is multiplied
36    */
37    public static void multiply(double[] data, double factor)
38    {
39       for (int i = 0; i < data.length; i++)
40       {
41          data[i] = data[i] * factor;
42       }
43    }
44
45    /**
46       Prints an array in reverse order.
47       @param data an array of numbers
48       @return an array that contains the elements of data in reverse order
49    */
50    public static void printReversed(double[] data)
51    {
52       // Traverse the array in reverse order, starting with the last element
53       for (int i = data.length - 1; i >= 0; i--)
54       {
55          System.out.print(data[i] + " ");
56       }
57       System.out.println();
58    }
```

```
59  }
```

Program Run

```
Enter 5 numbers:
12 25 20 0 10
100.0 0.0 200.0 250.0 120.0
```

SELF CHECK

19. How do you call the squares method to compute the first five squares and store the result in an array numbers?

20. Write a method fill that fills all elements of an array of integers with a given value. For example, the call fill(scores, 10) should fill all elements of the array scores with the value 10.

21. Describe the purpose of the following method:

```java
public static int[] mystery(int length, int n)
{
   int[] result = new int[length];
   for (int i = 0; i < result.length; i++)
   {
      result[i] = (int) (n * Math.random());
   }
   return result;
}
```

22. Consider the following method that reverses an array:

```java
public static int[] reverse(int[] values)
{
   int[] result = new int[values.length];
   for (int i = 0; i < values.length; i++)
   {
      result[i] = values[values.length - 1 - i];
   }
   return result;
}
```

Suppose the reverse method is called with an array values that contains the numbers 1, 4, and 9. What is the contents of values after the method call?

23. Provide a trace diagram of the reverse method when called with an array that contains the values 1, 4, and 9.

Practice It   Now you can try these exercises at the end of the chapter: R6.21, P6.5, P6.6.

HOW TO 6.1   Working with Arrays

In many data processing situations, you need to process a sequence of values. This How To walks you through the steps for storing input values in an array and carrying out computations with the array values.

Consider this example problem: You are given the quiz scores of a student. You are to compute the final quiz score, which is the sum of all scores after dropping the lowest one. For example, if the scores are

    8   7   8.5   9.5   7   5   10

then the final score is 50.

Step 1 Decompose your task into steps.

You will usually want to break down your task into multiple steps, such as

- Reading the data into an array.
- Processing the data in one or more steps.
- Displaying the results.

When deciding how to process the data, you should be familiar with the array algorithms in Section 6.3. Most processing tasks can be solved by using one or more of these algorithms.

In our sample problem, we will want to read the data. Then we will remove the minimum and compute the total. For example, if the input is 8 7 8.5 9.5 7 5 10, we will remove the minimum of 5, yielding 8 7 8.5 9.5 7 10. The sum of those values is the final score of 50.

Thus, we have identified three steps:

> Read inputs.
> Remove the minimum.
> Calculate the sum.

(It is possible to solve this problem using a different sequence of steps—see Exercise P6.3).

Step 2 Determine which algorithm(s) you need.

Sometimes, a step corresponds to exactly one of the basic array algorithms in Section 6.4. That is the case with calculating the sum (Section 6.3.2) and reading the inputs (Section 6.3.9). At other times, you need to combine several algorithms. To remove the minimum value, you can find the minimum value (Section 6.3.3), find its position (Section 6.3.5), and remove the element at that position (Section 6.3.6).

We have now refined our plan as follows:

> Read inputs.
> Find the minimum.
> Find its position.
> Remove the minimum.
> Calculate the sum.

This plan will work, but it is possible to do a bit better. It is easier to compute the sum and subtract the minimum. Then we don't have to find its position. The revised plan is

> Read inputs.
> Find the minimum.
> Calculate the sum.
> Subtract the minimum.

Step 3 Use methods to structure the program.

Even though it may be possible to put all steps into the main method, this is rarely a good idea. It is better to make each processing step into a separate method. In our example, we will implement three methods:

- readInputs
- sum
- minimum

The main method simply calls these methods:

```
double[] scores = readInputs();
double total = sum(scores) - minimum(scores);
System.out.println("Final score: " + total);
```

Step 4 Assemble and test the program.

Place your methods into a class. Review your code and check that you handle both normal and exceptional situations. What happens with an empty array? One that contains a single element? When no match is found? When there are multiple matches? Consider these boundary conditions and make sure that your program works correctly.

In our example, it is impossible to compute the minimum if the array is empty. In that case, we should terminate the program with an error message *before* attempting to call the `minimum` method.

What if the minimum value occurs more than once? That means that a student had more than one test with the same low score. We subtract only one of the occurrences of that low score, and that is the desired behavior.

The following table shows test cases and their expected output:

Test Case	Expected Output	Comment
8 7 8.5 9.5 7 5 10	50	See Step 1.
8 7 7 9	24	Only one instance of the low score should be removed.
8	0	After removing the low score, no score remains.
(no inputs)	**Error**	That is not a legal input.

Here's the complete program (ch06/scores/Scores.java).

```java
import java.util.Arrays;
import java.util.Scanner;

/**
    This program computes a final score for a series of quiz scores: the sum after dropping
    the lowest score. The program uses arrays.
*/
public class Scores
{
    public static void main(String[] args)
    {
        double[] scores = readInputs();
        if (scores.length == 0)
        {
            System.out.println("At least one score is required.");
        }
        else
        {
            double total = sum(scores) - minimum(scores);
            System.out.println("Final score: " + total);
        }
    }

    /**
        Reads a sequence of floating-point numbers.
        @return an array containing the numbers
    */
    public static double[] readInputs()
    {
        // Read the input values into an array

        final int INITIAL_SIZE = 10;
        double[] inputs = new double[INITIAL_SIZE];
        System.out.println("Please enter values, Q to quit:");
        Scanner in = new Scanner(System.in);
```

```java
      int currentSize = 0;
      while (in.hasNextDouble())
      {
         // Grow the array if it has been completely filled

         if (currentSize >= inputs.length)
         {
            inputs = Arrays.copyOf(inputs, 2 * inputs.length);
         }
         inputs[currentSize] = in.nextDouble();
         currentSize++;
      }

      return Arrays.copyOf(inputs, currentSize);
   }

   /**
      Computes the sum of the values in an array.
      @param data an array
      @return the sum of the values in data
   */
   public static double sum(double[] data)
   {
      double total = 0;
      for (double element : data)
      {
         total = total + element;
      }
      return total;
   }

   /**
      Gets the minimum value from an array.
      @param data an array of size >= 1
      @return the smallest element of data
   */
   public static double minimum(double[] data)
   {
      double smallest = data[0];
      for (int i = 1; i < data.length; i++)
      {
         if (data[i] < smallest)
         {
            smallest = data[i];
         }
      }
      return smallest;
   }
}
```

| WORKED EXAMPLE 6.1 | **Rolling the Dice** |

This Worked Example shows how to analyze a set of die tosses to see whether the die is "fair".

⊕ Available online in WileyPLUS and at www.wiley.com/college/horstmann.

6.5 Two-Dimensional Arrays

It often happens that you want to store collections of values that have a two-dimensional layout. Such data sets commonly occur in financial and scientific applications. An arrangement consisting of rows and columns of values is called a *two-dimensional array*, or a *matrix*.

Let's explore how to store the example data shown in Figure 11: the medal counts of the figure skating competitions at the 2006 Winter Olympics.

	Gold	Silver	Bronze
Canada	0	0	1
China	0	1	1
Japan	1	0	0
Russia	3	0	1
Switzerland	0	1	0
Ukraine	0	0	1
United States	0	2	0

Figure 11 Figure Skating Medal Counts

6.5.1 Declaring Two-Dimensional Arrays

Use a two-dimensional array to store tabular data.

In Java, you obtain a two-dimensional array by supplying the number of rows and columns. For example, new int[7][3] is an array with seven rows and three columns. You store a reference to such an array in a variable of type int[][]. Here is a complete declaration of a two-dimensional array, suitable for holding our medal count data:

```
final int COUNTRIES = 7;
final int MEDALS = 3;
int[][] counts = new int[COUNTRIES][MEDALS];
```

Alternatively, you can declare and initialize the array by grouping each row:

```
int[][] counts =
   {
      { 0, 0, 1 },
      { 0, 1, 1 },
      { 1, 0, 0 },
      { 3, 0, 1 },
      { 0, 1, 0 },
      { 0, 0, 1 },
      { 0, 2, 0 }
   };
```

As with one-dimensional arrays, you cannot change the size of a two-dimensional array once it has been declared.

Syntax 6.3 Two-Dimensional Array Declaration

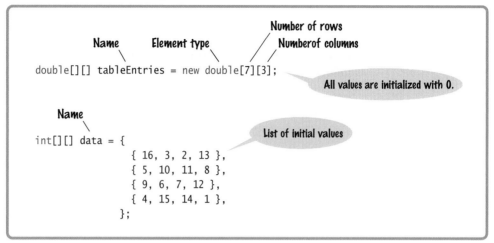

6.5.2 Accessing Elements

Individual elements in a two-dimensional array are accessed by using two index values, *array*[i][j].

To access a particular element in the two-dimensional array, you need to specify two index values in separate brackets to select the row and column, respectively (see Figure 12):

```
int value = counts[3][1];
```

To access all values in a two-dimensional array, you use two nested loops. For example, the following loop prints all elements of counts.

```
for (int i = 0; i < COUNTRIES; i++)
{
   // Process the ith row
   for (int j = 0; j < MEDALS; j++)
   {
      // Process the jth column in the ith row
      System.out.printf("%8d", counts[i][j]);
   }
   System.out.println(); // Start a new line at the end of the row
}
```

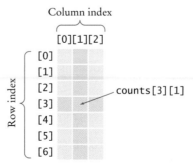

Figure 12 Accessing an Element in a Two-Dimensional Array

6.5.3 Computing Row and Column Totals

A common task is to compute row or column totals. In our example, the row totals give us the total number of medals won by a particular country.

Finding the right index values is a bit tricky, and it is a good idea to make a quick sketch. To compute the total of row i, we need to visit the following elements:

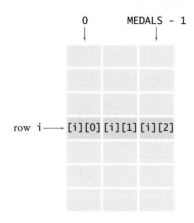

As you can see, we need to compute the sum of counts[i][j], where j ranges from 0 to MEDALS - 1. The following loop computes the total:

```
int total = 0;
for (int j = 0; j < MEDALS; j++)
{
    total = total + counts[i][j];
}
```

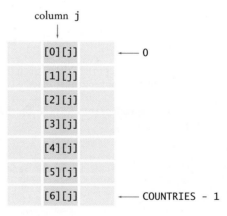

ANIMATION
Tracing a Nested Loop in a 2D Array

Computing column totals is similar. Form the sum of counts[i][j], where i ranges from 0 to COUNTRIES - 1.

```
int total = 0;
for (int i = 0; i < COUNTRIES; i++)
{
    total = total + counts[i][j];
}
```

Working with two-dimensional arrays is illustrated in the following program. The program prints out the medal counts and the row totals.

ch06/medal/Medals.java

```java
1   /**
2        This program prints a table of medal winner counts with row totals.
3   */
4   public class Medals
5   {
6      public static void main(String[] args)
7      {
8         final int COUNTRIES = 7;
9         final int MEDALS = 3;
10
11        String[] countries =
12           {
13              "Canada",
14              "China",
15              "Japan",
16              "Russia",
17              "Switzerland",
18              "Ukraine",
19              "United States"
20           };
21
22        int[][] counts =
23           {
24              { 0, 0, 1 },
25              { 0, 1, 1 },
26              { 1, 0, 0 },
27              { 3, 0, 1 },
28              { 0, 1, 0 },
29              { 0, 0, 1 },
30              { 0, 2, 0 }
31           };
32
33        System.out.println("        Country    Gold  Silver  Bronze    Total");
34
35        // Print countries, counts, and row totals
36
37        for (int i = 0; i < COUNTRIES; i++)
38        {
39           // Process the ith row
40
41           System.out.printf("%15s", countries[i]);
42
43           int total = 0;
44
45           // Print each row element and update the row total
46
47           for (int j = 0; j < MEDALS; j++)
48           {
49              System.out.printf("%8d", counts[i][j]);
50              total = total + counts[i][j];
51           }
52
53           // Display the row total and print a new line
54
55           System.out.printf("%8d\n", total);
56        }
57     }
58  }
```

Program Run

Country	Gold	Silver	Bronze	Total
Canada	0	0	1	1
China	0	1	1	2
Japan	1	0	0	1
Russia	3	0	1	4
Switzerland	0	1	0	1
Ukraine	0	0	1	1
United States	0	2	0	2

SELF CHECK

24. What results do you get if you total the columns in our sample data?

25. Consider an 8×8 array for a board game:

```
int[][] board = new int[8][8];
```

Using two nested loops, initialize the board so that zeroes and ones alternate, as on a checkerboard:

```
0 1 0 1 0 1 0 1
1 0 1 0 1 0 1 0
0 1 0 1 0 1 0 1
. . .
1 0 1 0 1 0 1 0
```

Hint: Check whether i + j is even.

26. Declare a two-dimensional array for representing a tic-tac-toe board. The board has three rows and columns and contains strings "x", "o", and " ".

27. Write an assignment statement to place an "x" in the upper-right corner of the tic-tac-toe board in Self Check 26.

28. Which elements are on the diagonal joining the upper-left and the lower-right corners of the tic-tac-toe board in Self Check 26?

Practice It Now you can try these exercises at the end of the chapter: R6.22, P6.12, P6.13.

WORKED EXAMPLE 6.2   **A World Population Table**

This Worked Example shows how to print world population data in a table with row and column headers, and with totals for each of the data columns.

6.6 Array Lists

An array list stores a sequence of values whose size can change.

When you write a program that collects values, you don't always know how many values you will have. In such a situation, an **array list** offers two significant advantages:

- Array lists can grow and shrink as needed.
- The ArrayList class supplies methods for common tasks, such as inserting and removing elements.

   Available online in WileyPLUS and at www.wiley.com/college/horstmann.

An array list expands to hold as many elements as needed.

In the following sections, you will learn how to work with array lists.

6.6.1 Declaring and Using Array Lists

Let us declare an array list of strings:

```
ArrayList<String> names = new ArrayList<String>();
```

The ArrayList class is contained in the java.util package. In order to use array lists in your program, you need to use the statement import java.util.ArrayList.

The ArrayList class is a generic class: ArrayList<*Type*> collects elements of the specified type.

The type ArrayList<String> denotes an array list of String values. The angle brackets around the String type tell you that String is a **type parameter**. You can replace String with any other class and get a different array list type. For that reason, ArrayList is called a **generic class**. However, you cannot use primitive types as type parameters—there is no ArrayList<int> or ArrayList<double>. Section 6.6.5 shows how you can collect numbers in an array list.

Syntax 6.4   Array Lists

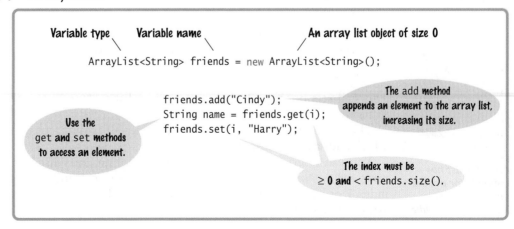

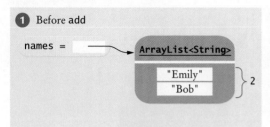

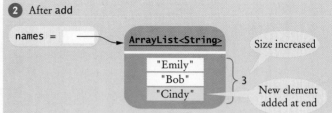

Figure 13 Adding an Element with add

It is a common error to forget the initialization:

```
ArrayList<String> names;
names.add("Harry"); // Error—names not initialized
```

Again, here is the proper initialization:

```
ArrayList<String> names = new ArrayList<String>();
```

Note the () after new ArrayList<String> on the right-hand side of the initialization. It indicates that the **constructor** of the ArrayList<String> class is being called. We will discuss constructors in Chapter 7.

> Use the size method to obtain the current size of an array list.

When the ArrayList<String> is first constructed, it has size 0. You use the add method to add an element to the end of the array list.

```
names.add("Emily"); // Now names has size 1 and element "Emily"
names.add("Bob"); // Now names has size 2 and elements "Emily", "Bob"
names.add("Cindy"); // names has size 3 and elements "Emily", "Bob", and "Cindy"
```

The size increases after each call to add (see Figure 13). The size method yields the current size of the array list.

> Use the get and set methods to access an array list element at a given index.

To obtain the value of an array list element, use the get method, not the [] operator. As with arrays, index values start at 0. For example, names.get(2) retrieves the name with index 2, the third element in the array list:

```
String name = names.get(2);
```

As with arrays, it is an error to access a nonexistent element. A very common bounds error is to use the following:

```
int i = names.size();
name = names.get(i);  // Error
```

The last valid index is names.size() - 1.

To set an array list element to a new value, use the set method.

```
names.set(2, "Carolyn");
```

This call sets position 2 of the names array list to "Carolyn", overwriting whatever value was there before.

The set method overwrites existing values. It is different from the add method, which adds a new element to the array list.

An array list has methods for adding and removing elements in the middle.

You can insert an element in the middle of an array list. For example, the call names.add(1, "Ann") adds a new element at position 1 and moves all elements with index 1 or larger by one position. After each call to the add method, the size of the array list increases by 1 (see Figure 14).

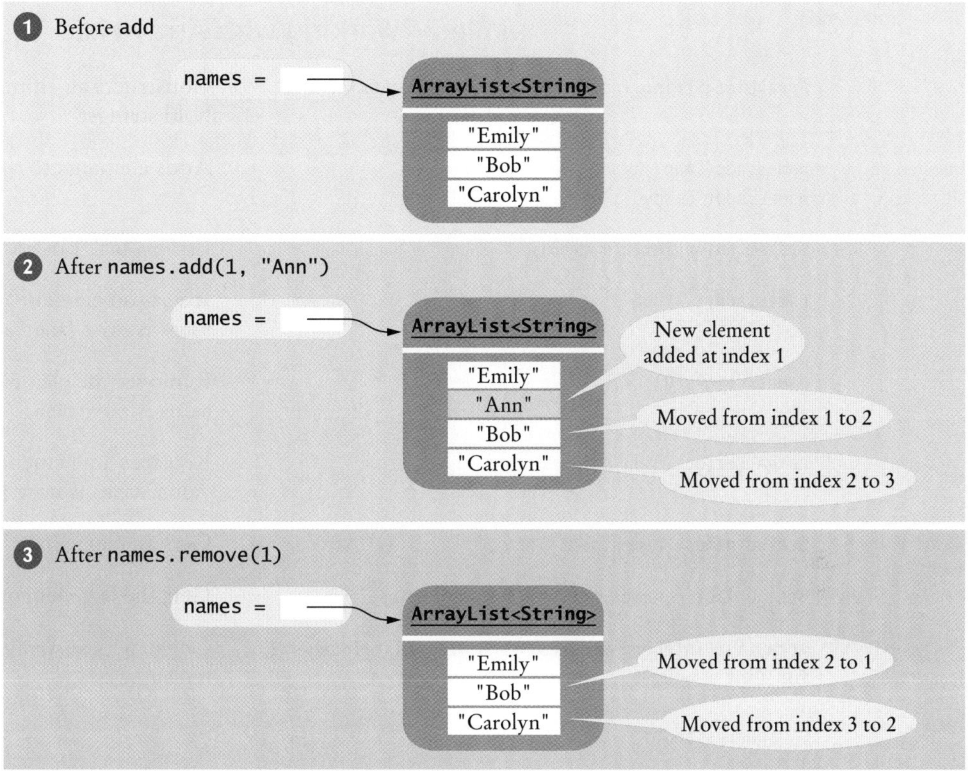

Figure 14 Adding and Removing Elements in the Middle of an Array List

Conversely, the remove method removes the element at a given position, moves all elements after the removed element down by one position, and reduces the size of the array list by 1. Part 3 of Figure 14 illustrates the result of names.remove(1).

Use the add and remove methods to add and remove array list elements.

With an array list, it is very easy to get a quick printout. Simply pass the array list to the println method:

```
System.out.println(names); // Prints [Emily, Bob, Carolyn]
```

6.6.2 Using the Enhanced for Loop with Array Lists

You can use the enhanced for loop to visit all elements of an array list. For example, the following loop prints all names:

```
ArrayList<String> names = . . . ;
for (String name : names)
{
   System.out.println(name);
}
```

This loop is equivalent to the following ordinary for loop:

```
for (int i = 0; i < names.size(); i++)
{
   String name = names.get(i);
   System.out.println(name);
}
```

Table 2 Working with Array Lists	
`ArrayList<String> names = new ArrayList<String>();`	Constructs an empty array list that can hold strings.
`names.add("Ann");` `names.add("Cindy");`	Adds elements to the end.
`System.out.println(names);`	Prints [Ann, Cindy].
`names.add(1, "Bob");`	Inserts an element at index 1. `names` is now `[Ann, Bob, Cindy]`.
`names.remove(0);`	Removes the element at index 0. `names` is now `[Bob, Cindy]`.
`names.set(0, "Bill");`	Replaces an element with a different value. `names` is now `[Bill, Cindy]`.
`String name = names.get(i);`	Gets an element.
`String last = names.get(names.size() - 1);`	Gets the last element.

`ArrayList<Integer> squares = new ArrayList<Integer>();`
`for (int i = 0; i < 10; i++)`
`{`
`    squares.add(i * i);`
`}`
	Constructs an array list holding the first ten squares.

6.6.3 Copying Array Lists

As with arrays, you need to remember that array list variables hold references. Copying the reference yields two references to the same array list (see Figure 15).

```
ArrayList<String> friends = names;
friends.add("Harry");
```

Now both `names` and `friends` reference the same array list to which the string `"Harry"` was added.

If you want to make a copy of an array list, construct the copy and pass the original list into the constructor:

```
ArrayList<String> newNames = new ArrayList<String>(names);
```

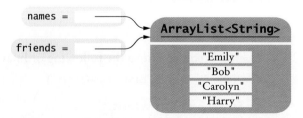

Figure 15 Copying an Array List Reference

6.6.4 Array Lists and Methods

Like arrays, array lists can be method parameters and return values. Here is an example: a method that receives a list of strings and returns the reversed list.

```java
public static ArrayList<String> reverse(ArrayList<String> names)
{
    // Allocate a list to hold the method result
    ArrayList<String> result = new ArrayList<String>();

    // Traverse the names list in reverse order, starting with the last element
    for (int i = names.size() - 1; i >= 0; i--)
    {
        // Add each name to the result
        result.add(names.get(i));
    }
    return result;
}
```

If this method is called with an array list containing the names Emily, Bob, Cindy, it returns a new array list with the names Cindy, Bob, Emily.

6.6.5 Wrappers and Auto-boxing

To collect numbers in array lists, you must use wrapper classes.

In Java, you cannot directly insert primitive type values—numbers, characters, or Boolean values—into array lists. For example, you cannot form an ArrayList<double>. Instead, you must use one of the following **wrapper classes**:

Primitive Type	Wrapper Class
byte	Byte
boolean	Boolean
char	Character
double	Double
float	Float
int	Integer
long	Long
short	Short

For example, to collect double values in an array list, you use an ArrayList<Double>. Note that the wrapper class names start with uppercase letters, and that two of them differ from the names of the corresponding primitive type: Integer and Character.

Conversion between primitive types and the corresponding wrapper classes is automatic. This process is called **auto-boxing** (even though *auto-wrapping* would have been more consistent).

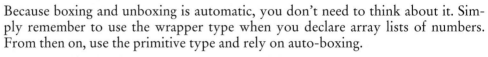

Figure 16 A Wrapper Class Variable

For example, if you assign a `double` value to a `Double` variable, the number is automatically "put into a box" (see Figure 16).

```
Double wrapper = 29.95;
```

Conversely, wrapper values are automatically "unboxed" to primitive types.

```
double x = wrapper;
```

Because boxing and unboxing is automatic, you don't need to think about it. Simply remember to use the wrapper type when you declare array lists of numbers. From then on, use the primitive type and rely on auto-boxing.

```
ArrayList<Double> data = new ArrayList<Double>();
data.add(29.95);
double x = data.get(0);
```

*Like truffles that must be in a wrapper to be sold,
a number must be placed in a wrapper to be stored in an array list.*

6.6.6 Array List Algorithms

The array algorithms in Section 6.3 can be converted to array lists simply by using the array list methods instead of the array syntax (see Table 3). For example, this code snippet computes the largest value in an array.

```
double largest = data[0];
for (int i = 1; i < data.length; i++)
{
   if (data[i] > largest)
   {
      largest = data[i];
   }
}
```

Here is the same algorithm, now using an array list:

```
double largest = data.get(0);
for (int i = 1; i < data.size(); i++)
{
   if (data.get(i) > largest)
   {
```

```
        largest = data.get(i);
    }
}
```

Array lists are *much* easier to use than arrays for collecting an unknown number of input values. Simply read inputs and add them to an array list:

```
ArrayList<Double> inputs = new ArrayList<Double>();
while (in.hasNextDouble())
{
    inputs.add(in.nextDouble());
}
```

6.6.7 Choosing Between Array Lists and Arrays

For most programming tasks, array lists are easier to use than arrays. Array lists can grow and shrink. On the other hand, arrays have a nicer syntax for element access and initialization.

Which of the two should you choose? Here are some recommendations.

- If the size of a collection never changes, use an array.

- If you collect a long sequence of primitive type values and you are concerned about efficiency, use an array.

- Otherwise, use an array list.

The following program shows how to mark the largest value in a sequence of values. This program uses an array list. Note how the program is an improvement over the array version on page 234. This program can process input sequences of arbitrary length.

Table 3 Comparing Array and Array List Operations		
Operation	Arrays	Array Lists
Get an element.	`x = data[4];`	`x = data.get(4)`
Replace an element.	`data[4] = 35;`	`data.set(4, 35);`
Number of elements.	`data.length`	`data.size()`
Number of filled elements.	`currentSize` (companion variable, see Section 6.1.3)	`data.size()`
Remove an element.	See Section 6.3.6	`data.remove(4);`
Add an element, growing the collection.	See Section 6.3.7	`data.add(35);`
Initializing a collection.	`int[] data = { 1, 4, 9 };`	No initializer list syntax; call add three times.

ch06/largest2/LargestInArrayList.java

```java
1   import java.util.ArrayList;
2   import java.util.Scanner;
3
4   /**
5      This program reads a sequence of values and prints them, marking the largest value.
6   */
7   public class LargestInArrayList
8   {
9      public static void main(String[] args)
10     {
11        ArrayList<Double> data = new ArrayList<Double>();
12
13        // Read inputs
14
15        System.out.println("Please enter values, Q to quit:");
16        Scanner in = new Scanner(System.in);
17        while (in.hasNextDouble())
18        {
19           data.add(in.nextDouble());
20        }
21
22        // Find the largest value
23
24        double largest = data.get(0);
25        for (int i = 1; i < data.size(); i++)
26        {
27           if (data.get(i) > largest)
28           {
29              largest = data.get(i);
30           }
31        }
32
33        // Print all values, marking the largest
34
35        for (double element : data)
36        {
37           System.out.print(element);
38           if (element == largest)
39           {
40              System.out.print(" <== largest value");
41           }
42           System.out.println();
43        }
44     }
45  }
```

Program Run

```
Please enter values, Q to quit:
35 80 115 44.5 Q
35
80
115 <== largest value
44.5
```

29. Declare an array list primes of integers that contains the first five prime numbers (2, 3, 5, 7, and 11).

30. Given the array list primes declared in Self Check 29, write a loop to print its elements in reverse order, starting with the last element.

31. What does the array list names contain after the following statements?

```
ArrayList<String> names = new ArrayList<String>;
names.add("Bob");
names.add(0, "Ann");
names.remove(1);
names.add("Cal");
```

32. What is wrong with this code snippet?

```
ArrayList<String> names;
names.remove(0);
```

33. Consider this method that appends the elements of one array list to another.

```
public static void append(ArrayList<String> target, ArrayList<String> source)
{
   for (int i = 0; i < source.size(); i++)
   {
      target.add(source.get(i));
   }
}
```

What are the contents of names1 and names2 after these statements?

```
ArrayList<String> names1 = new ArrayList<String>();
names1.add("Emily");
names1.add("Bob");
names1.add("Cindy");
ArrayList<String> names2 = new ArrayList<String>();
names2.add("Dave");
append(names1, names2);
```

34. Suppose you want to store the names of the weekdays. Should you use an array list or an array of seven strings?

35. The ch06/scores2 directory contains an alternate implementation of the problem solution in How To 6.1 on page 242. Compare the array and array list implementations. What is the primary advantage of the latter?

Practice It   Now you can try these exercises at the end of the chapter: R6.10, R6.23, P6.14, P6.16.

Common Error 6.4

Length and Size

Unfortunately, the Java syntax for determining the number of elements in an array, an array list, and a string is not at all consistent. It is a common error to confuse these. You just have to remember the correct syntax for every data type.

Data Type	Number of Elements
Array	a.length
Array list	a.size()
String	a.length()

Random Fact 6.2 The First Programmer

Before pocket calculators and personal computers existed, navigators and engineers used mechanical adding machines, slide rules, and tables of logarithms and trigonometric functions to speed up computations. Unfortunately, the tables—for which values had to be computed by hand—were notoriously inaccurate. The mathematician Charles Babbage (1791–1871) had the insight that if a machine could be constructed that produced printed tables automatically, both calculation and typesetting errors could be avoided. Babbage set out to develop a machine for this purpose, which he called a *Difference Engine*

because it used successive differences to compute polynomials. For example, consider the function $f(x) = x^3$. Write down the values for $f(1)$, $f(2)$, $f(3)$, and so on. Then take the *differences* between successive values:

```
1
     7
8
     19
27
     37
64
     61
125
     91
216
```

Repeat the process, taking the difference of successive values in the second column, and then repeat once again:

```
1
     7
8        12
     19       6
27       18
     37       6
64       24
     61       6
125      30
     91
216
```

Now the differences are all the same. You can retrieve the function values by a pattern of additions—you need to know the values at the fringe of the pattern and the constant difference. You can try it out yourself: Write the highlighted numbers on a sheet of paper, and fill in the others by adding the numbers that are in the north and northwest positions.

This method was very attractive, because mechanical addition machines had been known for some time. They consisted of cog wheels, with 10 cogs per wheel, to represent digits, and mechanisms to handle the carry from one digit to the next. Mechanical multiplication machines, on the other hand, were fragile and unreliable. Babbage built a successful prototype of the Difference Engine and, with his own money and government grants, proceeded to build the table-printing machine. However, because of funding problems and the difficulty of building the machine to the required precision, it was never completed.

While working on the Difference Engine, Babbage conceived of a much grander vision that he called the *Analytical Engine*. The Difference Engine was designed to carry out a limited set of computations—it was no smarter than a pocket calculator is today. But Babbage realized that such a machine could be made *programmable* by storing programs as well as data. The internal storage of the Analytical Engine was to consist of 1,000 registers of 50 decimal digits each. Programs and constants were to be stored on punched cards—a technique that was, at that time, commonly used on looms for weaving patterned fabrics.

Ada Augusta, Countess of Lovelace (1815–1852), the only child of Lord Byron, was a friend and sponsor of Charles Babbage. Ada Lovelace was one of the first people to realize the potential of such a machine, not just for computing mathematical tables but for processing data that were not numbers. She is considered by many to be the world's first programmer.

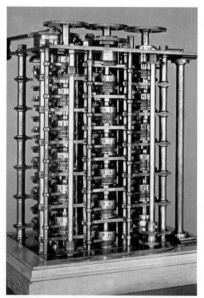

Replica of Babbage's Difference Engine

SCREENCAST 6.1   Game of Life

Conway's *Game of Life* simulates the growth of a population, using only two simple rules. This Screencast Video shows you how to implement this famous "game".

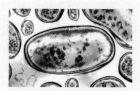

CHAPTER SUMMARY

- An array collects a sequence of values of the same type.
- Individual elements in an array `data` are accessed by an integer index `i`, using the notation `data[i]`.
- An array element can be used like any variable.
- An array index must be at least zero and less than the size of the array.
- A bounds error, which occurs if you supply an invalid array index, can cause your program to terminate.
- Use the expression *array*.`length` to find the number of elements in an array.

- An array variable specifies the location of an array. Copying the reference yields a second reference to the same array.
- With a partially filled array, keep a companion variable for the current size.

- You can use the enhanced `for` loop to visit all elements of an array.

- A linear search inspects elements in sequence until a match is found.
- Use the `Arrays.copyOf` method to copy the elements of an array into a new array.

- Arrays and array lists can occur as method parameters and return values.

- Use a two-dimensional array to store tabular data.
- Individual elements in a two-dimensional array are accessed by using two index values, *array*`[i][j]`.

- An array list stores a sequence of values whose size can change.
  - The `ArrayList` class is a generic class: `ArrayList<Type>` collects elements of the specified type.
  - Use the `size` method to obtain the current size of an array list.
  - Use the `get` and `set` methods to access an array list element at a given index.

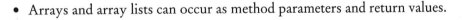

- Use the add and remove methods to add and remove array list elements.

- To collect numbers in array lists, you must use wrapper classes.

MEDIA RESOURCES

www.wiley.com/
college/
horstmann

- ***Worked Example*** Rolling the Dice
- ***Worked Example*** A World Population Table
- Guided Lab Exercises
- ➕ ***Animation*** Removing from an Array
- ➕ ***Animation*** Inserting into an Array
- ➕ ***Animation*** Tracing a Nested Loop in a 2D Array
- ➕ ***Screencast*** Game of Life
- ➕ Practice Quiz
- ➕ Code Completion Exercises

REVIEW EXERCISES

★★ **R6.1** Write code that fills an array data with each set of values below.

a. 1	2	3	4	5	6	7	8	9	10
b. 0	2	4	6	8	10	12	14	16	18 20
c. 1	4	9	16	25	36	49	64	81	100
d. 0	0	0	0	0	0	0	0	0	0
e. 1	4	9	16	9	7	4	9	11	
f. 0	1	0	1	0	1	0	1	0	1
g. 0	1	2	3	4	0	1	2	3	4

★★ **R6.2** Consider the following array:

```
int[] a = { 1, 2, 3, 4, 5, 4, 3, 2, 1, 0 };
```

What is the value of total after the following loops complete?

a. ```
int total = 0;
for (int i = 0; i < 10; i++) { total = total + a[i]; }
```

**b.** ```
int total = 0;
for (int i = 0; i < 10; i = i + 2) { total = total + a[i]; }
```

c. ```
int total = 0;
for (int i = 1; i < 10; i = i + 2) { total = total + a[i]; }
```

**d.** ```
int total = 0;
for (int i = 2; i <= 10; i++) { total = total + a[i]; }
```

e. ```
int total = 0;
for (int i = 1; i < 10; i = 2 * i) { total = total + a[i]; }
```
```

f. `int total = 0;`
`for (int i = 9; i >= 0; i--) { total = total + a[i]; }`

g. `int total = 0;`
`for (int i = 9; i >= 0; i = i - 2) { total = total + a[i]; }`

h. `int total = 0;`
`for (int i = 0; i < 10; i++) { total = a[i] - total; }`

★★ **R6.3** Consider the following array:

`int[] a = { 1, 2, 3, 4, 5, 4, 3, 2, 1, 0 };`

What are the contents of the array a after the following loops complete?

a. `for (int i = 1; i < 10; i++) { a[i] = a[i - 1]; }`

b. `for (int i = 9; i > 0; i--) { a[i] = a[i - 1]; }`

c. `for (int i = 0; i < 9; i++) { a[i] = a[i + 1]; }`

d. `for (int i = 8; i >= 0; i--) { a[i] = a[i + 1]; }`

e. `for (int i = 1; i < 10; i++) { a[i] = a[i] + a[i - 1]; }`

f. `for (int i = 1; i < 10; i = i + 2) { a[i] = 0; }`

g. `for (int i = 0; i < 5; i++) { a[i + 5] = a[i]; }`

h. `for (int i = 1; i < 5; i++) { a[i] = a[9 - i]; }`

★★★ **R6.4** Write a loop that fills an array data with ten random numbers between 1 and 100. Write code for two nested loops that fill data with ten *different* random numbers between 1 and 100.

★★ **R6.5** Write Java code for a loop that simultaneously computes both the maximum and minimum of an array.

★ **R6.6** What is wrong with each of the following code segments?

a. `int[] data = new int[10];`
```
for (int i = 1; i <= 10; i++)
{
    data[i] = i * i;
}
```

b. `int[] data;`
```
for (int i = 0; i < data.length; i++)
{
    data[i] = i * i;
}
```

★★ **R6.7** Write "for each" loops for the following tasks:

a. Printing all elements of an array in a single row, separated by spaces.

b. Computing the product of all elements in an array.

c. Counting how many elements in an array are negative.

★★ **R6.8** Rewrite the following loops without using the "for each" construct. Here, data is an array of double values.

a. `for (double x : data) { sum = sum + x; }`

b. `for (double x : data) { if (x == target) { return true; } }`

c. `int i = 0;`
`for (double x : data) { data[i] = 2 * x; i++; }`

★★ **R6.9** Rewrite the following loops, using the "for each" construct. Here, data is an array of double values.

    a. `for (int i = 0; i < data.length; i++) { sum = sum + data[i]; }`

    b. `for (int i = 1; i < data.length; i++) { sum = sum + data[i]; }`

    c.
```
for (int i = 0; i < data.length; i++)
{
    if (data[i] == target) { return i; }
}
```

★ **R6.10** What is wrong with each of the following code segments?

    a. `ArrayList<int> data = new ArrayList<int>();`

    b. `ArrayList<Integer> data = new ArrayList();`

    c. `ArrayList<Integer> data = new ArrayList<Integer>;`

    d.
```
ArrayList<Integer> data = new ArrayList<Integer>();
for (int i = 1; i <= 10; i++)
{
    data.set(i - 1, i * i);
}
```

    e.
```
ArrayList<Integer> data;
for (int i = 1; i <= 10; i++)
{
    data.add(i * i);
}
```

★ **R6.11** What is an index of an array? What are the legal index values? What is a bounds error?

★ **R6.12** Write a program that contains a bounds error. Run the program. What happens on your computer?

★ **R6.13** Trace the flow of the loop in Section 6.3.4 with the given example. Show two columns, one with the value of i and one with the output.

★ **R6.14** Consider this loop for collecting all values that match a condition; in this case, that the value is larger than 100:
```
ArrayList<Double> matches = new ArrayList<Double>();
for (double element : data)
{
    if (element > 100)
    {
        matches.add(element);
    }
}
```
Trace the flow of the loop, where data contains the values 110 90 100 120 80. Show two columns, for element and matches.

★ **R6.15** Trace the flow of the loop in Section 6.3.5, where data contains the values 80 90 100 120 110. Show two columns, for pos and found. Repeat the trace when data contains 80 90 120 70.

★★ **R6.16** Trace the algorithm for removing an element described in Section 6.3.6. Use an array data with values 110 90 100 120 80, and remove the element at index 2.

★★   **R6.17** Give pseudocode for an algorithm that rotates the elements of an array by one position, moving the initial element to the end of the array, like this:

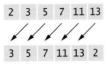

★★   **R6.18** Give pseudocode for an algorithm that removes all negative values from an array, preserving the order of the remaining elements.

★★   **R6.19** Suppose data is a *sorted* array of integers. Give pseudocode that describes how a new value can be inserted in its proper position so that the resulting array stays sorted.

★★★   **R6.20** A *run* is a sequence of adjacent repeated values. Give pseudocode for computing the length of the longest run in an array. For example, the longest run in the array with elements

    1 2 5 5 3 1 2 4 3 2 2 2 2 3 6 5 5 6 3 1

has length 4.

★★★   **R6.21** What is wrong with the following method that aims to fill an array with random numbers?

```
void fillWithRandomNumbers(double[] values)
{
    double[] numbers = new double[values.length];
    for (int i = 0; i < numbers.length; i++) { numbers[i] = Math.random(); }
    values = numbers;
}
```

★★   **R6.22** Write Java statements for performing the following tasks with an array declared as

    int[][] values = new int[ROWS][COLUMNS];

- Fill all entries with 0.
- Fill elements alternately with 0s and 1s in a checkerboard pattern.
- Fill only the elements at the top and bottom row with zeroes.
- Compute the sum of all elements.
- Print the array in tabular form.

★★   **R6.23** How do you perform the following tasks with array lists in Java?
  a. Test that two array lists contain the same elements in the same order.
  b. Copy one array list to another.
  c. Fill an array list with zeroes, overwriting all elements in it.
  d. Remove all elements from an array list.

PROGRAMMING EXERCISES

★★ **P6.1** Write a program that initializes an array with ten random integers and then prints four lines of output, containing

- Every element at an even index.
- Every even element.
- All elements in reverse order.
- Only the first and last element.

★ **P6.2** Modify the LargestInArray.java program to mark both the smallest and the largest elements.

★★ **P6.3** Reimplement How To 6.1 on page 242 by following the original plan: Remove the minimum from the array of scores, then compute the sum.

★★ **P6.4** Compute the *alternating sum* of all elements in an array. For example, if your program reads the input

$$1 \quad 4 \quad 9 \quad 16 \quad 9 \quad 7 \quad 4 \quad 9 \quad 11$$

then it computes

$$1 - 4 + 9 - 16 + 9 - 7 + 4 - 9 + 11 = -2$$

★ **P6.5** Write a method that reverses the sequence of elements in an array. For example, if you call the method with the array

$$1 \quad 4 \quad 9 \quad 16 \quad 9 \quad 7 \quad 4 \quad 9 \quad 11$$

then the array is changed to

$$11 \quad 9 \quad 4 \quad 7 \quad 9 \quad 16 \quad 9 \quad 4 \quad 1$$

★★★ **P6.6** Write a method that removes duplicates from a partially filled array. For example, if your array contains

$$1 \quad 4 \quad 9 \quad 16 \quad 9 \quad 7 \quad 4 \quad 9 \quad 11$$

then after the method has been called, it should contain

$$1 \quad 4 \quad 9 \quad 16 \quad 7 \quad 11$$

Your method should return the number of elements in the array after the call.

★★ **P6.7** A *run* is a sequence of adjacent repeated values. Write a program that generates a sequence of 20 random die tosses in an array and that prints the die values, marking the runs by including them in parentheses, like this:

1 2 (5 5) 3 1 2 4 3 (2 2 2 2) 3 6 (5 5) 6 3 1

Use the following pseudocode:

```
Set a boolean variable inRun to false.
For each valid index i in the array
    If inRun
        If values[i] is different from the preceding value
            Print ).
            inRun = false.
```

```
        If not inRun
            If values[i] is the same as the following value
                Print (.
                inRun = true.
        Print values[i].
    If inRun, print ).
```

★★★ **P6.8** Write a program that generates a sequence of 20 random die tosses in an array and that prints the die values, marking only the longest run, like this:

1 2 5 5 3 1 2 4 3 (2 2 2 2) 3 6 5 5 6 3 1

If there is more than one run of maximum length, mark the first one.

★★ **P6.9** Write a program that generates a sequence of 20 random values between 0 and 99 in an array, prints the sequence, sorts it, and prints the sorted sequence. Use the sort method from the standard Java library.

★★★ **P6.10** Write a program that produces ten random permutations of the numbers 1 to 10. To generate a random permutation, you need to fill an array with the numbers 1 to 10 so that no two entries of the array have the same contents. You could do it by brute force, by generating random values until you have a value that is not yet in the array. But that is inefficient. Instead, follow this algorithm.

```
Make a second array and fill it with the numbers 1 to 10.
Repeat 10 times
    Pick a random element from the second array.
    Remove it and append it to the permutation array.
```

★★ **P6.11** It is a well-researched fact that men in a restroom generally prefer to maximize their distance from already occupied stalls, by occupying the middle of the longest sequence of unoccupied places.

For example, consider the situation where ten stalls are empty.

_ _ _ _ _ _ _ _ _ _

The first visitor will occupy a middle position:

_ _ _ _ _ X _ _ _ _

The next visitor will be in the middle of the empty area at the left.

_ _ X _ _ X _ _ _ _

Write a program that reads the number of stalls and then prints out diagrams in the format given above when the stalls become filled, one at a time. _Hint:_ Use an array of boolean values to indicate whether a stall is occupied.

★★★ **P6.12** _Magic squares._ An $n \times n$ matrix that is filled with the numbers 1, 2, 3, . . ., n^2 is a magic square if the sum of the elements in each row, in each column, and in the two diagonals is the same value.

16	3	2	13
5	10	11	8
9	6	7	12
4	15	14	1

Write a program that reads in 16 values from the keyboard and tests whether they form a magic square when put into a 4 × 4 array. You need to test two features:

1. Does each of the numbers 1, 2, ..., 16 occur in the user input?

2. When the numbers are put into a square, are the sums of the rows, columns, and diagonals equal to each other?

★★★ **P6.13** Implement the following algorithm to construct magic $n \times n$ squares; it works only if n is odd.

```
Set row = n - 1, column = n / 2.
For k = 1 ... n * n
    Place k at [row][column].
    Increment row and column.
    If the row or column is n, replace it with 0.
    If the element at [row][column] has already been filled
        Set row and column to their previous value.
        Decrement row.
```

Here is the 5 × 5 square that you get if you follow this method:

11	18	25	2	9
10	12	19	21	3
4	6	13	20	22
23	5	7	14	16
17	24	1	8	15

Write a program whose input is the number n and whose output is the magic square of order n if n is odd.

★★ **P6.14** Write a program that reads a sequence of input values and displays a bar chart of the values in data, using asterisks, like this:

```
**********************
*******************************************
******************************
***************************
**************
```

You may assume that all values are positive. First figure out the maximum value in data. That value's bar should be drawn with 40 asterisks. Shorter bars should use proportionally fewer asterisks.

★★★ **P6.15** Improve the program of Exercise P6.14 to work correctly when data contains negative values.

★★ **P6.16** Improve the program of Exercise P6.14 by adding captions for each bar. Prompt the user for the captions and data values. The output should look like this:

```
      Egypt ************************
     France ******************************************
      Japan *****************************
    Uruguay ***************************
Switzerland **************
```

★★ **P6.17** A theater seating chart is implemented as a two-dimensional array of ticket prices, like this:

```
10 10 10 10 10 10 10 10 10 10
10 10 10 10 10 10 10 10 10 10
10 10 10 10 10 10 10 10 10 10
10 10 20 20 20 20 20 20 10 10
10 10 20 20 20 20 20 20 10 10
10 10 20 20 20 20 20 20 10 10
20 20 30 30 40 40 30 30 20 20
20 30 30 40 50 50 40 30 30 20
30 40 50 50 50 50 50 50 40 30
```

Write a program that prompts users to pick either a seat or a price. Mark sold seats by changing the price to 0. When a user specifies a seat, make sure it is available. When a user specifies a price, find any seat with that price.

★★★ **P6.18** Write a program that plays tic-tac-toe. The tic-tac-toe game is played on a 3 × 3 grid as in

The game is played by two players, who take turns. The first player marks moves with a circle, the second with a cross. The player who has formed a horizontal, vertical, or diagonal sequence of three marks wins. Your program should draw the game board, ask the user for the coordinates of the next mark, change the players after every successful move, and pronounce the winner.

ANSWERS TO SELF-CHECK QUESTIONS

1. `int primes[] = { 2, 3, 5, 7, 11 };`

2. `2, 3, 5, 3, 2`

3. `3, 4, 6, 8, 12`

4. `data[0] = 10;`
   `data[9] = 10;`   or better   `data[data.length - 1] = 10;`

5. `String[] words = new String[10];`

6. `String words[] = { "Yes", "No" };`

7. No. Because you don't store the values, you need to print them when you read them. But you don't know where to add the <= until you have seen all values.

8. It counts how many elements of `data` are zero.

9. `for (double x : data) { System.out.println(x); }`

10. `double product = 1;`
    `for (double f : factors) { product = product * f; }`

11. The loop writes a value into `data[i]`. The "for each" loop does not have the index variable `i`.

12. `20 <== largest value`
    `10`
    `20 <== largest value`

13. ```
    int count = 0;
    for (double x : data)
    {
       if (x == 0)
       {
          count++;
       }
    }
    ```

14. If all elements of `data` are negative, then the result is incorrectly computed as `0`.

15. ```
    for (int i = 0; i < data.length; i++)
    {
       System.out.print(data[i]);
       if (i < data.length - 1)
       {
          System.out.print(" | ");
       }
    }
    ```
    Now you know why we set up the loop the other way.

16. If the array has no elements, then the program terminates with an exception.

17. If there is a match, then `pos` is incremented before the loop exits.

18. This loop sets all elements to `data[pos]`.

19. `int[] numbers = squares(5);`

20. ```
    public static void fill(int[] data, int value)
    {
       for (int i = 0; i < data.length; i++) { data[i] = value; }
    }
    ```

21. The method returns an array whose length is given in the first parameter. The array is filled with random integers between 0 and n - 1.
    ```

22. The contents of `values` is unchanged. The `reverse` method returns a new array with the reversed numbers.

23.

values	result	i
[1, 4, 9]	[~~0, 0, 0~~]	~~2~~
	[~~9, 0, 0~~]	~~1~~
	[~~9, 4, 0~~]	0
	[9, 4, 1]	

24. You get the total number of gold, silver, and bronze medals in the competition. In our example, there are four of each.

25.
```
for (int i = 0; i < 8; i++)
{
    for (int j = 0; j < 8; j++)
    {
        board[i][j] = (i + j) % 2;
    }
}
```

26. `String[][] board = new String[3][3];`

27. `board[0][2] = "x";`

28. `board[0][0], board[1][1], board[2][2]`

29.
```
ArrayList<Integer> primes = new ArrayList<Integer>();
primes.add(2);
primes.add(3);
primes.add(5);
primes.add(7);
primes.add(11);
```

30.
```
for (int i = primes.size() - 1; i >= 0; i--)
{
    System.out.println(primes.get(i));
}
```

31. `"Ann", "Cal"`

32. The `names` variable has not been initialized.

33. `names1` contains "Emily", "Bob", "Cindy", "Dave";
`names2` contains "Dave"

34. Because the number of weekdays doesn't change, there is no disadvantage to using an array, and it is easier to initialize:
```
String[] weekdayNames = { "Monday", "Tuesday", "Wednesday", "Thursday",
    "Friday", "Saturday", "Sunday" };
```

35. Reading inputs into an array list is much easier.

OBJECTS AND CLASSES

This chapter introduces you to object-oriented programming, an important technique for writing complex programs. In an object-oriented program, you don't simply manipulate numbers and strings, but you work with objects that are meaningful for your application. Objects with the same behavior (such as the windmills to the left) are grouped into classes. A programmer provides the desired behavior by specifying and implementing methods for these classes. In this chapter, you will learn how to discover, specify, and implement your own classes, and how to use them in your programs.

7.1 Object-Oriented Programming

You have learned how to structure your programs by decomposing tasks into methods. This is an excellent practice, but experience shows that it does not go far enough. It is difficult to understand and update a program that consists of a large collection of methods.

To overcome this problem, computer scientists invented **object-oriented programming**, a programming style in which tasks are solved by collaborating objects. Each object has its own set of data, together with a set of methods that act upon the data.

You have already experienced this programming style when you used strings, the System.out object, or a Scanner object. Each of these objects has a set of methods. For example, you can use the length and substring methods to work with String objects.

When you develop an object-oriented program, you create your own objects that describe what is important in your application. For example, in a student database you might work with Student and Course objects. Of course, then you must supply methods for these objects.

A class describes objects with the same behavior. For example, a Car class describes all passenger vehicles that have a certain capacity and shape.

In Java, a programmer doesn't implement a single object. Instead, the programmer provides a **class**. A class describes a set of objects with the same behavior. For example, the String class describes the behavior of all strings. The class specifies how a string stores its characters, which methods can be used with strings, and how the methods are implemented.

> A class describes a set of objects with the same behavior.

In order to obtain objects from a class, you need to *construct* them. For example, the expression new Scanner(in) in the statement

```
Scanner in = new Scanner(System.in);
```

constructs a new object of the Scanner class. In Java, you use the new operator to construct objects.

> Use the new operator to construct objects from a class.

You have not yet seen many examples of object construction because the objects System.in and System.out have already been constructed by the System class, and you can obtain strings as literals (such as "Hello"). However, these are special cases. As you use other classes, you will frequently construct objects. For example, as you will see in Chapter 8, you construct an object of the PrintWriter class for file output like this:

```
PrintWriter out = new PrintWriter("output.txt");
```

Once an object has been constructed, you can call its methods. These methods are called **instance methods** because they are invoked on an object, unlike the static methods of Chapter 5. An instance method is invoked by specifying the object, then the method name and parameters, such as

> Methods that are invoked on objects are called instance methods.

```
out.println("Hello, World!");
```

When you work with an object, you do not know how it is implemented. You need not know how a String organizes a character sequence, or how a PrintWriter object sends data to a file. All you need to know is the **public interface**: the specifications for the methods that you can invoke. The process of providing a public interface, while hiding the implementation details, is called **encapsulation**.

> Every class has a public interface: a collection of methods through which the objects of the class can be manipulated.

You will want to use encapsulation for your own classes. That is, you will want to specify a set of methods and hide the implementation details. Other programmers on your team can then use your classes without having to know their implementations, just as you are able to make use of the String and Scanner classes.

> Encapsulation is the act of providing a public interface and hiding the implementation details.

You can drive a car by operating the steering wheel and pedals, without knowing how the engine works. Similarly, you use an object through its methods. The implementation is hidden.

A driver of an electric car doesn't have to learn new controls even though the car engine is very different. Neither does the programmer who uses an object with an improved implementation—as long as the public interface has not changed.

> **Encapsulation enables changes in the implementation without affecting users of a class.**

If you work on a program that is being developed over a long amount of time, it is common for implementation details to change, usually to make objects more efficient or more capable. When the implementation is hidden, the improvements do not affect the programmers that use the objects.

SELF CHECK

1. When using a String object, you do not know how it stores its characters. How can you access them?

2. Describe a way in which a String object might store its characters.

3. Suppose the providers of your Java compiler decide to change the way that a String object stores its characters, and they update the String method implementations accordingly. Which parts of your code do you need to change when you get the new compiler?

4. Construct two PrintWriter objects that can be used for writing data to the files output1.txt and output2.txt.

Practice It   Now you can try these exercises at the end of the chapter: R7.1, R7.4.

7.2 Specifying the Public Interface of a Class

When designing a class, you start by specifying its **public interface**. The public interface of a class consists of all methods that a user of the class may want to apply to its objects.

Let's consider a simple example. We want to use objects that simulate cash registers. A cashier who rings up a sale presses a key to start the sale, then rings up each item. A display shows the amount owed as well as the total number of items purchased.

In our simulation, we want to call the following methods on a cash register object:

- Add the price of an item.
- Get the total amount owed, and the count of items purchased.
- Clear the cash register to start a new sale.

Here is an outline of the CashRegister class. We supply comments for all of the methods to document their purpose.

Our first example of a class simulates a cash register.

```java
/**
    A simulated cash register that tracks the item
    count and the total amount due.
*/
public class CashRegister
{
    private data—see Section 7.3

    /**
        Adds an item to this cash register.
        @param price the price of this item
    */
    public void addItem(double price)
    {
        implementation—see Section 7.4
    }

    /**
        Gets the price of all items in the current sale.
        @return the total price
    */
    public double getTotal()
    {
        implementation—see page 286
    }

    /**
        Gets the number of items in the current sale.
        @return the item count
    */
    public int getCount()
    {
        implementation—see page 286
    }

    /**
        Clears the item count and the total.
    */
    public void clear()
    {
        implementation—see page 286
    }
}
```

The method declarations make up the *public interface* of the class. The data and the method bodies make up the *private implementation* of the class.

Note that the methods of the CashRegister class are instance methods. They are *not* declared as static. You invoke them on objects (or instances) of the CashRegister class.

To see an instance method in action, we first need to construct an object:

```java
CashRegister register1 = new CashRegister();
    // Constructs a CashRegister object
```

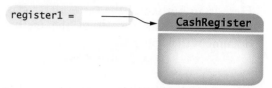

Figure 1 An Object Reference and an Object

This statement initializes the `register1` variable with a reference to a new `CashRegister` object—see Figure 1. (We discuss the process of object construction in Section 7.5 and object references in Section 7.8.)

Once the object has been constructed, we are ready to invoke a method.

```
register1.addItem(1.95); // Invokes a method
```

> A mutator method changes the object on which it operates.

When you look at the public interface of a class, it is useful to classify its methods as *mutators* and *accessors*. A **mutator** is a method that modifies the object on which it operates in some way. The `CashRegister` class has two mutators: `addItem` and `clear`. After you call either of these methods, the object has changed. You can observe that change by calling the `getTotal` or `getCount` method.

> An accessor method does not change the object on which it operates.

An **accessor** method just queries the object for some information without changing it. The `CashRegister` class has two accessors: `getTotal` and `getCount`. Applying either of these methods to a `CashRegister` object simply returns a value and does not modify the object. For example, the following statement prints the current total and count:

```
System.out.println(register1.getTotal()) + " " + register1.getCount());
```

Now we know *what* a `CashRegister` object can do, but not *how* it does it. Of course, to use `CashRegister` objects in our programs, we don't need to know.

In the next section, you will see how the `CashRegister` class is implemented.

SELF CHECK

5. What does the following code segment print?
   ```
   CashRegister reg = new CashRegister();
   reg.clear();
   reg.addItem(0.95);
   reg.addItem(0.95);
   System.out.println(reg.getCount() + " " + reg.getTotal());
   ```

6. What is wrong with the following code segment?
   ```
   CashRegister reg = new CashRegister();
   reg.clear();
   reg.addItem(0.95);
   System.out.println(reg.getAmountDue());
   ```

7. Declare a method `getDollars` of the `CashRegister` class that yields the amount of the total sale as a dollar value without the cents.

8. Name two accessor methods of the `String` class.

9. Is the `nextInt` method of the `Scanner` class an accessor or a mutator?

Practice It Now you can try these exercises at the end of the chapter: R7.2, R7.8.

7.3 Instance Variables

An object holds instance variables that are accessed by methods.

An object stores its data in **instance variables**. These are variables that are declared inside the class (see Syntax 7.1).

When implementing a class, you have to determine which data each object needs to store. The object needs to have all the information necessary to carry out any method call.

Go through all methods and consider their data requirements. It is a good idea to start with the accessor methods. For example, a CashRegister object must be able to return the correct value for the getTotal method. That means, it must either store all entered prices and compute the total in the method call, or it must store the total.

Now apply the same reasoning to the getCount method. If the cash register stores all entered prices, it can count them in the getCount method. Otherwise, you need to have a variable for the count.

The addItem method receives a price as a parameter, and it must record the price. If the CashRegister object stores an array of entered prices, then the addItem method appends the price. On the other hand, if we decide to store just the item total and count, then the addItem method updates these two variables.

Finally, the clear method must prepare the cash register for the next sale, either by emptying the array of prices or by setting the total and count to zero.

We have now discovered two different ways of representing the data that the object needs. Either of them will work, and we have to make a choice. We will choose the simpler one: variables for the total price and the item count. (Other options are explored in Exercises P7.1 and P7.2.)

The instance variables are declared in the class, but outside any methods, with the private modifier:

```java
public class CashRegister
{
    private int itemCount;
    private double totalPrice;
    . . .
}
```

Like a wilderness explorer who needs to carry all items that may be needed, an object needs to store the data required for any method calls.

Figure 2
Instance Variables of
CashRegister Objects

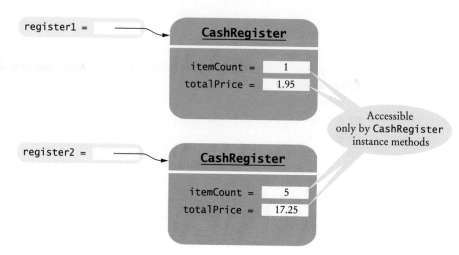

Every object has
its own set of
instance variables.

Every CashRegister object has a separate copy of these instance variables (see Figure 2). The values stored in these variables make up the **state** of the object. The state can change when a mutator method is applied to an object.

Because the instance variables are declared to be private, programmers using the CashRegister class cannot access the instance variables directly:

```java
public static void main(String[] args)
{
    . . .
    System.out.println(register1.itemCount); // Error
    . . .
}
```

Private instance
variables can only be
accessed by methods
of the same class.

They must use a method of the class to access the data in the instance variables:

```java
System.out.println(register1.getCount());
```

Thus, the instance variables of an object are effectively hidden from the programmer using the class. While it is possible in Java to leave instance variables unencapsulated (by declaring them as public), this is very uncommon in practice. We will always make all instance variables private in this book.

Syntax 7.1 Instance Variables

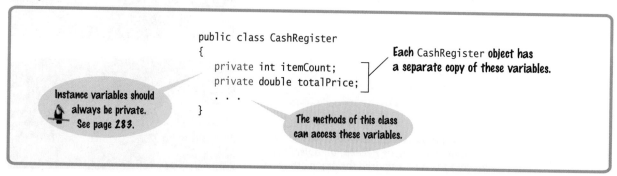

These clocks have common behavior, but each of them has a different state. Similarly, objects of a class can have their instance variables set to different values.

SELF CHECK

10. What is wrong with this code segment?

    ```
    CashRegister register2 = new CashRegister();
    register2.clear();
    register2.addItem(0.95);
    System.out.println(register2.totalPrice);
    ```

11. Consider a class Time that represents a point in time, such as 9 A.M. or 3:30 P.M. Give two sets of instance variables that can be used for implementing the Time class. (Hint for the second set: Military time.)

12. Suppose the implementor of the Time class changes from one implementation strategy to another, keeping the public interface unchanged. What do the programmers who use the Time class need to do?

13. Consider a class Grade that represents a letter grade, such as A+ or B. Give two different sets of instance variables that can be used for implementing the Grade class.

Practice It Now you can try these exercises at the end of the chapter: R7.5, R7.6.

7.4 Instance Methods

When implementing a class, you need to provide the bodies for all methods. Implementing an instance method is very similar to implementing static methods, with one essential difference: You can access the instance variables of the class in the method body.

For example, here is the implementation of the addItem method of the CashRegister class. (You can find the remaining methods at the end of the next section.)

```
public void addItem(double price)
{
    itemCount++;
    totalPrice = totalPrice + price;
}
```

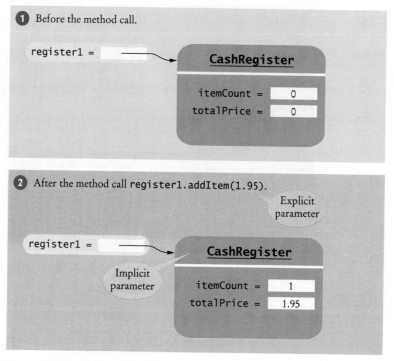

① Before the method call.

register1 =

CashRegister

itemCount = 0
totalPrice = 0

② After the method call `register1.addItem(1.95)`.

Explicit parameter

register1 =

CashRegister

Implicit parameter

itemCount = 1
totalPrice = 1.95

Figure 3 Implicit and Explicit Parameters

Whenever you use an instance variable, such as `itemCount` or `totalPrice`, in a method, it denotes that instance variable *of the object on which the method was invoked.* For example, consider the call

```
register1.addItem(1.95);
```

The first statement in the `addItem` method is

```
itemCount++;
```

> The object on which a method is applied is the implicit parameter.

Which `itemCount` is incremented? In this call, it is the `itemCount` of the `register1` object. (See Figure 3.)

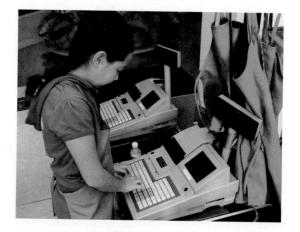

When an item is added, it affects the instance variables of the cash register object on which the method is invoked.

Syntax 7.2   Instance Methods

```
                        public class BankAccount
                        {                                        Explicit parameter
                          . . .
                          public void addItem(double price)
                          {
                              itemCount++;
                              totalPrice = totalPrice + price;
                          }
                          . . .
                        }
```

Instance variables of the implicit parameter

Explicit parameter

The object on which a method is invoked is called the **implicit parameter** of the method. In Java, you do not actually write the implicit parameter in the method declaration. For that reason, the parameter is called "implicit".

Explicit parameters of a method are listed in the method declaration.

In contrast, parameters that are explicitly mentioned in the method declaration, such as the price parameter, are called **explicit parameters**. Every method has exactly one implicit parameter and zero or more explicit parameters.

SELF CHECK

14. What is the value of register1.itemCount, register1.totalPrice, register2.item-Count, and register2.totalPrice after these statements?

```
CashRegister register1 = new CashRegister();
register1.addItem(0.90);
register1.addItem(0.95);
CashRegister register2 = new CashRegister();
register2.addItem(1.90);
```

15. Implement a method getDollars of the CashRegister class that yields the amount of the total sale as a dollar value without the cents.

16. Consider the substring method of the String class that is described in Section 2.6.6. How many parameters does it have, and what are their types?

17. Consider the length method of the String class. How many parameters does it have, and what are their types?

Practice It   Now you can try these exercises at the end of the chapter: R7.10, P7.1, P7.2, P7.4.

Programming Tip 7.1

All Instance Variables Should Be Private; Most Methods Should Be Public

It is possible to declare instance variables as public, but you should not do that in your own code. Always use encapsulation, with private instance variables that are manipulated with methods.

Typically, methods are public. However, sometimes you have a method that is used only as a helper method by other methods. In that case, you can make the helper method private. Simply use the private reserved word when declaring the method.

7.5 Constructors

A constructor initializes the instance variables of an object.

The name of a constructor is the same as the class name.

A **constructor** is a method that initializes the instance variables of an object. The constructor is automatically called whenever an object is created with the new operator. By supplying a constructor, you ensure that all instance variables are properly set before any methods act on an object.

The name of a constructor is identical to the name of its class. For example:

```java
public class CashRegister
{
   . . .

   /**
      Constructs a cash register with cleared item count and total.
   */
   public CashRegister() // A constructor
   {
      itemCount = 0;
      totalPrice = 0;
   }
}
```

Constructors never return values, but you do not use the void reserved word when declaring them.

A class can have multiple constructors.

Many classes have more than one constructor. This allows you to declare objects in different ways. Consider for example a BankAccount class that has two constructors:

```java
public class BankAccount
{
   . . .

   /**
      Constructs a bank account with a zero balance.
   */
   public BankAccount() { . . . }

   /**
      Constructs a bank account with a given balance.
      @param initialBalance the initial balance
   */
   public BankAccount(double initialBalance) { . . . }
}
```

A constructor is like a set of assembly instructions for an object.

Syntax 7.3 Constructors

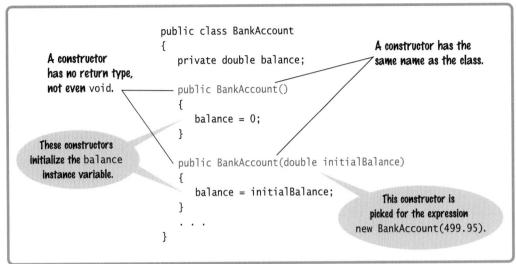

Both constructors have the same name as the class, BankAccount. The first constructor has no parameters, whereas the second constructor has a parameter of type double.

When you construct an object, the compiler chooses the constructor that matches the parameters that you supply. For example,

> The compiler picks the constructor that matches the construction parameters.

```
BankAccount joesAccount = new BankAccount();
    // Uses BankAccount() constructor
BankAccount lisasAccount = new BankAccount(499.95);
    // Uses BankAccount(double) constructor
```

If you do not initialize an instance variable in a constructor, it is automatically set to a default:

> By default, numbers are initialized as 0, Booleans as false, and object references as null.

- Numbers are set to zero.
- Boolean variables are initialized as false.
- Object and array references are set to the special value null that indicates that no object is associated with the variable (see Section 7.8). This is usually *not* desirable, and you should initialize object references in your constructors (see Common Error 7.1 on page 287).

In this regard, instance variables differ from local variables declared inside methods. The computer reports an error if you use a local variable that has not been explicitly initialized.

> If you do not provide a constructor, a constructor with no parameters is generated.

If you do not supply any constructor for a class, the compiler automatically generates a constructor. That constructor has no parameters, and it initializes all instance variables with their default values. Therefore, every class has at least one constructor.

You have now encountered all concepts that are necessary to implement the CashRegister class. The complete code for the class is given here. In the next section, you will see how to test the class.

ch07/register/CashRegister.java

```java
1   /**
2       A simulated cash register that tracks the item count and
3       the total amount due.
4   */
5   public class CashRegister
6   {
7       private int itemCount;
8       private double totalPrice;
9
10      /**
11          Constructs a cash register with cleared item count and total.
12      */
13      public CashRegister()
14      {
15          itemCount = 0;
16          totalPrice = 0;
17      }
18
19      /**
20          Adds an item to this cash register.
21          @param price the price of this item
22      */
23      public void addItem(double price)
24      {
25          itemCount++;
26          totalPrice = totalPrice + price;
27      }
28
29      /**
30          Gets the price of all items in the current sale.
31          @return the total amount
32      */
33      public double getTotal()
34      {
35          return totalPrice;
36      }
37
38      /**
39          Gets the number of items in the current sale.
40          @return the item count
41      */
42      public int getCount()
43      {
44          return itemCount;
45      }
46
47      /**
48          Clears the item count and the total.
49      */
50      public void clear()
51      {
52          itemCount = 0;
53          totalPrice = 0;
54      }
55  }
```

18. Consider this class:

```
public class Person
{
    private String name;

    public Person(String firstName, String lastName)
    {
        name = lastName + ", " + firstName;
    }
    . . .
}
```

If an object is constructed as

```
Person harry = new Person("Harry", "Morgan");
```

what is its `name` instance variable?

19. Provide an implementation for a `Person` constructor so that after the call

```
Person p = new Person();
```

the `name` instance variable of p is "unknown".

20. What happens if you supply no constructor for the `CashRegister` class?

21. Consider the following class:

```
public class Item
{
    private String description;
    private double price;

    public Item() { . . . }
    // Additional methods omitted
}
```

Provide an implementation for the constructor. Be sure that no instance variable is set to `null`.

22. Which constructors should be supplied in the `Item` class so that each of the following declarations compiles?

   a. `Item item2 = new Item("Corn flakes");`
   b. `Item item3 = new Item(3.95);`
   c. `Item item4 = new Item("Corn flakes", 3.95);`
   d. `Item item1 = new Item();`
   e. `Item item5;`

Practice It Now you can try these exercises at the end of the chapter: R7.12, P7.8, P7.10.

Common Error 7.1

Forgetting to Initialize Object References in a Constructor

Just as it is a common error to forget to initialize a local variable, it is easy to forget about instance variables. Every constructor needs to ensure that all instance variables are set to appropriate values.

If you do not initialize an instance variable, the Java compiler will initialize it for you. Numbers are initialized with 0, but object references—such as string variables—are set to the `null` reference.

Of course, 0 is often a convenient default for numbers. However, null is hardly ever a convenient default for objects. Consider this "lazy" constructor for a modified version of the BankAccount class:

```java
public class BankAccount
{
   private double balance;
   private String owner;
   . . .
   public BankAccount(double initialBalance)
   {
      balance = initialBalance;
   }
}
```

In this case, balance is initialized, but the owner variable is set to a null reference. This can be a problem—it is illegal to call methods on the null reference.

To avoid this problem, it is a good idea to initialize every instance variable:

```java
public BankAccount(double initialBalance)
{
   balance = initialBalance;
   owner = "None";
}
```

Common Error 7.2

Trying to Call a Constructor

There is only one way of invoking a constructor: through the new operator:

```java
CashRegister register1 = new CashRegister();
```

After an object has been constructed, you cannot invoke the constructor on that object again. For example, you cannot call the constructor to clear an object:

```java
   . . .
register1.CashRegister(); // Error
```

It is true that the constructor can set a *new* CashRegister object to the cleared state, but you cannot invoke a constructor on an *existing* object. However, you can *replace* the object with a new one:

```java
register1 = new CashRegister(); // OK
```

Common Error 7.3

Declaring a Constructor as void

Do not use the void reserved word when you declare a constructor:

```java
public void BankAccount()  // Error—don't use void!
```

This would declare a method with return type void and *not* a constructor. Unfortunately, the Java compiler does not consider this an error.

Special Topic 7.1

Overloading

When the same method name is used for more than one method, then the name is **overloaded**. In Java you can overload method names provided that the parameter types are different. For example, you can declare two methods, both called print:

```
void print(CashRegister register)
void print(BankAccount account)
```

When the print method is called,

```
print(x);
```

the compiler looks at the type of x. If x is a CashRegister object, the first method is called. If x is an BankAccount object, the second method is called. If x is neither, the compiler generates an error.

We have not used the overloading feature in this book. Instead, we gave each method a unique name, such as printRegister or printAccount. However, we have no choice with constructors. Java demands that the name of a constructor equal the name of the class. If a class has more than one constructor, then that name must be overloaded.

7.6 Testing a Class

In the preceding section, we completed the implementation of the CashRegister class. What can you do with it? Of course, you can compile the file CashRegister.java. However, you can't *execute* the CashRegister class. It doesn't contain a main method. That is normal—most classes don't contain a main method. They are meant to be combined with a class that has a main method.

> A unit test verifies that a class works correctly in isolation, outside a complete program.

In the long run, your class may become a part of a larger program that interacts with users, stores data in files, and so on. However, before integrating a class into a program, it is always a good idea to test it in isolation. Testing in isolation, outside a complete program, is called **unit testing**.

To test your class, you have two choices. Some interactive development environments (such as BlueJ, http://bluej.org, and Dr. Java, http://drjava.org) have commands for constructing objects and invoking methods. Then you can test a class

An engineer tests a part in isolation. This is an example of unit testing.

Figure 4
The Return Value of the
getTotal Method in BlueJ

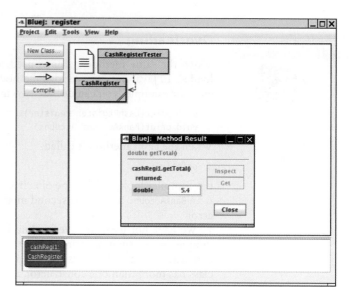

simply by constructing an object, calling methods, and verifying that you get the expected return values. Figure 4 shows the result of calling the getTotal method on a CashRegister object in BlueJ.

Alternatively, you can write a *tester class*. A tester class is a class with a main method that contains statements to run methods of another class. A tester class typically carries out the following steps:

To test a class, use an environment for interactive testing, or write a tester class to execute test instructions.

1. Construct one or more objects of the class that is being tested.

2. Invoke one or more methods.

3. Print out one or more results.

4. Print the expected results.

Here is a class to run methods of the CashRegister class. The main method constructs an object of type CashRegister, invokes the addItem method three times, and then displays the result of the getCount and getTotal methods.

ch07/register/CashRegisterTester.java

```java
1  /**
2      This program tests the CashRegister class.
3  */
4  public class CashRegisterTester
5  {
6      public static void main(String[] args)
7      {
8          CashRegister register1 = new CashRegister();
9          register1.addItem(1.95);
10         register1.addItem(0.95);
11         register1.addItem(2.50);
12         System.out.println(register1.getCount());
13         System.out.println("Expected: 3");
14         System.out.printf("%.2f\n", register1.getTotal());
15         System.out.println("Expected: 5.40");
16     }
17 }
```

Program Run

```
3
Expected: 3
5.40
Expected: 5.40
```

In our sample program, we add three items totaling $5.40. When displaying the method results, we also display messages that describe the values we expect to see.

This is a very important step. You want to spend some time thinking about what the expected result is before you run a test program. This thought process will help you understand how your program should behave, and it can help you track down errors at an early stage.

Determining the expected result in advance is an important part of testing.

To produce a program, you need to combine the CashRegister and the CashRegisterTester classes. The details for building the program depend on your compiler and development environment. In most environments, you need to carry out these steps:

1. Make a new subfolder for your program.
2. Make two files, one for each class.
3. Compile both files.
4. Run the test program.

Many students are surprised that such a simple program contains two classes. However, this is normal. The two classes have entirely different purposes. The CashRegister class describes objects that model cash registers. The CashRegisterTester class runs a test that puts a CashRegister object through its paces.

SELF CHECK

23. How would you enhance the tester class to test the clear method?

24. When you run the CashRegisterTester program, how many objects of class CashRegister are constructed? How many objects of type CashRegisterTester?

25. Why is the CashRegisterTester class unnecessary in development environments that allow interactive testing, such as BlueJ?

Practice It Now you can try these exercises at the end of the chapter: P7.9, P7.14, P7.17.

HOW TO 7.1   Implementing a Class

A very common task is to implement a class whose objects can carry out a set of specified actions. This How To walks you through the necessary steps.

As an example, consider a class Menu. An object of this class can display a menu such as

```
1) Open new account
2) Log into existing account
3) Help
4) Quit
```

Then the menu waits for the user to supply a value. If the user does not supply a valid value, the menu is redisplayed, and the user can try again.

Step 1   Get an informal list of the responsibilities of your objects.

Be careful that you restrict yourself to features that are actually required in the problem. With real-world items, such as cash registers or bank accounts, there are potentially dozens of features that might be worth implementing. But your job is not to faithfully model the real world. You need to determine only those responsibilities that you need for solving your specific problem.

In the case of the menu, you need to

Display the menu.
Get user input.

Now look for hidden responsibilities that aren't part of the problem description. How do objects get created? Which mundane activities need to happen, such as clearing the cash register at the beginning of each sale?

In the menu example, consider how a menu is produced. The programmer creates an empty menu object and then adds options "Open new account", "Help", and so on. That is another responsibility:

Add an option.

Step 2   Specify the public interface.

Turn the list in Step 1 into a set of methods, with specific types for the parameters and the return values. Many programmers find this step simpler if they write out method calls that are applied to a sample object, like this:

```
Menu mainMenu = new Menu();
mainMenu.addOption("Open new account");
// Add more options
int input = mainMenu.getInput();
```

Now we have a specific list of methods.

- `void addOption(String option)`

- `int getInput()`

What about displaying the menu? There is no sense in displaying the menu without also asking the user for input. However, getInput may need to display the menu more than once if the user provides a bad input. Thus, display is a good candidate for a private method.

To complete the public interface, you need to specify the constructors. Ask yourself what information you need in order to construct an object of your class. Sometimes you will want two constructors: one that sets all fields to a default and one that sets them to user-supplied values.

In the case of the menu example, we can get by with a single constructor that creates an empty menu.

Here is the public interface:

```
public class Menu
{
    public Menu() { . . . }
    public void addOption(String option) { . . . }
    public int getInput() { . . . }
}
```

Step 3   Document the public interface.

Supply a documentation comment for the class, then comment each method.

```
/**
    A menu that is displayed on a console.
*/
public class Menu
{
```

```
/**
    Constructs a menu with no options.
*/
public Menu() { . . . }

/**
    Adds an option to the end of this menu.
    @param option  the option to add
*/
public void addOption(String option) { . . . }

/**
    Displays the menu, with options numbered starting with 1,
    and prompts the user for input. Repeats until a valid input
    is supplied.
    @return  the number that the user supplied
*/
public int getInput() { . . . }
}
```

Step 4 Determine instance variables.

Ask yourself what information an object needs to store to do its job. The object needs to be able to process every method using just its instance variables and the method parameters.

Go through each method, perhaps starting with a simple one or an interesting one, and ask yourself what the object needs to carry out the method's task. Which data items are required in addition to the method parameters? Make instance variables for those data items.

In our example, let's start with the addOption method. We clearly need to store the added menu option so that the menu can be displayed later. How should we store the options? As an array list of strings? As one long string? Both approaches can be made to work. We will use an array list here. Exercise P7.5 asks you to implement the other approach.

```
public class Menu
{
    private ArrayList<String> options;
    . . .
}
```

Now consider the getInput method. It shows the stored options and reads an integer. When checking that the input is valid, we need to know the number of menu items. Because we store them in an array list, the number of menu items is simply obtained as the size of the array list. If you stored the menu items in one long string, you might want to keep another instance variable that stores the item count.

We will also need a scanner to read the user input, which we will add as another instance variable:

```
private Scanner in;
```

Step 5 Implement constructors and methods.

Implement the constructors and methods in your class, one at a time, starting with the easiest ones. For example, here is the implementation of the addOption method:

```
public void addOption(String option)
{
    options.add(option);
}
```

Here is the getInput method. This method is a bit more sophisticated. It loops until a valid input has been obtained, displaying the menu options before reading the input.

```
public int getInput()
{
```

```
      int input;
      do
      {
         for (int i = 0; i < options.size(); i++)
         {
            int choice = i + 1;
            System.out.println(choice + ") " + options.get(i));
         }
         input = in.nextInt();
      }
      while (input < 1 || input > options.size());
      return input;
   }
```

Finally, we need to supply a constructor to initialize the instance variables.

```
public Menu()
{
   options = new ArrayList<String>();
   in = new Scanner(System.in);
}
```

If you find that you have trouble with the implementation of some of your methods, you may need to rethink your choice of instance variables. It is common for a beginner to start out with a set of instance variables that cannot accurately describe the state of an object. Don't hesitate to go back and rethink your implementation strategy.

Once you have completed the implementation, compile your class and fix any compiler errors. (See ch07/menu/Menu.java in your book code for the completed class.)

Step 6   Test your class.

Write a short tester program and execute it. The tester program should carry out the method calls that you found in Step 2.

```
public class MenuTester
{
   public static void main(String[] args)
   {
      Menu mainMenu = new Menu();
      mainMenu.addOption("Open new account");
      mainMenu.addOption("Log into existing account");
      mainMenu.addOption("Help");
      mainMenu.addOption("Quit");
      int input = mainMenu.getInput();
      System.out.println("Input: " + input);
   }
}
```

Program Run

```
1) Open new account
2) Log into existing account
3) Help
4) Quit
5
1) Open new account
2) Log into existing account
3) Help
4) Quit
3
Input: 3
```

WORKED EXAMPLE 7.1 | **Implementing a Bank Account Class**

This Worked Example shows how to develop a class that simulates a bank account.

Random Fact 7.1 Electronic Voting Machines

In the 2000 presidential elections in the United States, votes were tallied by a variety of machines. Some machines processed cardboard ballots into which voters punched holes to indicate their choices. When voters were not careful, remains of paper—the now infamous "chads"—were partially stuck in the punch cards, causing votes to be miscounted. A manual recount was necessary, but it was not carried out everywhere due to time constraints and procedural wrangling. The election was very close, and there remain doubts in the minds of many people whether the election outcome would have been different if the voting machines had accurately counted the intent of the voters.

Punch Card Ballot

Subsequently, voting machine manufacturers have argued that electronic voting machines would avoid the problems caused by punch cards or optically scanned forms. In an electronic voting machine, voters indicate their preferences by pressing buttons or touching icons on a computer screen. Typically, each voter is presented with a summary screen for review before casting the ballot. The process is very similar to using an automatic bank teller machine.

It seems plausible that these machines make it more likely that a vote is counted in the same way that the voter intends. However, there has been significant controversy surrounding some types of electronic voting machines. If a machine simply records the votes and prints out the totals after the election has been completed, then how do you know that the machine worked correctly? Inside the machine is a computer that executes a program, and, as you may know from your own experience, programs can have bugs.

In fact, some electronic voting machines do have bugs. There have been isolated cases where machines reported tallies that were impossible. When a machine reports far more or far fewer votes than voters, then it is clear that it has malfunctioned. Unfortunately, it is then impossible to find out the actual votes. Over time, one would expect these bugs to be fixed in the software. More insidiously, if the results are plausible, nobody may ever investigate.

Many computer scientists have spoken out on this issue and confirmed that it is impossible, with today's technology, to tell that software is error free and has not been tampered with. Many of them recommend that electronic voting machines should employ a *voter-verifiable audit trail*. (A good source of information is http://verifiedvoting.org.) Typically, a voter-verifiable machine prints out a ballot. Each voter has a chance to review the printout, and then deposits it in an old-fashioned ballot box. If there is a problem with the electronic equipment, the printouts can be scanned or counted by hand.

What do you think? You probably use an automatic bank teller machine to get cash from your bank account. Do you review the paper record that the machine issues? Do you check your bank statement? Even if you don't, do you put your faith in other people who double-check their balances, so that the bank won't get away with widespread cheating?

Is the integrity of banking equipment more important or less important than that of voting machines? Won't every voting process have some room for error or fraud anyway? Is the added cost for equipment, paper, and staff time reasonable to combat a potentially slight risk of malfunction and fraud? Computer scientists cannot answer these questions—an informed society must make these tradeoffs. But, like all professionals, they have an obligation to speak out and give accurate testimony about the capabilities and limitations of computing equipment.

Touch Screen Voting Machine

Available online in WileyPLUS and at www.wiley.com/college/horstmann.

7.7 Discovering Classes

To discover classes, look for nouns in the problem description.

When you solve a problem using objects and classes, you need to determine the classes required for the implementation. You may be able to reuse existing classes, or you may need to implement new ones. One simple approach for discovering classes and methods is to look for the nouns and verbs in the problem description. Often, nouns correspond to classes, and verbs correspond to methods.

Concepts from the problem domain are good candidates for classes.

Concepts from the problem domain, be it science, business, or a game, often make good classes. Examples are

- Cannonball
- CashRegister
- Monster

The name for such a class should be a noun that describes the concept. Other frequently used classes represent system services such as files or menus.

What might not be a good class? If you can't tell from the class name what an object of the class is supposed to do, then you are probably not on the right track. For example, your homework assignment might ask you to write a program that prints paychecks. Suppose you start by trying to design a class PaycheckProgram. What would an object of this class do? An object of this class would have to do everything that the homework needs to do. That doesn't simplify anything. A better class would be Paycheck. Then your program can manipulate one or more Paycheck objects.

Another common mistake, often made by students who are used to writing programs that consist of methods, is to turn an action into a class. For example, if your homework assignment is to compute a paycheck, you may consider writing a class ComputePaycheck. But can you visualize a "ComputePaycheck" object? The fact that "ComputePaycheck" isn't a noun tips you off that you are on the wrong track. On the other hand, a Paycheck class makes intuitive sense. The word "paycheck" is a noun. You can visualize a paycheck object. You can then think about useful methods of the Paycheck class, such as computeTaxes, that help you solve the assignment.

When you analyze a problem description, you often find that you need multiple classes. It is then helpful to consider how these classes are related. One of the fundamental relationships between classes is the "aggregation" relationship (which is informally known as the "has-a" relationship).

In a class scheduling system, potential classes from the problem domain include Class, LectureHall, Instructor, and Student.

Figure 5 Class Diagram

A class aggregates another if its objects contain objects of the other class.

The **aggregation** relationship states that objects of one class contain objects of another class. Consider a quiz that is made up of questions. Because each quiz has one or more questions, we say that the class Quiz aggregates the class Question. There is a standard notation, called a UML (Unified Modeling Language) class diagram, to describe class relationships. In the UML notation, aggregation is denoted by a line with a diamond-shaped symbol (see Figure 5).

Finding out about aggregation is very helpful for deciding how to implement classes. For example, when you implement the Quiz class, you will want to store the questions of a quiz as an instance variable. Because a quiz can have any number of questions, an array list is a good choice for collecting them:

```java
public class Quiz
{
    private ArrayList<Question> questions;
    . . .
}
```

In summary, when you analyze a problem description, you will want to carry out these tasks:

- Find the concepts that you need to implement as classes. Often, these will be nouns in the problem description.
- Find the responsibilities of the classes. Often, these will be verbs in the problem description.
- Find relationships between the classes that you have discovered. In this section, we described the aggregation relationship. In Chapter 9, you will learn about another important relationship between classes, called inheritance.

A car has a motor and tires. In object-oriented design, this "has-a" relationship is called aggregation.

26. What is the rule of thumb for finding classes?

27. Your job is to write a program that plays chess. Might ChessBoard be an appropriate class? How about MovePiece?

28. In an e-mail system, messages are stored in a mailbox. Draw a UML diagram that shows the appropriate aggregation relationship.

29. You are implementing a system to manage a library, keeping track of which books are checked out by whom. Should the Book class aggregate Patron or the other way around?

30. In a library management system, what would be the relationship between classes Patron and Author?

Practice It Now you can try these exercises at the end of the chapter: R7.16, R7.19, P7.21.

Programming Tip 7.2

Make Parallel Arrays into Arrays of Objects

Sometimes, you find yourself using arrays or array lists of the same length, each of which stores a part of what conceptually should be an object. In that situation, it is a good idea to reorganize your program and use a single array or array list whose elements are objects.

For example, suppose an invoice contains a series of item descriptions and prices. One solution is to keep two arrays:

```
String[] descriptions;
double[] prices;
```

Each of the arrays will have the same length, and the ith *slice*, consisting of descriptions[i] and prices[i], contains data that needs to be processed together. These arrays are called **parallel arrays** (see Figure 6).

Parallel arrays become a headache in larger programs. The programmer must ensure that the arrays always have the same length and that each slice is filled with values that actually belong together. Moreover, any method that operates on a slice must get all values of the slice as parameters, which is tedious to program.

The remedy is simple. Look at the slice and find the *concept* that it represents. Then make the concept into a class. In this example, each slice contains the description and price of an *item*; turn this into a class.

```
public class Item
{
    private String description;
    private double price;
    . . .
}
```

Figure 6
Parallel Arrays

You can now eliminate the parallel arrays and replace them with a single array:

```
Item[] items;
```

Each slot in the resulting array corresponds to a slice in the set of parallel arrays (see Figure 7).

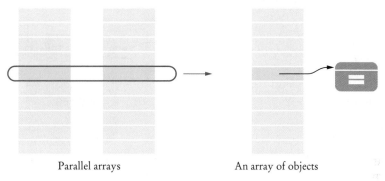

Parallel arrays   An array of objects

Figure 7 Eliminating Parallel Arrays

7.8 Object References

In Java, a variable whose type is a class does not actually hold an object. It merely holds the memory *location* of an object. The object itself is stored elsewhere—see Figure 8.

We use the technical term **object reference** to denote the memory location of an object. When a variable contains the memory location of an object, we say that it *refers* to an object. For example, after the statement

An object reference specifies the location of an object.

```
CashRegister reg1 = new CashRegister();
```

the variable reg1 refers to the CashRegister object that the new operator constructed. Technically speaking, the new operator returned a reference to the new object, and that reference is stored in the reg1 variable.

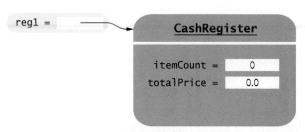

Figure 8 An Object Variable Containing an Object Reference

7.8.1 Shared References

Multiple object variables can contain references to the same object.

You can have two (or more) object variables that store references to the same object, for example by assigning one to the other.

```
CashRegister reg2 = reg1;
```

Now you can access the same CashRegister object both as reg1 and as reg2, as shown in Figure 9.

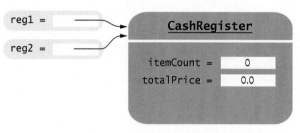

Figure 9 Two Object Variables Referring to the Same Object

Primitive type variables store values. Object variables store references.

In this regard, object variables differ from variables for primitive types (numbers, characters, and Boolean values). When you declare

```
int num1 = 0;
```

then the num1 variable holds the number 0, not a reference to the number (see Figure 10).

```
num1 =   0
```

Figure 10 A Variable of Type int Stores a Number

You can see the difference between primitive type variables and object variables when you make a copy of a variable. When you copy a number, the original and the copy of the number are independent values. But when you copy an object reference, both the original and the copy are references to the same object.

Consider the following code, which copies a number and then changes the copy (see Figure 11):

```
int num1 = 0;  ❶
int num2 = num1;  ❷
num2++;  ❸
```

Now the variable num1 contains the value 0, and num2 contains 1.

Now consider the seemingly analogous code with CashRegister objects (see Figure 12).

ANIMATION
Object References

```
CashRegister reg1 = new CashRegister();  ❶
CashRegister reg2 = reg1;  ❷
reg2.addItem(2.95);  ❸
```

Because reg1 and reg2 refer to the same cash register after step ❷, both variables now refer to a cash register with item count 1 and total price 2.95.

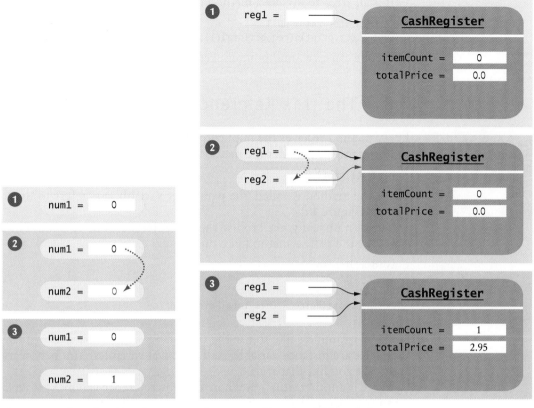

Figure 11 Copying Numbers   **Figure 12** Copying Object References

There is a reason for the difference between numbers and objects. In the computer, each number requires a small amount of memory. But objects can be very large. It is far more efficient to manipulate only the memory location.

7.8.2 The null Reference

The null reference refers to no object.

An object reference can have the special value null if it refers to no object at all. It is common to use the null value to indicate that a value has never been set. For example,

```
String middleInitial = null; // No middle initial
```

You use the == operator (and not equals) to test whether an object reference is a null reference:

```
if (middleInitial == null)
   System.out.println(firstName + " " + lastName);
else
   System.out.println(firstName + " " + middleInitial + ". " + lastName);
```

Note that the null reference is not the same as the empty string "". The empty string is a valid string of length 0, whereas a null indicates that a String variable refers to no string at all.

It is an error to invoke a method on a `null` reference. For example,

```
CashRegister reg = null;
System.out.println(reg.getTotal()); // Error—cannot invoke a method on null
```

This code causes a "null pointer exception" at run time.

7.8.3 The `this` Reference

In a method, the `this` reference refers to the implicit parameter.

Every method receives the implicit parameter in a variable called `this`.

For example, consider the method call

```
reg1.addItem(2.95);
```

When the method is called, the parameter variable `this` refers to the same object as `reg1` (see Figure 13).

You don't usually need to use the `this` reference, but you can. For example, you can write the `addItem` method like this:

```
void addItem(double price)
{
    this.itemCount++;
    this.totalPrice = this.totalPrice + price;
}
```

Some programmers like to use the `this` reference to make it clear that `itemCount` and `totalPrice` are instance variables and not local variables. You may want to try it out and see if you like that style.

There is another situation where the `this` reference can make your programs easier to read. Consider an instance method that calls another instance method *on the same object*. For example, the `CashRegister` constructor can call the `clear` method instead of duplicating its code:

```
public CashRegister()
{
    clear();
}
```

This call is easier to understand when you use the `this` reference:

```
public CashRegister()
{
    this.clear();
}
```

It is now more obvious that the method is invoked on the object that is being constructed.

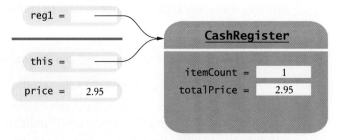

Figure 13 The Implicit Parameter of a Method Call

31. Suppose we have a variable

`String greeting = "Hello";`

What is the effect of this statement?

`String greeting2 = greeting;`

32. After calling `String greeting3 = greeting2.toUpperCase()`, what are the contents of `greeting` and `greeting2`?

33. What is the value of `s.length()` if `s` is

a. the empty string `""`?
b. `null`?

34. What is the type of `this` in the call `greeting.substring(1, 4)`?

35. Supply a method `addItems(int quantity, double price)` in the `CashRegister` class to add multiple instances of the same item. Your implementation should repeatedly call the `addItem` method. Use the `this` reference.

Practice It   Now you can try these exercises at the end of the chapter: R7.21, R7.22.

7.9 Static Variables and Methods

Sometimes, a value properly belongs to a class, not to any object of the class. You use a **static variable** for this purpose. Here is a typical example. We want to assign bank account numbers sequentially. That is, we want the bank account constructor to construct the first account with number 1001, the next with number 1002, and so on. To solve this problem, we need to have a single value of `lastAssignedNumber` that is a property of the *class*, not any object of the class. Such a variable is called a static variable, because you declare it using the static reserved word.

> A static variable belongs to the class, not to any object of the class.

```java
public class BankAccount
{
    private double balance;
    private int accountNumber;
    private static int lastAssignedNumber = 1000;

    public BankAccount()
    {
        lastAssignedNumber++;
        accountNumber = lastAssignedNumber;
    }
    . . .
}
```

The reserved word static *is a holdover from the C++ language. Its use in Java has no relationship to the normal use of the term.*

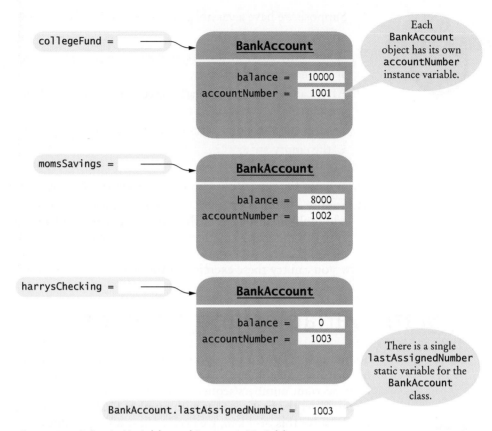

Figure 14 A Static Variable and Instance Variables

Every BankAccount object has its own balance and accountNumber instance variables, but there is only a single copy of the lastAssignedNumber variable (see Figure 14). That variable is stored in a separate location, outside any BankAccount objects.

Like instance variables, static variables should always be declared as private to ensure that methods of other classes do not change their values. The exception to this rule are static *constants*, which may be either private or public. For example, the BankAccount class can define a public constant value, such as

```java
public class BankAccount
{
    public static final double OVERDRAFT_FEE = 29.95;
    . . .
}
```

Methods from any class can refer to such a constant as BankAccount.OVERDRAFT_FEE.

Sometimes a class defines methods that are not invoked on an object. Such a method is called a **static method**. A typical example of a static method is the sqrt method in the Math class. Because numbers aren't objects, you can't invoke methods on them. For example, the call x.sqrt() can never be legal in Java. Therefore, the Math class provides a static method that is invoked as Math.sqrt(x). No object of the Math class is constructed. The Math qualifier simply tells the compiler where to find the sqrt method.

> A static method is not invoked on an object.

You can define your own static methods for use in other classes. Here is an example:

```java
public class Financial
{
    /**
       Computes a percentage of an amount.
       @param percentage the percentage to apply
       @param amount the amount to which the percentage is applied
       @return the requested percentage of the amount
    */
    public static double percentOf(double percentage, double amount)
    {
        return (percentage / 100) * amount;
    }
}
```

When calling this method, supply the name of the class containing it:

```java
double tax = Financial.percentOf(taxRate, total);
```

You had to use static methods in Chapter 5 before you knew how to implement your own objects. However, in object-oriented programming, static methods are not very common.

Nevertheless, the main method is always static. When the program starts, there aren't any objects. Therefore, the first method of a program must be a static method.

SELF CHECK

36. Name two static variables of the System class.

37. Name a static constant of the Math class.

38. The following method computes the average of an array of numbers:

```java
public static double average(double[] values)
```

Why should it not be defined as an instance method?

39. Harry tells you that he has found a great way to avoid those pesky objects: Put all code into a single class and declare all methods and variables static. Then main can call the other static methods, and all of them can access the static variables. Will Harry's plan work? Is it a good idea?

Practice It   Now you can try these exercises at the end of the chapter: P7.23, P7.24.

7.10 Packages

A Java program consists of a collection of classes. So far, most of your programs have consisted of a small number of classes. As programs get larger, however, simply distributing the classes over multiple files isn't enough. An additional structuring mechanism is needed.

A package is a set of related classes.

In Java, packages provide this structuring mechanism. A Java **package** is a set of related classes. For example, the Java library consists of dozens of packages, some of which are listed in Table 1. The following sections show how you can make use of packages in your programs.

Table 1	Important Packages in the Java Library	
Package	Purpose	Sample Class
`java.lang`	Language support	`Math`
`java.util`	Utilities	`Scanner`
`java.io`	Input and output	`PrintStream`
`java.awt`	Abstract Windowing Toolkit	`Color`
`java.applet`	Applets	`Applet`
`java.net`	Networking	`Socket`
`java.sql`	Database access through Structured Query Language	`ResultSet`
`javax.swing`	Swing user interface	`JButton`
`omg.w3c.dom`	Document Object Model for XML documents	`Document`

7.10.1 Organizing Related Classes into Packages

To put a class in a package, you must place

package *packageName*;

as the first statement in its source file. A package name consists of one or more identifiers separated by periods. (See Section 7.10.3 for tips on constructing package names.)

For example, let's put the `CashRegister` class introduced in this chapter into a package named `com.horstmann`. The `CashRegister.java` file must start as follows:

```
package com.horstmann;

public class CashRegister
{
   . . .
}
```

In Java, related classes are grouped into packages.

In addition to the named packages (such as java.util or com.horstmann), there is a special package, called the *default package*, which has no name. If you did not include any package statement at the top of your source file, its classes are placed in the default package.

7.10.2 Importing Packages

If you want to use a class from a package, you can refer to it by its full name (package name plus class name). For example, java.util.Scanner refers to the Scanner class in the java.util package:

```
java.util.Scanner in = new java.util.Scanner(System.in);
```

Naturally, that is somewhat inconvenient. You can instead *import* a name with an import statement:

```
import java.util.Scanner;
```

Then you can refer to the class as Scanner without the package prefix.

You can import *all classes* of a package with an import statement that ends in .*. For example, you can use the statement

```
import java.util.*;
```

to import all classes from the java.util package. That statement lets you refer to classes like Scanner or ArrayList without a java.util prefix.

However, you never need to import the classes in the java.lang package explicitly. That is the package containing the most basic Java classes, such as Math and Object. These classes are always available to you. In effect, an automatic import java.lang.*; statement has been placed into every source file.

Finally, you don't need to import other classes in the same package. For example, when you implement the class problem1.Tester, you don't need to import the class problem1.BankAccount. The compiler will find the BankAccount class without an import statement because it is located in the same package, problem1.

> The import directive lets you refer to a class from a package by its class name, without the package prefix.

7.10.3 Package Names

Placing related classes into a package is clearly a convenient mechanism to organize classes. However, there is a more important reason for packages: to avoid **name clashes**. In a large project, it is inevitable that two people will come up with the same name for the same concept. This even happens in the standard Java class library (which has now grown to thousands of classes). There is a class Timer in the java.util package and another class called Timer in the javax.swing package. You can still tell the Java compiler exactly which Timer class you need, simply by referring to them as java.util.Timer and javax.swing.Timer.

Of course, for the package-naming convention to work, there must be some way to ensure that package names are unique. It wouldn't be good if the car maker BMW placed all its Java code into the package bmw, and some other programmer (perhaps Britney M. Walters) had the same bright idea. To avoid this problem, the inventors of Java recommend that you use a package-naming scheme that takes advantage of the uniqueness of Internet domain names.

> Use a domain name in reverse to construct an unambiguous package name.

For example, I have a domain name horstmann.com, and there is nobody else on the planet with the same domain name. (I was lucky that the domain name horstmann.com had not been taken by anyone else when I applied. If your name is Walters, you will sadly find that someone else beat you to walters.com.) To get a package name, turn the domain name around to produce a package name prefix, such as com.horstmann.

If you don't have your own domain name, you can still create a package name that has a high probability of being unique by writing your e-mail address backwards. For example, if Britney Walters has an e-mail address walters@cs.sjsu.edu, then she can use a package name edu.sjsu.cs.walters for her own classes.

Some instructors will want you to place each of your assignments into a separate package, such as problem1, problem2, and so on. The reason is again to avoid name collision. You can have two classes, problem1.BankAccount and problem2.BankAccount, with slightly different properties.

7.10.4 How Classes Are Located

> The path of a class file must match its package name.

A package is located in a subdirectory that matches the package name. For example, a package homework1 is located in a directory homework1. If the package name has multiple parts, such as com.horstmann.javabook, then you use a subdirectory for each part: com/horstmann/javabook.

For example, if you do your homework assignment in a *base directory* /home/britney/assignments, then you can place the class files for the problem1 package into the directory /home/britney/assignments/problem1, as shown in Figure 15. (Here, we are using UNIX-style file names. Under Windows, you would use a directory such as c:\Users\Britney\assignments\problem1.)

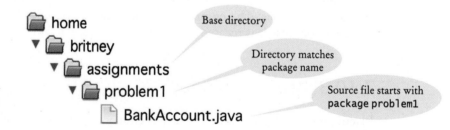

Figure 15
Base Directories
and Subdirectories
for Packages

SELF CHECK

40. Which of the following are packages?
    a. java
    b. java.lang
    c. java.util
    d. java.lang.Math

41. Is a Java program without import statements limited to using the default and java.lang packages?

42. Suppose your homework assignments are located in the directory /home/me/cs101 (c:\Users\me\cs101 on Windows). Your instructor tells you to place your

homework into packages. In which directory do you place the class `hw1.problem1.TicTacToeTester`?

Practice It Now you can try these exercises at the end of the chapter: P7.25, P7.26.

Random Fact 7.2 Open Source and Free Software

Most companies that produce software regard the source code as a trade secret. After all, if customers or competitors had access to the source code, they could study it and create similar programs without paying the original vendor. For the same reason, customers dislike secret source code. If a company goes out of business or decides to discontinue support for a computer program, its users are left stranded. They are unable to fix bugs or adapt the program to a new operating system.

Nowadays, some software packages are distributed with "open source" or "free software" licenses. Here, the term "free" doesn't refer to price, but to the freedom to inspect and modify the source code. Richard Stallman, a famous computer scientist and winner of a MacArthur "genius" grant, pioneered the concept of free software. He is the inventor of the Emacs text editor and the originator of the GNU project that aims to create an entirely free version of a UNIX-compatible operating system. All programs of the GNU project are licensed under the General Public License, or GPL. The GPL allows you to make as many copies as you wish, make any modifications to the source, and redistribute the original and modified programs, charging nothing at all or whatever the market will bear. In return, you

must agree that your modifications also fall under the GPL. If you produce an enhanced version, you must include the source code and allow anyone else to make use of your enhancements. The GPL, and similar open source licenses, form a social contract. Users of the software enjoy the freedom to use and modify the software, and in return they are obligated to share any improvements that they make. Many programs, such as the Linux operating system and the GNU C++ compiler, are distributed under the GPL.

Some commercial software vendors have attacked the GPL as "viral" and "undermining the commercial software sector". Other companies have a more nuanced strategy, producing proprietary software while also contributing to open source projects.

Frankly, open source is not a panacea and there is plenty of room for the commercial software sector. Open source software often lacks the polish of commercial software because many of the programmers are volunteers who are interested in solving their own problems, not in making a product that is easy to use by others. Some product categories are not available at all as open source software because the development work is unattractive when there is little promise of commercial gain. Open source software has been most successful in areas that

are of interest to programmers, such as the Linux operating system, web servers, and programming tools.

On the positive side, the open software community can be very competitive and creative. It is quite common to see several competing projects that take ideas from each other, all rapidly becoming more capable. Having many programmers involved, all reading the source code, often means that bugs get squashed quickly. Eric Raymond describes open source development in his famous article "The Cathedral and the Bazaar" (http://catb.org/~esr/writings/cathedral-bazaar/cathedral-bazaar/index.html). He writes, "Given enough eyeballs, all bugs are shallow."

Richard Stallman, a pioneer of the free source movement.

SCREENCAST 7.1 **Paying Off a Loan**

When you take out a loan, the bank tells you how much you need to pay and for how long. Where do these numbers come from? This Screencast Video uses a Loan object to demonstrate how a loan is paid off.

➕ Available online in WileyPLUS and at www.wiley.com/college/horstmann.

CHAPTER SUMMARY

- A class describes a set of objects with the same behavior.
  - Use the new operator to construct objects from a class.
  - Methods that are invoked on objects are called instance methods.
  - Every class has a public interface: a collection of methods through which the objects of the class can be manipulated.

  - Encapsulation is the act of providing a public interface and hiding the implementation details.

- Encapsulation enables changes in the implementation without affecting users of a class.

- A mutator method changes the object on which it operates.
- An accessor method does not change the object on which it operates.

- An object holds instance variables that are accessed by methods.
- Every object has its own set of instance variables.
- Private instance variables can only be accessed by methods of the same class.

- The object on which a method is applied is the implicit parameter.
- Explicit parameters of a method are listed in the method declaration.

- A constructor initializes the instance variables of an object.
- The name of a constructor is the same as the class name.
- A class can have multiple constructors.
- The compiler picks the constructor that matches the construction parameters.
- By default, numbers are initialized as 0, Booleans as false, and object references as null.
- If you do not provide a constructor, a constructor with no parameters is generated.

- A unit test verifies that a class works correctly in isolation, outside a complete program.
  - To test a class, use an environment for interactive testing, or write a tester class to execute test instructions.
  - Determining the expected result in advance is an important part of testing.

- To discover classes, look for nouns in the problem description.
- Concepts from the problem domain are good candidates for classes.

- A class aggregates another if its objects contain objects of the other class.
- Avoid parallel arrays by changing them into arrays of objects.

- An object reference specifies the location of an object.
- Multiple object variables can contain references to the same object.
- Primitive type variables store values. Object variables store references.
- The `null` reference refers to no object.
- In a method, the `this` reference refers to the implicit parameter.

- A static variable belongs to the class, not to any object of the class.
  - A static method is not invoked on an object.

- A package is a set of related classes.
- The `import` directive lets you refer to a class from a package by its class name, without the package prefix.
- Use a domain name in reverse to construct an unambiguous package name.
- The path of a class file must match its package name.

MEDIA RESOURCES

www.wiley.com/
college/
horstmann

- ***Worked Example*** Implementing a Bank Account Class
- Guided Lab Exercises
- ⊕ ***Animation*** Object References
- ⊕ ***Screencast*** Paying Off a Loan
- ⊕ Practice Quiz
- ⊕ Code Completion Exercises

REVIEW EXERCISES

★   **R7.1** What is encapsulation? Why is it useful?

★   **R7.2** What value is returned by the calls `reg1.getCount()`, `reg1.getTotal()`, `reg2.getCount()`, and `reg2.getTotal()` after these statements?

```
CashRegister reg1 = new CashRegister();
reg1.addItem(3.25);
reg1.addItem(1.95);
CashRegister reg2 = new CashRegister();
reg2.addItem(3.25);
reg2.clear();
```

★ **R7.3** Consider the Menu class in How To 7.1 on page 291. What is displayed when the following calls are executed?

```
Menu simpleMenu = new Menu();
simpleMenu.addOption("Ok");
simpleMenu.addOption("Cancel");
int response = simpleMenu.getInput();
```

★ **R7.4** What is the *public interface* of a class? How does it differ from the *implementation* of a class?

★★ **R7.5** Suppose the CashRegister needs to keep track of taxable and nontaxable items. Suppose the addItem method adds a tax-free item and the addTaxableItem method adds a taxable item. The getTotal method should apply sales tax to the taxable items. What instance variables should the modified CashRegister class have?

★★★ **R7.6** Suppose the CashRegister needs to support a method void undo() that undoes the addition of the preceding item. This enables a cashier to quickly undo a mistake. What instance variables should you add to the CashRegister class to support this modification?

★ **R7.7** What is an instance method, and how does it differ from a static method?

★ **R7.8** What is a mutator method? What is an accessor method?

★ **R7.9** What is an implicit parameter? How does it differ from an explicit parameter?

★ **R7.10** How many implicit parameters can an instance method have? How many implicit parameters can a static method have? How many explicit parameters can an instance method have?

★ **R7.11** What is a constructor?

★ **R7.12** How many constructors can a class have? Can you have a class with no constructors? If a class has more than one constructor, which of them gets called?

★★★ **R7.13** Instance variables are "hidden" by declaring them as private, but they aren't hidden very well at all. Anyone can read the class declaration. Explain to what extent the private reserved word hides the private implementation of a class.

★★★ **R7.14** You can read the itemCount instance variable of the CashRegister class with the getCount accessor method. Should there be a setCount mutator method to change it? Explain why or why not.

★★★ **R7.15** In a static method, it is easy to differentiate between calls to instance methods and calls to static methods. How do you tell them apart? Why is it not as easy for methods that are called from an instance method?

★★ **R7.16** Consider the following problem description:

> Users place coins in a vending machine and select a product by pushing a button. If the inserted coins are sufficient to cover the purchase price of the product, the product is dispensed and change is given. Otherwise, the inserted coins are returned to the user.

What classes should you use to implement a solution?

★★ **R7.17** Consider the following problem description:

> Employees receive their biweekly paychecks. They are paid their hourly rates for each hour worked; however, if they worked more than 40 hours per week, they are paid overtime at 150 percent of their regular wage.

What classes should you use to implement a solution?

★★ **R7.18** Consider the following problem description:

> Customers order products from a store. Invoices are generated to list the items and quantities ordered, payments received, and amounts still due. Products are shipped to the shipping address of the customer, and invoices are sent to the billing address.

What classes should you use to implement a solution?

★★ **R7.19** Suppose a vending machine contains products, and users insert coins into the vending machine to purchase products. Draw a UML diagram showing the aggregation relationships between the classes VendingMachine, Coin, and Product.

★★ **R7.20** Suppose an Invoice object contains descriptions of the products ordered, and the billing and shipping addresses of the customer. Draw a UML diagram showing the aggregation relationships between the classes Invoice, Address, Customer, and Product.

★★ **R7.21** What is the this reference? Why would you use it?

★★ **R7.22** What is the the difference between the number zero, the null reference, the value false, and the empty string?

PROGRAMMING EXERCISES

★★ **P7.1** Reimplement the CashRegister class so that it keeps track of the price of each added item in an ArrayList<Double>. Remove the itemCount and totalPrice instance variables. Reimplement the clear, addItem, getTotal, and getCount methods. Add a method displayAll that displays the prices of all items in the current sale.

★★ **P7.2** Reimplement the CashRegister class so that it keeps track of the total price as an integer: the total cents of the price. For example, instead of storing 17.29, store the integer 1729. Such an implementation is commonly used because it avoids the accumulation of roundoff errors. Do not change the public interface of the class.

★★ **P7.3** Add a feature to the CashRegister class for computing sales tax. The tax rate should be supplied when constructing a CashRegister object. Add addTaxableItem and getTotalTax methods. (Items added with addItem are not taxable.)

★★ **P7.4** After closing time, the store manager would like to know how much business was transacted during the day. Modify the CashRegister class to enable this functionality. Supply methods getSalesTotal and getSalesCount to get the total amount of all sales and the number of sales. Supply a method resetSales that resets any counters and totals so that the next day's sales start from zero.

★★★ **P7.5** Reimplement the Menu class so that it stores all menu items in one long string. *Hint:* Keep a separate counter for the number of options. When a new option is added, append the option count, the option, and a newline character.

★★ **P7.6** Implement a class Address. An address has a house number, a street, an optional apartment number, a city, a state, and a postal code. Supply two constructors: one with an apartment number and one without. Supply a print method that prints the address with the street on one line and the city, state, and postal code on the next line. Supply a method public boolean comesBefore (Address other) that tests whether this address comes before another when the addresses are compared by postal code.

★★ **P7.7** Implement a class Portfolio. This class has two objects, checking and savings, of the type BankAccount that was developed in Worked Example 7.1 (ch07/account/Bank-Account.java in your code files). Implement four methods:

```
public void deposit(double amount, String account)
public void withdraw(double amount, String account)
public void transfer(double amount, String account)
public void printBalances()
```

Here the account string is "S" or "C". For the deposit or withdrawal, it indicates which account is affected. For a transfer, it indicates the account from which the money is taken; the money is automatically transferred to the other account.

★ **P7.8** Implement a class SodaCan with methods getSurfaceArea() and get-Volume(). In the constructor, supply the height and radius of the can.

★★ **P7.9** Implement a class Car with the following properties. A car has a certain fuel efficiency (measured in miles/gallon) and a certain amount of fuel in the gas tank. The efficiency is specified in the constructor, and the initial fuel level is 0. Supply a method drive that simulates driving the car for a certain distance, reducing the fuel level in the gas tank, and methods getGasLevel, to return the current fuel level, and addGas, to tank up. Sample usage:

```
Car myHybrid = new Car(50); // 50 miles per gallon
myHybrid.addGas(20); // Tank 20 gallons
myHybrid.drive(100); // Drive 100 miles
System.out.println(myHybrid.getGasLevel()); // Print fuel remaining
```

★★ **P7.10** Implement a class Student. For the purpose of this exercise, a student has a name and a total quiz score. Supply an appropriate constructor and methods getName(), addQuiz(int score), getTotalScore(), and getAverageScore(). To compute the latter, you also need to store the *number of quizzes* that the student took.

★★ **P7.11** Modify the Student class of Exercise P7.10 to compute grade point averages. Methods are needed to add a grade and get the current GPA. Specify grades as elements of a class Grade. Supply a constructor that constructs a grade from a string, such as "B+". You will also need a method that translates grades into their numeric values (for example, "B+" becomes 3.3).

★★★ **P7.12** Declare a class ComboLock that works like the combination lock in a gym locker, as shown here. The lock is constructed with a combination—three numbers between 0 and 39. The reset method resets the dial so that it points to 0. The turnLeft and turnRight methods turn the dial by a given number of ticks to the left or right. The open method attempts to open the lock. The lock opens if the user first turned it right to the first number in the combination, then left to the second, and then right to the third.

```
public class ComboLock
{
    . . .
    public ComboLock(int secret1, int secret2, int secret3) { . . . }
    public void reset() { . . . }
    public void turnLeft(int ticks) { . . . }
    public void turnRight(int ticks) { . . . }
    public boolean open() { . . . }
}
```

★★ **P7.13** Declare a class Country that stores the name of the country, its population, and its area. Using that class, write a program that reads in a set of countries and prints

- The country with the largest area.
- The country with the largest population.
- The country with the largest population density (people per square kilometer (or mile)).

★★ **P7.14** Design a class Message that models an e-mail message. A message has a recipient, a sender, and a message text. Support the following methods:

- A constructor that takes the sender and recipient
- A method append that appends a line of text to the message body
- A method toString that makes the message into one long string like this: "From: Harry Morgan\nTo: Rudolf Reindeer\n . . ."

Write a program that uses this class to make a message and print it.

★★ **P7.15** Design a class Mailbox that stores e-mail messages, using the Message class of Exercise P7.14.

Implement the following methods:

```
public void addMessage(Message m)
public Message getMessage(int i)
public void removeMessage(int i)
```

★★ **P7.16** Implement a VotingMachine class that can be used for a simple election. Have methods to clear the machine state, to vote for a Democrat, to vote for a Republican, and to get the tallies for both parties. Extra credit if your program gives the nod to your favored party if the votes are tallied after 8 P.M. on the first Tuesday in November, but acts normally on all other dates. (*Hint:* Use the GregorianCalendar class to get the current date.)

★★ **P7.17** Provide a class for authoring a simple letter. In the constructor, supply the names of the sender and the recipient:

```
public Letter(String from, String to)
```

Supply a method

```
public void addLine(String line)
```

to add a line of text to the body of the letter. Supply a method

```
public String getText()
```

that returns the entire text of the letter. The text has the form:

Dear *recipient name*:
blank line
first line of the body

second line of the body
. . .
last line of the body
blank line
Sincerely,
blank line
sender name

Also supply a main method that prints this letter.

```
Dear John:

I am sorry we must part.
I wish you all the best.

Sincerely,

Mary
```

Construct an object of the Letter class and call addLine twice.

★★ **P7.18** Write a class Bug that models a bug moving along a horizontal line. The bug moves either to the right or left. Initially, the bug moves to the right, but it can turn to change its direction. In each move, its position changes by one unit in the current direction. Provide a constructor

```
public Bug(int initialPosition)
```

and methods

```
public void turn()
public void move()
public int getPosition()
```

Sample usage:

```
Bug bugsy = new Bug(10);
bugsy.move(); // Now the position is 11
bugsy.turn();
bugsy.move(); // Now the position is 10
```

Your main method should construct a bug, make it move and turn a few times, and print the actual and expected positions.

★★ **P7.19** Implement a class Moth that models a moth flying in a straight line. The moth has a position, the distance from a fixed origin. When the moth moves toward a point of light, its new position is halfway between its old position and the position of the light source. Supply a constructor

```
public Moth(double initialPosition)
```

and methods

```
public void moveToLight(double lightPosition)
public void getPosition()
```

Your main method should construct a moth, move it toward a couple of light sources, and check that the moth's position is as expected.

★★★ **P7.20** Design a class Cannonball to model a cannonball that is fired into the air. A ball has

- An x- and a y-position.
- An x- and a y-velocity.

Supply the following methods:

- A constructor with an x-position (the y-position is initially 0)
- A method `move(double sec)` that moves the ball to the next position (First compute the distance traveled in sec seconds, using the current velocities, then update the x- and y-positions; then update the y-velocity by taking into account the gravitational acceleration of -9.81 m/sec^2; the x-velocity is unchanged.) (See Exercise P4.22 for additional details.)
- Methods `getX` and `getY` that get the current location of the cannonball
- A method `shoot` whose parameters are the angle α and initial velocity v (Compute the x-velocity as $v \cos \alpha$ and the y-velocity as $v \sin \alpha$; then keep calling `move` with a time interval of 0.1 seconds until the y-position is 0; call `getX` and `getY` after every move and display the position.)

Use this class in a program that prompts the user for the starting angle and the initial velocity. Then call `shoot`.

★★★ **P7.21** Write a program that simulates a vending machine. Supply a user interface for showing the products available for sale, paying and receiving change, and restocking the machine. Your solution should include a class `VendingMachine` and a class `Product`.

★★★ **P7.22** Design and implement a simple e-mail messaging system. A message has a recipient, a sender, and a message text. A mailbox can store messages. Supply a number of mailboxes for different users and a user interface for users to log in, send messages to other users, read their own messages, and log out. Use classes `Message`, `Mailbox`, and `MailSystem` in your solution.

★★ **P7.23** Write static methods
- `public static double sphereVolume(double r)`
- `public static double sphereSurface(double r)`
- `public static double cylinderVolume(double r, double h)`
- `public static double cylinderSurface(double r, double h)`
- `public static double coneVolume(double r, double h)`
- `public static double coneSurface(double r, double h)`

that compute the volume and surface area of a sphere with radius r, a cylinder with circular base with radius r and height h, and a cone with circular base with radius r and height h. Place them into a class `Geometry`. Then write a program that prompts the user for the values of r and h, calls the six methods, and prints the results.

★★ **P7.24** Solve Exercise P7.23 by implementing classes `Sphere`, `Cylinder`, and `Cone`. Which approach is more object-oriented?

★ **P7.25** Place the `CashRegister` class into the package `com.horstmann`. Keep the `CashRegister-Tester` class in the default package.

★ **P7.26** Place the `BankAccount` class from Worked Example 7.1 in a package whose name is derived from your e-mail address, as described in Section 7.10. Keep the `BankAccountTester` class in the default package.

ANSWERS TO SELF-CHECK QUESTIONS

1. Through the substring and charAt methods.
2. As an ArrayList<Character>. As a char array.
3. None. The methods will have the same effect, and your code could not have manipulated String objects in any other way.
4.
```
PrintWriter out1 = new PrintWriter("output1.txt");
PrintWriter out2 = new PrintWriter("output2.txt");
```
5. 2 1.90
6. There is no method named getAmountDue.
7. `int getDollars();`
8. length, substring. In fact, *all* methods of the String class are accessors.
9. A mutator. Getting the next number removes it from the input, thereby modifying it. Not convinced? Consider what happens if you call the nextInt method twice. You will usually get two different numbers. But if you call an accessor twice on an object (without a mutation between the two calls), you are sure to get the same result.
10. The code tries to access a private instance variable.
11. (1)
```
int hours; // Between 1 and 12
int minutes; // Between 0 and 59
boolean pm; // True for P.M., false for A.M.
```
   (2)
```
int hours; // Military time, between 0 and 23
int minutes; // Between 0 and 59
```
   (3)
```
int totalMinutes // Between 0 and 60 * 24 - 1
```
12. They need not change their programs at all because the public interface has not changed. They need to recompile with the new version of the Time class.
13. (1) `String letterGrade; // "A+", "B"`
    (2) `double numberGrade; // 4.3, 3.0`
14. 2 1.85 1 1.90
15.
```
public int getDollars()
{
    int dollars = (int) totalPrice; // Truncates cents
    return dollars;
}
```
16. Three parameters: two explicit parameters of type int, and one implicit parameter of type String.
17. One parameter: the implicit parameter of type String. The method has no explicit parameters.
18. `"Morgan, Harry"`
19. `public Person() { name = "unknown"; }`
20. A constructor is generated that has the same effect as the constructor provided in this section. It sets both instance variables to zero.
21.
```
public Item()
{
```

```
    price = 0;
    description = "";
}
```

The price instance variable need not be initialized because it is set to zero by default, but it is clearer to initialize it explicitly.

22. (a) Item(String) (b) Item(double) (c) Item(String, double)
    (d) Item() (e) No constructor has been called.

23. Add these lines:

```
register1.clear();
System.out.println(register1.getCount());
System.out.println("Expected: 0");
System.out.printf("%.2f\n", register1.getTotal());
System.out.println("Expected: 0.00");
```

24. 1, 0

25. These environments allow you to call methods on an object without creating a main method.

26. Look for nouns in the problem description.

27. Yes (ChessBoard) and no (MovePiece).

28.

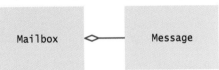

29. Typically, a library system wants to track which books a patron has checked out, so it makes more sense to have Patron aggregate Book. However, there is not always one true answer in design. If you feel strongly that it is important to identify the patron who had checked out a particular book (perhaps to notify the patron to return it because it was requested by someone else), then you can argue that the aggregation should go the other way around.

30. There would be no relationship.

31. Both greeting and greeting2 refer to the same string "Hello".

32. They both still refer to the string "Hello". The toUpperCase method computes the string "HELLO", but it is not a mutator—the original string is unchanged.

33. (a) 0
    (b) A null pointer exception is thrown.

34. It is a reference of type String.

35.
```
public void addItems(int quantity, double price)
{
    for (int i = 1; i <= quantity; i++)
    {
        this.addItem(price);
    }
}
```

36. System.in and System.out

37. Math.PI

38. The method needs no data of any object. The only required input is the values parameter.

39. Yes, it works. Static methods can call each other and access static variables—any method can. But it is a terrible idea. A program that consists of a single class with many methods is hard to understand.

40. (a) No; (b) Yes; (c) Yes; (d) No

41. No—you simply use fully qualified names for all other classes, such as `java.util.Random` and `java.awt.Rectangle`.

42. `/home/me/cs101/hw1/problem1` or, on Windows, `c:\Users\me\cs101\hw1\problem1`.

CHAPTER 8

INPUT/OUTPUT AND EXCEPTION HANDLING

CHAPTER GOALS

To be able to read and write text files

To process command line arguments

To learn how to throw and catch exceptions

To understand the difference between checked and unchecked exceptions

CHAPTER CONTENTS

In this chapter, you will learn how to read and write files—a very useful skill for processing real world data. As an application, you will learn how to encrypt data. (The Enigma machine shown at left is an encryption device used by Germany in World War II. Pioneering British computer scientists broke the code and were able to intercept encoded messages, which was a significant help in winning the war.) The remainder of this chapter tells you how your programs can report and recover from exceptional conditions (such as missing files or malformed content).

8.1 Reading and Writing Text Files

We begin this chapter by discussing the common task of reading and writing files that contain text. Examples of text files include not only files that are created with a simple text editor, such as Windows Notepad, but also Java source code and HTML files.

Use the Scanner class for reading text files.

In Java, the most convenient mechanism for reading text is to use the Scanner class. You already know how to use a Scanner for reading console input. To read input from a disk file, the Scanner class relies on another class, File, which describes disk files and directories. (The File class has many methods that we do not discuss in this book; for example, methods that delete or rename a file.)

To begin, construct a File object with the name of the input file:

```
File inputFile = new File("input.txt");
```

Then use the File object to construct a Scanner object:

```
Scanner in = new Scanner(inputFile);
```

This Scanner object reads text from the file input.txt. You can use the Scanner methods (such as next, nextLine, nextInt, and nextDouble) to read data from the input file.

For example, you can use the following loop to process all lines in the file:

```
while (in.hasNextLine())
{
    String line = in.nextLine();
    Process line
}
```

When writing text files, use the PrintWriter class and the print/ println/printf methods.

To write output to a file, you construct a PrintWriter object with the given file name, for example

```
PrintWriter out = new PrintWriter("output.txt");
```

If the output file already exists, it is emptied before the new data are written into it. If the file doesn't exist, an empty file is created.

The PrintWriter class is an enhancement of the PrintStream class that you already know—System.out is a PrintStream object. You can use the familiar print, println, and printf methods with any PrintWriter object:

```
out.println("Hello, World!");
out.printf("Total: %8.2f\n", totalPrice);
```

Close all files when you are done processing them.

When you are done processing a file, be sure to *close* the `Scanner` or `PrintWriter`:

```
in.close();
out.close();
```

If your program exits without closing the `PrintWriter`, some of the output may not be written to the disk file.

The following program puts these concepts to work. It reads all lines of an input file and sends them to the output file, preceded by *line numbers*. If the input file is

```
Mary had a little lamb
Whose fleece was white as snow.
And everywhere that Mary went,
The lamb was sure to go!
```

then the program produces the output file

```
/* 1 */ Mary had a little lamb
/* 2 */ Whose fleece was white as snow.
/* 3 */ And everywhere that Mary went,
/* 4 */ The lamb was sure to go!
```

The line numbers are enclosed in `/*  */` delimiters so that the program can be used for numbering Java source files.

There is one additional issue that we need to tackle. If the input or output file for a `Scanner` doesn't exist, a `FileNotFoundException` occurs when the `Scanner` object is constructed. The compiler insists that we specify what the program should do when that happens. Similarly, the `PrintWriter` constructor generates this exception if it cannot open the file for writing. (This can happen if the name is illegal or the user does not have the authority to create a file in the given location.) In our sample program, we want to terminate the `main` method if the exception occurs. To achieve this, we label the `main` method with a `throws` declaration:

```
public static void main(String[] args) throws FileNotFoundException
```

You will see in Section 8.4 how to deal with exceptions in a more professional way.

The `File`, `PrintWriter`, and `FileNotFoundException` classes are contained in the `java.io` package.

ch08/lines/LineNumberer.java

```
 1   import java.io.File;
 2   import java.io.FileNotFoundException;
 3   import java.io.PrintWriter;
 4   import java.util.Scanner;
 5
 6   /**
 7      This program applies line numbers to a file.
 8   */
 9   public class LineNumberer
10   {
11      public static void main(String[] args) throws FileNotFoundException
12      {
13         // Prompt for the input and output file names
14
15         Scanner console = new Scanner(System.in);
16         System.out.print("Input file: ");
17         String inputFileName = console.next();
18         System.out.print("Output file: ");
```

```
19      String outputFileName = console.next();
20
21      // Construct the Scanner and PrintWriter objects for reading and writing
22
23      File inputFile = new File(inputFileName);
24      Scanner in = new Scanner(inputFile);
25      PrintWriter out = new PrintWriter(outputFileName);
26      int lineNumber = 1;
27
28      // Read the input and write the output
29
30      while (in.hasNextLine())
31      {
32         String line = in.nextLine();
33         out.println("/* " + lineNumber + " */ " + line);
34         lineNumber++;
35      }
36
37      in.close();
38      out.close();
39   }
40 }
```

SELF CHECK

1. What happens when you supply the same name for the input and output files to the LineNumberer program? Try it out if you are not sure.

2. What happens when you supply the name of a nonexistent input file to the Line-Numberer program? Try it out if you are not sure.

3. The output of a longer file doesn't look very pretty because the numbers don't line up.

   ```
   /* 9 */ And so the teacher turned it out
   /* 10 */ But still it lingered near
   ```

   How do you improve the program so that the line numbers line up? (Assume there are less than 1,000 input lines.)

4. How can you modify the program so that it prints each *word* in a separate line, with a line number?

5. Suppose you wanted to add the line numbers to an existing file instead of writing a new file. Self Check 1 indicates that you cannot simply do this by specifying the same file for input and output. How can you achieve this task? Provide the pseudocode for the solution.

Practice It Now you can try these exercises at the end of the chapter: R8.1, R8.2, P8.1.

Common Error 8.1

Backslashes in File Names

When you specify a file name as a string literal, and the name contains backslash characters (as in a Windows file name), you must supply each backslash twice:

```
File inputFile = new File("c:\\homework\\input.dat");
```

A single backslash inside a quoted string is an **escape character** that is combined with the following character to form a special meaning, such as \n for a newline character. The \\ combination denotes a single backslash.

When a user supplies a file name to a program, however, the user should not type the backslash twice.

Constructing a Scanner with a String

When you construct a PrintWriter with a string, it writes to a file:

    PrintWriter out = new PrintWriter("output.txt");

However, this does *not* work for a Scanner. The statement

    Scanner in = new Scanner("input.txt"); // Error?

does *not* open a file. Instead, it simply reads through the string: in.nextLine() returns the string "input.txt". (This is occasionally useful—see Section 8.2.2.)

You must simply remember to use File objects in the Scanner constructor:

    Scanner in = new Scanner(new File("input.txt")); // OK

Reading Web Pages

You can read the contents of a web page with this sequence of commands.

    String address = "http://horstmann.com/index.html";
    URL pageLocation = new URL(address);
    Scanner in = new Scanner(pageLocation.openStream());

Now simply read the contents of the web page with the Scanner in the usual way. The URL constructor and the openStream method can throw an IOException, so you need to tag the main method with throws IOException. (See Section 8.4.3 for more information on the throws clause.)

The URL class is contained in the java.net package.

Reading and Writing Binary Data

You use the Scanner and PrintWriter classes to read and write text files. Text files contain sequences of characters. Other files, such as images, are not made up of characters but of bytes. A **byte** is a fundamental storage unit in a computer—a number consisting of eight binary digits. The Java library has a different set of classes, called streams, for working with binary files. While modifying binary files is quite challenging and beyond the scope of this book, we give you a simple example of copying binary data from a web site to a file.

You use an InputStream to read binary data, for example

    URL imageLocation = new URL("http://horstmann.com/java4everyone/duke.gif");
    InputStream in = imageLocation.openStream();

To write binary data to a file, use a FileOutputStream:

    FileOutputStream out = new FileOutputStream("duke.gif");

The read method of an input stream reads a single byte and returns –1 when no further input is available. The write method of an output stream writes a single byte.

The following loop copies all bytes from an input stream to an output stream:

```
boolean done = false;
while (!done)
{
    int input = in.read(); // -1 or a byte between 0 and 255
    if (input == -1) { done = true; }
    else { out.write(input); }
}
```

8.2 Processing Text Input

In the following sections, you will learn how to process text with complex contents, such as that which often occurs in real life situations.

8.2.1 Reading Words

In the preceding example, we read input a line at a time. Sometimes, it is useful to read words rather than lines. For example, consider the loop

```
while (in.hasNext())
{
    String input = in.next();
    System.out.println(input);
}
```

With our sample input, this loop would print a word on every line:

```
Mary
had
a
little
lamb
```

However, the words can contain punctuation marks and other symbols. The next method returns any sequence of characters that is not white space. White space includes spaces, tab characters, and the newline characters that separate lines. For example, the following strings are considered "words" by the next method:

```
snow.
1729
C++
```

(Note the period after snow—it is considered a part of the word because it is not white space.)

Here is precisely what happens when the next method is executed. Input characters that are *white space* are *consumed*—that is, removed from the input. However, they do not become part of the word. The first character that is not white space becomes the first character of the word. More characters are added until either another white space character occurs, or the end of the input has been reached. If no characters are available after consuming the initial white space, a "no such element exception" occurs.

Sometimes, you want to read just the words and discard anything that isn't a letter. You achieve this task by calling the useDelimiter method on your Scanner object:

```
Scanner in = new Scanner(. . .);
in.useDelimiter("[^A-Za-z]+");
```

Here, we set the character pattern that separates words to "any sequence of characters other than letters". (The notation used for describing the character pattern is beyond the scope of this book. Search the Internet for "regular expression tutorial" if you are interested in the details.) With this setting, punctuation and numbers are not included in the words returned by the next method.

8.2.2 Reading Lines

When each line of a file is a data record, it is often best to read entire lines with the nextLine method:

```
String line = in.nextLine();
```

The next input line (without the newline character) is placed into the string line. You can then take the line apart for further processing.

Here is a typical example of processing lines in a file. A file with population data from the CIA Fact Book site (http://www.cia.gov/library/publications/the-world-factbook/) contains lines such as the following:

```
China    1330044605
India    1147995898
United States 303824646
. . .
```

Because some country names have more than one word, it would be tedious to read this file using the next method. For example, after reading United, how would your program know that it still needs to read another word before reading the population count?

Instead, read each input line into a string. Use the isDigit and isWhiteSpace methods introduced in Chapter 3 to find out where the name ends and the number starts.

Locate the first digit:

```
int i = 0;
while (!Character.isDigit(line.charAt(i))) { i++; }
```

Then extract the country name and population:

```
String countryName = line.substring(0, i);
String population = line.substring(i);
```

However, the country name contains one or more spaces at the end. Use the trim method to remove them:

```
countryName = countryName.trim();
```

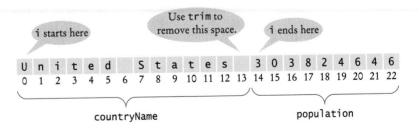

The `trim` method returns the string with all white space at the beginning and end removed.

There is one additional problem. The population is stored in a string, not a number. Use the `Integer.parseInt` method to convert it:

```
int populationValue = Integer.parseInt(population);
```

You need to be careful when calling the `Integer.parseInt` method. Its parameter must be a string containing the digits of an integer, without any additional characters. Not even spaces are allowed! In our situation, we happen to know that there won't be any spaces at the beginning of the string, but there might be some at the end. Therefore, we use the `trim` method:

```
int populationValue = Integer.parseInt(population.trim());
```

How To 8.1 on page 334 continues this example.

Here you saw how to break a string into parts by looking at individual characters. Another approach is occasionally easier. You can use a `Scanner` object to read the characters from a string:

```
Scanner lineScanner = new Scanner(line);
```

Then you can use `lineScanner` like any other `Scanner` object, reading words and numbers:

```
String countryName = lineScanner.next();
while (!lineScanner.hasNextInt())
{
    countryName = countryName + " " + lineScanner.next();
}
int populationValue = lineScanner.nextInt();
```

8.2.3 Reading Numbers

You have used the `nextInt` and `nextDouble` methods of the `Scanner` class many times, but here we will have a look at what happens in "abnormal" situations. Suppose you call

```
double value = in.nextDouble();
```

The `nextDouble` method recognizes floating-point numbers such as 3.14159, -21, or 1E12 (a billion in scientific notation). However, if there is *no number* in the input, then a "no such element exception" occurs.

Now consider an input containing the characters

```
2 1 s t   c e n t u r y
```

White space is consumed and the word 21st is read. However, this word is not a properly formatted number. In this situation, an "input mismatch exception" occurs.

To avoid exceptions, use the `hasNextDouble` method to screen the input. For example,

```
if (in.hasNextDouble())
{
    double value = in.nextDouble();
    . . .
}
```

Similarly, you should call the `hasNextInt` method before calling `nextInt`.

Note that the nextInt and nextDouble methods *do not* consume the white space that follows a number. This can be a problem if you alternate between calling nextInt/nextDouble and nextLine. Suppose a file contains country names and population values in this format:

```
China
1330044605
India
1147995898
United States
303824646
```

Now suppose you read the file with these instructions:

```
while (in.hasNextInt())
{
    String countryName = in.nextLine();
    int population = in.nextInt();
    Process the country name and population
}
```

Initially, the input contains

> C h i n a \n 1 3 3 0 0 4 4 6 0 5 \n I n d i a \n

After the first call to the nextLine method, the input contains

> 1 3 3 0 0 4 4 6 0 5 \n I n d i a \n

After the call to nextInt, the input contains

> \n I n d i a \n

Note that the nextInt call did *not* consume the newline character. Therefore, the second call to nextLine reads an empty string!

The remedy is to add a call to nextLine after reading the population value:

```
String countryName = in.nextLine();
int population = in.nextInt();
in.nextLine(); // Consume the newline
```

The call to nextLine consumes any remaining white space and the newline character.

8.2.4 Reading Characters

Sometimes, you want to read a file one character at a time. You will see an example in Section 8.3 where we encrypt the characters of a file. You achieve this task by calling the useDelimiter method on your Scanner object with an empty string:

```
Scanner in = new Scanner(. . .);
in.useDelimiter("");
```

Now each call to next returns a string consisting of a single character. Here is how you can process the characters:

```
while (in.hasNext())
{
    char ch = in.next().charAt(0);
    Process ch
}
```

SELF CHECK

6. Suppose the input contains the characters Hello, World!. What are the values of word1 and word2 after this code fragment?

```
String word = in.next();
String input = in.nextLine();
```

7. Suppose the input contains the characters 995.0. What are the values of number and input after this code fragment?

```
int number = in.nextInt();
String input = in.next();
```

8. Suppose the input contains the characters 6E6 6,995.00. What are the values of x1 and x2 after this code fragment?

```
double x1 = in.nextDouble();
double x2 = in.nextDouble();
```

9. Your input file contains a sequence of numbers, but sometimes a value is not available and is marked as N/A. How can you read the numbers and skip over the markers?

10. How can you remove spaces from the country name in Section 8.2.2 without using the trim method?

Practice It   Now you can try these exercises at the end of the chapter: P8.2, P8.4, P8.5.

8.3 Command Line Arguments

Depending on the operating system and Java development environment used, there are different methods of starting a program—for example, by selecting "Run" in the compilation environment, by clicking on an icon, or by typing the name of the program at the prompt in a command shell window. The latter method is called "invoking the program from the command line". When you use this method, you must of course type the name of the program, but you can also type in additional information that the program can use. These additional strings are called **command line arguments**. For example, if you start a program with the command line

```
java ProgramClass -v input.dat
```

then the program receives two command line arguments: the strings "-v" and "input.dat". It is entirely up to the program what to do with these strings. It is customary to interpret strings starting with a hyphen (-) as program options.

Should you support command line arguments for your programs, or should you prompt users, perhaps with a graphical user interface? For a casual and infrequent user, an interactive user interface is much better. The user interface guides the user along and makes it possible to navigate the application without much knowledge. But for a frequent user, a command line interface has a major advantage: it is easy to automate. If you need to process hundreds of files every day, you could spend all your time typing file names into file chooser dialog boxes. However, by using batch files or shell scripts (a feature of your computer's operating system), you can automatically call a program many times with different command line arguments.

Your program receives its command line arguments in the args parameter of the main method:

```
public static void main(String[] args)
```

Programs that start from the command line receive the command line arguments in the main method.

In our example, args is an array of length 2, containing the strings

```
args[0]:   "-v"
args[1]:   "input.dat"
```

Let us write a program that *encrypts* a file—that is, scrambles it so that it is unreadable except to those who know the decryption method. Ignoring 2,000 years of progress in the field of encryption, we will use a method familiar to Julius Caesar, replacing A with a D, B with an E, and so on (see Figure 1).

The program takes the following command line arguments:

- An optional -d flag to indicate decryption instead of encryption
- The input file name
- The output file name

For example,

```
java CaesarCipher input.txt encrypt.txt
```

encrypts the file input.txt and places the result into encrypt.txt.

```
java CaesarCipher -d encrypt.txt output.txt
```

decrypts the file encrypt.txt and places the result into output.txt.

The emperor Julius Caesar used a simple scheme to encrypt messages.

Figure 1
Caesar Cipher

Plain text

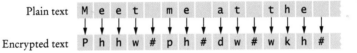

Encrypted text

ch08/cipher/CaesarCipher.java

```java
1  import java.io.File;
2  import java.io.FileNotFoundException;
3  import java.io.PrintWriter;
4  import java.util.Scanner;
5
6  /**
7     This program encrypts a file using the Caesar cipher.
8  */
9  public class CaesarCipher
10 {
11    public static void main(String[] args) throws FileNotFoundException
12    {
13       final int DEFAULT_KEY = 3;
14       int key = DEFAULT_KEY;
15       String inFile = null;
16       String outFile = null;
17
18       for (int i = 0; i < args.length; i++)
19       {
20          String arg = args[i];
```

```
21        if (arg.charAt(0) == '-')
22        {
23           // It is a command line option
24
25           char option = arg.charAt(1);
26           if (option == 'd') { key = -key; }
27           else { usage(); return; }
28        }
29        else
30        {
31           // It is a file name
32
33           if (inFile == null) { inFile = arg; }
34           else if (outFile == null) { outFile = arg; }
35           else { usage(); return; }
36        }
37     }
38     if (inFile == null || outFile == null) { usage(); return; }
39
40     Scanner in = new Scanner(new File(inFile));
41     in.useDelimiter(""); // Process individual characters
42     PrintWriter out = new PrintWriter(outFile);
43     while (in.hasNext())
44     {
45        char from = in.next().charAt(0);
46        char to = (char) (from + key);
47        out.print(to);
48     }
49     in.close();
50     out.close();
51   }
52
53   /**
54      Prints a message describing proper usage.
55   */
56   public static void usage()
57   {
58      System.out.println("Usage: java CaesarCipher [-d] infile outfile");
59   }
60 }
```

SELF CHECK

11. If the program is invoked with java CaesarCipher -d file1.txt, what are the elements of args?

12. Trace the program when it is invoked as in Self Check 11.

13. Will the program run correctly if the program is invoked with java CaesarCipher file1.txt file2.txt -d? If so, why? If not, why not?

14. Encrypt CAESAR using the Caesar cipher.

15. How can you modify the program so that the user can specify an encryption key other than 3 with a -k option, for example

    java CaesarCipher -k15 input.txt output.txt

Practice It   Now you can try these exercises at the end of the chapter: R8.4, P8.8, P8.9.

Random Fact 8.1 Encryption Algorithms

The exercises at the end of this chapter give a few algorithms to encrypt text. Don't actually use any of those methods to send secret messages to your lover. Any skilled cryptographer can *break* these schemes in a very short time—that is, reconstruct the original text without knowing the secret keyword.

In 1978 Ron Rivest, Adi Shamir, and Leonard Adleman introduced an encryption method that is much more powerful. The method is called *RSA encryption*, after the last names of its inventors. The exact scheme is too complicated to present here, but it is not actually difficult to follow. You can find the details in http://theory.lcs.mit.edu/~rivest/rsapaper.pdf.

RSA is a remarkable encryption method. There are two keys: a public key and a private key. (See the figure.) You can print the public key on your business card (or in your e-mail signature block) and give it to anyone. Then anyone can send you messages that only you can decrypt. Even though everyone else knows the public key, and even if they intercept all the messages coming to you, they cannot break the scheme and actually read the messages. In 1994, hundreds of researchers, collaborating over the Internet, cracked an RSA message encrypted with a 129-digit key. Messages encrypted with a key of 230 digits or more are expected to be secure.

The inventors of the algorithm obtained a *patent* for it. A patent is a deal that society makes with an inventor. For a period of 20 years, the inventor has an exclusive right for its commercialization, may collect royalties from others wishing to manufacture the invention, and may even stop competitors from using it altogether. In return, the inventor must publish the invention, so that others may learn from it, and must relinquish all claim to it after the monopoly period ends. The presumption is that in the absence of patent law, inventors would be reluctant to go through the trouble of inventing, or they would try to cloak their techniques to prevent others from copying their devices.

There has been some controversy about the RSA patent. Had there not been patent protection, would the inventors have published the method anyway, thereby giving the benefit to society without the cost of the 20-year monopoly? In this case, the answer is probably yes. The inventors were academic researchers, who live on salaries rather than sales receipts and are usually rewarded for their discoveries by a boost in their reputation and careers. Would their followers have been as active in discovering (and patenting) improvements? There is no way of knowing, of course. Is an algorithm even patentable, or is it a mathematical fact that belongs to nobody? The patent office did take the latter attitude for a long time. The RSA inventors and many others described their inventions in terms of imaginary electronic devices, rather than algorithms, to circumvent that restriction. Nowadays, the patent office will award software patents.

There is another interesting aspect to the RSA story. A programmer, Phil Zimmermann, developed a program called PGP (for *Pretty Good Privacy*) that is based on RSA. Anyone can use the program to encrypt messages, and decryption is not feasible even with the most powerful computers. You can get a copy of a free PGP implementation from the GNU project (http://www.gnupg.org). The existence of strong encryption methods bothers the United States government to no end. Criminals and foreign agents can send communications that the police and intelligence agencies cannot decipher. The government considered charging Zimmermann with breaching a law that forbids the unauthorized export of munitions, arguing that he should have known that his program would appear on the Internet. There have been serious proposals to make it illegal for private citizens to use these encryption methods, or to keep the keys secret from law enforcement.

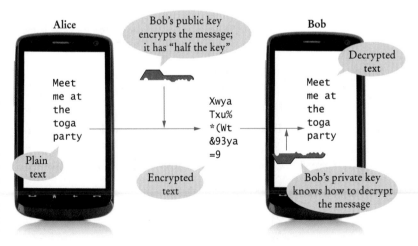

Public-Key Encryption

HOW TO 8.1

Processing Text Files

Processing text files that contain real data can be surprisingly challenging. This How To gives you step-by-step guidance.

As an example, we will consider this task: Read two country data files, `worldpop.txt` and `worldarea.txt` (supplied with your book code). Both files contain the same countries in the same order. Write a file `world_pop_density.txt` that contains country names and population densities (people per square km), with the country names aligned left and the numbers aligned right:

```
Afghanistan         50.56
Akrotiri           127.64
Albania            125.91
Algeria             14.18
American Samoa     288.92
    . . .
```

Singapore is one of the most densely populated countries in the world.

Step 1   Understand the processing task.

As always, you need to have a clear understanding of the task before designing a solution. Can you carry out the task by hand (perhaps with smaller input files)? If not, get more information about the problem.

One important aspect that you need to consider is whether you can process the data as it becomes available, or whether you need to store it first. For example, if you are asked to write out sorted data, you first need to collect all input, perhaps by placing it in an array list. However, it is often possible to process the data "on the go", without storing it.

In our example, we can read each file a line at a time and compute the density for each line because our input files store the population and area data in the same order.

The following pseudocode describes our processing task.

> **While there are more lines to be read**
>   Read a line from each file.
>   Extract the country name.
>   population = number following the country name in the line from the first file
>   area = number following the country name in the line from the second file
>   If area != 0
>   density = population / area
>   Print country name and density.

Step 2   Determine which files you need to read and write.

This should be clear from the problem. In our example, there are two input files, the population data and the area data, and one output file.

Step 3   Choose a mechanism for obtaining the file names.

There are three options:

- Hard-coding the file names (such as `"worldpop.txt"`).

- Asking the user:

```
Scanner in = new Scanner(System.in);
System.out.print("Enter filename: ");
String inFile = in.nextLine();
```

- Using command-line arguments for the file names.

In our example, we use hard-coded file names for simplicity.

Step 4   Choose between line, word, and character-based input.

As a rule of thumb, read lines if the input data is grouped by lines. That is the case with tabular data, such as in our example, or when you need to report line numbers.

When gathering data that can be distributed over several lines, then it makes more sense to read words. Keep in mind that you lose all white space when you read words.

Reading characters is mostly useful for tasks that require access to individual characters. Examples include analyzing character frequencies, changing tabs to spaces, or encryption.

Step 5   With line-oriented input, extract the required data.

It is simple to read a line of input with the `nextLine` method. Then you need to get the data out of that line. You can extract substrings, as described in Section 8.2.2.

Typically, you will use methods such as `Character.isWhitespace` and `Character.isDigit` to find the boundaries of substrings.

If you need any of the substrings as numbers, you must convert them, using `Integer.parseInt` or `Double.parseDouble`.

Step 6   Use methods to factor out common tasks.

Processing input files usually has repetitive tasks, such as skipping over white space or extracting numbers from strings. It really pays off to develop a set of methods to handle these tedious operations.

In our example, we have two common tasks that call for helper methods: extracting the country name and the value that follows. We will implement methods

```java
public static String extractCountry(String line)
public static double extractValue(String line)
```

These methods are implemented as described in Section 8.2.2.

Here is the complete source code (ch08/population/PopulationDensity.java).

```java
import java.io.File;
import java.io.FileNotFoundException;
import java.io.PrintWriter;
import java.util.Scanner;

/**
   This program reads data files of country populations and areas and prints the
   population density for each country.
*/
public class PopulationDensity
{
   public static void main(String[] args) throws FileNotFoundException
   {
      // Construct Scanner objects for input files
      Scanner in1 = new Scanner(new File("worldpop.txt"));
      Scanner in2 = new Scanner(new File("worldarea.txt"));

      // Construct PrintWriter for the output file

      PrintWriter out = new PrintWriter("world_pop_density.txt");

      // Read lines from each file

      while (in1.hasNextLine() && in2.hasNextLine())
      {
         String line1 = in1.nextLine();
         String line2 = in2.nextLine();
```

```java
      // Extract country and associated value
      String country = extractCountry(line1);
      double population = extractValue(line1);
      double area = extractValue(line2);

      // Compute and print the population density
      double density = 0;
      if (area != 0) // Protect against division by zero
      {
         density = population / area;
      }
      out.printf("%-40s%15.2f\n", country, density);
   }

   in1.close();
   in2.close();
   out.close();
}

/**
   Extracts the country from an input line.
   @param line  a line containing a country name, followed by a number
   @return  the country name
*/
public static String extractCountry(String line)
{
   int i = 0; // Locate the start of the first digit
   while (!Character.isDigit(line.charAt(i))) { i++; }
   return line.substring(0, i).trim(); // Extract the country name
}

/**
   Extracts the value from an input line.
   @param line  a line containing a country name, followed by a value
   @return  the value associated with the country
*/
public static double extractValue(String line)
{
   int i = 0; // Locate the start of the first digit
   while (!Character.isDigit(line.charAt(i))) { i++; }
   // Extract and convert the value
   return Double.parseDouble(line.substring(i).trim());
}
}
```

WORKED EXAMPLE 8.1   **Analyzing Baby Names**

In this worked example, you will use data from the
Social Security Administration to analyze the most
popular baby names.

8.4 Exception Handling

There are two aspects to dealing with program errors: *detection* and *handling*. For example, the Scanner constructor can detect an attempt to read from a non-existent file. However, it cannot handle that error. A satisfactory way of handling the error might be to terminate the program, or to ask the user for another file name. The Scanner class cannot choose between these alternatives. It needs to report the error to another part of the program.

In Java, *exception handling* provides a flexible mechanism for passing control from the point of error detection to a handler that can deal with the error. In the following sections, we will look into the details of this mechanism.

8.4.1 Throwing Exceptions

To signal an exceptional condition, use the throw statement to throw an exception object.

When you detect an error condition, your job is really easy. You just *throw* an appropriate exception object, and you are done. For example, suppose someone tries to withdraw too much money from a bank account.

```
if (amount > balance)
{
   // Now what?
}
```

First look for an appropriate exception class. The Java library provides many classes to signal all sorts of exceptional conditions. Figure 2 shows the most useful ones. (The classes are arranged as a tree-shaped hierarchy, with more specialized classes at the bottom of the tree. We will discuss such hierarchies in more detail in Chapter 9.)

When you throw an exception, the normal control flow is terminated. This is similar to a circuit breaker that cuts off the flow of electricity in a dangerous situation.

Look around for an exception type that might describe your situation. How about the ArithmeticException? Is it an arithmetic error to have a negative balance? No—Java can deal with negative numbers. Is the value of the amount parameter

Syntax 8.1   Throwing an Exception

> Most exception objects can be constructed with an error message.

```
if (amount > balance)
{
   throw new IllegalArgumentException("Amount exceeds balance");
}
balance = balance - amount;
```

A new exception object is constructed, then thrown.

> This line is not executed when the exception is thrown.

illegal? Indeed it is. It is just too large. Therefore, let's throw an `IllegalArgument-Exception`. (The term **argument** is an alternative term for a parameter value.)

When you throw an exception, processing continues in an exception handler.

```
if (amount > balance)
{
    throw new IllegalArgumentException("Amount exceeds balance");
}
```

When you throw an exception, execution does not continue with the next statement but with an **exception handler**. That is the topic of the next section.

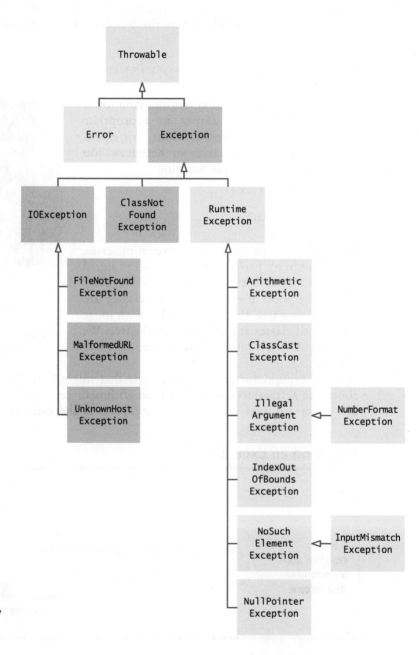

Figure 2
A Part of the Hierarchy
of Exception Classes

8.4.2 Catching Exceptions

Every exception should be handled somewhere in your program. If an exception has no handler, an error message is printed, and your program terminates. Of course, such an unhandled exception is confusing to program users.

You handle exceptions with the try/catch statement. Place the statement into a location of your program that knows how to handle a particular exception. The try block contains one or more statements that may cause an exception of the kind that you are willing to handle. Each catch clause contains the handler for an exception type. Here is an example:

```
try
{
   String filename = . . .;
   Scanner in = new Scanner(new File(filename));
   String input = in.next();
   int value = Integer.parseInt(input);
   . . .
}
catch (IOException exception)
{
   exception.printStackTrace();
}
catch (NumberFormatException exception)
{
   System.out.println("Input was not a number");
}
```

Three exceptions may be thrown in this try block:

- The Scanner constructor can throw a FileNotFoundException.
- Scanner.next can throw a NoSuchElementException.
- Integer.parseInt can throw a NumberFormatException.

If any of these exceptions is actually thrown, then the rest of the instructions in the try block are skipped. Here is what happens for the various exception types:

- If a FileNotFoundException is thrown, then the catch clause for the IOException is executed. (If you look at Figure 2, you will note that that FileNotFoundException is a descendant of IOException.)
- If a NumberFormatException occurs, then the second catch clause is executed.
- A NoSuchElementException is *not caught* by any of the catch clauses. The exception remains thrown until it is caught by another try block.

Each catch clause contains a handler. When the catch (IOException exception) block is executed, then some method in the try block has failed with an IOException (or one

ANIMATION
Exception Handling

You should only catch those exceptions that you can handle.

Syntax 8.2   Catching Exceptions

> This constructor can throw a
> `FileNotFoundException`.

```
try
{
    Scanner in = new Scanner(new File("input.txt"));
    String input = in.next();
    process(input);
}
catch (IOException exception)
{
    System.out.println("Could not open input file");
}
```

When an `IOException` is thrown,
execution resumes here.

This is the exception that was thrown.

Additional catch clauses
can appear here.

A `FileNotFoundException`
is a special case of an `IOException`.

of its descendants). In the handler, we produce a printout of the chain of method calls that led to the exception, by calling

```
exception.printStackTrace()
```

In this sample catch clause, we merely inform the user of the source of the problem. A better way of dealing with the exception would be to give the user another chance to provide a correct input—see Section 8.5 for a solution.

8.4.3 Checked Exceptions

In Java, the exceptions that you can throw and catch fall into three categories.

- Internal errors are reported by descendants of the type `Error`. One example is the `OutOfMemoryError`, which is thrown when all available computer memory has been used up. These are fatal errors that happen rarely, and we will not consider them in this book.

- Descendants of `RuntimeException`, such as as `IndexOutOfBoundsException`, `IllegalArgumentException`, and `NullPointerException`, indicate errors in your code. They are called **unchecked exceptions**.

- All other exceptions are **checked exceptions**. These exceptions indicate that something has gone wrong for some external reason beyond your control. In Figure 2, the checked exceptions are shaded in a darker color.

> Checked exceptions are due to external circumstances that the programmer cannot prevent. The compiler checks that your program handles these exceptions.

Why have two kinds of exceptions? A checked exception describes a problem that can occur, no matter how careful you are. For example, an `IOException` can be caused by forces beyond your control, such as a disk error or a broken network connection. The compiler takes checked exceptions very seriously and ensures that they are handled.

The unchecked exceptions, on the other hand, are your fault. The compiler doesn't check whether you handle a `NullPointerException`. After all, you should test

Syntax 8.3   The throws Clause

```
                public static String readData(String filename)
                    throws FileNotFoundException, NumberFormatException
```

You must specify all checked exceptions that this method may throw.

You may also list unchecked exceptions.

your references for `null` before using them rather than install a handler for that exception.

If you have a handler for a checked exception in the same method that may throw it, then the compiler is satisfied. For example,

```
try
{
    File inFile = new File(filename);
    Scanner in = new Scanner(inFile); // Throws FileNotFoundException
    . . .
}
catch (FileNotFoundException exception) // Exception caught here
{
    . . .
}
```

Add a throws clause to a method that can throw a checked exception.

However, it commonly happens that the current method *cannot handle* the exception. In that case, you need to tell the compiler that you are aware of this exception and that you want your method to be terminated when it occurs. You supply a method with a `throws` clause.

```
public static String readData(String filename) throws FileNotFoundException
{
    File inFile = new File(filename);
    Scanner in = new Scanner(inFile);
    . . .
}
```

The `throws` clause signals the caller of your method that it may encounter a `FileNotFoundException`. Then the caller needs to make the same decision—handle the exception, or declare that the exception may be thrown.

It sounds somehow irresponsible not to handle an exception when you know that it happened. Actually, the opposite is true. Java provides an exception handling facility so that an exception can be sent to the *appropriate* handler. Some methods detect errors, some methods handle them, and some methods just pass them along. The `throws` clause simply ensures that no exceptions get lost along the way.

Just as trucks with large or hazardous loads carry warning signs, the throws *clause warns the caller that an exception may occur.*

8.4.4 The finally Clause

Occasionally, you need to take some action whether or not an exception is thrown. The finally construct is used to handle this situation. Here is a typical situation.

It is important to close a PrintWriter to ensure that all output is written to the file. In the following code segment, we open a stream, call one or more methods, and then close the stream:

```
PrintWriter out = new PrintWriter(filename);
writeData(out);
out.close(); // May never get here
```

Now suppose that one of the methods before the last line throws an exception. Then the call to close is never executed! You solve this problem by placing the call to close inside a finally clause:

```
PrintWriter out = new PrintWriter(filename);
try
{
    writeData(out);
}
finally
{
    out.close();
}
```

In a normal case, there will be no problem. When the try block is completed, the finally clause is executed, and the writer is closed. However, if an exception occurs, the finally clause is also executed before the exception is passed to its handler.

Use the finally clause whenever you need to do some clean up, such as closing a file, to ensure that the clean up happens no matter how the method exits.

Once a try block is entered, the statements in a finally clause are guaranteed to be executed, whether or not an exception is thrown.

All visitors to a foreign country have to go through passport control, no matter what happened on their trip. Similarly, the code in a finally clause is always executed, even when an exception has occurred.

Syntax 8.4   The finally Clause

```
                                    This variable must be declared outside the try block
                                    so that the finally clause can access it.

                           PrintWriter out = new PrintWriter(filename);
 This code may             try
 throw exceptions.     ┌─  {
                       └─     writeData(out);
                           }
                           finally
 This code is          ┌─  {
 always executed,      └─     out.close();
 even if an exception occurs.  }
```

16. Suppose balance is 100 and amount is 200. What is the value of balance after these statements?

```
if (amount > balance)
{
    throw new IllegalArgumentException("Amount exceeds balance");
}
balance = balance - amount;
```

17. When depositing an amount into a bank account, we don't have to worry about overdrafts—except when the amount is negative. Write a statement that throws an appropriate exception in that case.

18. Consider the method

```
public static void main(String[] args)
{
    try
    {
        Scanner in = new Scanner(new File("input.txt"));
        int value = in.nextInt();
        System.out.println(value);
    }
    catch (IOException exception)
    {
        System.out.println("Error opening file.");
    }
}
```

Suppose the file with the given file name exists and has no contents. Trace the flow of execution.

19. Why is a NullPointerException not a checked exception?

20. Is there a difference between catching checked and unchecked exceptions?

21. What is wrong with the following code, and how can you fix it?

```
public static void writeAll(String[] lines, String filename)
{
    PrintWriter out = new PrintWriter(filename);
    for (String line : lines) { out.println(line.toUpperCase()); }
    out.close();
}
```

Practice It Now you can try these exercises at the end of the chapter: R8.7, R8.8, R8.9.

Programming Tip 8.1

Throw Early, Catch Late

When a method detects a problem that it cannot solve, it is better to throw an exception rather than try to come up with an imperfect fix. For example, suppose a method expects to read a number from a file, and the file doesn't contain a number. Simply using a zero value would be a poor choice because it hides the actual problem and perhaps causes a different problem elsewhere.

> Throw an exception as soon as a problem is detected. Catch it only when the problem can be handled.

Conversely, a method should only catch an exception if it can really remedy the situation. Otherwise, the best remedy is simply to have the exception propagate to its caller, allowing it to be caught by a competent handler.

These principles can be summarized with the slogan "throw early, catch late".

Programming Tip 8.2

Do Not Squelch Exceptions

When you call a method that throws a checked exception and you haven't specified a handler, the compiler complains. In your eagerness to continue your work, it is an understandable impulse to shut the compiler up by squelching the exception:

```
try
{
    Scanner in = new Scanner(new File(filename));
    // Compiler complained about FileNotFoundException
    . . .
}
catch (FileNotFoundException e) {} // So there!
```

The do-nothing exception handler fools the compiler into thinking that the exception has been handled. In the long run, this is clearly a bad idea. Exceptions were designed to transmit problem reports to a competent handler. Installing an incompetent handler simply hides an error condition that could be serious.

Programming Tip 8.3

Do Not Use catch and finally in the Same try Statement

It is possible to have a finally clause following one or more catch clauses. Then the code in the finally clause is executed whenever the try block is exited in any of three ways:

1. After completing the last statement of the try block
2. After completing the last statement of a catch clause, if this try block caught an exception
3. When an exception was thrown in the try block and not caught

It is tempting to combine catch and finally clauses, but the resulting code can be hard to understand, and it is often incorrect. Instead, use two statements:

- a try/finally statement to close resources
- a separate try/catch statement to handle errors

For example,

```
try
{
    PrintWriter out = new PrintWriter(filename);
    try
    {
        Write output
    }
    finally
    {
        out.close();
    }
}
catch (IOException exception)
{
    Handle exception
}
```

Note that the nested statements work correctly if the PrintWriter constructor throws an exception, too.

Special Topic 8.3

Automatic Resource Management in Java 7

In Java 7, you can use a new form of the try block that automatically closes a PrintWriter or Scanner object. Here is the syntax:

```
try (PrintWriter out = new PrintWriter(filename))
{
    Write output to out
}
```

The close method is automatically invoked on the out object when the try block ends, whether or not an exception has occurred. A finally statement is not required.

Random Fact 8.2 The Ariane Rocket Incident

The European Space Agency (ESA), Europe's counterpart to NASA, had developed a rocket model called Ariane that it had successfully used several times to launch satellites and scientific experiments into space. However, when a new version, the Ariane 5, was launched on June 4, 1996, from ESA's launch site in Kourou, French Guiana, the rocket veered off course about 40 seconds after liftoff. Flying at an angle of more than 20 degrees, rather than straight up, exerted such an aerodynamic force that the boosters separated, which triggered the automatic self-destruction mechanism. The rocket blew itself up.

The ultimate cause of this accident was an unhandled exception! The rocket contained two identical devices (called inertial reference systems) that processed flight data from measuring devices and turned the data into information about the rocket's position. The onboard computer used the position information for controlling the boosters. The same inertial reference systems and computer software had worked fine on the Ariane 4.

However, due to design changes to the rocket, one of the sensors measured a larger acceleration force than had been encountered in the Ariane 4. That value, expressed as a floating-point value, was stored in a 16-bit integer (like a short variable in Java). Unlike Java, the Ada language, used for the device software, generates an exception if a floating-point number is too large to be converted to an integer. Unfortunately, the programmers of the device had decided that this situation would never happen and didn't provide an exception handler.

When the overflow did happen, the exception was triggered and, because there was no handler, the device shut itself off. The onboard computer sensed the failure and switched over to the backup device. However, that device had shut itself off for exactly the same reason, something that the designers of the rocket had not expected. They figured that the devices might fail for mechanical reasons, and the chances of two devices having the same mechanical failure was considered remote. At that point, the rocket was without reliable position information and went off course. Perhaps it would have been better if the software hadn't been so thorough? If it had ignored the overflow, the device wouldn't have been shut off. It would have computed bad data. But then the device would have reported wrong position data, which could have been just as fatal. Instead, a correct implementation should have caught overflow exceptions and come up with some strategy to recompute the flight data. Clearly, giving up was not a reasonable option in this context.

The advantage of the exception-handling mechanism is that it makes these issues explicit to programmers—something to think about when you curse the Java compiler for complaining about uncaught exceptions.

The Explosion of the Ariane Rocket

8.5 Application: Handling Input Errors

This section walks through an example program that includes exception handling. The program, DataAnalyzer.java, asks the user for the name of a file. The file is expected to contain data values. The first line of the file should contain the total number of values, and the remaining lines contain the data. A typical input file looks like this:

```
3
1.45
-2.1
0.05
```

What can go wrong? There are two principal risks.

- The file might not exist.
- The file might have data in the wrong format.

Who can detect these faults? The Scanner constructor will throw an exception when the file does not exist. The methods that process the input values need to throw an exception when they find an error in the data format.

What exceptions can be thrown? The Scanner constructor throws a FileNot-FoundException when the file does not exist, which is appropriate in our situation. When there are fewer data items than expected, or when the file doesn't start with the count of values, the program will throw an NoSuchElementException. Finally, when there are more inputs than expected, an IOException should be thrown.

Who can remedy the faults that the exceptions report? Only the main method of the DataAnalyzer program interacts with the user, so it catches the exceptions, prints appropriate error messages, and gives the user another chance to enter a correct file:

```
// Keep trying until there are no more exceptions
boolean done = false;
while (!done)
{
   try
   {
      Prompt user for file name

      double[] data = readFile(filename);

      Process data

      done = true;
   }
   catch (NoSuchElementException exception)
   {
      System.out.println("File contents invalid.");
   }
   catch (FileNotFoundException exception)
   {
      System.out.println("File not found.");
   }
   catch (IOException exception)
   {
      exception.printStackTrace();
   }
}
```

The first two catch clauses in the main method give a human-readable error report if bad data was encountered or the file was not found. However, if another IOException occurs, then it prints a stack trace so that a programmer can diagnose the problem.

The following readFile method constructs the Scanner object and calls the readData method. It does not handle any exceptions. If there is a problem with the input file, it simply passes the exception to its caller.

```
public static double[] readFile(String filename) throws IOException
{
   File inFile = new File(filename);
   Scanner in = new Scanner(inFile);
   try
   {
      return readData(in);
   }
   finally
   {
      in.close();
   }
}
```

Note how the finally clause ensures that the file is closed even when an exception occurs.

Also note that the throws clause of the readFile method need not include the File-NotFoundException class because it is a special case of an IOException.

The readData method reads the number of values, constructs an array, and fills it with the data values.

```
public static double[] readData(Scanner in) throws IOException
{
   int numberOfValues = in.nextInt(); // May throw NoSuchElementException
   double[] data = new double[numberOfValues];

   for (int i = 0; i < numberOfValues; i++)
   {
      data[i] = in.nextDouble(); // May throw NoSuchElementException
   }

   if (in.hasNext())
   {
      throw new IOException("End of file expected");
   }
   return data;
}
```

As discussed in Section 8.2.3, the calls to the nextInt and nextDouble methods can throw a NoSuchElementException when there is no input at all or an InputMismatchException if the input is not a number. As you can see from Figure 2 on page 340, an InputMismatchException is a special case of a NoSuchElementException.

You need not declare the NoSuchElementException in the throws clause because it is not a checked exception, but you can include it for greater clarity.

There are three potential errors:

- The file might not start with an integer.
- There might not be a sufficient number of data values.
- There might be additional input after reading all data values.

In the first two cases, the Scanner throws a NoSuchElementException. Note again that this is *not* a checked exception—we could have avoided it by calling hasNextInt/hasNextDouble first. However, this method does not know what to do in this case, so it allows the exception to be sent to a handler elsewhere.

When we find that there is additional unexpected input, we throw an IOException. To see the exception handling at work, look at a specific error scenario.

1. main calls readFile.

2. readFile calls readData.

3. readData calls Scanner.nextInt.

4. There is no integer in the input, and Scanner.nextInt throws a NoSuchElement-Exception.

5. readData has no handler for the exception and terminates immediately.

6. readFile has no handler for the exception and terminates immediately after executing the finally clause and closing the file.

7. main has a handler for a NoSuchElementException. That handler prints a message to the user. Afterward, the user is given another chance to enter a file name. Note that the statements for processing the data have been skipped.

This example shows the separation between error detection (in the readData method) and error handling (in the main method). In between the two is the readFile method, which simply passes the exceptions along.

ch08/data/DataAnalyzer.java

```java
1   import java.io.File;
2   import java.io.FileNotFoundException;
3   import java.io.EOFException;
4   import java.io.IOException;
5   import java.util.Scanner;
6   import java.util.NoSuchElementException;
7
8   /**
9      This program processes a file containing a count followed by data values.
10     If the file doesn't exist or the format is incorrect, you can specify another file.
11  */
12  public class DataAnalyzer
13  {
14     public static void main(String[] args)
15     {
16        Scanner in = new Scanner(System.in);
17
18        // Keep trying until there are no more exceptions
19
20        boolean done = false;
21        while (!done)
22        {
23           try
24           {
25              System.out.print("Please enter the file name: ");
26              String filename = in.next();
27
28              double[] data = readFile(filename);
29
```

```
30            // As an example for processing the data, we compute the sum
31
32            double sum = 0;
33            for (double d : data) { sum = sum + d; }
34            System.out.println("The sum is " + sum);
35
36            done = true;
37         }
38         catch (NoSuchElementException exception)
39         {
40            System.out.println("File contents invalid.");
41         }
42         catch (FileNotFoundException exception)
43         {
44            System.out.println("File not found.");
45         }
46         catch (IOException exception)
47         {
48            exception.printStackTrace();
49         }
50      }
51   }
52
53   /**
54      Opens a file and reads a data set.
55      @param filename the name of the file holding the data
56      @return the data in the file
57   */
58   public static double[] readFile(String filename) throws IOException
59   {
60      File inFile = new File(filename);
61      Scanner in = new Scanner(inFile);
62      try
63      {
64         return readData(in);
65      }
66      finally
67      {
68         in.close();
69      }
70   }
71
72   /**
73      Reads a data set.
74      @param in the scanner that scans the data
75      @return the data set
76   */
77   public static double[] readData(Scanner in) throws IOException
78   {
79      int numberOfValues = in.nextInt(); // May throw NoSuchElementException
80      double[] data = new double[numberOfValues];
81
82      for (int i = 0; i < numberOfValues; i++)
83      {
84         data[i] = in.nextDouble(); // May throw NoSuchElementException
85      }
86
87      if (in.hasNext())
88      {
```

```
89              throw new IOException("End of file expected");
90          }
91      return data;
92      }
93  }
```

22. Why doesn't the readFile method catch any exceptions?
23. Consider the try/finally statement in the readFile method. Why was the in variable declared outside the try block?
24. Suppose the user specifies a file that exists and is empty. Trace the flow of execution in the DataAnalyzer program.
25. Why didn't the readData method call hasNextInt/hasNextDouble to ensure that the NoSuchElementException is not thrown?

Practice It   Now you can try these exercises at the end of the chapter: R8.15, R8.16, P8.13.

SCREENCAST 8.1   **Detecting Accounting Fraud**

In this Screencast Video, you will see how to detect accounting fraud by analyzing digit distributions. You will learn how to read data from the Internet and handle exceptional situations.

CHAPTER SUMMARY

- Use the Scanner class for reading text files.
- When writing text files, use the PrintWriter class and the print/println/printf methods.
- Close all files when you are done processing them.

- Programs that start from the command line receive the command line arguments in the main method.

- To signal an exceptional condition, use the throw statement to throw an exception object.
- When you throw an exception, processing continues in an exception handler.

- Place the statements that can cause an exception inside a `try` block, and the handler inside a `catch` clause.
- Checked exceptions are due to external circumstances that the programmer cannot prevent. The compiler checks that your program handles these exceptions.

- Add a `throws` clause to a method that can throw a checked exception.
  - Once a `try` block is entered, the statements in a `finally` clause are guaranteed to be executed, whether or not an exception is thrown.

  - Throw an exception as soon as a problem is detected. Catch it only when the problem can be handled.

MEDIA RESOURCES

WILEY PLUS

www.wiley.com/
college/
horstmann

- **_Worked Example_** Analyzing Baby Names
- Guided Lab Exercises
- ➕ **_Animation_** Exception Handling
- ➕ **_Screencast_** Detecting Accounting Fraud
- ➕ Practice Quiz
- ➕ Code Completion Exercises

REVIEW EXERCISES

★★ **R8.1** What happens if you try to open a file for reading that doesn't exist? What happens if you try to open a file for writing that doesn't exist?

★★ **R8.2** What happens if you try to open a file for writing, but the file or device is write-protected (sometimes called read-only)? Try it out with a short test program.

★ **R8.3** How do you open a file whose name contains a backslash, like `c:\temp\output.dat`?

★ **R8.4** If a program Woozle is started with the command

```
java Woozle -Dname=piglet -I\eeyore -v heff.txt a.txt lump.txt
```

what are the values of `args[0]`, `args[1]`, and so on?

★ **R8.5** What is the difference between throwing an exception and catching an exception?

★ **R8.6** What is a checked exception? What is an unchecked exception? Give an example for each. Which exceptions do you need to declare with the `throws` reserved word?

★★ **R8.7** Why don't you need to declare that your method might throw an `IndexOutOfBounds-Exception`?

★★ **R8.8** When your program executes a `throw` statement, which statement is executed next?

★★ **R8.9** What happens if an exception does not have a matching `catch` clause?

★★ **R8.10** What can your program do with the exception object that a `catch` clause receives?

★★ **R8.11** Is the type of the exception object always the same as the type declared in the catch clause that catches it? If not, why not?

★ **R8.12** What is the purpose of the `finally` clause? Give an example of how it can be used.

★★★ **R8.13** What happens when an exception is thrown, the code of a `finally` clause executes, and that code throws an exception of a different kind than the original one? Which one is caught by a surrounding catch clause? Write a sample program to try it out.

★★ **R8.14** Which exceptions can the `next` and `nextInt` methods of the `Scanner` class throw? Are they checked exceptions or unchecked exceptions?

★★ **R8.15** Suppose the program in Section 8.5 reads a file containing the following values:

```
1
2
3
4
```

What is the outcome? How could the program be improved to give a more accurate error report?

★★ **R8.16** Can the `readFile` method in Section 8.5 throw a `NullPointerException`? If so, how?

PROGRAMMING EXERCISES

★ **P8.1** Write a program that carries out the following tasks:

> Open a file with the name hello.txt.
> Store the message "Hello, World!" in the file.
> Close the file.
> Open the same file again.
> Read the message into a string variable and print it.

★ **P8.2** Write a program that reads a file containing floating-point numbers. Print the average of the numbers in the file. Prompt the user for the file name.

★ **P8.3** Repeat Exercise P8.2, but allow the user to specify the file name on the command-line. If the user doesn't specify any file name, then prompt the user for the name.

★ **P8.4** Write a program that reads a file containing two columns of floating-point numbers. Prompt the user for the file name. Print the average of each column.

★★ **P8.5** Write a program that asks the user for a file name and prints the number of characters, words, and lines in that file.

★★ **P8.6** Write a program `Find` that searches all files specified on the command line and prints out all lines containing a specified word. For example, if you call

```
java Find ring report.txt address.txt Homework.java
```

then the program might print

```
report.txt: has broken up an international ring of DVD bootleggers that
address.txt: Kris Kringle, North Pole
address.txt: Homer Simpson, Springfield
Homework.java: String filename;
```

The specified word is always the first command line argument.

★★ **P8.7** Write a program that checks the spelling of all words in a file. It should read each word of a file and check whether it is contained in a word list. A word list is available on most Linux systems in the file /usr/share/dict/words. (If you don't have access to a Linux system, your instructor should be able to get you a copy.) The program should print out all words that it cannot find in the word list.

★★ **P8.8** Write a program that replaces each line of a file with its reverse. For example, if you run

```
java Reverse HelloPrinter.java
```

then the contents of HelloPrinter.java are changed to

```
retnirPolleH ssalc cilbup
{
)sgra ][gnirtS(niam diov citats cilbup
{
wodniw elosnoc eht ni gniteerg a yalpsiD //

;)"!dlroW ,olleH"(nltnirp.tuo.metsyS
}
}
```

Of course, if you run Reverse twice on the same file, you get back the original file.

★★ **P8.9** Write a program that reads each line in a file, reverses its lines, and writes them to another file. For example, if the file input.txt contains the lines

```
Mary had a little lamb
Its fleece was white as snow
And everywhere that Mary went
The lamb was sure to go.
```

and you run

```
reverse input.txt output.txt
```

then output.txt contains

```
The lamb was sure to go.
And everywhere that Mary went
Its fleece was white as snow
Mary had a little lamb
```

★★ **P8.10** Get the data for names in prior decades from the Social Security Administration. Paste the table data in files named babynames80s.txt, etc. Modify the BabyNames.java program so that it prompts the user for a file name. The numbers in the files have comma separators, so modify the program to handle them. Can you spot a trend in the frequencies?

★★ **P8.11** Write a program that reads in babynames.txt and produces two files, boynames.txt and girlnames.txt, separating the data for the boys and girls.

★★★ **P8.12** Write a program that reads a file in the same format as babynames.txt and prints all names that are both boy and girl names (such as Alexis or Morgan).

★★ **P8.13** Write a program that asks the user to input a set of floating-point values. When the user enters a value that is not a number, give the user a second chance to enter the value. After two chances, quit reading input. Add all correctly specified values and print the sum when the user is done entering data. Use exception handling to detect improper inputs.

★★ **P8.14** Using the mechanism described in Special Topic 8.1 on page 325, write a program that reads all data from a web page and writes them to a file. Prompt the user for the web page URL and the file.

★★ **P8.15** Using the mechanism described in Special Topic 8.1 on page 325, write a program that reads all data from a web page and prints all hyperlinks of the form

```
<a href="link">link text</a>
```

Extra credit if your program can follow the links that it finds and find links in those web pages as well. (This is the method that search engines such as Google use to find web sites.)

ANSWERS TO SELF-CHECK QUESTIONS

1. When the PrintWriter object is created, the output file is emptied. Sadly, that is the same file as the input file. The input file is now empty and the while loop exits immediately.

2. The program throws a FileNotFoundException and terminates.

3. Replace

```
out.println("/* " + lineNumber + " */ " + line);
```

with

```
out.printf("/* %4d */ %s\n", lineNumber, line);
```

4. Change lines 30–32 to

```
while (in.hasNext())
{
    String line = in.next();
```

5. Let input be a scanner for the file.
   Let lineList be an ArrayList of strings.
   lineNumber = 1
   For each line in the input
      Set numberedLine to commented lineNumber and line.
      Add numberedLine to lineList.
      Increment lineNumber.
   Close the input.
   Let output be a PrintWriter for the same file.
   For each line in lineList
      Print line to output.
   Close the output.

6. word is "Hello," and input is "World!"

7. Because 995.0 is not a properly formatted *integer*, the first statement causes an input mismatch exception. Neither number nor input is set.

8. x1 is set to 6000000. Because a comma is not considered a part of a floating-point number in Java, the second call to nextDouble causes an input mismatch exception and x2 is not set.

9. Read them as strings, and convert those strings to numbers that are not equal to N/A:

```
String input = in.next();
if (!input.equals("N/A"))
{
    double value = Double.parseDouble(input);
    Process value
}
```

10. Locate the last character of the country name:

```
int j = i - 1;
while (!Character.isWhiteSpace(line.charAt(j))) { j--; }
```

Then extract the country name:

```
String countryName = line.substring(0, j + 1);
```

11. args[0] is "-d" and args[1] is "file1.txt"

12.

key	inFile	outFile	i	arg
~~3~~	~~null~~	null	~~0~~	~~-d~~
-3	file1.txt		~~1~~	file1.txt
			2	

Then the program prints a message

```
Usage: java CaesarCipher [-d] infile outfile
```

13. The program will run correctly. The loop that parses the options does not depend on the positions in which the options appear.

14. FDHVDU

15. Add the lines

```
else if (option == 'k')
{
    key = Integer.parseInt(args[i].substring(2));
}
```

after line 26 and update the usage information.

16. It is still 100. The last statement was not executed because the exception was thrown.

17. `if (amount < 0) { throw new IllegalArgumentException("Negative amount"); }`

18. The Scanner constructor succeeds because the file exists. The nextInt method throws a NoSuchElementException. This is *not* an IOException. Therefore, the error is not caught. Because there is no other handler, an error message is printed and the program terminates.

19. Because programmers should simply check for null pointers instead of trying to handle a NullPointerException.

20. No. You can catch both exception types in the same way, as you can see in the code example on page 339.

21. There are two mistakes. The PrintWriter constructor can throw a FileNotFoundException. You should supply a throws clause. And if one of the array elements is null, a NullPointerException is thrown. In that case, the out.close() statement is never executed. You should use a try/finally statement.

22. The exceptions are better handled in the main method.

23. If it had been declared inside the try block, its scope would only have extended until the end of the try block, and it would not have been accessible in the `finally` clause.

24. `main` calls `readFile`, which calls `readData`. The call `in.nextInt()` throws a `NoSuchElement-Exception`. The `readFile` method doesn't catch it, so it propagates back to `main`, where it is caught. An error message is printed, and the user can specify another file.

25. We *want* to throw that exception, so that someone else can handle the problem of a bad data file.

INHERITANCE AND INTERFACES

Objects from related classes usually share common behavior. For example, shovels, rakes, and clippers all perform gardening tasks. In this chapter, you will learn how the notion of inheritance expresses the relationship between specialized and general classes. By using inheritance, you will be able to share code between classes and provide services that can be used by multiple classes.

9.1 Inheritance Hierarchies

> A subclass inherits data and behavior from a superclass.

In object-oriented design, **inheritance** is a relationship between a more general class (called the **superclass**) and a more specialized class (called the **subclass**). The subclass inherits data and behavior from the superclass. For example, consider the relationships between different kinds of vehicles depicted in Figure 1.

Every car *is a* vehicle. Cars share the common traits of all vehicles, such as the ability to transport people from one place to another. We say that the class Car inherits from the class Vehicle. In this relationship, the Vehicle class is the superclass and the Car class is the subclass. In Figure 2, the superclass and subclass are joined with an arrow that points to the superclass.

> You can always use a subclass object in place of a superclass object.

Suppose we have an algorithm that manipulates a Vehicle object. Because a car is a special kind of vehicle, we can use a Car object in such an algorithm, and it will work correctly. The **substitution principle** states that you can always use a subclass

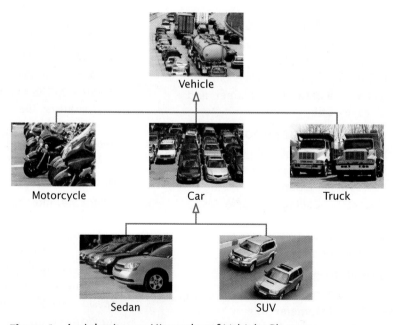

Figure 1 An Inheritance Hierarchy of Vehicle Classes

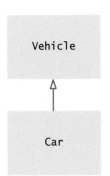

Figure 2
An Inheritance Diagram

object when a superclass object is expected. For example, consider a method that takes a parameter of type Vehicle.

```
void processVehicle(Vehicle v)
```

Because Car is a subclass of Vehicle, you can call that method with a Car object:

```
Car myCar = new Car(. . .);
processVehicle(myCar);
```

Why provide a method that processes Vehicle objects instead of Car objects? That method is more useful because it can handle *any* kind of vehicle (including Truck and Motorcycle objects).

In this chapter, we will consider a simpler hierarchy of classes. Most likely, you have taken computer-graded quizzes. A quiz consists of questions, and there are different kinds of questions:

- Fill-in-the-blank
- Choice (single or multiple)
- Numeric (where an approximate answer is ok; e.g., 1.33 when the actual answer is 4/3)
- Free response

We will develop a simple but flexible quiz-taking program to illustrate inheritance.

Figure 3 shows an inheritance hierarchy for these question types.

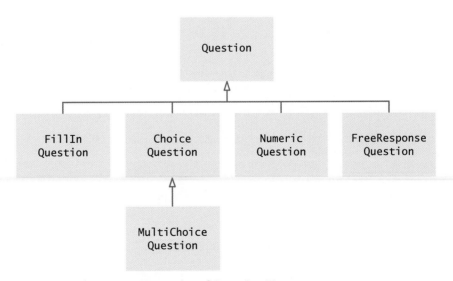

Figure 3 Inheritance Hierarchy of Question Types

At the root of this hierarchy is the Question type. A question can display its text, and it can check whether a given response is a correct answer.

ch09/questions/Question.java

```
1   /**
2       A question with a text and an answer.
3   */
4   public class Question
5   {
6      private String text;
7      private String answer;
8
9      /**
10         Constructs a question with empty question and answer.
11      */
12      public Question()
13      {
14         text = "";
15         answer = "";
16      }
17
18      /**
19         Sets the question text.
20         @param questionText the text of this question
21      */
22      public void setText(String questionText)
23      {
24         text = questionText;
25      }
26
27      /**
28         Sets the answer for this question.
29         @param correctResponse the answer
30      */
31      public void setAnswer(String correctResponse)
32      {
33         answer = correctResponse;
34      }
35
36      /**
37         Checks a given response for correctness.
38         @param response the response to check
39         @return true if the response was correct, false otherwise
40      */
41      public boolean checkAnswer(String response)
42      {
43         return response.equals(answer);
44      }
45
46      /**
47         Displays this question.
48      */
49      public void display()
50      {
51         System.out.println(text);
52      }
53   }
```

How the text is displayed depends on the question type. Later in this chapter, you will see some variations, but the superclass simply sends the question text to System.out. How the response is checked also depends on the question type. As already mentioned, a numeric question might accept approximate answers (see Exercise P9.1). In Exercise P9.3, you will see another way of checking the response. But in the superclass, we will simply require that the response match the correct answer exactly.

In the following sections, you will see how to form subclasses of the Question class.

Here is a simple test program for the Question class.

ch09/questions/QuestionDemo1.java

```java
1   import java.util.ArrayList;
2   import java.util.Scanner;
3
4   /**
5      This program shows a simple quiz with one question.
6   */
7   public class QuestionDemo1
8   {
9      public static void main(String[] args)
10     {
11        Scanner in = new Scanner(System.in);
12
13        Question q = new Question();
14        q.setText("Who was the inventor of Java?");
15        q.setAnswer("James Gosling");
16
17        q.display();
18        System.out.print("Your answer: ");
19        String response = in.nextLine();
20        System.out.println(q.checkAnswer(response));
21     }
22  }
```

Program Run

```
Who was the inventor of Java?
Your answer: James Gosling
true
```

SELF CHECK

1. Consider classes Manager and Employee. Which should be the superclass and which should be the subclass?
2. What are the inheritance relationships between classes BankAccount, CheckingAccount, and SavingsAccount?
3. Figure 8.1 shows an inheritance diagram of exception classes in Java. List all superclasses of the class RuntimeException.
4. Consider the method doSomething(Car c). List all vehicle classes from Figure 1 whose objects *cannot* be passed to this method.
5. Should a class Quiz inherit from the class Question? Why or why not?

Practice It   Now you can try these exercises at the end of the chapter: R9.1, R9.7, R9.9.

Use a Single Class for Variation in Values, Inheritance for Variation in Behavior

The purpose of inheritance is to model objects with different *behavior*. When students first learn about inheritance, they have a tendency to overuse it, by creating multiple classes even though the variation could be expressed with a simple instance variable.

Consider a program that tracks the fuel efficiency of a fleet of cars by logging the distance traveled and the refueling amounts. Some cars in the fleet are hybrids. Should you create a subclass `HybridCar`? Not in this application. Hybrids don't behave any differently than other cars when it comes to driving and refueling. They just have a better fuel efficiency. A single `Car` class with an instance variable

```
double milesPerGallon;
```

is entirely sufficient.

However, if you write a program that shows how to repair different kinds of vehicles, then it makes sense to have a separate class `HybridCar`. When it comes to repairs, hybrid cars behave differently from other cars.

9.2 Implementing Subclasses

In this section, you will see how to form a subclass and how a subclass automatically inherits functionality from its superclass.

Consider the task of implementing a `ChoiceQuestion` class to handle questions such as the following:

```
In which country was the inventor of Java born?
1. Australia
2. Canada
3. Denmark
4. United States
```

You could write this class from scratch, with methods to set up the question, display it, and check the answer. But you don't have to. Instead, use inheritance and implement the `ChoiceQuestion` as a subclass of the `Question` class.

In Java, you form a subclass by specifying what makes the subclass different from its superclass.

Subclass objects automatically have the instance variables that are declared in the superclass. You only declare instance variables that are not part of the superclass objects.

> A subclass inherits all methods that it does not override.

The subclass inherits all public methods from the superclass. You declare any methods that are *new* to the subclass, and *change* the implementation of inherited methods if the inherited behavior is not appropriate. When you supply a new implementation for an inherited method, you **override** the method.

> A subclass can override a superclass method by providing a new implementation.

A `ChoiceQuestion` object differs from a `Question` object in three ways:

- Its objects store the various choices for the answer.
- There is a method for adding answer choices.
- The `display` method of the `ChoiceQuestion` class shows these choices so that the respondent can choose one of them.

Figure 4
Data Layout of Subclass Object

ChoiceQuestion

Question portion

text =

answer =

- - - - - - - - - - - - - - - - - -

choices =

When the ChoiceQuestion class inherits from the Question class, it needs to spell out these three differences:

```
public class ChoiceQuestion extends Question
{
    // This instance variable is added to the subclass
    private ArrayList<String> choices;

    // This method is added to the subclass
    public void addChoice(String choice, boolean correct) { . . . }

    // This method overrides a method from the superclass
    public void display() { . . . }
}
```

The reserved word extends denotes inheritance.

Figure 4 shows the layout of a ChoiceQuestion object. It has the text and answer instance variables that are declared in the Question superclass, and it adds an additional instance variable, choices.

The addChoice method is specific to the ChoiceQuestion class. You can only apply it to ChoiceQuestion objects, not general Question objects.

In contrast, the display method is a method that already exists in the superclass. The subclass overrides this method, so that the choices can be properly displayed.

All other methods of the Question class are automatically inherited by the Choice-Question class.

You can call the inherited methods on a subclass object:

```
choiceQuestion.setAnswer("2");
```

However, the instance variables of the superclass are inaccessible. Because these variables are private data of the superclass, only the superclass has access to them. The subclass has no more access rights than any other class.

In particular, the ChoiceQuestion methods cannot directly access the instance variable answer. These methods must use the public interface of the Question class to access its private data, just like every other method.

Like the manufacturer of a stretch limo, who starts with a regular car and modifies it, a programmer makes a subclass by modifying another class.

Syntax 9.1 Subclass Declaration

The reserved word extends denotes inheritance.

Declare instance variables that are added to the subclass.

Subclass

Superclass

```
public class ChoiceQuestion extends Question
{
    private ArrayList<String> choices
```

Declare methods that are added to the subclass.

```
    public void addChoice(String choice, boolean correct) { . . . }
```

Declare methods that the subclass overrides.

```
    public void display() { . . . }
}
```

To illustrate this point, let's implement the addChoice method. The method has two parameters: the choice to be added (which is appended to the list of choices), and a Boolean value to indicate whether this choice is correct. If it is true, the method sets the answer to the number of the current choice (which is equal to the size of the list of choices).

```java
public void addChoice(String choice, boolean correct)
{
    choices.add(choice);
    if (correct)
    {
        // Convert choices.size() to string
        String choiceString = "" + choices.size();
        setAnswer(choiceString);
    }
}
```

You can't just access the answer variable in the superclass. Fortunately, the Question class has a setAnswer method. You can call that method. On which object? The question that you are currently modifying—that is, the implicit parameter of the Choice-Question.addChoice method. As you saw in Chapter 7, if you invoke a method on the implicit parameter, you don't specify the parameter but just write the method name:

```java
setAnswer(choiceString);
```

The compiler interprets this call as

```java
this.setAnswer(choiceString);
```

SELF CHECK

6. Suppose q is an object of the class Question and cq an object of the class Choice-Question. Which of the following calls are legal?

a. q.setAnswer(response)

b. cq.setAnswer(response)

c. q.addChoice(choice, true)

d. cq.addChoice(choice, true)

7. Suppose the class `Employee` is declared as follows:

```java
public class Employee
{
    private String name;
    private double baseSalary;

    public void setName(String newName) { . . . }
    public void setBaseSalary(double newSalary) { . . . }
    public String getName() { . . . }
    public double getSalary() { . . . }
}
```

Declare a class `Manager` that inherits from the class `Employee` and adds an instance variable `bonus` for storing a salary bonus. Omit constructors and methods.

8. Which instance variables does the `Manager` class from Self Check 7 have?

9. In the `Manager` class, provide the method header (but not the implementation) for a method that overrides the `getSalary` method from the class `Employee`.

10. Which methods does the `Manager` class from Self Check 9 inherit?

Practice It   Now you can try these exercises at the end of the chapter: R9.3, P9.6, P9.14.

Common Error 9.1

Replicating Instance Variables from the Superclass

A subclass has no access to the private instance variables of the superclass.

```java
public ChoiceQuestion(String questionText)
{
    text = questionText; // Error—tries to access private superclass variable
}
```

When faced with a compiler error, beginners commonly "solve" this issue by adding *another* instance variable with the same name to the subclass:

```java
public class ChoiceQuestion extends Question
{
    private ArrayList<String> choices;
    private String text; // Don't!
    . . .
}
```

Sure, now the constructor compiles, but it doesn't set the correct text! Such a `ChoiceQuestion` object has two instance variables, both named `text`. The constructor sets one of them, and the `display` method displays the other.

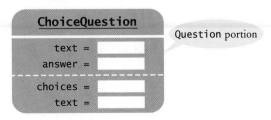

Confusing Super- and Subclasses

If you compare an object of type ChoiceQuestion with an object of type Question, then you find that

- The reserved word extends suggests that the ChoiceQuestion object is an extended version of a Question.
- The ChoiceQuestion object is larger; it has an added instance variable, choices.
- The ChoiceQuestion object is more capable; it has an addChoice method.

It seems a superior object in every way. So why is ChoiceQuestion called the *subclass* and Question the *superclass*?

The *super/sub* terminology comes from set theory. Look at the set of all questions. Not all of them are ChoiceQuestion objects; some of them are other kinds of questions. Therefore, the set of ChoiceQuestion objects is a *subset* of the set of all Question objects, and the set of Question objects is a *superset* of the set of ChoiceQuestion objects. The more specialized objects in the subset have a richer state and more capabilities.

9.3 Overriding Methods

The subclass inherits the methods from the superclass. If you are not satisfied with the behavior of an inherited method, you override it by specifying a new implementation in the subclass.

Consider the display method of the ChoiceQuestion class. It needs to override the superclass display method in order to show the choices for the answer. Specifically, the subclass method needs to

- Display the question text.
- Display the answer choices.

The second part is easy because the answer choices are an instance variable of the subclass.

```
public class ChoiceQuestion
{
    . . .
    public void display()
    {
        // Display the question text
        . . .
        // Display the answer choices
        for (int i = 0; i < choices.size(); i++)
        {
            int choiceNumber = i + 1;
            System.out.println(choiceNumber + ": " + choices.get(i));
        }
    }
}
```

But how do you get the question text? You can't access the text variable of the superclass directly because it is private.

Instead, you can call the display method of the superclass, by using the reserved word super:

```java
public void display()
{
   // Display the question text
   super.display(); // OK
   // Display the answer choices
   . . .
}
```

If you omit the reserved word super, then the method will not work as intended.

```java
public void display()
{
   // Display the question text
   display(); // Error—invokes this.display()
   . . .
}
```

Because the implicit parameter this is of type ChoiceQuestion, and there is a method named display in the ChoiceQuestion class, that method will be called—but that is just the method you are currently writing! The method would call itself over and over.

When you override a method, you usually want to *extend* the functionality of the superclass version. In that case, the subclass method should invoke the superclass method. However, you have no obligation to do so. Occasionally, a subclass overrides a superclass method and specifies an entirely different functionality.

Here is the complete program that lets you take a quiz consisting of a plain Question object and a ChoiceQuestion object. We construct both objects and pass them to a method presentQuestion. That method displays the question to the user and checks whether the user response is correct.

ch09/questions/QuestionDemo2.java

```java
 1  import java.util.Scanner;
 2
 3  /**
 4     This program shows a simple quiz with two question types.
 5  */
 6  public class QuestionDemo2
 7  {
 8     public static void main(String[] args)
 9     {
10        Question first = new Question();
11        first.setText("Who was the inventor of Java?");
12        first.setAnswer("James Gosling");
13
14        ChoiceQuestion second = new ChoiceQuestion();
15        second.setText("In which country was the inventor of Java born?");
16        second.addChoice("Australia", false);
17        second.addChoice("Canada", true);
18        second.addChoice("Denmark", false);
19        second.addChoice("United States", false);
20
21        presentQuestion(first);
22        presentQuestion(second);
23     }
```

Use the reserved word super to call a superclass method.

ANIMATION
Inheritance

```
24
25      /**
26         Presents a question to the user and checks the response.
27         @param q the question
28      */
29      public static void presentQuestion(Question q)
30      {
31         q.display();
32         System.out.print("Your answer: ");
33         Scanner in = new Scanner(System.in);
34         String response = in.nextLine();
35         System.out.println(q.checkAnswer(response));
36      }
37  }
```

ch09/questions/ChoiceQuestion.java

```
1   import java.util.ArrayList;
2
3   /**
4      A question with multiple choices.
5   */
6   public class ChoiceQuestion extends Question
7   {
8      private ArrayList<String> choices;
9
10     /**
11        Constructs a choice question with no choices.
12     */
13     public ChoiceQuestion()
14     {
15        choices = new ArrayList<String>();
16     }
17
18     /**
19        Adds an answer choice to this question.
20        @param choice the choice to add
21        @param correct true if this is the correct choice, false otherwise
22     */
23     public void addChoice(String choice, boolean correct)
24     {
25        choices.add(choice);
26        if (correct)
27        {
28           // Convert choices.size() to string
29           String choiceString = "" + choices.size();
30           setAnswer(choiceString);
31        }
32     }
33
34     public void display()
35     {
36        // Display the question text
37        super.display();
38        // Display the answer choices
39        for (int i = 0; i < choices.size(); i++)
40        {
41           int choiceNumber = i + 1;
42           System.out.println(choiceNumber + ": " + choices.get(i));
```

```
43         }
44      }
45  }
```

Program Run

```
Who was the inventor of Java?
Your answer: Bjarne Stroustrup
false
In which country was the inventor of Java born?
1: Australia
2: Canada
3: Denmark
4: United States
Your answer: 2
true
```

SELF CHECK

11. What is wrong with the following implementation of the display method?

```java
public class ChoiceQuestion
{
    . . .
    public void display()
    {
        System.out.println(text);
        for (int i = 0; i < choices.size(); i++)
        {
            int choiceNumber = i + 1;
            System.out.println(choiceNumber + ": " + choices.get(i));
        }
    }
}
```

12. What is wrong with the following implementation of the display method?

```java
public class ChoiceQuestion
{
    . . .
    public void display()
    {
        this.display();
        for (int i = 0; i < choices.size(); i++)
        {
            int choiceNumber = i + 1;
            System.out.println(choiceNumber + ": " + choices.get(i));
        }
    }
}
```

13. Look again at the implementation of the addChoice method that calls the setAnswer method of the superclass. Why don't you need to call super.setAnswer?

14. In the Manager class of Self Check 7, override the getName method so that managers have a * before their name (such as *Lin, Sally).

15. In the Manager class of Self Check 9, override the getSalary method so that it returns the sum of the salary and the bonus.

Practice It   Now you can try these exercises at the end of the chapter: P9.1, P9.2, P9.15.

Accidental Overloading

In Java, two methods can have the same name, provided they have *different* method parameters. For example, the `PrintStream` class has methods called `println` with headers

```
void println(int x)
```

and

```
void println(String x)
```

These are different methods, each with its own implementation. The Java compiler considers them to be completely unrelated. We say that the `println` name is **overloaded**. This is different from overriding, where a subclass method provides an implementation of a method with the *same* method parameters.

If you mean to override a method but supply a different parameter type, then you accidentally introduce an overloaded method. For example,

```
public class ChoiceQuestion extends Question
{
   . . .
   public void display(PrintStream out) // Does not override void display()
   {
      . . .
   }
}
```

The compiler will not complain. It thinks that you want to provide a method just for `Print-Stream` parameters, while inheriting another method `void display()`.

When overriding a method, be sure to check that the parameter types match exactly.

Forgetting to Use super When Invoking a Superclass Method

A common error in extending the functionality of a superclass method is to forget the reserved word super. For example, to compute the salary of a manager, get the salary of the underlying `Employee` object and add a bonus:

```
public class Manager
{
   . . .
   public double getSalary()
   {
      double baseSalary = getSalary();
         // Error: should be super.getSalary()
      return baseSalary + bonus;
   }
}
```

Here `getSalary()` refers to the `getSalary` method applied to the implicit parameter of the method. The implicit parameter is of type `Manager`, and there is a `getSalary` method in the `Manager` class. Calling that method is a recursive call, which will never stop. Instead, you must tell the compiler to invoke the superclass method.

Whenever you call a superclass method from a subclass method with the same name, be sure to use the reserved word super.

Calling the Superclass Constructor

Consider the process of constructing a subclass object. A subclass constructor can only initialize the instance variables of the subclass. But the superclass instance variables also need to be initialized. Unless you specify otherwise, the superclass instance variables are initialized with the constructor of the superclass that has no parameters.

> Unless specified otherwise, the subclass constructor calls the superclass constructor with no parameters.

In order to specify another constructor, you use the super reserved word, together with the parameters of the superclass constructor, as the *first statement* of the subclass constructor.

For example, suppose the Question superclass had a constructor for setting the question text. Here is how a subclass constructor could call that superclass constructor:

> To call a superclass constructor, use the super reserved word in the first statement of the subclass constructor.

```
public ChoiceQuestion(String questionText)
{
    super(questionText);
    choices = new ArrayList<String>();
}
```

In our example program, we used the superclass constructor with no parameters. However, if all superclass constructors have parameters, you must use the super syntax and provide the parameter values for a superclass constructor.

> The constructor of a subclass can pass parameters to a superclass constructor, using the reserved word super.

When the reserved word super is followed by a parenthesis, it indicates a call to the superclass constructor. When used in this way, the constructor call must be the first statement of the subclass constructor. If super is followed by a period and a method name, on the other hand, it indicates a call to a superclass method, as you saw in the preceding section. Such a call can be made anywhere in any subclass method.

Syntax 9.2   Constructor with Superclass Initializer

The superclass constructor is called first.

The constructor body can contain additional statements.

```
public ChoiceQuestion(String questionText)
{
    super(questionText);
    choices = new ArrayList<String>;
}
```

> If you omit the superclass constructor call, the superclass constructor with no parameters is invoked.

9.4 Polymorphism

In the QuestionDemo2 program, we passed a Question object, then a ChoiceQuestion object to the presentQuestion method. That method is declared to have a parameter of type Question:

```
public static void presentQuestion(Question q)
```

Variable of type
ChoiceQuestion

second =

ChoiceQuestion

text =
answer =

q =

choices =

Variable of type
Question

Figure 5 Variables of Different Types Referring to the Same Object

As discussed in Section 9.1, we can substitute a subclass object whenever a super-class object is expected:

```
ChoiceQuestion second = new ChoiceQuestion();
. . .
presentQuestion(second); // OK to pass a ChoiceQuestion
```

> A subclass reference can be used when a superclass reference is expected.

When the presentQuestion method executes, the object references stored in second and q refer to the same object of type ChoiceQuestion (see Figure 5).

However, the *variable* q knows less than the full story about the object to which it refers (see Figure 6).

Because q is a variable of type Question, you can call the display and checkAnswer methods. You cannot call the addChoice method, though—it is not a method of the Question superclass.

This is as it should be. After all, it happens that in this method call, q refers to a ChoiceQuestion. In another method call, q might refer to a plain Question or an entirely different subclass of Question.

Now let's have a closer look inside the presentQuestion method. It starts with the call

```
q.display(); // Does it call Question.display or ChoiceQuestion.display?
```

ANIMATION
Polymorphism

Which display method is called? If you look at the program output on page 369, you will see that the method called depends on the contents of the parameter q. In the first case, q refers to a Question object, so the Question.display method is called. But in the second case, q refers to a ChoiceQuestion, so the ChoiceQuestion.display method is called, showing the list of choices.

q =

?

text =
answer =

Variable of type
Question

Figure 6 A Question Reference Can Refer to an Object of Any Subclass of Question

In the same way that vehicles can differ in their method of locomotion, polymorphic objects carry out tasks in different ways.

Polymorphism ("having multiple shapes") allows us to manipulate objects that share a set of tasks, even though the tasks are executed in different ways.

In Java, method calls *are always determined by the type of the actual object*, not the type of the variable containing the object reference. This is called **dynamic method lookup**.

Dynamic method lookup allows us to treat objects of different classes in a uniform way. This feature is called **polymorphism**. We ask multiple objects to carry out a task, and each object does so in its own way.

Polymorphism makes programs *easily extensible*. Suppose we want to have a new kind of question for calculations, where we are willing to accept an approximate answer. All we need to do is to declare a new class NumericQuestion, with its own checkAnswer method. Then we can call the presentQuestion method with a mixture of plain questions, choice questions, and numeric questions. The presentQuestion method need not be changed at all! Thanks to dynamic method lookup, method calls to the display and checkAnswer methods automatically select the correct method of the newly declared classes.

SELF CHECK

16. Assuming SavingsAccount is a subclass of BankAccount, which of the following code fragments are valid in Java?

    a. `BankAccount account = new SavingsAccount();`
    b. `SavingsAccount account2 = new BankAccount();`
    c. `BankAccount account = null;`
    d. `SavingsAccount account2 = account;`

17. If account is a variable of type BankAccount that holds a non-null reference, what do you know about the object to which account refers?

18. Declare an array quiz that can hold a mixture of Question and ChoiceQuestion objects.

19. Consider the code fragment

    ```
    ChoiceQuestion cq = . . .; // A non-null value
    cq.display();
    ```

    Which actual method is being called?

20. Is the method call Math.sqrt(2) resolved through dynamic method lookup?

Practice It   Now you can try these exercises at the end of the chapter: R9.6, P9.4, P9.7.

Dynamic Method Lookup and the Implicit Parameter

Suppose we add the `presentQuestion` method to the `Question` class itself:

```java
void presentQuestion()
{
    display();
    System.out.print("Your answer: ");
    Scanner in = new Scanner(System.in);
    String response = in.nextLine();
    System.out.println(checkAnswer(response));
}
```

Now consider the call

```java
ChoiceQuestion cq = new ChoiceQuestion();
cq.setText("In which country was the inventor of Java born?");
. . .
cq.presentQuestion();
```

Which `display` and `checkAnswer` method will the `presentQuestion` method call? If you look inside the code of the `presentQuestion` method, you can see that these methods are executed on the implicit parameter.

```java
public class Question
{
    public void presentQuestion()
    {
        this.display();
        System.out.print("Your answer: ");
        Scanner in = new Scanner(System.in);
        String response = in.nextLine();
        System.out.println(this.checkAnswer(response));
    }
}
```

The implicit parameter `this` in our call is a reference to an object of type `ChoiceQuestion`. Because of dynamic method lookup, the `ChoiceQuestion` versions of the `display` and `check-Answer` methods are called automatically. This happens even though the `presentQuestion` method is declared in the `Question` class, which has *no knowledge* of the `ChoiceQuestion` class.

As you can see, polymorphism is a very powerful mechanism. The `Question` class supplies a `presentQuestion` method that specifies the common nature of presenting a question, namely to display it and check the response. How the displaying and checking are carried out is left to the subclasses.

Abstract Classes

When you extend an existing class, you have the choice whether or not to override the methods of the superclass. Sometimes, it is desirable to *force* programmers to override a method. That happens when there is no good default for the superclass, and only the subclass programmer can know how to implement the method properly.

Here is an example. Suppose the First National Bank of Java decides that every account type must have some monthly fees. Therefore, a `deductFees` method should be added to the `Account` class:

```java
public class Account
{
    public void deductFees() { . . . }
    . . .
```

```
    }
```

But what should this method do? Of course, we could have the method do nothing. But then a programmer implementing a new subclass might simply forget to implement the deductFees method, and the new account would inherit the do-nothing method of the superclass. There is a better way—declare the deductFees method as an **abstract method:**

```
public abstract void deductFees();
```

An abstract method has no implementation. This forces the implementors of subclasses to specify concrete implementations of this method. (Of course, some subclasses might decide to implement a do-nothing method, but then that is their choice—not a silently inherited default.)

> An abstract method is a method whose implementation is not specified.

You cannot construct objects of classes with abstract methods. For example, once the Account class has an abstract method, the compiler will flag an attempt to create a new Account() as an error.

A class for which you cannot create objects is called an **abstract class.** A class for which you can create objects is sometimes called a **concrete class.** In Java, you must declare all abstract classes with the reserved word abstract:

> An abstract class is a class that cannot be instantiated.

```
public abstract class Account
{
    public abstract void deductFees();
    . . .
}

public class SavingsAccount extends Account // Not abstract
{
    . . .
    public void deductFees() // Provides an implementation
    {
        . . .
    }
}
```

Note that you cannot construct an *object* of an abstract class, but you can still have an *object reference* whose type is an abstract class. Of course, the actual object to which it refers must be an instance of a concrete subclass:

```
Account anAccount; // OK
anAccount = new Account(); // Error—Account is abstract
anAccount = new SavingsAccount(); // OK
anAccount = null; // OK
```

The reason for using abstract classes is to force programmers to create subclasses. By specifying certain methods as abstract, you avoid the trouble of coming up with useless default methods that others might inherit by accident.

Special Topic 9.4

Protected Access

We ran into a hurdle when trying to implement the display method of the ChoiceQuestion class. That method wanted to access the instance variable text of the superclass. Our remedy was to use the appropriate method of the superclass to display the text.

Java offers another solution to this problem. The superclass can declare an instance variable as *protected:*

```
public class Question
{
```

```
        protected String text;
        . . .
    }
```

Protected data in an object can be accessed by the methods of the object's class and all its subclasses. For example, `ChoiceQuestion` inherits from `Question`, so its methods can access the protected instance variables of the `Question` superclass.

> Protected features can be accessed by all subclasses and all classes in the same package.

Some programmers like the protected access feature because it seems to strike a balance between absolute protection (making instance variables private) and no protection at all (making instance variables public). However, experience has shown that protected instance variables are subject to the same kinds of problems as public instance variables. The designer of the superclass has no control over the authors of subclasses. Any of the subclass methods can corrupt the superclass data. Furthermore, classes with protected variables are hard to modify. Even if the author of the superclass would like to change the data implementation, the protected variables cannot be changed, because someone somewhere out there might have written a subclass whose code depends on them.

In Java, protected variables have another drawback—they are accessible not just by subclasses, but also by other classes in the same package.

It is best to leave all data private. If you want to grant access to the data to subclass methods only, consider making the *accessor* method protected.

HOW TO 9.1   Developing an Inheritance Hierarchy

When you work with a set of classes, some of which are more general and others more specialized, you want to organize them into an inheritance hierarchy. This enables you to process objects of different classes in a uniform way.

As an example, we will consider a bank that offers customers the following account types:

- A savings account that earns interest. The interest compounds monthly and is based on the minimum monthly balance.

- A checking account that has no interest, gives you three free withdrawals per month, and charges a $1 transaction fee for each additional withdrawal.

The program will manage a set of accounts of both types, and it should be structured so that other account types can be added without affecting the main processing loop. Supply a menu

```
D)eposit  W)ithdraw  M)onth end  Q)uit
```

For deposits and withdrawals, query the account number and amount. Print the balance of the account after each transaction.

In the "Month end" command, accumulate interest or clear the transaction counter, depending on the type of the bank account. Then print the balance of all accounts.

Step 1   List the classes that are part of the hierarchy.

In our case, the problem description yields two classes: `SavingsAccount` and `CheckingAccount`. Of course, you could implement each of them separately. But that would not be a good idea because the classes would have to repeat common functionality, such as updating an account balance. We need another class that can be responsible for that common functionality. The problem statement does not explicitly mention such a class. Therefore, we need to discover it. Of course, in this case, the solution is simple. Savings accounts and checking accounts are special cases of a bank account. Therefore, we will introduce a common superclass `BankAccount`.

Step 2 Organize the classes into an inheritance hierarchy.

Draw an inheritance diagram that shows super- and subclasses. Here is the diagram for our example.

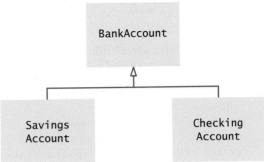

Step 3 Determine the common responsibilities.

In Step 2, you will have identified a class at the base of the hierarchy. That class needs to have sufficient responsibilities to carry out the tasks at hand. To find out what those tasks are, write pseudocode for processing the objects.

```
For each user command
    If it is a deposit or withdrawal
        Deposit or withdraw the amount from the specified account.
        Print the balance.
    If it is month end processing
        For each account
            Call month end processing.
            Print the balance.
```

From the pseudocode, we obtain the following list of common responsibilities that every bank account must carry out:

```
Deposit money.
Withdraw money.
Get the balance.
Carry out month end processing.
```

Step 4 Decide which methods are overridden in subclasses.

For each subclass and each of the common responsibilities, decide whether the behavior can be inherited or whether it needs to be overridden. Be sure to declare any methods that are inherited or overridden in the root of the hierarchy.

```java
public class BankAccount
{
    . . .
    /**
        Makes a deposit into this account.
        @param amount  the amount of the deposit
    */
    public void deposit(double amount) { . . . }

    /**
        Makes a withdrawal from this account, or charges a penalty if
        sufficient funds are not available.
        @param amount  the amount of the withdrawal
    */
    public void withdraw(double amount) { . . . }
```

```
/**
   Carries out the end of month processing that is appropriate
   for this account.
*/
public void monthEnd() { . . . }

/**
   Gets the current balance of this bank account.
   @return the current balance
*/
public double getBalance() { . . . }
}
```

The `SavingsAccount` and `CheckingAccount` classes both override the `monthEnd` method. The `SavingsAccount` class must also override the `withdraw` method to track the minimum balance. The `CheckingAccount` class must update a transaction count in the `withdraw` method.

Step 5 Declare the public interface of each subclass.

Typically, subclasses have responsibilities other than those of the superclass. List those, as well as the methods that need to be overridden. You also need to specify how the objects of the subclasses should be constructed.

In this example, we need a way of setting the interest rate for the savings account. In addition, we need to specify constructors and overridden methods.

```
public class SavingsAccount extends BankAccount
{
   . . .
   /**
      Constructs a savings account with a zero balance.
   */
   public SavingsAccount() { . . . }

   /**
      Sets the interest rate for this account.
      @param rate the monthly interest rate in percent
   */
   public void setInterestRate(double rate) { . . . }

   // These methods override superclass methods
   public void withdraw(double amount) { . . . }
   public void monthEnd() { . . . }
}

public class CheckingAccount extends BankAccount
{
   . . .
   /**
      Constructs a checking account with a zero balance.
   */
   public CheckingAccount() { . . . }

   // These methods override superclass methods
   public void withdraw(double amount) { . . . }
   public void monthEnd() { . . . }
}
```

Step 6 Identify instance variables.

List the instance variables for each class. If you find an instance variable that is common to all classes, be sure to place it in the base of the hierarchy.

All accounts have a balance. We store that value in the BankAccount superclass.

```
public class BankAccount
{
   private double balance;
   . . .
}
```

The SavingsAccount class needs to store the interest rate. It also needs to store the minimum monthly balance, which must be updated by all withdrawals.

```
public class SavingsAccount extends BankAccount
{
   private double interestRate;
   private double minBalance;
   . . .
}
```

The CheckingAccount class needs to count the withdrawals, so that the charge can be applied after the free withdrawal limit is reached.

```
public class CheckingAccount extends BankAccount
{
   private int withdrawals;
   . . .
}
```

Step 7   Implement constructors and methods.

The methods of the BankAccount class update or return the balance.

```
public void deposit(double amount)
{
   balance = balance + amount;
}

public void withdraw(double amount)
{
   balance = balance - amount;
}

public double getBalance()
{
   return balance;
}
```

At the level of the BankAccount superclass, we can say nothing about end of month processing. We choose to make that method do nothing.

```
public void monthEnd()
{
}
```

In the withdraw method of the SavingsAccount class, the minimum balance is updated. Note the call to the superclass method.

```
public void withdraw(double amount)
{
   super.withdraw(amount);
   double balance = getBalance();
   if (balance < minBalance)
   {
      minBalance = balance;
   }
}
```

In the `monthEnd` method of the `SavingsAccount` class, the interest is deposited into the account. We must call the `deposit` method because we have no direct access to the `balance` instance variable. The minimum balance is reset for the next month.

```java
public void monthEnd()
{
    double interest = minBalance * interestRate / 100;
    deposit(interest);
    minBalance = getBalance();
}
```

The `withdraw` method of the `CheckingAccount` class needs to check the withdrawal count. If there have been too many withdrawals, a charge is applied. Again, note how the method invokes the superclass method.

```java
public void withdraw(double amount)
{
    final int FREE_WITHDRAWALS = 3;
    final int WITHDRAWAL_FEE = 1;

    super.withdraw(amount);
    withdrawals++;
    if (withdrawals > FREE_WITHDRAWALS)
    {
        super.withdraw(WITHDRAWAL_FEE);
    }
}
```

End of month processing for a checking account simply resets the withdrawal count.

```java
public void monthEnd()
{
    withdrawals = 0;
}
```

Step 8 Construct objects of different subclasses and process them.

In our sample program, we allocate 5 checking accounts and 5 savings accounts and store their addresses in an array of bank accounts. Then we accept user commands and execute deposits, withdrawals, and monthly processing.

```java
BankAccount[] accounts = . . .;

Scanner in = new Scanner(System.in);
boolean done = false;
while (!done)
{
    System.out.print("D)eposit  W)ithdraw  M)onth end  Q)uit: ");
    String input = in.next();
    if (input.equals("D") || input.equals("W")) // Deposit or withdrawal
    {
        System.out.print("Enter account number and amount: ");
        int num = in.nextInt();
        double amount = in.nextDouble();

        if (input.equals("D")) { accounts[num].deposit(amount); }
        else { accounts[num].withdraw(amount); }

        System.out.println("Balance: " + accounts[num].getBalance());
    }
    else if (input.equals("M")) // Month end processing
    {
```

```
            for (int n = 0; n < accounts.length; n++)
            {
               accounts[n].monthEnd();
               System.out.println(n + " " + accounts[n].getBalance());
            }
         }
         else if (input == "Q")
         {
            done = true;
         }
      }
   }
```

The complete program is contained in the ch09/accounts directory of your source code.

 **WORKED EXAMPLE 9.1**   **Implementing an Employee Hierarchy for Payroll Processing**

This Worked Example shows how to implement payroll processing that works for different kinds of employees.

9.5 Object: The Cosmic Superclass

In Java, every class that is declared without an explicit extends clause automatically extends the class Object. That is, the class Object is the direct or indirect superclass of *every* class in Java (see Figure 7). The methods of the Object class are very general. In Chapter 10, you will see how to make use of the equals and hashCode methods of the Object class. In the next section, we discuss the toString method.

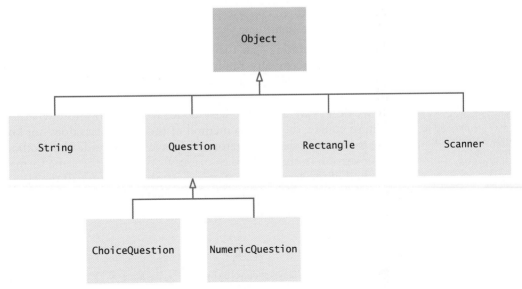

Figure 7 The Object Class Is the Superclass of Every Java Class

➕ Available online in WileyPLUS and at www.wiley.com/college/horstmann.

9.5.1 Overriding the `toString` Method

The `toString` method returns a string representation for each object. It is often used for debugging. For example, consider the `Rectangle` class in the standard Java library. Its `toString` method shows the state of a rectangle:

```
Rectangle box = new Rectangle(5, 10, 20, 30);
String s = box.toString();
    // Sets s to "java.awt.Rectangle[x=5,y=10,width=20,height=30]"
```

The `toString` method is called automatically whenever you concatenate a string with an object. Here is an example:

```
"box=" + box;
```

On one side of the + concatenation operator is a string, but on the other side is an object reference. The Java compiler automatically invokes the `toString` method to turn the object into a string. Then both strings are concatenated. In this case, the result is the string

```
"box=java.awt.Rectangle[x=5,y=10,width=20,height=30]"
```

The compiler can invoke the `toString` method, because it knows that *every* object has a `toString` method: Every class extends the `Object` class, and that class declares `toString`.

As you know, numbers are also converted to strings when they are concatenated with other strings. For example,

```
int age = 18;
String s = "Harry's age is " + age;
    // Sets s to "Harry's age is 18"
```

In this case, the `toString` method is *not* involved. Numbers are not objects, and there is no `toString` method for them. Fortunately, there is only a small set of primitive types, and the compiler knows how to convert them to strings.

Let's try the `toString` method for the `BankAccount` class:

```
BankAccount momsSavings = new BankAccount(5000);
String s = momsSavings.toString();
    // Sets s to something like "BankAccount@d24606bf"
```

That's disappointing—all that's printed is the name of the class, followed by the **hash code**, a seemingly random code. The hash code can be used to tell objects apart—different objects are likely to have different hash codes. (See Chapter 10 for the details.)

We don't care about the hash code. We want to know what is inside the object. But, of course, the `toString` method of the `Object` class does not know what is inside the `BankAccount` class. Therefore, we have to override the method and supply our own version in the `BankAccount` class. We'll follow the same format that the `toString` method of the `Rectangle` class uses: first print the name of the class, and then the values of the instance variables inside brackets.

> Override the toString method to yield a string that describes the object's state.

```
public class BankAccount
{
    . . .
    public String toString()
    {
        return "BankAccount[balance=" + balance + "]";
    }
}
```

This works better:

```
BankAccount momsSavings = new BankAccount(5000);
String s = momsSavings.toString();
   // Sets s to "BankAccount[balance=5000]"
```

9.5.2 Casts and the instanceof Operator

As you have seen, it is legal to store a subclass reference in a superclass variable:

```
ChoiceQuestion cq = new ChoiceQuestion();
Question q = cq; // OK
Object obj = cq; // OK
```

Very occasionally, you need to carry out the opposite conversion, from a superclass reference to a subclass reference.

For example, you may have a variable of type Object, and you happen to know that it actually holds a Question reference. In that case, you can use a cast to convert the type:

```
Question q = (Question) obj;
```

However, this cast is somewhat dangerous. If you are wrong, and obj actually refers to an object of an unrelated type, then a "class cast" exception is thrown.

The instanceof operator tests whether an object belongs to a particular type.

To protect against bad casts, you can use the instanceof operator. It tests whether an object belongs to a particular type. For example,

```
obj instanceof Question
```

returns true if the type of obj is convertible to Question. This happens if obj refers to an actual Question or to a subclass such as ChoiceQuestion. Using the instanceof operator, a safe cast can be programmed as follows:

```
if (obj instanceof Question)
{
   Question q = (Question) obj;
}
```

Syntax 9.3   The instanceof and Cast Operators

If anObject is null, instanceof returns false.

Returns true if anObject can be cast to a Question.

The object may belong to a subclass of Question.

```
if (anObject instanceof Question)
{
      Question q = (Question) anObject;
      . . .
}
```

You can invoke Question methods on this variable.

Two references to the same object.

Casts and the `instanceof` operator are most commonly used with very generic mechanisms—see Special Topic 9.7 on page 392 for an example.

You should *not* use them to bypass polymorphism:

```java
if (q instanceof ChoiceQuestion) // Don't do this—see Common Error 9.5 on page 384
{
    // Do the task the ChoiceQuestion way
}
else if (q instanceof Question)
{
    // Do the task the Question way
}
```

In this case, you should implement a method `doTheTask` in the `Question` class, override it in `ChoiceQuestion`, and call

```java
q.doTheTask();
```

SELF CHECK

21. Why does the call

```java
System.out.println(System.out);
```

produce a result such as `java.io.PrintStream@7a84e4`?

22. Will the following code fragment compile? Will it run? If not, what error is reported?

```java
Object obj = "Hello";
System.out.println(obj.length());
```

23. Will the following code fragment compile? Will it run? If not, what error is reported?

```java
Object obj = "Who was the inventor of Java?";
Question q = (Question) obj;
q.display();
```

24. Why don't we simply store all objects in variables of type `Object`?

25. Assuming that x is an object reference, what is the value of `x instanceof Object`?

Practice It Now you can try these exercises at the end of the chapter: P9.11, P9.12, P9.16.

Common Error 9.5

Don't Use Type Tests

Some programmers use specific type tests in order to implement behavior that varies with each class:

```java
if (q instanceof ChoiceQuestion) // Don't do this
{
    // Do the task the ChoiceQuestion way
}
else if (q instanceof Question)
{
    // Do the task the Question way
}
```

This is a poor strategy. If a new class is such as NumericQuestion is added, then you need to revise all parts of your program that make a type test, adding another case:

```
else if (q instanceof NumericQuestion)
{
    // Do the task the NumericQuestion way
}
```

In contrast, consider the addition of a class NumericQuestion to our quiz program. *Nothing* needs to change in that program because it uses polymorphism, not type tests.

Whenever you find yourself trying to use type tests in a hierarchy of classes, reconsider and use polymorphism instead. Declare a method doTheTask in the superclass, override it in the subclasses, and call

```
q.doTheTask();
```

Special Topic 9.5

Inheritance and the toString Method

You just saw how to write a toString method: Form a string consisting of the class name and the names and values of the instance variables. However, if you want your toString method to be usable by subclasses of your class, you need to work a bit harder. Instead of hardcoding the class name, call the getClass method (which every class inherits from the Object class) to obtain an object that describes a class and its properties. Then invoke the getName method to get the name of the class:

```
public String toString()
{
    return getClass().getName() + "[balance=" + balance + "]";
}
```

Then the toString method prints the correct class name when you apply it to a subclass, say a SavingsAccount.

```
SavingsAccount momsSavings = . . . ;
System.out.println(momsSavings);
// Prints "SavingsAccount[balance=10000]"
```

Of course, in the subclass, you should override toString and add the values of the subclass instance variables. Note that you must call super.toString to get the instance variables of the superclass—the subclass can't access them directly.

```
public class SavingsAccount extends BankAccount
{
    . . .
    public String toString()
    {
        return super.toString() + "[interestRate=" + interestRate + "]";
    }
}
```

Now a savings account is converted to a string such as SavingsAccount[balance= 10000][interestRate=5]. The brackets show which variables belong to the superclass.

9.6 Interface Types

It is often possible to make a mechanism for processing objects more general and more reusable by focusing on the essential operations that are carried out. *Interface types* are used to express these common operations.

9.6.1 Defining an Interface

Use interface types to make a mechanism for processing objects available to multiple classes.

Consider the following method that computes the average balance in an array of BankAccount objects:

```java
public static double average(BankAccount[] objs)
{
    if (objs.length == 0) return 0;
    double sum = 0;
    for (BankAccount obj : objs)
    {
        sum = sum + obj.getBalance();
    }
    return sum / objs.length;
}
```

Now suppose you have an array of Country objects and want to determine the average of the areas:

```java
public static double average(Country[] objs)
{
    if (objs.length == 0) return 0;
    double sum = 0;
    for (Country obj : objs)
    {
        sum = sum + obj.getArea();
    }
    return sum / objs.length;
}
```

Clearly, the algorithm for computing the result is the same in both cases, but the details of measurement differ.

Suppose that the various classes agree on a single method getMeasure that obtains the measure to be used in the data analysis. For bank accounts, getMeasure returns the balance. For countries, getMeasure returns the area, and so on. Then we can implement a single method that computes

```java
sum = sum + obj.getMeasure();
```

What is the type of the variable obj? Any class that has a getMeasure method.

A Java interface type declares a set of methods and their signatures.

In Java, an **interface type** is used to specify required operations. We will declare an interface type that we call Measurable:

```java
public interface Measurable
{
    double getMeasure();
}
```

The interface declaration lists all methods that the interface type requires. The Measurable interface type requires a single method, but in general, an interface type can require multiple methods. (Note that the Measurable type is not a type in the standard library—it is a type that was created specifically for this book.)

Syntax 9.4   Interface Types

Interface methods
are always public.

```
public interface Measurable
{
    double getMeasure();
}
```

Interface methods
have no implementation.

```
public class BankAccount implements Measurable
{
    . . .

    public double getMeasure()
    {
        return balance;
    }
}
```

Other
BankAccount
methods.

A class can implement one
or more interface types.

Implementation for the method that
was declared in the interface type.

Unlike a class, an
interface type
provides no
implementation.

An interface type is similar to a class, but there are several important differences:

- All methods in an interface type are *abstract;* that is, they have a name, parameters, and a return type, but they don't have an implementation.
- All methods in an interface type are automatically public.
- An interface type cannot have instance variables.
- An interface type cannot have static methods.

We can use the interface type Measurable to implement a "universal" method for computing averages:

```
public static double average(Measurable[] objs)
{
    if (objs.length == 0) return 0;
    double sum = 0;
    for (Measurable obj : objs)
    {
        sum = sum + obj.getMeasure();
    }
    return sum / objs.length;
}
```

*This standmixer provides the "rotation"
service to any attachment that
conforms to a common interface.*

9.6.2 Implementing an Interface

Use the implements reserved word to indicate that a class implements an interface type.

The average method is usable for objects of any class that **implements** the Measurable interface. A class implements an interface type if it declares the interface in an implements clause, and if it implements the method or methods that the interface requires. Let's modify the BankAccount class to implement the Measurable interface.

```
public class BankAccount implements Measurable
{
    public double getMeasure()
    {
        return balance;
    }
    . . .
}
```

Note that the class must declare the method as public, whereas the interface type need not—all methods in an interface type are public.

Similarly, it is an easy matter to implement a Country class that implements the Measurable interface.

```
public class Country implements Measurable
{
    public double getMeasure()
    {
        return area;
    }
    . . .
}
```

A reference to a BankAccount or Country can be converted to a Measurable reference. The sample program at the end of this section shows how the same average method can compute the average of a collection of bank accounts or countries.

In summary, the Measurable interface expresses what all measurable objects have in common. This commonality makes it possible to write methods such as average that are usable for many classes.

Figure 8 shows a diagram of the classes and interfaces in this program. A dotted arrow with a triangular tip denotes the "implements" relationship.

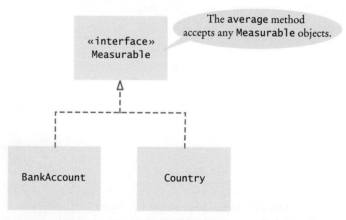

Figure 8 Classes that Implement the Measurable Interface

ch09/measure/MeasurableDemo.java

```java
1   /**
2      This program demonstrates the measurable BankAccount and Country classes.
3   */
4   public class MeasurableDemo
5   {
6      public static void main(String[] args)
7      {
8         Measurable[] accounts = new Measurable[3];
9         accounts[0] = new BankAccount(0);
10        accounts[1] = new BankAccount(10000);
11        accounts[2] = new BankAccount(2000);
12
13        System.out.println("Average balance: "
14           + average(accounts));
15
16        Measurable[] countries = new Measurable[3];
17        countries[0] = new Country("Uruguay", 176220);
18        countries[1] = new Country("Thailand", 514000);
19        countries[2] = new Country("Belgium", 30510);
20
21        System.out.println("Average area: "
22           + average(countries));
23     }
24
25     /**
26        Computes the average of the measures of the given objects.
27        @param objs an array of Measurable objects
28        @return the average of the measures
29     */
30     public static double average(Measurable[] objs)
31     {
32        if (objs.length == 0) { return 0; }
33        double sum = 0;
34        for (Measurable obj : objs)
35        {
36           sum = sum + obj.getMeasure();
37        }
38        return sum / objs.length;
39     }
40  }
```

Program Run

```
Average balance: 4000.0
Average area: 240243.33333333334
```

9.6.3 The Comparable Interface

In the preceding sections, we defined the Measurable interface and provided an average method that works with any classes implementing that interface. In this section, you will learn about the Comparable interface of the standard Java library.

The Measurable interface is used for measuring a single object. The Comparable interface is more complex because comparisons involve two objects. The interface declares a compareTo method. The call

```
a.compareTo(b)
```

must return a negative number if a should come before b, zero if a and b are the same, and a positive number otherwise.

In order to express the fact that we want a and b to have the same type, the Comparable interface uses a type parameter. You have already seen type parameters in the ArrayList class. A type parameter is enclosed in angle brackets, such as ArrayList<String>. Here is the declaration of the Comparable interface:

```
public interface Comparable<T>
{
    int compareTo(T other);
}
```

The type parameter T specifies the type of the other parameter. This type should be the same as the implementing class. For example, the BankAccount class can implement Comparable<BankAccount>, like this:

```
public class BankAccount implements Comparable<BankAccount>
{
    . . .
    public int compareTo(BankAccount other)
    {
        if (balance < other.getBalance()) { return -1; }
        if (balance > other.getBalance()) { return 1; }
        return 0;
    }
    . . .
}
```

This compareTo method compares bank accounts by their balance.

Once the BankAccount class implements the Comparable interface, you can sort an array of bank accounts with the Arrays.sort method:

```
BankAccount[] accounts = new BankAccount[3];
accounts[0] = new BankAccount(10000);
accounts[1] = new BankAccount(0);
accounts[2] = new BankAccount(2000);
Arrays.sort(accounts);
```

The accounts array is now sorted by increasing balance.

The compareTo *method checks whether another object is larger or smaller.*

26. Suppose you want to use the average method to find the average salary of Employee objects. What condition must the Employee class fulfill?

27. Why can't the average method have a parameter of type Object[]?

28. Why can't you use the average method to find the average length of String objects?

29. What is wrong with this code?

```
Measurable meas = new Measurable();
System.out.println(meas.getMeasure());
```

30. How can you sort an array of Country objects by increasing area?

31. Can you use the Arrays.sort method to sort an array of String objects? Check the API documentation for the String class.

Practice It   Now you can try these exercises at the end of the chapter: R9.14, P9.19, P9.20.

Common Error 9.6

Forgetting to Declare Implementing Methods as Public

The methods in an interface are not declared as public, because they are public by default. However, the methods in a class are not public by default. It is a common error to forget the public reserved word when declaring a method from an interface:

```
public class BankAccount implements Measurable
{
   double getMeasure() // Oops—should be public
   {
      return balance;
   }
   . . .
}
```

Then the compiler complains that the method has a weaker access level, namely package access instead of public access. The remedy is to declare the method as public.

Special Topic 9.6

Constants in Interfaces

Interfaces cannot have instance variables, but it is legal to specify **constants**.

When declaring a constant in an interface, you can (and should) omit the reserved words public static final, because all variables in an interface are automatically public static final. For example,

```
public interface Measurable
{
   double OUNCES_PER_LITER = 33.814;
   . . .
}
```

To use this constant in your programs, add the interface name:

```
Measurable.OUNCES_PER_LITER
```

Common Error 9.7

The compareTo Method Can Return Any Integer, Not Just –1, 0, and 1

The call a.compareTo(b) is allowed to return *any* negative integer to denote that a should come before b, not necessarily the value –1. That is, the test

```
if (a.compareTo(b) == -1) // ERROR!
```

is generally wrong. Instead, you should test

```
if (a.compareTo(b) < 0) // OK
```

Why would a compareTo method ever want to return a number other than –1, 0, or 1? Sometimes, it is convenient to just return the difference of two integers. For example, the compareTo method of the String class compares characters in matching positions:

```
char c1 = charAt(i);
char c2 = other.charAt(i);
```

If the characters are different, then the method simply returns their difference:

```
if (c1 != c2) { return c1 - c2; }
```

This difference is a negative number if c1 is less than c2, but it is not necessarily the number –1.

Special Topic 9.7

Function Objects

In the preceding section, you saw how the Measurable interface type makes it possible to provide services that work for many classes—provided they are willing to implement the interface type. But what can you do if a class does not do so? For example, we might want to compute the average length of a collection of strings, but String does not implement Measurable.

Let's rethink our approach. The average method needs to measure each object. When the objects are required to be of type Measurable, the responsibility for measuring lies with the objects themselves, which is the cause of the limitation that we noted. It would be better if another object could carry out the measurement. Let's move the measurement method into a different interface:

```
public interface Measurer
{
    double measure(Object anObject);
}
```

The measure method measures an object and returns its measurement. We use a parameter of type Object, the "lowest common denominator" of all classes in Java, because we do not want to restrict which classes can be measured.

We add a Measurer parameter to the average method:

```
public static double average(Object[] objs, Measurer meas)
{
    if (objs.length == 0) { return 0; }
    double sum = 0;
    for (Object obj : objs)
    {
        sum = sum + meas.measure(obj);
    }
    return sum / objs.length;
}
```

When calling the method, you need to supply a Measurer object. That is, you need to implement a class with a measure method, and then create an object of that class. Let's do that for measuring strings:

```
public class StringMeasurer implements Measurer
{
    public double measure(Object obj)
    {
        String str = (String) obj; // Cast obj to String type
        return str.length();
    }
}
```

Note that the `measure` method must accept a parameter of type `Object`, even though this particular measurer just wants to measure strings. The method signature must match the signature of the `measure` method in the `Measurer` interface. Therefore, the `Object` parameter is cast to the `String` type.

Finally, we are ready to compute the average length of an array of strings:

```
String[] words = { "Mary", "had", "a", "little", "lamb" };
Measurer strMeas = new StringMeasurer();
double result = average(words, strMeas); // result is set to 3.6
```

An object such as `strMeas` is called a *function object*. The sole purpose of the object is to execute a single method, in our case `measure`. (In mathematics, as well as many other programming languages, the term "function" is used where Java uses "method".)

See ch09/measure2 for a complete sample program. The `Comparator` interface, discussed in Special Topic 10.2, is another example of an interface for function objects.

Random Fact 9.1 Databases and Privacy

Most companies use computers to keep huge databases of customer records and other business information. Databases not only lower the cost of doing business, they improve the quality of service that companies can offer. Nowadays it is almost unimaginable how time-consuming it used to be to withdraw money from a bank branch or to make travel reservations.

As these databases became ubiquitous, they started creating problems for citizens. Consider the "no fly list" maintained by the U.S. government, which lists names used by suspected terrorists. Unfortunately the list was not very accurate, and quite a few innocent travelers were denied boarding passes at the airport. Many of them had serious difficulties trying to get themselves off the list.

Problems such as these have become commonplace. Companies and the government routinely merge multiple databases, derive information about us that may be quite inaccurate, and then use that information to make decisions. An insurance company may deny coverage, or charge a higher premium, if it finds that you have too many relatives with a certain disease. You may be denied a job because of a credit or medical report. You do not usually know what information about yourself is stored or how it is used. In cases where the information can be checked—such as credit reports—it is often difficult to correct errors.

Another issue of concern is privacy. Most people do something, at one time or another in their life, that they do not want everyone to know about. As Judge Louis Brandeis wrote in 1928, "Privacy is the right to be alone—the most comprehensive of rights, and the right most valued by civilized man." When employers can see your old Facebook posts, divorce lawyers have access to tollroad records, and Google mines your searches to present you "targeted" advertising, you have little privacy left.

The 1948 "universal declaration of human rights" by the United Nations states, "No one shall be subjected to arbitrary interference with his privacy, family, home or correspondence, nor to attacks upon his honour and reputation. Everyone has the right to the protection of the law against such interference or attacks." The United States has surprisingly few legal protections against privacy invasion. Other industrialized countries have gone much further and recognize every citizen's right to control what information about themselves should be communicated to others and under what circumstances.

If you pay tolls with an electronic pass, your records may not be private.

CHAPTER SUMMARY

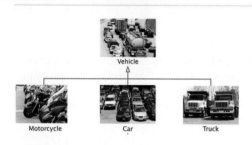

- A subclass inherits data and behavior from a superclass.
- You can always use a subclass object in place of a superclass object.

- A subclass inherits all methods that it does not override.
- A subclass can override a superclass method by providing a new implementation.

- Use the reserved word super to call a superclass method.
- Unless specified otherwise, the subclass constructor calls the superclass constructor with no parameters.
- To call a superclass constructor, use the super reserved word in the first statement of the subclass constructor.
- The constructor of a subclass can pass parameters to a superclass constructor, using the reserved word super.

- A subclass reference can be used when a superclass reference is expected.
- Polymorphism ("having multiple shapes") allows us to manipulate objects that share a set of tasks, even though the tasks are executed in different ways.
- An abstract method is a method whose implementation is not specified.
- An abstract class is a class that cannot be instantiated.
- Protected features can be accessed by all subclasses and all classes in the same package.

- Override the toString method to yield a string that describes the object's state.
- The instanceof operator tests whether an object belongs to a particular type.

➕ Available online in WileyPLUS and at www.wiley.com/college/horstmann.

- Use interface types to make a mechanism for processing objects available to multiple classes.
- A Java interface type declares a set of methods and their signatures.
- Unlike a class, an interface type provides no implementation.
- Use the `implements` reserved word to indicate that a class implements an interface type.

MEDIA RESOURCES

www.wiley.com/
college/
horstmann

- **Worked Example** Implementing an Employee Hierarchy for Payroll Processing
- Guided Lab Exercises
- ⊕ **Animation** Inheritance
- ⊕ **Animation** Polymorphism
- ⊕ **Screencast** Drawing Geometric Shapes
- ⊕ Practice Quiz
- ⊕ Code Completion Exercises

REVIEW EXERCISES

★ **R9.1** Identify the superclass and subclass in each of the following pairs of classes.

     a. Employee, Manager
     b. GraduateStudent, Student
     c. Person, Student
     d. Employee, Professor
     e. BankAccount, CheckingAccount
     f. Vehicle, Car
     g. Vehicle, Minivan
     h. Car, Minivan
     i. Truck, Vehicle

★ **R9.2** Consider a program for managing inventory in a small appliance store. Why isn't it useful to have a superclass SmallAppliance and subclasses Toaster, CarVacuum, Travel-Iron, and so on?

★ **R9.3** Which methods does the ChoiceQuestion class inherit from its superclass? Which methods does it override? Which methods does it add?

★ **R9.4** Which methods does the SavingsAccount class in How To 9.1 on page 376 inherit from its superclass? Which methods does it override? Which methods does it add?

★ **R9.5** List the instance variables of a CheckingAccount object from How To 9.1 on page 376.

★★ **R9.6** Suppose the class Sub extends the class Sandwich. Which of the following assignments are legal?

```
Sandwich x = new Sandwich();
Sub y = new Sub();
```

     a. x = y;   **c.** y = new Sandwich();
     b. y = x;   **d.** x = new Sub();

★   **R9.7** Draw an inheritance diagram that shows the inheritance relationships between the classes:

- Person
- Employee
- Student
- Instructor
- Classroom
- Object

★   **R9.8** In an object-oriented traffic simulation system, we have the following classes:

- Vehicle
- Car
- Truck
- Sedan
- Coupe
- PickupTruck
- SportUtilityVehicle
- Minivan
- Bicycle
- Motorcycle

Draw an inheritance diagram that shows the relationships between these classes.

★   **R9.9** What inheritance relationships would you establish among the following classes?

- Student
- Professor
- TeachingAssistant
- Employee
- Secretary
- DepartmentChair
- Janitor
- SeminarSpeaker
- Person
- Course
- Seminar
- Lecture
- ComputerLab

★★   **R9.10** How does a cast such as (BankAccount) x differ from a cast of number values such as (int) x?

★★★   **R9.11** Which of these conditions returns true? Check the Java documentation for the inheritance patterns. Recall that System.out is an object of the PrintStream class.

a. System.out instanceof PrintStream
b. System.out instanceof OutputStream
c. System.out instanceof LogStream
d. System.out instanceof Object
e. System.out instanceof Closeable
f. System.out instanceof Writer

★★   **R9.12** Suppose C is a class that implements the interfaces I and J. Which of the following assignments require a cast?

```
C c = . . .;
I i = . . .;
J j = . . .;
```

a. c = i;
b. j = c;
c. i = j;

★★ **R9.13** Suppose C is a class that implements the interfaces I and J, and suppose i is declared as

```
I i = new C();
```

Which of the following statements will throw an exception?

a. C c = (C) i;
b. J j = (J) i;
c. i = (I) null;

★★ **R9.14** Suppose the class Sandwich implements the Edible interface, and you are given the variable declarations

```
Sandwich sub = new Sandwich();
Rectangle cerealBox = new Rectangle(5, 10, 20, 30);
Edible e = null;
```

Which of the following assignment statements are legal?

a. e = sub;
b. sub = e;
c. sub = (Sandwich) e;
d. sub = (Sandwich) cerealBox;
e. e = cerealBox;
f. e = (Edible) cerealBox;
g. e = (Rectangle) cerealBox;
h. e = (Rectangle) null;

PROGRAMMING EXERCISES

★★ **P9.1** Add a class NumericQuestion to the question hierarchy of Section 9.1. If the response and the expected answer differ by no more than 0.01, then accept the response as correct.

★★ **P9.2** Add a class FillInQuestion to the question hierarchy of Section 9.1. Such a question is constructed with a string that contains the answer, surrounded by _ _, for example, "The inventor of Java was _James Gosling_". The question should be displayed as

```
The inventor of Java was _____
```

★ **P9.3** Modify the checkAnswer method of the Question class so that it does not take into account different spaces or upper/lowercase characters. For example, the response "JAMES gosling" should match an answer of "James Gosling".

★★ **P9.4** Add a class AnyCorrectChoiceQuestion to the question hierarchy of Section 9.1 that allows multiple correct choices. The respondent should provide any one of the correct choices. The answer string should contain all of the correct choices, separated by spaces. Provide instructions in the question text.

★★ **P9.5** Add a class MultiChoiceQuestion to the question hierarchy of Section 9.1 that allows multiple correct choices. The respondent should provide all correct choices, separated by spaces. Provide instructions in the question text.

★★ **P9.6** Add a method addText to the Question superclass and provide a different implementation of ChoiceQuestion that calls addText rather than storing an array list of choices.

★★ **P9.7** Change the CheckingAccount class in How To 9.1 so that a $1 fee is levied for deposits or withdrawals in excess of three free monthly transactions. Place the code for computing the fee into a separate method that you call from the deposit and withdraw methods.

★★★ **P9.8** Implement a superclass Appointment and subclasses Onetime, Daily, Weekly, and Monthly. An appointment has a description (for example, "see the dentist") and a date and time. Write a method occursOn(int year, int month, int day) that checks whether the appointment occurs on that date. For example, for a monthly appointment, you must check whether the day of the month matches. Then fill an array of Appointment objects with a mixture of appointments. Have the user enter a date and print out all appointments that occur on that date.

★★★ **P9.9** Improve the appointment book program of Exercise P9.8. Give the user the option to add new appointments. The user must specify the type of the appointment, the description, and the date and time.

★★★ **P9.10** Improve the appointment book program of Exercises P9.8 and P9.9 by letting the user save the appointment data to a file and reload the data from a file. The saving part is straightforward: Make a method save. Save the type, description, date, and time to a file. The loading part is not so easy. First determine the type of the appointment to be loaded, create an object of that type, and then call a load method to load the data.

★ **P9.11** Provide toString methods for the Question and ChoiceQuestion classes.

★★ **P9.12** Implement a superclass Person. Make two classes, Student and Instructor, that inherit from Person. A person has a name and a year of birth. A student has a major, and an instructor has a salary. Write the class declarations, the constructors, and the methods toString for all classes. Supply a test program that tests these classes and methods.

★★ **P9.13** Make a class Employee with a name and salary. Make a class Manager inherit from Employee. Add an instance variable, named department, of type String. Supply a method toString that prints the manager's name, department, and salary. Make a class Executive inherit from Manager. Supply appropriate toString methods for all classes. Supply a test program that tests these classes and methods.

★★ **P9.14** The Rectangle class of the standard Java library does not supply a method to compute the area or the perimeter of a rectangle. Provide a subclass BetterRectangle of the Rectangle class that has getPerimeter and getArea methods. *Do not add any instance variables.* In the constructor, call the setLocation and setSize methods of the Rectangle class. Provide a program that tests the methods that you supplied.

★★★ **P9.15** Repeat Exercise P9.14, but in the BetterRectangle constructor, invoke the superclass constructor.

★★ **P9.16** A labeled point has *x*- and *y*-coordinates and a string label. Provide a class Labeled-Point with a constructor LabeledPoint(int x, int y, String label) and a toString method that displays x, y, and the label.

★★ **P9.17** Reimplement the `LabeledPoint` class of Exercise P9.16 by storing the location in a `java.awt.Point` object. Your `toString` method should invoke the `toString` method of the `Point` class.

★★ **P9.18** Modify the `SodaCan` class of Exercise P7.8 to implement the `Measurable` interface. The measure of a square should be its area. Write a program that computes the average area of an array of squares.

★★ **P9.19** A person has a name and a height in centimeters. Use the `average` method in Section 9.4 to process a collection of `Person` objects.

★★★ **P9.20** Write a method

```
public static Measurable maximum(Measurable[] objs)
```

that returns the object with the largest measure. Use that method to determine the country with the largest area from an array of countries.

★★★ **P9.21** Declare an interface `Filter` as follows:

```
public interface Filter
{
    boolean accept(Object x);
}
```

Write a method

```
public static ArrayList<Object> collectAll(ArrayList<Object> objs, Filter f)
```

that returns all objects in the `objs` array that are accepted by the given filter.

Provide a class `ShortWordFilter` whose `filter` method accepts all strings of length < 5.

Then write a program that reads all words from `System.in`, puts them into an `Array-List<Object>`, calls `collectAll`, and prints a list of the short words.

★★★ **P9.22** The `System.out.printf` method has predefined formats for printing integers, floating-point numbers, and other data types. But it is also extensible. If you use the `S` format, you can print any class that implements the `Formattable` interface. That interface has a single method:

```
void formatTo(Formatter formatter, int flags, int width, int precision)
```

In this exercise, you should make the `BankAccount` class implement the `Formattable` interface. Ignore the flags and precision and simply format the bank balance, using the given width. In order to achieve this task, you need to get an `Appendable` reference like this:

```
Appendable a = formatter.out();
```

`Appendable` is another interface with a method

```
void append(CharSequence sequence)
```

`CharSequence` is yet another interface that is implemented by (among others) the `String` class. Construct a string by first converting the bank balance into a string and then padding it with spaces so that it has the desired width. Pass that string to the `append` method.

★★★ **P9.23** Enhance the `formatTo` method of Exercise P9.22 by taking into account the precision.

ANSWERS TO SELF-CHECK QUESTIONS

1. Because every manager is an employee but not the other way around, the `Manager` class is more specialized. It is the subclass, and `Employee` is the superclass.

2. `CheckingAccount` and `SavingsAccount` both inherit from the more general class `Bank-Account`.

3. `Exception`, `Throwable`

4. Vehicle, truck, motorcycle

5. It shouldn't. A quiz isn't a question; it *has* questions.

6. a, b, d

7. ```
   public class Manager extends Employee
   {
       private double bonus;
       // Constructors and methods omitted
   }
   ```

8. `name`, `baseSalary`, and `bonus`

9. ```
   public class Manager extends Employee
   {
       . . .
       public double getSalary() { . . . }
   }
   ```

10. `getName`, `setName`, `setBaseSalary`

11. The method is not allowed to access the instance variable text from the superclass.

12. The type of the `this` reference is `ChoiceQuestion`. Therefore, the `display` method of `ChoiceQuestion` is selected, and the method calls itself.

13. Because there is no ambiguity. The subclass doesn't have a `setAnswer` method.

14. ```
    public String getName()
    {
        return "*" + super.getName();
    }
    ```

15. ```
    public double getSalary()
    {
        return super.getSalary() + bonus;
    }
    ```

16. a only.

17. It belongs to the class `BankAccount` or one of its subclasses.

18. `Question[] quiz = new Question[SIZE];`

19. You cannot tell from the fragment—cq may be initialized with an object of a subclass of `ChoiceQuestion`. The `display` method of whatever object `cq` references is invoked.

20. No. This is a static method of the `Math` class. There is no implicit parameter object that could be used to dynamically look up a method.

21. Because the implementor of the `PrintStream` class did not supply a `toString` method.

22. The second line will not compile. The class `Object` does not have a method `length`.

23. The code will compile, but the second line will throw a class cast exception because `Question` is not a subclass of `String`.

24. There are only a few methods that can be invoked on variables of type `Object`.

25. The value is `false` if `x` is `null` and `true` otherwise.

26. It must implement the `Measurable` interface and provide a `getMeasure` method returning the salary.

27. The `Object` class doesn't have a `getMeasure` method.

28. You cannot modify the `String` class to implement `Measurable`—it is a library class. See Special Topic 9.7 on page 392 for a solution.

29. `Measurable` is not a class. You cannot construct objects of type `Measurable`.

30. Have the `Country` class implement the `Comparable` interface, as shown below, and call `Arrays.sort`.

```
public class Country implements Comparable<Country>
{
   . . .
   public int compareTo(Country other)
   {
      if (area < other.area) return -1;
      if (area > other.area) return 1;
      return 0;
   }
}
```

31. Yes, you can, because `String` implements `Comparable<String>`.

CHAPTER 10

COLLECTIONS AND MAPS

CHAPTER GOALS

To learn how to use the collection
classes supplied in the Java library

To be able to use iterators to traverse collections

To choose appropriate collections for solving programming problems

CHAPTER CONTENTS

If you want to write a program that collects objects (such as the stamps to the left), you have a number of choices. Of course, you can use an array list, but computer scientists have invented other mechanisms that may be better suited for the task. In this chapter, we introduce the collection classes and interfaces that the Java library offers. You will learn how to ensure that your objects work with a particular collection type, and how to choose the most appropriate type for a particular problem.

10.1 The Java Collections Framework

When you need to organize multiple objects in your program, you can place them into a **collection**. The ArrayList class that was introduced in Chapter 6 is one of many collection classes that the standard Java library supplies. In this chapter, you will learn about the Java *collections framework*, a hierarchy of interface types and classes for collecting objects. Each interface type is implemented by one or more classes (see Figure 1).

A collection groups together elements and allows them to be retrieved later.

At the root of the hierarchy is the Collection interface. Table 1 shows the most commonly used methods in that interface. These methods are available for all collection classes. For example, the size method reports the number of elements in any collection.

The ArrayList class implements the List interface. In Java, a *list* is a collection that remembers the order of its elements (see Figure 2). The Java library supplies another class, LinkedList, that also implements the List interface. Unlike an array list, a linked list allows speedy insertion and removal of elements in the middle of the list. We will discuss that class in the next section.

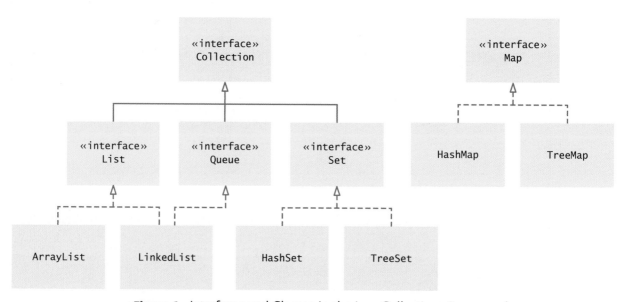

Figure 1 Interfaces and Classes in the Java Collections Framework

Table 1	Methods of the Collection Interface
int size()	Gets the size of the collection.
boolean add(*ElementType* e)	Adds the element to the collection.
boolean remove(*ElementType* e)	Removes the element from the collection.
boolean contains(*ElementType* e)	Checks whether this collection contains a given element.
String toString()	Returns a string with all elements in the collection.
Iterator<*ElementType*> iterator()	Provides a mechanism for visiting all elements in the collection (see Section 10.2).

A list is a collection that remembers the order of its elements.

You use a list whenever you want to retain the order that you established. For example, in your bookshelf, you may order books by topic. A list is an appropriate data structure for such a collection because the ordering matters to you.

However, in many applications, you don't really care about the order of the elements in a collection. Consider a mail-order dealer of books. Without customers browsing the shelves, there is no need to order books by topic. Such a collection without an intrinsic order is called a **set**—see Figure 3.

A set is an unordered collection of unique elements.

Because a set does not track the order of the elements, it can arrange them in a way that speeds up the operations of finding, adding, and removing elements. Computer scientists have invented two different mechanisms for this purpose, called *hash tables* and *binary search trees*. The Java library provides set implementations based upon both of these mechanisms. You will learn in this chapter how to choose between them.

Another way of gaining efficiency in a collection is to reduce the number of operations. A **stack** remembers the order of its elements, but it does not allow you to insert elements in every position. You can only add and remove elements at the top—see Figure 4.

In a **queue**, you add items to one end (the tail) and remove them from the other end (the head). For example, you could keep a queue of books, adding required reading at the tail and taking a book from the head whenever you have time to read another one. We will discuss stacks and queues in Section 10.3.

Figure 2 A List of Books

Figure 3 A Set of Books

Figure 4 A Stack of Books

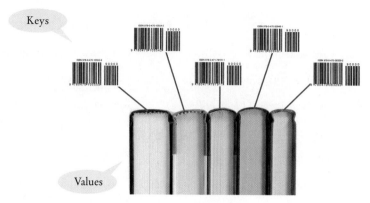

Keys

Values

Figure 5 A Map from Bar Codes to Books

A map keeps associations between key and value objects.

Finally, a **map** manages associations between *keys* and *values*. Every key in the map has an associated value. The map stores the keys, values, and the associations between them. For an example, consider a library that puts a bar code on each book. The program that processes checkouts and checkins needs to look up the book associated with each bar code. A map associating bar codes with books can solve this problem—see Figure 5. We will discuss maps in Section 10.5.

Table 2 Using the Collection Interface	
`Collection<String> coll = new ArrayList<String>();`	The `ArrayList` class implements the `Collection` interface.
`int n = coll.size();`	Gets the size of the collection. n is now 0.
`coll.add("Harry");` `coll.add("Sally");`	Adds elements to the collection.
`String s = coll.toString();`	Returns a string with all elements in the collection. s is now `"[Harry, Sally]"`
`System.out.println(coll);`	Invokes the `toString` method and prints `[Harry, Sally]`.
`coll.remove("Harry");` `boolean b = coll.remove("Tom");`	Removes an element from the collection, returning `false` if the element is not present. b is false.
`b = coll.contains("Sally");`	Checks whether this collection contains a given element. b is now `true`

`for (String s : coll)`
`{`
`   System.out.println(s);`
`}`
	You can use the "for each" loop with any collection. This loop prints the elements on separate lines.

`Iterator<String> iter = coll.iterator()`	Provides a mechanism for visiting all elements in the collection (see Section 10.2).

SELF CHECK

1. A gradebook application stores a collection of quizzes. Should it use a list or a set?

2. A student information system stores a collection of student records in a university. Should it use a list or a set?

3. Why is a queue of books a better choice than a stack for organizing your required reading?

4. As you can see from Figure 1, the Java collections framework does not consider a map a collection. Give a reason for this decision.

Practice It Now you can try these exercises at the end of the chapter: R10.1, R10.2, R10.3.

10.2 Linked Lists

A **linked list** is a data structure used for collecting a sequence of objects that allows efficient addition and removal of elements in the middle of the sequence.

To understand the need for such a data structure, imagine a program that maintains a sequence of employee objects, sorted by the last names of the employees. When a new employee is hired, an object needs to be inserted into the sequence. Unless the company happens to hire employees in alphabetical order, the new object probably needs to be inserted somewhere near the middle of the sequence. If we use an array to store the objects, then all objects following the new hire must be moved toward the end.

Each node in a linked list is connected to the neighboring nodes.

> *A linked list consists of a number of nodes, each of which has a reference to the next node.*

> *Adding and removing elements in the middle of a linked list is efficient.*

Conversely, if an employee leaves the company, the object must be removed, and the hole in the sequence needs to be closed up by moving all objects that come after it. Moving a large number of elements can involve a substantial amount of processing time. A linked list structures the data in a way that minimizes this cost.

Rather than storing the values in an array, a linked list uses a sequence of *nodes*. A node is an object that stores a value and references to the neighboring nodes in the sequence (see Figure 6). When you insert a new node into a linked list, only the

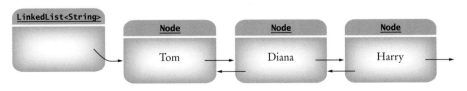

Figure 6 A Linked List

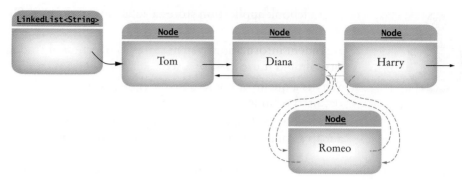

Figure 7 Inserting a Node into a Linked List

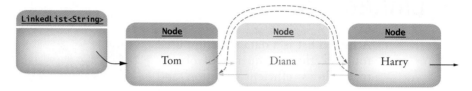

Figure 8 Removing a Node from a Linked List

neighboring node references need to be updated (see Figure 7). The same is true when you remove a node (see Figure 8). What's the catch? Linked lists allow speedy insertion and removal, but element access can be slow.

For example, suppose you want to locate the fifth element. You must first traverse the first four. This is a problem if you need to access the elements in arbitrary order. The term "random access" is used in computer science to describe an access pattern in which elements are accessed in arbitrary (not necessarily random) order. In contrast, sequential access visits the elements in sequence.

Of course, if you mostly visit all elements in sequence (for example, to display or print the elements), the inefficiency of random access is not a problem. You use linked lists when you are concerned about the efficiency of inserting or removing elements and you rarely need element access in random order.

The Java library provides a LinkedList class in the java.util package. It is a **generic class**, just like the ArrayList class. That is, you specify the type of the list elements in angle brackets, such as LinkedList<String> or LinkedList<Employee>.

> Visiting the elements of a linked list in sequential order is efficient, but random access is not.

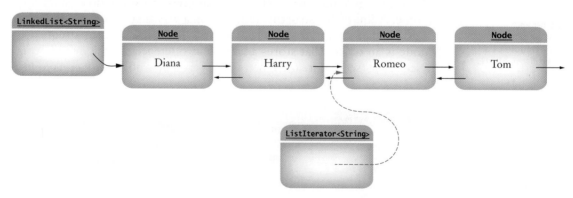

Figure 9 A List Iterator

Table 3	LinkedList Methods
`LinkedList<String> list = new LinkedList<String>();`	An empty list.
`list.addLast("Harry");`	Adds an element to the end of the list. Same as add.
`list.addFirst("Sally");`	Adds an element to the beginning of the list. `list` is now `[Sally, Harry]`.
`list.getFirst();`	Gets the element stored at the beginning of the list; here `"Sally"`.
`list.getLast();`	Gets the element stored at the end of the list; here `"Harry"`.
`String removed = list.removeFirst();`	Removes the first element of the list and returns it. `removed` is `"Sally"` and `list` is `[Harry]`. Use removeLast to remove the last element.
`ListIterator<String> iter = list.listIterator()`	Provides an iterator for visiting all list elements (see Table 4 on page 410).

Table 3 shows important methods of the `LinkedList` class. (Remember that the `LinkedList` class also inherits the methods of the `Collection` interface in Table 1 on page 405.)

As you can see from Table 3, there are methods for accessing the beginning and the end of the list directly. However, to visit the other elements, you need a list **iterator**. An iterator encapsulates a position anywhere inside the linked list (see Figure 9).

> You use a list iterator to access elements inside a linked list.

Conceptually, you should think of the iterator as pointing between two elements, just as the cursor in a word processor points between two characters (see Figure 10). In the conceptual view, think of each element as being like a letter in a word processor, and think of the iterator as being like the blinking cursor between letters.

You obtain a list iterator with the `listIterator` method of the `LinkedList` class:

```
LinkedList<String> employeeNames = . . .;
ListIterator<String> iterator = employeeNames.listIterator();
```

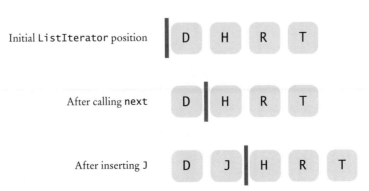

Initial `ListIterator` position   D   H   R   T

After calling next   D   H   R   T

After inserting J   D   J   H   R   T

Figure 10 A Conceptual View of the List Iterator

ANIMATION
List Iterators

Note that the iterator class is also a generic type. A `ListIterator<String>` iterates through a list of strings; a `ListIterator<Book>` visits the elements in a `LinkedList<Book>`.

Initially, the iterator points before the first element. You can move the iterator position with the `next` method:

```
iterator.next();
```

The `next` method throws a `NoSuchElementException` if you are already past the end of the list. You should always call the method `hasNext` before calling `next`—it returns `true` if there is a next element.

```
if (iterator.hasNext())
{
    iterator.next();
}
```

The `next` method returns the element that the iterator is passing. When you use a `ListIterator<String>`, the return type of the `next` method is `String`. In general, the return type of the `next` method matches the list iterator's type parameter (which reflects the type of the elements in the list).

You traverse all elements in a linked list of strings with the following loop:

```
while (iterator.hasNext())
{
    String name = iterator.next();
    Do something with name
}
```

As a shorthand, if your loop simply visits all elements of the linked list, you can use the "for each" loop:

```
for (String name : employeeNames)
{
    Do something with name
}
```

Table 4 Methods of the `Iterator` and `ListIterator` Interfaces	
`String s = iter.next();`	Assume that `iter` points to the beginning of the list `[Sally]` before calling `next`. After the call, `s` is `"Sally"` and the iterator points to the end.
`iter.hasNext()`	Returns `false` because the iterator is at the end of the collection.

`if (iter.hasPrevious())`
`{`
`    s = iter.previous();`
`}`
	`hasPrevious` returns `true` because the iterator is not at the beginning of the list. `previous` and `hasPrevious` are `ListIterator` methods.

`iter.add("Diana");`	Adds an element before the iterator position (`ListIterator` only). The list is now `[Diana, Sally]`.
`iter.next();` `iter.remove();`	`remove` removes the last element returned by `next` or `previous`. The list is now `[Diana]`.

Then you don't have to worry about iterators at all. Behind the scenes, the for loop uses an iterator to visit all list elements.

The nodes of the LinkedList class store two links: one to the next element and one to the previous one. Such a list is called a **doubly linked list**. You can use the previous and hasPrevious methods of the ListIterator interface to move the iterator position backwards.

The add method adds an object after the iterator, then moves the iterator position past the new element.

```
iterator.add("Juliet");
```

You can visualize insertion to be like typing text in a word processor. Each character is inserted after the cursor, and then the cursor moves past the inserted character (see Figure 10). Most people never pay much attention to this—you may want to try it out and watch carefully how your word processor inserts characters.

The remove method removes the object that was returned by the last call to next or previous. For example, the following loop removes all names that fulfill a certain condition:

```
while (iterator.hasNext())
{
   String name = iterator.next();
   if (condition is fulfilled for name)
   {
      iterator.remove();
   }
}
```

You have to be careful when calling remove. It can be called only *once* after calling next or previous, and you cannot call it immediately after a call to add. If you call the method improperly, it throws an IllegalStateException.

Table 4 summarizes the methods of the ListIterator interface. The ListIterator interface extends a more general Iterator interface that is suitable for arbitrary collections, not just lists. The table indicates which methods are specific to list iterators.

Here is a sample program that inserts strings into a list and then iterates through the list, adding and removing elements. Finally, the entire list is printed. The comments indicate the iterator position.

ch10/list/ListTester.java

```
 1  import java.util.LinkedList;
 2  import java.util.ListIterator;
 3
 4  /**
 5     A program that tests the LinkedList class.
 6  */
 7  public class ListTester
 8  {
 9     public static void main(String[] args)
10     {
11        LinkedList<String> staff = new LinkedList<String>();
12        staff.addLast("Diana");
13        staff.addLast("Harry");
14        staff.addLast("Romeo");
15        staff.addLast("Tom");
```

```
16
17    // | in the comments indicates the iterator position
18
19    ListIterator<String> iterator = staff.listIterator(); // |DHRT
20    iterator.next(); // D|HRT
21    iterator.next(); // DH|RT
22
23    // Add more elements after second element
24
25    iterator.add("Juliet"); // DHJ|RT
26    iterator.add("Nina"); // DHJN|RT
27
28    iterator.next(); // DHJNR|T
29
30    // Remove last traversed element
31
32    iterator.remove(); // DHJN|T
33
34    // Print all elements
35
36    System.out.println(staff);
37    System.out.println("Expected: [Diana, Harry, Juliet, Nina, Tom]");
38    }
39 }
```

Random Fact 10.1 Standardization

You encounter the benefits of standardization every day. When you buy a light bulb, you can be assured that it fits the socket without having to measure the socket at home and the light bulb in the store. In fact, you may have experienced how painful the lack of standards can be if you have ever purchased a flashlight with nonstandard bulbs. Replacement bulbs for such a flashlight can be difficult and expensive to obtain.

Programmers have a similar desire for standardization. Consider the important goal of platform independence for Java programs. After you compile a Java program into class files, you can execute the class files on any computer that has a Java virtual machine. For this to work, the behavior of the virtual machine has to be strictly defined. If all virtual machines don't behave exactly the same way, then the slogan of "write once, run anywhere" turns into "write once, debug everywhere". In order for multiple implementors to create compatible virtual machines, the virtual machine needed to be *standardized*. That is, someone needed to create a definition of the virtual machine and its expected behavior.

Who creates standards? Some of the most successful standards have been created by volunteer groups such as the Internet Engineering Task Force (IETF) and the World Wide Web Consortium (W3C). The IETF standardizes protocols used in the Internet, such as the protocol for exchanging e-mail messages. The W3C standardizes the Hypertext Markup Language (HTML), the format for web pages. These standards have been instrumental in the creation of the World Wide Web as an open platform that is not controlled by any one company.

Many programming languages, such as C++ and Scheme, have been standardized by independent standards organizations, such as the American National Standards Institute (ANSI) and the International Organization for Standardization—called ISO

Program Run

```
[Diana, Harry, Juliet, Nina, Tom]
Expected: [Diana, Harry, Juliet, Nina, Tom]
```

SELF CHECK

5. Do linked lists take more storage space than arrays of the same size?

6. Why don't we need iterators with arrays?

7. Suppose the list lst contains elements "A", "B", "C", and "D". Draw the contents of the list and the iterator position for the following operations:

```
ListIterator<String> iter = letters.iterator();
iter.next();
iter.next();
iter.remove();
iter.next();
iter.add("E");
iter.next();
iter.add("F");
```

8. Write a loop that removes all strings of length < 4 from a linked list of strings called words.

9. Write a loop that prints every second element of a linked list of strings.

Practice It   Now you can try these exercises at the end of the chapter: R10.4, R10.7, P10.1.

---

for short (not an acronym; see http://www.iso.ch/iso/en/aboutiso/introduction/whatisISO.html). ANSI and ISO are associations of industry professionals who develop standards for everything from car tires and credit card shapes to programming languages.

When a company invents a new technology, it has an interest in its invention becoming a standard, so that other vendors produce tools that work with the invention and thus increase its likelihood of success. On the other hand, by handing over the invention to a standards committee, especially one that insists on a fair process, the company may lose control over the standard. For that reason, Sun Microsystems, the inventor of Java, never agreed to have a third-party organization standardize the Java language. They put in place their own standardization process, involving other companies but refusing to relinquish control. Another unfortunate but common tactic is to create a weak standard. For example, Netscape and Microsoft chose the European Computer Manufacturers Association (ECMA) to standardize the JavaScript language. ECMA was willing to settle for something less than truly useful, standardizing the behavior of the core language and just a few of its libraries.

Of course, many important pieces of technology aren't standardized at all. Consider the Windows operating system. Although Windows is often called a de-facto standard, it really is no standard at all. Nobody has ever attempted to define formally what the Windows operating system should do. The behavior changes at the whim of its vendor. That suits Microsoft just fine, because it makes it impossible for a third party to create its own version of Windows.

As a computer professional, there will be many times in your career when you need to make a decision whether to support a particular standard. Consider a simple example. In this chapter, you learn about the collection classes from the standard Java library. However, many computer scientists dislike these classes because of their numerous design issues. Should you use the Java collections in your own code, or should you implement a better set of collections? If you do the former, you have to deal with a design that is less than optimal. If you do the latter, other programmers may have a hard time understanding your code because they aren't familiar with your classes.

10.3 Queues and Stacks

In this section we will consider two common data types that allow insertion and removal of items at the ends only, not in the middle.

> A queue is a collection of elements with "first in, first out" retrieval.

A **queue** lets you add items to one end of the queue (the *tail*) and remove them from the other end of the queue (the *head*). Queues store items in a *first in, first out* or *FIFO* fashion. Items are removed in the same order in which they have been added.

There are many uses of queues in computer science. A typical example is a print queue. A printer may be accessed by several applications, perhaps running on different computers. If each of the applications tried to access the printer at the same time, the printout would be garbled. Instead, each application places its print data into a file and adds that file to the print queue. When the printer is done printing one file, it retrieves the next one from the queue. Therefore, print jobs are printed using the "first in, first out" rule, which is a fair arrangement for users of the shared printer.

The Queue interface in the standard Java library has methods add to add an element to the tail of the queue, remove to remove the head of the queue, and peek to get the head element of the queue without removing it.

The standard library provides a number of queue classes for programs in which multiple activities, called threads, run in parallel. These queues are useful for sharing work between threads. We do not discuss those classes in this book. The LinkedList class also implements the Queue interface, and you can use it when a queue is required:

```
Queue<String> q = new LinkedList<String>();
```

> A stack is a collection of elements with "last in, first out" retrieval.

A **stack** lets you insert and remove elements at only one end, traditionally called the *top* of the stack. New items can be added to the top of the stack. Items are removed from the top of the stack as well. Therefore, they are removed in the order that is opposite from the order in which they have been added, called *last in, first out* or *LIFO* order. For example, if you add items A, B, and C and then remove them, you obtain C, B, and A. Traditionally, the addition and removal operations are called push and pop.

To visualize a queue, simply think of people lining up.

Table 5   Working with Queues and Stacks

`Queue<Integer> q = new LinkedList<Integer>();`	The `LinkedList` class implements the `Queue` interface.
`q.add(1); q.add(2); q.add(3);`	Adds to the tail of the queue; q is now `[1, 2, 3]`.
`int head = q.remove();`	Removes the head of the queue; head is set to 1 and q is `[2, 3]`.
`head = q.peek();`	Gets the head of the queue without removing it; head is set to 2.
`Stack<Integer> s = new Stack<Integer>();`	Constructs an empty stack.

`s.push(1);`
`s.push(2);`
`s.push(3);`
	Adds to the top of the stack; s is now `[1, 2, 3]`. (Following the `toString` method of the `Stack` class, we show the top of the stack at the end.)

`int top = s.pop();`	Removes the top of the stack; top is set to 3 and s is now `[1, 2]`.
`head = s.peek();`	Gets the top of the stack without removing it; head is set to 2.

For example, you can use a stack to find a path through a maze. Whenever you encounter an intersection, push the location on the stack, and then explore the first branch. If that branch is a dead end, return to the location at the top of the stack. If all branches are dead ends, pop the location off the stack. Now the top of the stack is a previously encountered intersection. Move to it and continue exploring it.

Another important example is the **run-time stack** that a processor or virtual machine keeps to organize the variables of nested methods. Whenever a new method is called, its parameters and local variables are pushed onto a stack. When the method exits, they are popped off again.

The Java library provides a `Stack` class that implements the abstract stack type's `push` and `pop` operations. The following sample code shows how to use that class.

```
Stack<String> s = new Stack<String>();
s.push("A");
s.push("B");
s.push("C");
// The following loop prints C, B, and A
while (s.size() > 0) { System.out.println(s.pop()); }
```

Here's an example of a stack for evaluating expressions. Consider how you write arithmetic expressions, such as $(3 + 4) \times 5$. The parentheses are needed so that 3 and 4 are added before multiplying the result by 5.

In the 1920s, the Polish mathematician Jan Łukasiewicz noticed that if you wrote the operators first, before the operands, the need for parentheses was eliminated. Thirty years later, Australian computer scientist Charles Hamblin noted that an even better scheme would be to have the operators *follow* the operands. This was termed *reverse Polish notation*. In reverse Polish notation the expression would be written as $3\ 4 + 5 \times$. Table 6 shows some other examples.

In 1972, the HP 35 was the world's first handheld scientific calculator. It used reverse Polish notation. No parentheses or = key were required, and Hewlett-Packard marketed it as "the calculator that has no equal".

Table 6	
Standard Notation	Reverse Polish Notation
3 + 4	3 4 +
3 + 4 × 5	3 4 5 × +
3 × (4 + 5)	3 4 5 + ×
(3 + 4) × (5 + 6)	3 4 + 5 6 + ×
3 + 4 + 5	3 4 + 5 +

Evaluation of reverse Polish notation is simple if you have a stack. Each operand is pushed on the stack. Each operator pops its arguments from the stack, performs the operation, and pushes the result back onto the stack.

The following program simulates a reverse Polish calculator.

ch10/calc/Calculator.java

```java
import java.util.Scanner;
import java.util.Stack;

/**
   This calculator uses the reverse polish notation.
*/
public class Calculator
{
   public static void main(String[] args)
   {
      Scanner in = new Scanner(System.in);
      Stack<Integer> results = new Stack<Integer>();
      System.out.println("Enter one number or operator per line, Q to quit. ");
      boolean done = false;
      while (!done)
      {
         String input = in.nextLine();

         // If the command is an operator, pop the arguments and push the result

         if (input.equals("+"))
         {
            results.push(results.pop() + results.pop());
         }
         else if (input.equals("-"))
         {
```

```
27              Integer arg2 = results.pop();
28              results.push(results.pop() - arg2);
29           }
30           else if (input.equals("*") || input.equals("x"))
31           {
32              results.push(results.pop() * results.pop());
33           }
34           else if (input.equals("/"))
35           {
36              Integer arg2 = results.pop();
37              results.push(results.pop() / arg2);
38           }
39           else if (input.equals("Q") || input.equals("q"))
40           {
41              done = true;
42           }
43           else
44           {
45              // Not an operator--push the input value
46
47              results.push(Integer.parseInt(input));
48           }
49           System.out.println(results);
50        }
51     }
52 }
```

Program Run

```
Enter one number or operator per line, Q to quit.
3
[3]
4
[3, 4]
+
[7]
5
[7, 5]
*
[35]
```

SELF CHECK

10. Why would you want to declare a variable as

   `Queue<String> q = new LinkedList<String>()`

   instead of simply declaring it as a linked list?

11. Why wouldn't you want to use an array list for implementing a queue?

12. What does this code print?

```
Queue<String> s = new LinkedList<String>();
q.push("A");
q.push("B");
q.push("C");
while (q.size() > 0) { System.out.print(q.remove() + " "); }
```

13. Why wouldn't you want to use a stack to manage print jobs?

14. What is the value of the reverse Polish notation expression 2 3 4 + 5 ×x?

15. Why does the branch for the subtraction operator in the `Calculator` program not simply execute

```
results.push(results.pop() - results.pop());
```

Practice It   Now you can try these exercises at the end of the chapter: R10.12, P10.3, P10.4.

10.4 Sets

> Sets don't have duplicates. Adding a duplicate of an element that is already present is silently ignored.

As you learned in Section 10.1, a **set** is an unordered collection. The collection does not keep track of the order in which elements have been added. Therefore, it can carry out its operations more efficiently than an ordered collection.

As in mathematics, a set collection in Java rejects duplicates. Adding an element has no effect if the element is already in the set. Similarly, attempting to remove an element that isn't in the set is silently ignored.

The `Set` interface in the standard Java library has the same methods as the `Collection` interface, shown in Table 1 on page 405. The `HashSet` and `TreeSet` classes implement the `Set` interface. These two classes provide set implementations based on two different mechanisms, called **hash tables** and **binary search trees**. Both implementations arrange the set elements so that finding, adding, and removing elements is fast, but they use different strategies.

> The HashSet and TreeSet classes both implement the Set interface.

> Set implementations arrange the elements so that they can locate them quickly.

The basic idea of a hash table is simple. Set elements are grouped into smaller collections of elements that share the same characteristic. You can imagine a hash set of books as having a group for each color, so that books of the same color are in the same group. To find whether a book is already present, you just need to check it against the books in the same color group. Actually, hash tables don't use colors, but integer values (called hash codes) that can be computed from the elements.

In order to use a hash table, the elements must have a method to compute those integer values. The method is called `hashCode`. The elements must also have a method called `equals` for checking whether an element equals another.

On this shelf, books of the same color are grouped together. Similarly, in a hash table, objects with the same hash code are placed in the same group.

Many classes in the standard library implement these methods, for example `String`, `Integer`, `Point`, `Rectangle`, `Color`, and all the collection classes. Therefore, you can form a `HashSet<String>`, `HashSet<Rectangle>`, or even a `HashSet<HashSet<Integer>>`.

Suppose you want to form a set of a class that you declared, such as a `Hash-Set<Book>`. Then you need to provide `hashCode` and `equals` methods for the element class `Book`. Read Section 10.6 for the details. There is one exception to this rule. If all elements are distinct (for example, if your program never has two Book objects with the same author and title), then you can simply inherit the hashCode and equals methods of the Object class.

The TreeSet class uses a different strategy for arranging its elements. Elements are kept in sorted order. For example, a set of books might be arranged by height, or alphabetically by author and title. The elements are not stored in an array—that would make adding and removing elements too slow. Instead, they are stored in nodes, like in a linked list. However, the nodes are not arranged in a linear sequence but in a tree shape. See Section 10.7 for the details.

In order to use a TreeSet, it must be possible to compare the elements and determine which one is "larger". You can use a TreeSet for classes such as String and Integer that

A tree set keeps its elements in sorted order.

implement the Comparable interface. Section 9.6.3 shows you how you can implement comparison methods for your own classes.

Now let's look at using a set of strings. First, construct the set, either as

```
Set<String> names = new HashSet<String>();
```

or

```
Set<String> names = new TreeSet<String>();
```

Note that we store the reference to the HashSet<String> object in a Set<String> variable. After you construct the collection object, the implementation no longer matters; only the interface is important.

Adding and removing set elements are accomplished with the add and remove methods:

```
names.add("Romeo");
names.remove("Juliet");
```

The contains method tests whether an element is contained in the set:

```
if (names.contains("Juliet")) . . .
```

Finally, to list all elements in the set, get an iterator. As with list iterators, you use the next and hasNext methods to step through the set.

```
Iterator<String> iter = names.iterator();
while (iter.hasNext())
{
    String name = iter.next();
    Do something with name
}
```

As with arrays and lists, you can use the "for each" loop instead of explicitly using an iterator:

```
for (String name : names)
{
    Do something with name
}
```

A set iterator visits the elements in the order in which the set implementation keeps them.

A set iterator visits the elements in the order in which the set implementation keeps them. This is not necessarily the order in which you inserted them. The order of elements in a hash set seems quite random because the hash code spreads the elements into different groups. When you visit elements of a tree set, they always appear in sorted order, even if you inserted them in a different order.

There is an important difference between the Iterator that you obtain from a set and the ListIterator that a list yields. The ListIterator has an add method to add an element at the list iterator position. The Iterator interface has no such method. It makes no sense to add an element at a particular position in a set, because the set can order the elements any way it likes. Thus, you always add elements directly to a set, never to an iterator of the set.

You cannot add an element to a set at an iterator position.

However, you can remove a set element at an iterator position, just as you do with list iterators.

Also, the Iterator interface has no previous method to go backwards through the elements. Because the elements are not ordered, it is not meaningful to distinguish between "going forward" and "going backward".

The following test program shows a practical application of sets. We read in all words from a dictionary file that contains correctly spelled words and place them into a set. We then read all words from a document into a second set—here, the book "Alice in Wonderland." Finally, we print all words from that set that are not in the dictionary set. These are the potential misspellings. (As you can see from the output, we used an American dictionary, and words with British spelling, such as *clamour*, are flagged as potential errors.)

ch10/spellcheck/SpellCheck.java

```java
import java.util.HashSet;
import java.util.Scanner;
import java.util.Set;
import java.io.File;
import java.io.FileNotFoundException;

/**
   This program checks which words in a file are not present in a dictionary.
*/
public class SpellCheck
{
   public static void main(String[] args)
      throws FileNotFoundException
   {
      // Read the dictionary and the document

      Set<String> dictionaryWords = readWords("words");
      Set<String> documentWords = readWords("alice30.txt");

      // Print all words that are in the document but not the dictionary

      for (String word : documentWords)
      {
         if (!dictionaryWords.contains(word))
         {
            System.out.println(word);
         }
      }
```

```
29      }
30
31      /**
32          Reads all words from a file.
33          @param filename  the name of the file
34          @return  a set with all lowercased words in the file. Here, a
35          word is a sequence of upper- and lowercase letters.
36      */
37      public static Set<String> readWords(String filename)
38          throws FileNotFoundException
39      {
40          Set<String> words = new HashSet<String>();
41          Scanner in = new Scanner(new File(filename));
42          // Use any characters other than a-z or A-Z as delimiters
43          in.useDelimiter("[^a-zA-Z]+");
44          while (in.hasNext())
45          {
46              words.add(in.next().toLowerCase());
47          }
48          return words;
49      }
50  }
```

Program Run

```
neighbouring
croqueted
pennyworth
dutchess
comfits
xii
dinn
clamour
...
```

SELF CHECK

16. Arrays and lists remember the order in which you added elements; sets do not. Why would you want to use a set instead of an array or list?

17. Why are set iterators different from list iterators?

18. What is wrong with the following test to check whether the Set<String> s contains the elements "Tom", "Diana", and "Harry"?

    `if (s.toString().equals("[Tom, Diana, Harry]")) . . .`

19. How can you correctly implement the test of Self Check 18?

20. Write a loop that prints all elements that are in both Set<String> s and Set<String> t.

21. Suppose you changed line 40 of the SpellCheck program to use a TreeSet instead of a HashSet. How would the output change?

Practice It   Now you can try these exercises at the end of the chapter: P10.7, P10.8, P10.13.

Programming Tip 10.1

Use Interface References to Manipulate Data Structures

It is considered good style to store a reference to a HashSet or TreeSet in a variable of type Set.

```
Set<String> words = new HashSet<String>();
```

This way, you have to change only one line if you decide to use a TreeSet instead.

If a method can operate on arbitrary collections, use the Collection interface type for the parameter:

```
public static void removeLongWords(Collection<String> words)
```

In theory, we should make the same recommendation for the List interface, namely to save ArrayList and LinkedList references in variables of type List. However, the List interface has get and set methods for random access, even though these methods are very inefficient for linked lists. You can't write efficient code if you don't know whether the methods that you are calling are efficient or not. This is plainly a serious design error in the standard library, and it makes the List interface somewhat unattractive.

10.5 Maps

The HashMap and TreeMap classes both implement the Map interface.

A **map** allows you to associate elements from a *key set* with elements from a *value collection*. You use a map when you want to look up objects by using a key. For example, Figure 11 shows a map from the names of people to their favorite colors.

Just as there are two kinds of set implementations, the Java library has two implementations for the Map interface: HashMap and TreeMap.

After constructing a HashMap or TreeMap, you can store the reference to the map object in a Map reference:

```
Map<String, Color> favoriteColors = new HashMap<String, Color>();
```

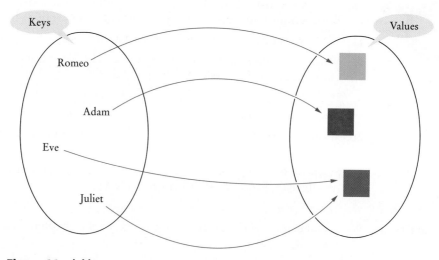

Figure 11 A Map

Use the put method to add an association:

```
favoriteColors.put("Juliet", Color.RED);
```

You can change the value of an existing association, simply by calling put again:

```
favoriteColors.put("Juliet", Color.BLUE);
```

The get method returns the value associated with a key.

```
Color julietsFavoriteColor = favoriteColors.get("Juliet");
```

If you ask for a key that isn't associated with any values, then the get method returns null.

To remove an association, call the remove method with the key:

```
favoriteColors.remove("Juliet");
```

Using a Map

To find all keys and values in a map, iterate through the key set and find the values that correspond to the keys.

Sometimes you want to enumerate all keys in a map. The keySet method yields the set of keys. You can then ask the key set for an iterator and get all keys. From each key, you can find the associated value with the get method. Thus, the following instructions print all key/value pairs in a map m:

```
Set<String> keySet = m.keySet();
for (String key : keySet)
{
    Color value = m.get(key);
    System.out.println(key + "->" + value);
}
```

Table 7 Working with Maps

`Map<String, Integer> scores;`	Keys are strings, values are Integer wrappers. Use the interface type for variable declarations.
`scores = new TreeMap<String, Integer>();`	Use a HashMap if you don't need to visit the keys in sorted order.
`scores.put("Harry", 90);` `scores.put("Sally", 95);`	Adds keys and values to the map.
`scores.put("Sally", 100);`	Modifies the value of an existing key.
`int n = scores.get("Sally");` `Integer n2 = scores.get("Diana");`	Gets the value associated with a key, or null if the key is not present. n is 100, n2 is null.
`System.out.println(scores);`	Prints scores.toString(), a string of the form {Harry=90, Sally=100}

`for (String key : scores.keySet())`
`{`
`    Integer value = scores.get(key);`
`    . . .`
`}`
	Iterates through all map keys and values.

`scores.remove("Sally");`	Removes the key and value.

The following sample program shows a map in action.

ch10/map/MapDemo.java

```
1   import java.awt.Color;
2   import java.util.HashMap;
3   import java.util.Map;
4   import java.util.Set;
5
6   /**
7       This program demonstrates a map that maps names to colors.
8   */
9   public class MapDemo
10  {
11     public static void main(String[] args)
12     {
13        Map<String, Color> favoriteColors = new HashMap<String, Color>();
14        favoriteColors.put("Juliet", Color.BLUE);
15        favoriteColors.put("Romeo", Color.GREEN);
16        favoriteColors.put("Adam", Color.RED);
17        favoriteColors.put("Eve", Color.BLUE);
18
19        // Print all keys and values in the map
20
21        Set<String> keySet = favoriteColors.keySet();
22        for (String key : keySet)
23        {
24           Color value = favoriteColors.get(key);
25           System.out.println(key + " : " + value);
26        }
27     }
28  }
```

Program Run

```
Juliet : java.awt.Color[r=0,g=0,b=255]
Adam : java.awt.Color[r=255,g=0,b=0]
Eve : java.awt.Color[r=0,g=0,b=255]
Romeo : java.awt.Color[r=0,g=255,b=0]
```

SELF CHECK

22. What is the difference between a set and a map?

23. Why is the collection of the keys of a map a set and not a list?

24. Why is the collection of the values of a map not a set?

25. Suppose you want to track how many times each word occurs in a document. Declare a suitable map variable.

26. What is a `Map<String, HashSet<String>>`? Give a possible use for such a structure.

Practice It   Now you can try these exercises at the end of the chapter: R10.19, P10.9, P10.14.

Special Topic 10.1

Enhancements to Collection Classes in Java 7

Java 7 provides several syntactical conveniences for working with collection classes.

Type parameters in constructors can be inferred from variable types. You no longer have to repeat them in the variable declaration and the constructor. For example,

```
Set<String> names = new HashSet<>(); // Constructs a HashSet<String>
Map<String, Integer> scores = new TreeMap<>(); // Constructs a TreeMap<String, Integer>
```

You can obtain collection literals of type List, Set, and Map, with the following syntax:

```
["Tom", "Diana", "Harry"];
{ 2, 3, 5, 7, 11 };
{ "Juliet" : Color.BLUE, "Romeo" : Color.GREEN, "Eve" : Color.BLUE };
```

These objects are immutable: you cannot change the contents of the list, set, or map literal. The objects are instances of classes that implements the List, Set, and Map interfaces, but you don't know what those classes are.

You can pass collection or map literals to methods, for example

```
names.addAll(["Tom", "Diana", "Harry"]);
```

If you want to store a literal in a variable, you must use the interface type for the variable declaration:

```
List<String> friends = ["Tom", "Diana", "Harry"];
```

Alternatively, you can initialize a collection with a literal:

```
ArrayList<String> friends = new ArrayList<>(["Tom", "Diana", "Harry"]);
```

This works because all Java collection and map classes have constructors that copy entries from another collection or map.

Finally, you can use the [] operator instead of the get, set, or put methods. For example,

```
String name = names[0];
names[0] = "Fred";
scores["Fred"] = 13;
int score = scores["Fred"];
```

HOW TO 10.1

Choosing a Collection

Suppose you need to store objects in a collection. You have now seen a number of different data structures. This How To reviews how to pick an appropriate collection for your application.

Step 1 Determine how you access the values.

You store values in a collection so that you can later retrieve them. How do you want to access individual values? You have several choices.

- Values are accessed by an integer position. Use an ArrayList. Go to Step 2, then stop.
- Values are accessed by a key that is not a part of the object. Use a map.
- It doesn't matter. Values are always accessed "in bulk", by traversing the collection and doing something with each value.

Step 2   Determine the element types or key/value types.

For a list or set, determine the type of the elements that you want to store. For example, if you collect a set of books, then the element type is Book.

   Similarly, for a map, determine the types of the keys and the associated values. If you want to look up books by ID, you can use a Map<Integer, Book> or Map<String, Book>, depending on your ID type.

Step 3   Determine whether element or key order matters.

When you visit elements from a collection or keys from a map, do you care about the order in which they are visited? You have several choices.

- Elements or keys must be sorted. Use a TreeSet or TreeMap. Go to Step 6.
- Elements must be in the same order in which they were inserted. Your choice is now narrowed down to a LinkedList or an ArrayList.
- It doesn't matter. As long as you get to visit all elements, you don't care in which order. If you chose a map in Step 1, use a HashMap and go to Step 5.

Step 4   For a collection, determine which operations must be fast.

You have several choices.

- Finding elements must be fast. Use a HashSet and go to Step 5.
- Adding and removing elements at the beginning or the middle must be fast. Use a LinkedList.
- You only insert at the end, or you collect so few elements that you aren't concerned about speed. Use an ArrayList.

Step 5   For hash sets and maps, decide whether you need to implement the equals and hashCode methods.

If your elements or keys belong to a class that someone else declared, check whether the class implements hashCode and equals methods. If so, you are all set. This is the case for most classes in the standard Java library, such as String, Integer, Rectangle, and so on.

   If not, decide whether you can compare the elements by identity. Are all elements distinct in your program? That is, can it never happen that you have two different elements with the same instance variables? In that case, you need not do anything—the hashCode and equals methods of the Object class are appropriate.

   If you need to implement your own equals and hashCode methods, turn to Section 10.6.

Step 6   If you use a tree, decide whether to supply a comparator.

Look at the class of the set elements or map keys. Does that class implement the Comparable interface? If so, is the sort order given by the compareTo method the one you want? If yes, then you don't need to do anything further. This is the case for many classes in the standard library, in particular for String and Integer.

   If no, then your element class must implement the Comparable interface (Section 9.6.3), or you must declare a class that implements the Comparator interface (see Special Topic 10.2 on page 438).

WORKED EXAMPLE 10.1   **Word Frequency**

In this Worked Example, we read a text file and print a list of all words in the file in alphabetical order, together with a count that indicates how often each word occurred in the file.

10.6 Hash Tables

In the following sections, you will see how the technique of **hashing** can be used to find elements in a set data structure quickly, without making a linear search through all elements.

10.6.1 Hash Codes

A hash function computes an integer value from an object.

A **hash function** is a function that computes an integer value, the **hash code**, from an object, in such a way that different objects are likely to yield different hash codes. Because hashing is so important, the Object class has a hashCode method. The call

```
int h = x.hashCode();
```

computes the hash code of any object x. If you want to put objects of a given class into a HashSet or use the objects as keys in a HashMap, the class should override this method. The method should be implemented so that different objects are likely to have different hash codes.

A good hash function produces different hash values for each object so that they are scattered about in a hash table.

A good hash function minimizes *collisions*—identical hash codes for different objects.

For example, the String class declares a hash function for strings that does a good job of producing different integer values for different strings. Table 8 shows some examples of strings and their hash codes. You will see in Section 10.6.3 how these values are obtained.

Table 8	Sample Strings and Their Hash Codes
String	Hash Code
"Adam"	2035631
"Eve"	70068
"Harry"	69496448
"Jim"	74478
"Joe"	74656
"Juliet"	−2065036585
"Katherine"	2079199209
"Sue"	83491

It is possible for two or more distinct objects to have the same hash code; this is called a *collision*. For example, the strings "VII" and "Ugh" happen to have the same hash code, but these collisions are very rare for strings (see Exercise P10.12).

In general, a hash function should be chosen so that it minimizes collisions. Section 10.6.3 explains how you should override the hashCode method for your classes.

10.6.2 Hash Tables

A hash code is used as an array index into a **hash table**. In the simplest implementation of a hash table, you could make an array and insert each object at the location of its hash code (see Figure 12).

Then it is a very simple matter to find out whether an object is already present in the set or not. Compute its hash code and check whether the array position with that hash code is already occupied. This doesn't require a search through the entire array!

However, there are two problems with this simplistic approach. First, it is not possible to allocate an array that is large enough to hold all possible integer index positions. Therefore, we must pick an array of some reasonable size and then reduce the hash code to fall inside the array:

```
int h = x.hashCode();
if (h < 0) { h = -h; }
h = h % tableSize;
```

After reducing the hash code modulo a smaller array size, it becomes more likely that several objects will collide and need to share a position in the array.

> A hash table can be implemented as an array of *buckets*—lists of nodes that hold elements with the same hash code.

To store multiple objects in the same array position, use linked lists for the elements with the same hash code (see Figure 13). These lists are called **buckets**.

Here is the algorithm for finding an object x in a hash table.

1. Compute the hash code and reduce it modulo the table size. This gives an index h into the hash table.

2. Iterate through the elements of the bucket at position h. For each element of the bucket, check whether it is equal to x.

3. If a match is found among the elements of that bucket, then x is in the set. Otherwise, it is not.

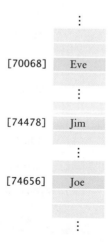

Figure 12
A Simplistic Implementation
of a Hash Table

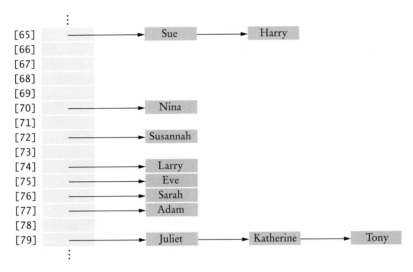

Figure 13 A Hash Table with Buckets to Store Elements with the Same Hash Code

Adding an element is an extension of the algorithm for finding an object. First compute the hash code to locate the bucket in which the element should be inserted. Try finding the object in that bucket. If it is already present, do nothing. Otherwise, insert it.

Removing an element is similar: First compute the hash code to locate the bucket in which the element should be inserted. Try finding the object in that bucket. If it is present, remove it. Otherwise, do nothing.

As long as the bucket sizes are small, these operations are very fast and independent of the number of elements in the table. Of course, as you add more elements, the buckets will get longer. In that case, the HashSet class in the Java library automatically switches to a larger table. In practice, hash tables perform very well as long as the hash function does a good job placing the added elements into different buckets.

> If there are no or only a few collisions, then adding, finding, and removing hash table elements is independent of the table size.

10.6.3 Computing Hash Codes

A hash function computes an integer hash code from an object in such a way that different objects are likely to have different hash codes. Let us first look at how you can compute a hash code from a string. The task is to combine the character values of the string to yield some integer. You could, for example, add up the character values:

```
int h = 0;
for (int i = 0; i < s.length(); i++)
{
   h = h + s.charAt(i);
}
```

However, that would not be a good idea. It doesn't scramble the character values enough. Strings that are permutations of another (such as "eat" and "tea") would all have the same hash code.

Here is the method the standard library uses to compute the hash code for a string.

```
final int HASH_MULTIPLIER = 31;
int h = 0;
for (int i = 0; i < s.length(); i++)
{
    h = HASH_MULTIPLIER * h + s.charAt(i);
}
```

For example, the hash code of "eat" is

31 * (31 * 'e' + 'a') + 't' = 100184

The hash code of "tea" is quite different, namely

31 * (31 * 't' + 'e') + 'a' = 114704

(Use the Unicode table from Appendix A to look up the character values: 'a' is 97, 'e' is 101, and 't' is 116.)

For your own classes, you should make up a hash code that combines the hash codes of the instance variables in a similar way. For example, let us declare a hashCode method for the Country class from Section 9.6. There are two instance variables: the country name and the area. First, compute their hash code. You know how to compute the hash code of a string. To compute the hash code of a floating-point number, first wrap the floating-point number into a Double object, and then compute its hash code.

```
public class Country
{
    public int hashCode()
    {
        int h1 = name.hashCode();
        int h2 = new Double(area).hashCode();
        . . .
    }
}
```

Then combine the two hash codes.

```
final int HASH_MULTIPLIER = 29;
int h = HASH_MULTIPLIER * h1 + h2;
return h;
```

Use a prime number as the hash multiplier—it scrambles the values well.

If you have more than two instance variables, then combine their hash codes as follows:

```
int h = HASH_MULTIPLIER * h1 + h2;
h = HASH_MULTIPLIER * h + h3;
h = HASH_MULTIPLIER * h + h4;
. . .
return h;
```

If one of the instance variables is an integer, just use the value as its hash code.

10.6.4 Implementing the equals Method

Consider again what happens when finding an element in a hash table. First, the hash code determines the bucket index. Then we traverse the bucket to see if any of the elements equals the one we are trying to find. How can the hash table determine whether two objects are equal?

The hash table relies on the equals method of the element type. The equals method is called to check whether two objects have the same contents:

```
if (country1.equals(country2)) . . .
   // Contents are the same—see Figure 14
```

This is different from the test with the == operator, which tests whether the two references are to the *same object*:

```
if (country1 == country2) . . .
   // Objects are the same—see Figure 15
```

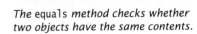

The equals method checks whether two objects have the same contents.

Let's implement the equals method for the Country class. You need to override the equals method of the Object class:

```
public class Country
{
   . . .
   public boolean equals(Object otherObject)
   {
      . . .
   }
   . . .
}
```

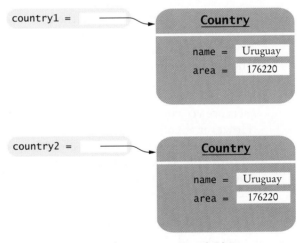

Figure 14 Two References to Equal Objects

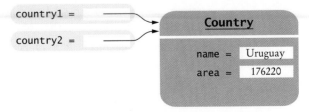

Figure 15 Two References to the Same Object

Now you have a slight problem. The Object class knows nothing about countries, so it declares the otherObject parameter of the equals method to have the type Object. When overriding the method, you are not allowed to change the method signature. Cast the parameter to the class Country:

```
Country other = (Country) otherObject;
```

Then you can compare the two countries.

```
public boolean equals(Object otherObject)
{
    Country other = (Country) otherObject;
    return name.equals(other.name)
        && area == other.area;
}
```

Note that you must use equals to compare instance variables that are objects, but use == to compare numbers.

The equals and hashCode methods must be *compatible* with each other. Two objects that are equal must yield the same hash code:

- If x.equals(y), then x.hashCode() == y.hashCode()

After all, if x and y are equal to each other, then you don't want to insert both of them into a set—sets don't store duplicates. But if their hash codes are different, x and y may end up in different buckets, and the add method would never notice that they are actually duplicates.

For the Country class, the compatibility condition holds. We declare two countries to be equal to each other if their names and values are equal. In that case, their hash codes will also be equal, because the hash code is computed from the hash codes of the name and area instance variables.

You get into trouble if your class declares an equals method but not a hashCode method. Suppose we forget to declare a hashCode method for the Country class. Then it inherits the hash code method from the Object superclass. That method computes a hash code from the *memory location* of the object. The effect is that any two objects are very likely to have a different hash code.

However, if you declare *neither* equals *nor* hashCode, then there is no problem. The equals method of the Object class considers two objects equal only if their memory location is the same. That is, the Object class has compatible equals and hashCode methods. Of course, then the notion of equality is very restricted: Only identical objects are considered equal. That can be a perfectly valid notion of equality, depending on your application.

Whenever you use a hash set or hash map, you need to make sure that appropriate hashCode and equals methods exist for the set elements or map keys. There are three possibilities:

- Use an existing class such as String. Its hashCode and equals methods have already been implemented to work correctly.
- Implement both hashCode and equals. Derive the hash code from the instance variables that the equals method compares, so that equal objects have the same hash code.
- Implement neither hashCode nor equals. Then only identical objects are considered to be equal.

ch10/hashcode/Country.java

```java
1   /**
2       A country with a name and area.
3   */
4   public class Country
5   {
6      private String name;
7      private double area;
8
9      /**
10         Constructs a country.
11         @param aName the name of the country
12         @param anArea the area of the country
13      */
14      public Country(String aName, double anArea)
15      {
16         name = aName;
17         area = anArea;
18      }
19
20      /**
21         Gets the country name.
22         @return the name
23      */
24      public String getName()
25      {
26         return name;
27      }
28
29      /**
30         Gets the area of the country.
31         @return the area
32      */
33      public double getArea()
34      {
35         return area;
36      }
37
38      public int hashCode()
39      {
40         int h1 = name.hashCode();
41         int h2 = new Double(area).hashCode();
42         final int HASH_MULTIPLIER = 29;
43         int h = HASH_MULTIPLIER * h1 + h2;
44         return h;
45      }
46
47      public boolean equals(Object otherObject)
48      {
49         Country other = (Country) otherObject;
50         return name.equals(other.name)
51            && area == other.area;
52      }
53
54      public String toString()
55      {
56         return getClass().getName() + "[name=" + name
57            + ",area=" + area + "]";
58      }
```

```
59 }
```

ch10/hashcode/HashCodePrinter.java

```java
1  import java.util.HashSet;
2  import java.util.Set;
3
4  /**
5     A program that prints hash codes of countries.
6  */
7  public class HashCodePrinter
8  {
9     public static void main(String[] args)
10    {
11       Country country1 = new Country("Belgium", 30510);
12       Country country2 = new Country("Thailand", 514000);
13       Country country3 = new Country("Belgium", 30510);
14
15       System.out.println("hash code of country1=" + country1.hashCode());
16       System.out.println("hash code of country2=" + country2.hashCode());
17       System.out.println("hash code of country3=" + country3.hashCode());
18
19       Set<Country> countries = new HashSet<Country>();
20       countries.add(country1);
21       countries.add(country2);
22       countries.add(country3);
23
24       // Print the set. Note that the set has two elements.
25
26       System.out.println(countries);
27    }
28 }
```

Program Run

```
hash code of country1=-96800969
hash code of country2=1640026923
hash code of country3=-96800969
[Country[name=Thailand,area=514000.0], Country[name=Belgium,area=30510.0]]
```

SELF CHECK

27. What is the hash code of the string "to"?

28. What is the hash code of new Integer(13)?

29. If a hash function returns 0 for all values, will the HashSet work correctly?

30. Suppose the equals method of the Country class only compares the country names. After all, if we have two country objects with name "Belgium", they must surely mean the same country. How do you change the implementation of the hashCode method so that it stays compatible?

31. Suppose the Country class did not implement the hashCode and equals methods. How would the output of the HashCodePrinter program be affected?

Practice It   Now you can try these exercises at the end of the chapter: R10.22, P10.17, P10.18.

10.7 Binary Search Trees

Both the HashSet and the TreeSet classes implement the Set interface. Thus, if you need a set of objects, you have a choice.

If you have a good hash function for your objects, then hashing is usually faster than tree-based algorithms. But the balanced trees used in the TreeSet class can *guarantee* reasonable performance, whereas the HashSet is entirely at the mercy of the hash function. Tree sets have another advantage: The iterators visit elements in *sorted order* rather than the completely random order given by the hash codes.

As the name indicates, tree sets are implemented as a data structure in which nodes are arranged in a tree-like shape (see Figure 16).

Like a linked list, a **binary tree** is made up of nodes. Each node stores an element and a reference to a left and right child node. Child nodes are themselves trees, which can have more children, and so on. We call the node on top of the tree the *root* node. Nodes without children are called *leaf* nodes. (It is traditional to draw the trees upside-down.) A **binary search tree** has the additional property that values in a left child subtree of any node are less than the value held by the node, and values in the right child subtree are greater than the value of the node.

For example, in Figure 16, the values to the left of the root are "Adam", "Eve", and "Harry". They are less than the root value "Juliet" in lexicographic order (see Special Topic 3.2). The values to the right of the root, "Romeo" and "Tom", are greater.

For a binary tree to be a search tree, it is not sufficient to check this property for the root. It must also hold for the other nodes in the tree.

Finding a value in a binary search tree is a simple matter. Compare the value to be found with the element that is stored in the root node. If it is the same, you have

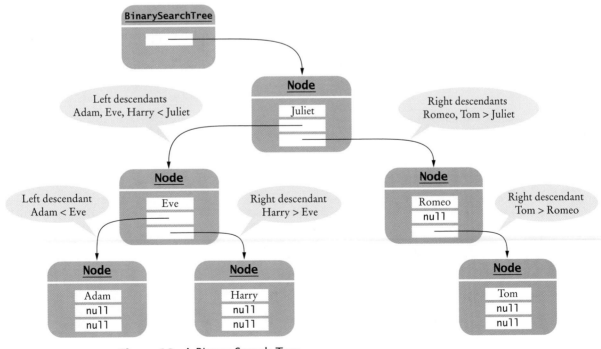

Figure 16 A Binary Search Tree

In computer science, trees are drawn with the root on top.

found the value. If it is smaller, keep looking in the left subtree. Otherwise, keep looking in the right subtree.

For example, to see if the name Harry is in the tree shown, you compare the name to the topmost node. Because the value of Harry is less than Juliet, you know that if the name occurs at all it must be in the left subtree. A comparison to Eve leads you down the right subtree, because Harry comes after Eve. Finally you locate Harry in three steps.

This algorithm is efficient provided the tree is *balanced*. In a balanced tree, all paths from the root to one of the leaf nodes have approximately the same length. The largest of these path lengths is called the *height* of the tree. The tree in Figure 16 has height 3. An important property of search trees is that the set operations take time proportional to the height of the tree, and not to the total number of nodes.

> Adding, finding, and removing an element in a tree set is proportional to the height of the tree.

To see why this is such a benefit, consider a fully populated balanced binary tree. Figure 17 shows such a tree of height 4.

It contains $1 + 2 + 4 + 8 = 15 = 2^4 - 1$ nodes. In general, a tree of height h can have up to $2^h - 1$ nodes. For example, a tree of height 10 can hold up to 1,023 nodes (because $2^{10} = 1024$), and a tree of height 20 can have approximately 1,000,000 nodes (because $2^{20} = 2^{10} \times 2^{10} = 1024 \times 1024 \approx 1000 \times 1000$). In such a tree, you can find any element in at most 20 steps. That is a lot faster than traversing 1,000,000 elements in a list.

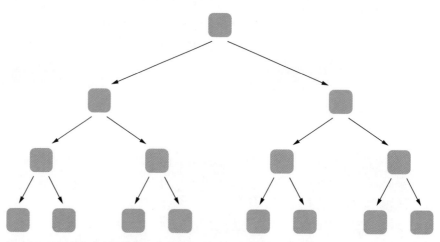

Figure 17 A Balanced Binary Tree of Height 4

To use a tree set, the elements must be comparable.

To use a TreeSet, your objects must belong to a class that implements the Comparable interface (see Section 9.6.3), or you must supply an object of a class that implements the Comparator interface (see Special Topic 10.2).

Several classes in the standard Java library, such as the String and Integer classes, implement the Comparable interface. Thus, you can use strings and integers in tree sets and tree maps with no additional work.

You can use other classes in tree sets and tree maps if you make them implement the Comparable interface. For example, you can modify the Country class like this:

```java
public class Country implements Comparable<Country>
{
    . . .
    public int compareTo(Country other)
    {
        if (area < other.area) return -1;
        if (area > other.area) return 1;
        return 0;
    }
}
```

This compareTo method compares countries by area.

The following program demonstrates a tree set. Note that the iterator visits the elements in sorted order.

ch10/treeset/TreeSetDemo.java

```java
 1  import java.util.Set;
 2  import java.util.TreeSet;
 3
 4  /**
 5     This program tests a tree set with a class that implements the Comparable interface.
 6  */
 7  public class TreeSetDemo
 8  {
 9     public static void main(String[] args)
10     {
11        Country country1 = new Country("Uruguay", 176220);
12        Country country2 = new Country("Thailand", 514000);
13        Country country3 = new Country("Belgium", 30510);
14
15        Set<Country> countries = new TreeSet<Country>();
16
17        countries.add(country1);
18        countries.add(country2);
19        countries.add(country3);
20        countries.add(country1); // Has no effect
21        countries.remove(country3);
22        countries.remove(country3); // Has no effect
23        countries.add(country3);
24
25        System.out.println(countries);
26     }
27  }
```

Program Run

```
[Country[name=Belgium,area=30510.0], Country[name=Uruguay,area=176220.0], Country[name=Thailand,area=514000.0]]
```

32. Suppose you want to keep a set of rectangle objects, using the Rectangle class in the standard library. Would you use a HashSet or a TreeSet? (Look up the API documentation for the Rectangle class.)

33. What happens if you add two countries with the same area into a TreeSet<Country>?

34. When you implement the equals method, you need a cast for the explicit parameter (see Section 10.6). Why is a cast not required in the implementation of the compareTo method?

35. Verify the binary search tree property for all nodes in the tree of Figure 16.

36. What is the height of a balanced binary tree with a billion elements? A trillion?

Practice It Now you can try these exercises at the end of the chapter: R10.24, R10.25, P10.20.

The Comparator Interface

Sometimes, you want to compare objects, but the objects don't belong to a class that implements the Comparable interface. Or, perhaps, you want to compare them in a different order. For example, you may want to sort countries by name rather than by area.

You wouldn't want to change the implementation of a class just in order to put them into a TreeSet. Fortunately, there is an alternative. One TreeSet constructor does not require that the objects belong to classes that implement the Comparable interface. Instead, you can supply arbitrary objects, together with an object whose job is to compare set elements. That object must belong to a class that implements the Comparator interface.

```
public interface Comparator<T>
{
    int compare(T a, T b);
}
```

The Comparator interface is a parameterized type. The type parameter T specifies the type of the compare parameters. For example, a class that implements the Comparator<Country> interface must supply a method

```
public int compare(Country a, Country b)
```

If comp is a comparator object, the call

```
comp.compare(a, b)
```

must return a negative number if a should come before b, 0 if a and b are the same, and a positive number otherwise.

For example, here is a Comparator class for countries that allows you to compare them by name, not area:

```
public class CountryComparatorByName implements Comparator<Country>
{
    public int compare(Country a, Country b)
    {
        return a.getName().compareTo(b.getName());
    }
}
```

To use this comparator in a TreeSet, construct the set as follows:

```
Comparator<Country> comp = new CountryComparatorByName();
Set<Country> countries = new TreeSet<Country>(comp);
```

SCREENCAST 10.1   **Building a Table of Contents**

In this Screencast Video, you will see how to build a table of contents for a book.

CHAPTER SUMMARY

- A collection groups together elements and allows them to be retrieved later.

- A list is a collection that remembers the order of its elements.

- A set is an unordered collection of unique elements.

- A map keeps associations between key and value objects.

- A linked list consists of a number of nodes, each of which has a reference to the next node.
- Adding and removing elements in the middle of a linked list is efficient.
- Visiting the elements of a linked list in sequential order is efficient, but random access is not.
- You use a list iterator to access elements inside a linked list.

- A queue is a collection of elements with "first in first out" retrieval.
  - A stack is a collection of elements with "last in, first out" retrieval.

- Sets don't have duplicates. Adding a duplicate of an element that is already present is silently ignored.
- The HashSet and TreeSet classes both implement the Set interface.
- Set implementations arrange the elements so that they can locate them quickly.
- A set iterator visits the elements in the order in which the set implementation keeps them.
- You cannot add an element to a set at an iterator position.

➕ Available online in WileyPLUS and at www.wiley.com/college/horstmann.

- The HashMap and TreeMap classes both implement the Map interface.
  - To find all keys and values in a map, iterate through the key set and find the values that correspond to the keys.

- A hash function computes an integer value from an object.
  - A good hash function minimizes *collisions*—identical hash codes for different objects.
  - A hash table can be implemented as an array of *buckets*—lists of nodes that hold elements with the same hash code.
  - If there are no or only a few collisions, then adding, finding, and removing hash table elements is independent of the table size.
  - Override hashCode methods in your own classes by combining the hash codes for the instance variables.
  - Override the equals method to test whether two objects have equal state.
  - Your hashCode method must be compatible with the equals method.

- Adding, finding, and removing an element in a tree set is proportional to the height of the tree.
- To use a tree set, the elements must be comparable.

MEDIA RESOURCES

www.wiley.com/
college/
horstmann

- ***Worked Example*** Word Frequency
- Guided Lab Exercises
- ➕ ***Animation*** List Iterators
- ➕ ***Animation*** Using a Map
- ➕ ***Screencast*** Building a Table of Contents
- ➕ Practice Quiz
- ➕ Code Completion Exercises

REVIEW EXERCISES

★★ **R10.1** An invoice contains a collection of purchased items. Should that collection be implemented as a list or set? Explain your answer.

★★ **R10.2** Consider a program that manages an appointment calendar. Should it place the appointments into a list, stack, or queue? Explain your answer.

★★★ **R10.3** One way of implementing a calendar is as a map from date objects to event objects. However, that only works if there is a single event for a given date. How can you use another collection type to allow for multiple events on a given date?

★ **R10.4** Explain what the following code prints. Draw a picture of the linked list after each step.

```
LinkedList<String> staff = new LinkedList<String>();
staff.addFirst("Harry");
staff.addFirst("Diana");
staff.addFirst("Tom");
System.out.println(staff.removeFirst());
System.out.println(staff.removeFirst());
System.out.println(staff.removeFirst());
```

★ **R10.5** Explain what the following code prints. Draw a picture of the linked list after each step.

```
LinkedList<String> staff = new LinkedList<String>();
staff.addFirst("Harry");
staff.addFirst("Diana");
staff.addFirst("Tom");
System.out.println(staff.removeLast());
System.out.println(staff.removeFirst());
System.out.println(staff.removeLast());
```

★ **R10.6** Explain what the following code prints. Draw a picture of the linked list after each step.

```
LinkedList<String> staff = new LinkedList<String>();
staff.addFirst("Harry");
staff.addLast("Diana");
staff.addFirst("Tom");
System.out.println(staff.removeLast());
System.out.println(staff.removeFirst());
System.out.println(staff.removeLast());
```

★ **R10.7** Explain what the following code prints. Draw a picture of the linked list and the iterator position after each step.

```
LinkedList<String> staff = new LinkedList<String>();
ListIterator<String> iterator = staff.listIterator();
iterator.add("Tom");
iterator.add("Diana");
iterator.add("Harry");
iterator = staff.listIterator();
if (iterator.next().equals("Tom"))
    iterator.remove();
while (iterator.hasNext())
    System.out.println(iterator.next());
```

★ **R10.8** Explain what the following code prints. Draw a picture of the linked list and the iterator position after each step.

```
LinkedList<String> staff = new LinkedList<String>();
ListIterator<String> iterator = staff.listIterator();
iterator.add("Tom");
iterator.add("Diana");
iterator.add("Harry");
iterator = staff.listIterator();
iterator.next();
```

```
iterator.next();
iterator.add("Romeo");
iterator.next();
iterator.add("Juliet");
iterator = staff.listIterator();
iterator.next();
iterator.remove();
while (iterator.hasNext())
    System.out.println(iterator.next());
```

★★ **R10.9** What advantages do linked lists have over arrays? What disadvantages do they have?

★★ **R10.10** Suppose you needed to organize a collection of telephone numbers for a company division. There are currently about 6,000 employees, and you know that the phone switch can handle at most 10,000 phone numbers. You expect several hundred look-ups against the collection every day. Would you use an array list or a linked list to store the information?

★★ **R10.11** Suppose you needed to keep a collection of appointments. Would you use a linked list or an array list of Appointment objects?

★ **R10.12** Suppose you write a program that models a card deck. Cards are taken from the top of the deck and given out to players. As cards are returned to the deck, they are placed on the bottom of the deck. Would you store the cards in a stack or a queue?

★ **R10.13** Suppose the strings "A" . . . "Z" are pushed onto a stack. Then they are popped off the stack and pushed onto a second stack. Finally, they are all popped off the second stack and printed. In which order are the strings printed?

★★ **R10.14** Consider the following algorithm for traversing a maze such as this one:

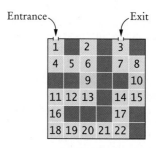

Make the cell at the entrance the current cell. Take the following actions, then repeat:
- If the current cell is adjacent to the exit, stop.
- Mark the current cell as visited.
- Add all unvisited neighbors to the north, east, south, and west to a queue.
- Remove the next element from the queue and make it the current cell.

In which order will the cells of the sample maze be visited?

★★ **R10.15** Repeat Exercise R10.14, using a stack instead of a queue.

★ **R10.16** What is the difference between a set and a map?

★★ **R10.17** The union of two sets A and B is the set of all elements that are contained in A, B, or both. The intersection is the set of all elements that are contained in A and B. How can you compute the union and intersection of two sets, using the add and contains methods, together with an iterator?

★★ **R10.18** How can you compute the union and intersection of two sets, using some of the methods that the java.util.Set interface provides, but without using an iterator? (Look up the interface in the API documentation.)

★ **R10.19** Can a map have two keys with the same value? Two values with the same key?

★★ **R10.20** A map can be implemented as a set of (*key, value*) pairs. Explain.

★★★ **R10.21** Verify the hash codes of the strings "Jim" and "Joe" in Table 8.

★★★ **R10.22** Verify that the strings "VII" and "Ugh" have the same hash code.

★★★ **R10.23** From the hash codes in Table 8, show that Figure 13 accurately shows the locations of the strings if the hash table size is 101.

★★ **R10.24** Draw a balanced binary search tree that contains the names

Adam Eve Romeo Juliet Tom Diana Harry

★★ **R10.25** Consider the following algorithm for processing a binary search tree:

Process the left subtree (using the same algorithm).
Print the value in the root.
Process the right subtree.

What is the output when the algorithm is applied to the tree in Figure 16?

PROGRAMMING EXERCISES

★★ **P10.1** Using only the public interface of the linked list class, write a method

public static void downsize(LinkedList<String> employeeNames, int n)

that removes every nth employee from a linked list.

★★ **P10.2** Using only the public interface of the linked list class, write a method

public static void reverse(LinkedList<String> strings)

that reverses the entries in a linked list.

★★★ **P10.3** In a paint program, a "flood fill" fills all empty pixels of a drawing with a given color, stopping when it reaches occupied pixels. In this exercise, you will implement a simple variation of this algorithm, flood-filling a 10 × 10 array of integers that are initially 0.

Prompt for the starting row and column.
Push the (row, column) pair onto a stack. (You will need to provide a simple Pair class.)

Repeat the following operations until the stack is empty.

Pop off the (row, column) pair from the top of the stack.
If it has not yet been filled, fill the corresponding array location now. (Fill in numbers 1, 2, 3, and so on, to show the order in which the square is filled.)
Push the coordinates of any unfilled neighbors in the north, east, south, or west direction on the stack.

When you are done, print the entire array.

★★★ **P10.4** Repeat Exercise P10.3, but use a queue instead.

★★★ **P10.5** Use a stack to enumerate all permutations of a string. Suppose you want to find all permutations of the string meat. Push the string +meat on the stack. Now repeat the following operations until the stack is empty.
- Pop off the top of the stack.
- If that string ends in a + (such as tame+), remove the + and print the string
- Otherwise, remove each letter in turn from the right of the +, insert it just before the +, and push the resulting string on the stack. For example, after popping e+mta, you push em+ta, et+ma, and ea+mt.

★★★ **P10.6** Repeat Exercise P10.5, but use a queue instead.

★ **P10.7** Write a program that reads text from a file and breaks it up into individual words. Insert the words into a tree set. At the end of the input file, print all words, followed by the size of the resulting set. This program determines how many unique words a text file has.

★★ **P10.8** Implement the *sieve of Eratosthenes:* a method for computing prime numbers, known to the ancient Greeks. This method will compute all prime numbers up to n. Choose an n. First insert all numbers from 2 to n into a set. Then erase all multiples of 2 (except 2); that is, 4, 6, 8, 10, 12, ... Erase all multiples of 3; that is, 6, 9, 12, 15, ... Go up to $\sqrt{n}$. Then print the set.

★★ **P10.9** Write a program that keeps a map in which both keys and values are strings—the names of students and their course grades. Prompt the user of the program to add or remove students, to modify grades, or to print all grades. The printout should be sorted by name and formatted like this:

```
Carl: B+
Joe: C
Sarah: A
```

★★★ **P10.10** Reimplement Exercise P10.9 so that the keys of the map are objects of class Student. A student should have a first name, a last name, and a unique integer ID. For grade changes and removals, lookup should be by ID. The printout should be sorted by last name. If two students have the same last name, then use the first name as tie breaker. If the first names are also identical, then use the integer ID. *Hint:* Use two maps.

★★★ **P10.11** Write a class Polynomial that stores a polynomial such as

$$p(x) = 5x^{10} + 9x^7 - x - 10$$

as a linked list of terms. A term contains the coefficient and the power of x. For example, you would store $p(x)$ as

$$(5,10),(9,7),(-1,1),(-10,0)$$

Supply methods to add, multiply, and print polynomials. Supply a constructor that makes a polynomial from a single term. For example, the polynomial p can be constructed as

```
Polynomial p = new Polynomial(new Term(-10, 0));
p.add(new Polynomial(new Term(-1, 1)));
p.add(new Polynomial(new Term(9, 7)));
p.add(new Polynomial(new Term(5, 10)));
```

Then compute $p(x) \times p(x)$.

```
Polynomial q = p.multiply(p);
q.print();
```

★★★ **P10.12** Repeat Exercise P10.11, but use a Map<Integer, Double> for the coefficients.

★ **P10.13** Insert all words from a large file (such as the novel "War and Peace", which is available on the Internet) into a hash set and a tree set. Time the results. Which data structure is faster?

★★★ **P10.14** Write a program that reads a Java source file and produces an index of all identifiers in the file. For each identifier, print all lines in which it occurs.

Hint: Call in.useDelimiter("[^A-Za-z0-9_]+"). Then each call to next returns a string consisting only of letters, numbers, and underscores.

★★ **P10.15** Try to find two words with the same hash code in a large file. Keep a Map<Integer, HashSet<String>>. When you read in a word, compute its hash code h and put the word in the set whose key is h. Then iterate through all keys and print the sets whose size is > 1.

★★ **P10.16** Supply compatible hashCode and equals methods to the Student class described in Exercise P10.10. Test the hash code by adding Student objects to a hash set.

★ **P10.17** Supply compatible hashCode and equals methods to the BankAccount class of Chapter 7. Test the hashCode method by printing out hash codes and by adding BankAccount objects to a hash set.

★★ **P10.18** A labeled point has x- and y-coordinates and a string label. Provide a class LabeledPoint with a constructor LabeledPoint(int x, int y, String label) and hashCode and equals methods. Two labeled points are considered the same when they have the same location and label.

★★ **P10.19** Reimplement the LabeledPoint class of the preceding exercise by storing the location in a java.awt.Point object. Your hashCode and equals methods should call the hashCode and equals methods of the Point class.

★★ **P10.20** Modify the LabeledPoint class of Exercise P10.18 so that it implements the Comparable interface. Sort points first by their x-coordinates. If two points have the same x-coordinate, sort them by their y-coordinates. If two points have the same x- and y-coordinates, sort them by their label. Write a tester program that checks all cases by inserting points into a TreeSet.

1. A list is a better choice because the application will want to retain the order in which the quizzes are given.

2. A set is a better choice. There is no intrinsically useful ordering for the students. For example, the registrar's office has little use for a list of all students by their GPA. By storing them in a set, adding, removing, and finding students can be fast.

3. With a stack, you would always read the latest required reading, and you might never get to the oldest readings.

4. A collection stores elements, but a map stores associations between elements.

5. Yes, for two reasons. A linked list needs to store the neighboring node references, which are not needed in an array, Moreover, there is some overhead for storing an object. In a linked list, each node is a separate object that incurs this overhead, whereas an array is a single object.

6. We can simply access each array element with an integer index.

7. |ABCD A|BCD AB|CD A|CD AC|D ACE|D ACED| ACEDF|

8. ```
ListIterator<String> iter = words.iterator();
while (iter.hasNext())
{
    String str = iter.next();
    if (str.length() < 4) { iter.remove(); }
}
```

9. ```
ListIterator<String> iter = words.iterator();
while (iter.hasNext())
{
    System.out.println(iter.next());
    if (iter.hasNext()) { iter.next(); } // Skip the next element
}
```

10. This way, we can ensure that only queue operations can be invoked on the q object.

11. Depending on whether you consider the 0 position the head or the tail of the queue, you would either add or remove elements at that position. Both are expensive operations.

12. A B C

13. Stacks use a "last in, first out" discipline. If you are the first one to submit a print job and lots of people add print jobs before the printer has a chance to deal with your job, they get their printouts first, and you have to wait until all other jobs are completed.

14. 70.

15. It would then subtract the first argument from the second. Consider the input 5 3 –. The stack contains 5 and 3, with the 3 on the top. Then results.pop() - results.pop() computes 3 – 5.

16. Adding and removing elements as well as testing for membership is faster with sets.

17. Sets do not have an ordering, so it doesn't make sense to add an element at a particular iterator position, or to traverse a set backwards.

18. You do not know in which order the set keeps the elements.

19. Here is one possibility:
```
if (s.size() == 3 && s.contains("Tom") && s.contains("Diana") && s.contains("Harry"))
    . . .
```

20.
```
for (String str : s)
{
    if (t.contains(str)) { System.out.println(str); }
}
```

21. The words would be listed in sorted order.

22. A set stores elements. A map stores associations between keys and values.

23. The ordering does not matter, and you cannot have duplicates.

24. Because it might have duplicates.

25. `Map<String, Integer> wordFrequency;`

Note that you cannot use a `Map<String, int>` because you cannot use primitive types as type parameters in Java.

26. It associates strings with sets of strings. One application would be a thesaurus that lists synonyms for a given word. For example, the key `"improve"` might have as its value the set `["ameliorate", "better", "enhance", "enrich", "perfect", "refine"]`.

27. $31 \times 116 + 111 = 3707$.

28. 13.

29. Yes, but all elements will end up in a single bucket. In effect, the `HashSet` has become a linked list.

30. Only compute the hash code of the `name` instance variable.

31. The hash codes will be different—they are now derived from the object locations. More importantly, the set now has three elements.

32. Because `Rectangle` does not implement the `Comparable` interface, use a `HashSet`.

33. Only the first one is added. The second one is considered identical to the first because `compareTo` was implemented to compare the area.

34. The explicit parameter of the `compareTo` method can be given the same type as the implicit parameter because you can set the type parameter of the `Comparable` interface. But the `equals` method is declared in the `Object` class, and its explicit parameter is always of type `Object`.

35. We already did this for the root. Let's move on to "Eve". There is a single smaller value to the left, "Adam", and a single larger value to the right, "Harry", so the condition is fulfilled for the "Eve" node.

The "Romeo" node has no values to the left, so there is nothing to check. There is one value to the right, "Tom", and it is larger than "Romeo".

The remaining nodes are leaf nodes without subtrees, so they trivially fulfill the property.

36. Approximately 30 and 40.

THE BASIC LATIN AND LATIN-1 SUBSETS OF UNICODE

This appendix lists the Unicode characters that are most commonly used for processing Western European languages. A complete listing of Unicode characters can be found at http://unicode.org.

Table 1 Selected Control Characters			
Character	Code	Decimal	Escape Sequence
Tab	'\u0009'	9	'\t'
Newline	'\u000A'	10	'\n'
Return	'\u000D'	13	'\r'
Space	'\u0020'	32	

Table 2   The Basic Latin (ASCII) Subset of Unicode

Char.	Code	Dec.	Char.	Code	Dec.	Char.	Code	Dec.
			@	'\u0040'	64	`	'\u0060'	96
!	'\u0021'	33	A	'\u0041'	65	a	'\u0061'	97
"	'\u0022'	34	B	'\u0042'	66	b	'\u0062'	98
#	'\u0023'	35	C	'\u0043'	67	c	'\u0063'	99
$	'\u0024'	36	D	'\u0044'	68	d	'\u0064'	100
%	'\u0025'	37	E	'\u0045'	69	e	'\u0065'	101
&	'\u0026'	38	F	'\u0046'	70	f	'\u0066'	102
'	'\u0027'	39	G	'\u0047'	71	g	'\u0067'	103
(	'\u0028'	40	H	'\u0048'	72	h	'\u0068'	104
)	'\u0029'	41	I	'\u0049'	73	i	'\u0069'	105
*	'\u002A'	42	J	'\u004A'	74	j	'\u006A'	106
+	'\u002B'	43	K	'\u004B'	75	k	'\u006B'	107
,	'\u002C'	44	L	'\u004C'	76	l	'\u006C'	108
-	'\u002D'	45	M	'\u004D'	77	m	'\u006D'	109
.	'\u002E'	46	N	'\u004E'	78	n	'\u006E'	110
/	'\u002F'	47	O	'\u004F'	79	o	'\u006F'	111
0	'\u0030'	48	P	'\u0050'	80	p	'\u0070'	112
1	'\u0031'	49	Q	'\u0051'	81	q	'\u0071'	113
2	'\u0032'	50	R	'\u0052'	82	r	'\u0072'	114
3	'\u0033'	51	S	'\u0053'	83	s	'\u0073'	115
4	'\u0034'	52	T	'\u0054'	84	t	'\u0074'	116
5	'\u0035'	53	U	'\u0055'	85	u	'\u0075'	117
6	'\u0036'	54	V	'\u0056'	86	v	'\u0076'	118
7	'\u0037'	55	W	'\u0057'	87	w	'\u0077'	119
8	'\u0038'	56	X	'\u0058'	88	x	'\u0078'	120
9	'\u0039'	57	Y	'\u0059'	89	y	'\u0079'	121
:	'\u003A'	58	Z	'\u005A'	90	z	'\u007A'	122
;	'\u003B'	59	[	'\u005B'	91	{	'\u007B'	123
<	'\u003C'	60	\	'\u005C'	92	|	'\u007C'	124
=	'\u003D'	61	]	'\u005D'	93	}	'\u007D'	125
>	'\u003E'	62	^	'\u005E'	94	~	'\u007E'	126
?	'\u003F'	63	_	'\u005F'	95			

Table 3   The Latin-1 Subset of Unicode

Char.	Code	Dec.	Char.	Code	Dec.	Char.	Code	Dec.
			À	'\u00C0'	192	à	'\u00E0'	224
¡	'\u00A1'	161	Á	'\u00C1'	193	á	'\u00E1'	225
¢	'\u00A2'	162	Â	'\u00C2'	194	â	'\u00E2'	226
£	'\u00A3'	163	Ã	'\u00C3'	195	ã	'\u00E3'	227
¤	'\u00A4'	164	Ä	'\u00C4'	196	ä	'\u00E4'	228
¥	'\u00A5'	165	Å	'\u00C5'	197	å	'\u00E5'	229
¦	'\u00A6'	166	Æ	'\u00C6'	198	æ	'\u00E6'	230
§	'\u00A7'	167	Ç	'\u00C7'	199	ç	'\u00E7'	231
¨	'\u00A8'	168	È	'\u00C8'	200	è	'\u00E8'	232
©	'\u00A9'	169	É	'\u00C9'	201	é	'\u00E9'	233
ª	'\u00AA'	170	Ê	'\u00CA'	202	ê	'\u00EA'	234
«	'\u00AB'	171	Ë	'\u00CB'	203	ë	'\u00EB'	235
¬	'\u00AC'	172	Ì	'\u00CC'	204	ì	'\u00EC'	236
	'\u00AD'	173	Í	'\u00CD'	205	í	'\u00ED'	237
®	'\u00AE'	174	Î	'\u00CE'	206	î	'\u00EE'	238
¯	'\u00AF'	175	Ï	'\u00CF'	207	ï	'\u00EF'	239
°	'\u00B0'	176	Ð	'\u00D0'	208	ð	'\u00F0'	240
±	'\u00B1'	177	Ñ	'\u00D1'	209	ñ	'\u00F1'	241
²	'\u00B2'	178	Ò	'\u00D2'	210	ò	'\u00F2'	242
³	'\u00B3'	179	Ó	'\u00D3'	211	ó	'\u00F3'	243
´	'\u00B4'	180	Ô	'\u00D4'	212	ô	'\u00F4'	244
µ	'\u00B5'	181	Õ	'\u00D5'	213	õ	'\u00F5'	245
¶	'\u00B6'	182	Ö	'\u00D6'	214	ö	'\u00F6'	246
·	'\u00B7'	183	×	'\u00D7'	215	÷	'\u00F7'	247
¸	'\u00B8'	184	Ø	'\u00D8'	216	ø	'\u00F8'	248
¹	'\u00B9'	185	Ù	'\u00D9'	217	ù	'\u00F9'	249
º	'\u00BA'	186	Ú	'\u00DA'	218	ú	'\u00FA'	250
»	'\u00BB'	187	Û	'\u00DB'	219	û	'\u00FB'	251
¼	'\u00BC'	188	Ü	'\u00DC'	220	ü	'\u00FC'	252
½	'\u00BD'	189	Ý	'\u00DD'	221	ý	'\u00FD'	253
¾	'\u00BE'	190	Þ	'\u00DE'	222	þ	'\u00FE'	254
¿	'\u00BF'	191	ß	'\u00DF'	223	ÿ	'\u00FF'	255

JAVA OPERATOR SUMMARY

The operators are listed in groups of decreasing precedence in the table below. The horizontal lines in the table indicate a change in operator precedence. For example, z = x - y; means z = (x - y); because = has lower precedence than -.

The prefix unary operators, conditional operator, and the assignment operators associate right-to-left. All other operators associate left-to-right.

Operator	Description	Associativity
.	Access class feature	
[]	Array subscript	Left to right
()	Function call	
++	Increment	
--	Decrement	
!	Boolean *not*	
~	Bitwise *not*	
+ *(unary)*	(Has no effect)	Right to left
- *(unary)*	Negative	
(*TypeName*)	Cast	
new	Object allocation	
*	Multiplication	
/	Division or integer division	Left to right
%	Integer remainder	
+	Addition, string concatenation	Left to right
-	Subtraction	

Operator	Description	Associativity
<<	Shift left	
>>	Right shift with sign extension	Left to right
>>>	Right shift with zero extension	
<	Less than	
<=	Less than or equal	
>	Greater than	Left to right
>=	Greater than or equal	
instanceof	Tests whether an object's type is a given type or a subtype thereof	
==	Equal	Left to right
!=	Not equal	
&	Bitwise *and*	Left to right
^	Bitwise exclusive *or*	Left to right
|	Bitwise *or*	Left to right
&&	Boolean "short circuit" *and*	Left to right
||	Boolean "short circuit" *or*	Left to right
? :	Conditional	Right to left
=	Assignment	Right to left
op=	Assignment with binary operator (*op* is one of +, -, *, /, &, |, ^, <<, >>, >>>)	

JAVA RESERVED
WORD SUMMARY

Reserved Word	Description
abstract	An abstract class or method
assert	An assertion that a condition is fulfilled
boolean	The Boolean type
break	Breaks out of the current loop or labeled statement
byte	The 8-bit signed integer type
case	A label in a switch statement
catch	The handler for an exception in a try block
char	The 16-bit Unicode character type
class	Defines a class
const	Not used
continue	Skip the remainder of a loop body
default	The default label in a switch statement
do	A loop whose body is executed at least once
double	The 64-bit double-precision floating-point type
else	The alternative clause in an if statement
enum	An enumeration type
extends	Indicates that a class is a subclass of another class
final	A value that cannot be changed after it has been initialized, a method that cannot be overridden, or a class that cannot be extended
finally	A clause of a try block that is always executed
float	The 32-bit single-precision floating-point type
for	A loop with initialization, condition, and update expressions
goto	Not used

Reserved Word	Description
if	A conditional branch statement
implements	Indicates that a class realizes an interface
import	Allows the use of class names without the package name
instanceof	Tests whether an object's type is a given type or a subtype thereof
int	The 32-bit integer type
interface	An abstract type with only abstract methods and constants
long	The 64-bit integer type
native	A method implemented in non-Java code
new	Allocates an object
package	A collection of related classes
private	A feature that is accessible only by methods of the same class
protected	A feature that is accessible only by methods of the same class, a subclass, or another class in the same package
public	A feature that is accessible by all methods
return	Returns from a method
short	The 16-bit integer type
static	A feature that is defined for a class, not for individual instances
strictfp	Use strict rules for floating-point computations
super	Invoke the superclass constructor or a superclass method
switch	A selection statement
synchronized	A block of code that is accessible to only one thread at a time
this	The implicit parameter of a method; or invocation of another constructor of the same class
throw	Throws an exception
throws	The exceptions that a method may throw
transient	Instance variables that should not be serialized
try	A block of code with exception handlers or a finally handler
void	Tags a method that doesn't return a value
volatile	A variable that may be accessed by multiple threads without synchronization
while	A loop statement

THE JAVA LIBRARY

This appendix lists all classes and methods from the standard Java library that are used in this book.

In the following inheritance hierarchy, superclasses that are not used in this book are shown in gray type. Some classes implement interfaces not covered in this book; they are omitted. Classes used in the graphics chapters are in purple type. Classes are sorted first by package, then alphabetically within a package.

```
java.lang.Object
    java.awt.BorderLayout
    java.awt.Color
    java.awt.Component
        java.awt.Container
            javax.swing.JComponent
                javax.swing.AbstractButton
                    javax.swing.JButton
                    javax.swing.JMenuItem
                        javax.swing.JMenu
                    javax.swing.JToggleButton
                        javax.swing.JCheckBox
                        javax.swing.JRadioButton
                javax.swing.JComboBox
                javax.swing.JFileChooser
                javax.swing.JLabel
                javax.swing.JMenuBar
                javax.swing.JPanel
                javax.swing.JOptionPane
                javax.swing.JScrollPane
                javax.swing.JSlider
                javax.swing.text.JTextComponent
                    javax.swing.JTextArea
                    javax.swing.JTextField
            java.awt.Panel
                java.applet.Applet
                    javax.swing.JApplet
        java.awt.Window
            java.awt.Frame
                javax.swing.JFrame
    java.awt.Dimension2D
        java.awt.Dimension
    java.awt.FlowLayout
    java.awt.Font
    java.awt.Graphics
        java.awt.Graphics2D;
    java.awt.GridLayout
    java.awt.event.MouseAdapter implements MouseListener
    java.awt.geom.Line2D
        java.awt.geom.Line2D.Double
    java.awt.geom.Point2D
        java.awt.geom.Point2D.Double
```

```
            java.awt.geom.RectangularShape
                java.awt.geom.Rectangle2D
                  java.awt.Rectangle
                java.awt.geom.Ellipse2D
                    java.awt.geom.Ellipse2D.Double
        java.io.File implements Comparable<File>
        java.io.Writer
            java.io.PrintWriter
        java.lang.Boolean implements Comparable<Boolean>
        java.lang.Character implements Comparable<Character>
        java.lang.Math
        java.lang.Number
            java.lang.Double implements Comparable<Double>
            java.lang.Integer implements Comparable<Integer>
        java.lang.String implements Comparable<String>
        java.lang.System
        java.lang.Throwable
          java.lang.Error
          java.lang.Exception
            java.io.IOException
                java.io.EOFException
                java.io.FileNotFoundException
            java.lang.RuntimeException
                java.lang.IllegalArgumentException
                    java.lang.NumberFormatException
                java.lang.IllegalStateException
                java.util.NoSuchElementException
                    java.util.InputMismatchException
                java.lang.NullPointerException
        java.net.URL
        java.util.AbstractCollection<E>
            java.util.AbstractList<E>
                java.util.AbstractSequentialList<E>
                java.util.LinkedList<E> implements List<E>
                java.util.ArrayList<E> implements List<E>
            java.util.AbstractSet<E>
                java.util.HashSet<E> implements Set<E>
                java.util.TreeSet<E> implements SortedSet<E>
        java.util.AbstractMap<K, V>
            java.util.HashMap<K, V> implements Map<K, V>
            java.util.TreeMap<K, V> implements Map<K, V>
        java.util.Arrays
        java.util.Collections
        java.util.EventObject
            java.awt.AWTEvent
                java.awt.event.ActionEvent
                java.awt.event.ComponentEvent
                    java.awt.event.InputEvent
                        java.awt.event.MouseEvent
            javax.swing.event.ChangeEvent
        java.util.Scanner
        javax.swing.ButtonGroup
        javax.swing.ImageIcon
        javax.swing.Timer
        javax.swing.border.AbstractBorder
            javax.swing.border.EtchedBorder
            javax.swing.border.TitledBorder
    java.lang.Comparable<T>
    java.util.Collection<E>
        java.util.List<E>
```

```
      java.util.Set<E>
          java.util.SortedSet<E>
  java.util.Comparator<T>
  java.util.EventListener
      java.awt.event.ActionListener
      java.awt.event.MouseListener
      javax.swing.event.ChangeListener
  java.util.Iterator<E>
      java.util.ListIterator<E>
  java.util.Map<K, V>
```

In the following descriptions, the phrase "this object" ("this component", "this container", and so forth) means the object (component, container, and so forth) on which the method is invoked (the implicit parameter, `this`).

Package `java.applet`

Class `java.applet.Applet`

- void **destroy**()
  This method is called when the applet is about to be terminated, after the last call to `stop`.
- void **init**()
  This method is called when the applet has been loaded, before the first call to `start`. Applets override this method to carry out applet-specific initialization and to read applet parameters.
- void **start**()
  This method is called after the `init` method and each time the applet is revisited.
- void **stop**()
  This method is called whenever the user has stopped watching this applet.

Package `java.awt`

Class `java.awt.BorderLayout`

- **BorderLayout**()
  This constructs a border layout. A border layout has five regions for adding components, called "North", "East", "South", "West", and "Center".
- static final int CENTER
  This value identifies the center position of a border layout.
- static final int EAST
  This value identifies the east position of a border layout.
- static final int NORTH
  This value identifies the north position of a border layout.
- static final int SOUTH
  This value identifies the south position of a border layout.
- static final int WEST
  This value identifies the west position of a border layout.

Class java.awt.Color

- **Color**(int red, int green, int blue)
  This creates a color with the specified red, green, and blue values between 0 and 255.
  Parameters: red The red component
  green The green component
  blue The blue component

Class java.awt.Component

- void **addMouseListener**(MouseListener listener)
  This method adds a mouse listener to the component.
  Parameters: listener The mouse listener to be added
- int **getHeight**()
  This method gets the height of this component.
  Returns: The height in pixels.
- int **getWidth**()
  This method gets the width of this component.
  Returns: The width in pixels.
- void **repaint**()
  This method repaints this component by scheduling a call to the paint method.
- void **setPreferredSize**(Dimension preferredSize)
  This method sets the preferred size of this component.
- void **setSize**(int width, int height)
  This method sets the size of this component.
  Parameters: width the component width
  height the component height
- void **setVisible**(boolean visible)
  This method shows or hides the component.
  Parameters: visible true to show the component, or false to hide it

Class java.awt.Container

- void **add**(Component c)
- void **add**(Component c, Object position)
  These methods add a component to the end of this container. If a position is given, the layout manager is called to position the component.
  Parameters: c The component to be added
  position An object expressing position information for the layout manager
- void **setLayout**(LayoutManager manager)
  This method sets the layout manager for this container.
  Parameters: manager A layout manager

Class java.awt.Dimension

- **Dimension**(int width, int height)
  This constructs a Dimension object with the given width and height.
  Parameters: width The width
  height The height

Class java.awt.FlowLayout

- FlowLayout()
  This constructs a new flow layout. A flow layout places as many components as possible in a row, without changing their size, and starts new rows when necessary.

Class java.awt.Font

- Font(String name, int style, int size)
  This constructs a font object from the specified name, style, and point size.
  Parameters: name The font name, either a font face name or a logical font name, which must be one of "Dialog", "DialogInput", "Monospaced", "Serif", or "SansSerif"

  style One of Font.PLAIN, Font.ITALIC, Font.BOLD, or Font.ITALIC+Font.BOLD

  size The point size of the font

Class java.awt.Frame

- void **setTitle**(String title)
  This method sets the frame title.
  Parameters: title The title to be displayed in the border of the frame

Class java.awt.Graphics

- void **setColor**(Color c)
  This method sets the current color. From now on, all graphics operations use this color.
  Parameters: c The new drawing color

Class java.awt.Graphics2D

- void **draw**(Shape s)
  This method draws the outline of the given shape. Many classes—among them Rectangle and Line2D.Double—implement the Shape interface.
  Parameters: s The shape to be drawn
- void **drawString**(String s, int x, int y)
- void **drawString**(String s, float x, float y)
  These methods draw a string in the current font.
  Parameters: s The string to draw

  x,y The basepoint of the first character in the string
- void **fill**(Shape s)
  This method draws the given shape and fills it with the current color.
  Parameters: s The shape to be filled

Class java.awt.GridLayout

- GridLayout(int rows, int cols)
  This constructor creates a grid layout with the specified number of rows and columns. The components in a grid layout are arranged in a grid with equal widths and heights. One, but not both, of rows and cols can be zero, in which case any number of objects can be placed in a row or in a column, respectively.
  Parameters: rows The number of rows in the grid

  cols The number of columns in the grid

Class `java.awt.Rectangle`

- `Rectangle()`
  This constructs a rectangle whose top-left corner is at (0, 0) and whose width and height are both zero.

- `Rectangle(int x, int y, int width, int height)`
  This constructs a rectangle with given top-left corner and size.
  Parameters: `x,y` The top-left corner
  　　　　　　　　`width` The width
  　　　　　　　　`height` The height

- `double getHeight()`
- `double getWidth()`
  These methods get the height and width of the rectangle.

- `double getX()`
- `double getY()`
  These methods get the x- and y-coordinates of the top-left corner of the rectangle.

- `void grow(int dw, int dh)`
  This method adjusts the width and height of this rectangle.
  Parameters: `dw`   The amount to add to the right and left (can be negative)
  　　　　　　　　`dh`   The amount to add to the top and bottom (can be negative)

- `Rectangle intersection(Rectangle other)`
  This method computes the intersection of this rectangle with the specified rectangle.
  Parameters: `other` A rectangle
  Returns: The largest rectangle contained in both `this` and `other`

- `void setLocation(int x, int y)`
  This method moves this rectangle to a new location.
  Parameters: `x,y` The new top-left corner

- `void setSize(int width, int height)`
  This method sets the width and height of this rectangle to new values.
  Parameters: `width` The new width
  　　　　　　　　`height` The new height

- `void translate(int dx, int dy)`
  This method moves this rectangle.
  Parameters: `dx` The distance to move along the x-axis
  　　　　　　　　`dy` The distance to move along the y-axis

- `Rectangle union(Rectangle other)`
  This method computes the union of this rectangle with the specified rectangle. This is not the set-theoretic union but the smallest rectangle that contains both `this` and `other`.
  Parameters: `other` A rectangle
  Returns: The smallest rectangle containing both `this` and `other`

Interface `java.awt.Shape`

The `Shape` interface describes shapes that can be drawn and filled by a `Graphics2D` object.

Package java.awt.event

Interface java.awt.event.ActionListener

- void **actionPerformed**(ActionEvent e)
  The event source calls this method when an action occurs.

Class java.awt.event.MouseEvent

- int **getX**()
  This method returns the horizontal position of the mouse as of the time the event occurred.
  Returns: The x-position of the mouse
- int **getY**()
  This method returns the vertical position of the mouse as of the time the event occurred.
  Returns: The y-position of the mouse

Interface java.awt.event.MouseListener

- void **mouseClicked**(MouseEvent e)
  This method is called when the mouse has been clicked (that is, pressed and released in quick succession).
- void **mouseEntered**(MouseEvent e)
  This method is called when the mouse has entered the component to which this listener was added.
- void **mouseExited**(MouseEvent e)
  This method is called when the mouse has exited the component to which this listener was added.
- void **mousePressed**(MouseEvent e)
  This method is called when a mouse button has been pressed.
- void **mouseReleased**(MouseEvent e)
  This method is called when a mouse button has been released.

Package java.awt.geom

Class java.awt.geom.Ellipse2D.Double

- **Ellipse2D.Double**(double x, double y, double w, double h)
  This constructs an ellipse from the specified coordinates.
  Parameters: x, y   The top-left corner of the bounding rectangle
  w   The width of the bounding rectangle
  h   The height of the bounding rectangle

Class java.awt.geom.Line2D

- double **getX1**()
- double **getX2**()
- double **getY1**()
- double **getY2**()

These methods get the requested coordinate of an endpoint of this line.

Returns: The *x*- or *y*-coordinate of the first or second endpoint

- void **setLine**(double x1, double y1, double x2, double y2)

This method sets the endpoints of this line.

Parameters: x1, y1 A new endpoint of this line
x2, y2 The other new endpoint

Class java.awt.geom.Line2D.Double

- **Line2D.Double**(double x1, double y1, double x2, double y2)

This constructs a line from the specified coordinates.

Parameters: x1, y1 One endpoint of the line
x2, y2 The other endpoint

- **Line2D.Double**(Point2D p1, Point2D p2)

This constructs a line from the two endpoints.

Parameters: p1, p2 The endpoints of the line

Class java.awt.geom.Point2D

- double **getX**()
- double **getY**()

These methods get the requested coordinates of this point.

Returns: The *x*- or *y*-coordinate of this point

- void **setLocation**(double x, double y)

This method sets the *x*- and *y*-coordinates of this point.

Parameters: x, y The new location of this point

Class java.awt.geom.Point2D.Double

- **Point2D.Double**(double x, double y)

This constructs a point with the specified coordinates.

Parameters: x, y The coordinates of the point

Class java.awt.geom.RectangularShape

- int **getHeight**()
- int **getWidth**()

These methods get the height or width of the bounding rectangle of this rectangular shape.

Returns: The height or width, respectively

- double **getCenterX**()
- double **getCenterY**()
- double **getMaxX**()
- double **getMaxY**()
- double **getMinX**()
- double **getMinY**()

These methods get the requested coordinate value of the corners or center of the bounding rectangle of this shape.

Returns: The center, maximum, or minimum x- and y-coordinates

Package java.io

Class java.io.EOFException

- **EOFException**(String message)

This constructs an "end of file" exception object.

Parameters: message The detail message

Class java.io.File

- **File**(String name)

This constructs a File object that describes a file (which may or may not exist) with the given name.

Parameters: name The name of the file

Class java.io.FileNotFoundException

This exception is thrown when a file could not be opened.

Class java.io.IOException

This type of exception is thrown when an input/output error is encountered.

Class java.io.PrintStream/Class java.io.PrintWriter

- **PrintStream**(String name)
- **PrintWriter**(String name)

This constructs a PrintStream or PrintWriter and opens the named file. If the file cannot be opened for writing, a FileNotFoundException is thrown.

Parameters: name The name of the file to be opened for writing

- void **close**()

This method closes this stream or writer and releases any associated system resources.

- void **print**(int x)
- void **print**(double x)
- void **print**(Object x)
- void **print**(String x)
- void **println**()
- void **println**(int x)
- void **println**(double x)
- void **println**(Object x)
- void **println**(String x)

These methods print a value to this PrintStream or PrintWriter. The println methods print a newline after the value. Objects are printed by converting them to strings with their toString methods.

Parameters: x   The value to be printed

- PrintStream **printf**(String format, Object... values)
- PrintWriter **printf**(String format, Object... values)

This method prints the format string to this PrintStream or PrintWriter, substituting the given values for placeholders that start with %.

Parameters: format   The format string

values   The values to be printed. You can supply any number of values

Returns: The implicit parameter

Package java.lang

Class java.lang.Boolean

The wrapper class for the primitive type boolean.

Class java.lang.Character

- static boolean **isDigit**(ch)
  This method tests whether a given character is a Unicode digit.
  Parameters: ch   The character to test
  Returns: true if the character is a digit
- static boolean **isLetter**(ch)
  This method tests whether a given character is a Unicode letter.
  Parameters: ch   The character to test
  Returns: true if the character is a letter
- static boolean **isLowerCase**(ch)
  This method tests whether a given character is a lowercase Unicode letter.
  Parameters: ch   The character to test
  Returns: true if the character is a lowercase letter
- static boolean **isUpperCase**(ch)
  This method tests whether a given character is an uppercase Unicode letter.
  Parameters: ch   The character to test
  Returns: true if the character is an uppercase letter

Interface java.lang.Comparable<T>

- int **compareTo**(T other)
  This method compares this object with the other object.
  Parameters: other   The object to be compared
  Returns: A negative integer if this object is less than the other, zero if they are equal, or a positive integer otherwise

Class java.lang.Double

- **Double**(double value)
  This constructs a wrapper object for a double-precision floating-point number.
  Parameters: value   The value to store in this object
- double **doubleValue**()
  This method returns the floating-point value stored in this Double wrapper object.
  Returns: The value stored in the object
- static double **parseDouble**(String s)
  This method returns the floating-point number that the string represents. If the string cannot be interpreted as a number, a NumberFormatException is thrown.
  Parameters: s   The string to be parsed
  Returns: The value represented by the string parameter

Class java.lang.Error

This is the superclass for all unchecked system errors.

Class java.lang.IllegalArgumentException

- **IllegalArgumentException**()
  This constructs an IllegalArgumentException with no detail message.

Class java.lang.IllegalStateException

This exception is thrown if the state of an object indicates that a method cannot currently be applied.

Class java.lang.Integer

- **Integer**(int value)
  This constructs a wrapper object for an integer.
  Parameters: value   The value to store in this object
- int **intValue**()
  This method returns the integer value stored in this wrapper object.
  Returns: The value stored in the object
- static int **parseInt**(String s)
  This method returns the integer that the string represents. If the string cannot be interpreted as an integer, a NumberFormatException is thrown.
  Parameters: s   The string to be parsed
  Returns: The value represented by the string parameter

- `static final int MAX_VALUE`
  This constant is the largest value of type `int`.
- `static final int MIN_VALUE`
  This constant is the smallest (negative) value of type `int`.

Class java.lang.Math

- `static double` **abs**`(double x)`
  This method returns the absolute value $|x|$.
  Parameters: x   A floating-point value
  Returns: The absolute value of the parameter
- `static double` **ceil**`(double x)`
  This method returns the smallest integer $\geq x$ (as a `double`).
  Parameters: x   A floating-point value
  Returns: The "ceiling integer" of the parameter
- `static double` **cos**`(double radians)`
  This method returns the cosine of an angle given in radians.
  Parameters: radians   An angle, in radians
  Returns: The cosine of the parameter
- `static double` **log10**`(double x)`
  This method returns the decimal (base 10) logarithm of x.
  Parameters: x   A number greater than 0.0
  Returns: The decimal logarithm of the parameter
- `static double` **pow**`(double x, double y)`
  This method returns the value x^y ($x > 0$, or $x = 0$ and $y > 0$, or $x < 0$ and y is an integer).
  Parameters: x, y   Two floating-point values
  Returns: The value of the first parameter raised to the power of the second parameter
- `static double` **random**`()`
  This method returns a floating-point value greater than or equal to 0 and less than 1.
- `static long` **round**`(double x)`
  This method returns the closest `long` integer to the parameter.
  Parameters: x   A floating-point value
  Returns: The value of the parameter rounded to the nearest `long` value
- `static double` **sin**`(double radians)`
  This method returns the sine of an angle given in radians.
  Parameters: radians   An angle, in radians
  Returns: The sine of the parameter
- `static double` **sqrt**`(double x)`
  This method returns the square root of x, $\sqrt{x}$.
  Parameters: x   A nonnegative floating-point value
  Returns: The square root of the parameter
- `static double` **tan**`(double radians)`
  This method returns the tangent of an angle given in radians.
  Parameters: radians   An angle, in radians
  Returns: The tangent of the parameter
- `static final double PI`
  This constant is the value of π.

Class java.lang.NullPointerException

This exception is thrown when a program tries to use an object through a `null` reference.

Class java.lang.NumberFormatException

This exception is thrown when a program tries to parse the numerical value of a string that is not a number.

Class java.lang.Object

- boolean **equals**(Object other)
  This method tests whether `this` and the other object are equal. This method tests only whether the object references are to the same object. Subclasses should redefine this method to compare the instance variables.
  Parameters: other   The object with which to compare
  Returns: true if the objects are equal, false otherwise

- String **toString**()
  This method returns a string representation of this object. This method produces only the class name and locations of the objects. Subclasses should redefine this method to print the instance variables.
  Returns: A string describing this object

Class java.lang.RuntimeException

This is the superclass for all unchecked exceptions.

Class java.lang.String

- int **compareTo**(String other)
  This method compares this string and the other string lexicographically.
  Parameters: other   The other string to be compared
  Returns: A value less than 0 if this string is lexicographically less than the other, 0 if the strings are equal, and a value greater than 0 otherwise.

- boolean **equals**(String other)
  This method tests whether two strings are equal.
  Parameters: other   The other string to be compared
  Returns: true if the strings are equal

- static String **format**(String format, Object... values)
  This method formats the given string by substituting placeholders that start with % with the given values.
  Parameters: format   The string with the placeholders
                  values   The values to be substituted for the placeholders
  Returns: The formatted string, with the placeholders replaced by the given values

- int **length**()
  This method returns the length of this string.
  Returns: The count of characters in this string

- String **substring**(int begin)
- String **substring**(int begin, int pastEnd)

These methods return a new string that is a substring of this string, made up of all characters starting at position begin and up to either position pastEnd - 1, if it is given, or the end of the string.

Parameters: begin The beginning index, inclusive

pastEnd The ending index, exclusive

Returns: The specified substring

- String **toLowerCase**()

This method returns a new string that consists of all characters in this string converted to lowercase.

Returns: A string with all characters in this string converted to lowercase

- String **toUpperCase**()

This method returns a new string that consists of all characters in this string converted to uppercase.

Returns: A string with all characters in this string converted to uppercase

Class java.lang.System

- static void **exit**(int status)

This method terminates the program.

Parameters: status Exit status. A nonzero status code indicates abnormal termination

- static final InputStream in

This object is the "standard input" stream. Reading from this stream typically reads keyboard input.

- static final PrintStream out

This object is the "standard output" stream. Printing to this stream typically sends output to the console window.

Class java.lang.Throwable

This is the superclass of exceptions and errors.

- void **printStackTrace**()

This method prints a stack trace to the "standard error" stream. The stack trace contains a printout of this object and of all calls that were pending at the time it was created.

Package java.net

Class java.net.URL

- URL(String s)

This constructs an URL object from a string containing the URL.

Parameters: s The URL string, such as "http://horstmann.com/index.html"

- InputStream **openStream**()

This method gets the input stream through which the client can read the information that the server sends.

Returns: The input stream associated with this URL

Package `java.util`

Class `java.util.ArrayList<E>`

- `ArrayList()`
  This constructs an empty array list.

- `boolean` **`add`**`(E element)`
  This method appends an element to the end of this array list.
  Parameters: `element` The element to add
  Returns: `true` (This method returns a value because it overrides a method in the `List` interface.)

- `void` **`add`**`(int index, E element)`
  This method inserts an element into this array list.
  Parameters: `index` Insert position
                       `element` The element to insert

- `E` **`get`**`(int index)`
  This method gets the element at the specified position in this array list.
  Parameters: `index` Position of the element to return
  Returns: The requested element

- `E` **`remove`**`(int index)`
  This method removes the element at the specified position in this array list and returns it.
  Parameters: `index` Position of the element to remove
  Returns: The removed element

- `E` **`set`**`(int index, E element)`
  This method replaces the element at a specified position in this array list.
  Parameters: `index` Position of element to replace
                       `element` Element to be stored at the specified position
  Returns: The element previously at the specified position

- `int` **`size`**`()`
  This method returns the number of elements in this array list.
  Returns: The number of elements in this array list

Class `java.util.Arrays`

- `static T[]` **`copyOf`**`(T[] a, int newLength)`
  This method copies the elements of the array `a`, or the first `newLength` elements if `a.length < newLength`, into an array of length `newLength` and returns that array. *T* can be a primitive type, class, or interface type.
  Parameters: `a` The array to be copied
                 `key` The value to be searched for
  Returns: The position of the search key, if it is contained in the array; otherwise, –*index* – 1, where *index* is the position where the element may be inserted

- `static void` **`sort`**`(Object[] a)`
  This method sorts the specified array of objects into ascending order. Its elements must implement the `Comparable` interface.
  Parameters: `a` The array to be sorted

- static String **toString**(*T*[] a)

  This method creates and returns a string containing the array elements. *T* can be a primitive type, class, or interface type.

  Parameters: a An array

  Returns: A string containing a comma-separated list of string representations of the array elements, surrounded by brackets.

Interface java.util.Collection<E>

- boolean **add**(E element)

  This method adds an element to this collection.

  Parameters: element The element to add

  Returns: true if adding the element changes the collection

- boolean **contains**(E element)

  This method tests whether an element is present in this collection.

  Parameters: element The element to find

  Returns: true if the element is contained in the collection

- Iterator **iterator**()

  This method returns an iterator that can be used to traverse the elements of this collection.

  Returns: An object of a class implementing the Iterator interface

- boolean **remove**(E element)

  This method removes an element from this collection.

  Parameters: element The element to remove

  Returns: true if removing the element changes the collection

- int **size**()

  This method returns the number of elements in this collection.

  Returns: The number of elements in this collection

Class java.util.Collections

- static <T> void **sort**(T[] a)

  This method sorts the specified list of objects into ascending order. Its elements must implement the Comparable interface.

  Parameters: a The list to be sorted

Interface java.util.Comparator<T>

- int **compare**(T first, T second)

  This method compares the given objects.

  Parameters: first, second The objects to be compared

  Returns: A negative integer if the first object is less than the second, zero if they are equal, or a positive integer otherwise

Class java.util.HashMap<K, V>

- **HashMap**<K, V>()

  This constructs an empty hash map.

Class java.util.HashSet<E>

- `HashSet<E>()`
  This constructs an empty hash set.

Class java.util.InputMismatchException

This exception is thrown if the next available input item does not match the type of the requested item.

Interface java.util.Iterator<E>

- `boolean hasNext()`
  This method checks whether the iterator is past the end of the list.
  Returns: true if the iterator is not yet past the end of the list

- `E next()`
  This method moves the iterator over the next element in the linked list. This method throws an exception if the iterator is past the end of the list.
  Returns: The object that was just skipped over

- `void remove()`
  This method removes the element that was returned by the last call to next or previous. This method throws an exception if there was an add or remove operation after the last call to next or previous.

Class java.util.LinkedHashMap<K, V>

- `LinkedHashMap<K, V>()`
  This constructs an empty linked hash map. The iterator of a linked hash map visits the entries in the order in which they were added to the map.

Class java.util.LinkedList<E>

- `void addFirst(E element)`
- `void addLast(E element)`
  These methods add an element before the first or after the last element in this list.
  Parameters: element   The element to be added

- `E getFirst()`
- `E getLast()`
  These methods return a reference to the specified element from this list.
  Returns: The first or last element

- `E removeFirst()`
- `E removeLast()`
  These methods remove the specified element from this list.
  Returns: A reference to the removed element

Interface java.util.List<E>

- `ListIterator<E> listIterator()`
  This method gets an iterator to visit the elements in this list.
  Returns: An iterator that points before the first element in this list

Interface java.util.ListIterator<E>

Objects implementing this interface are created by the listIterator methods of list classes.

- void **add**(E element)

  This method adds an element after the iterator position and moves the iterator after the new element.

  Parameters: element The element to be added

- boolean **hasPrevious**()

  This method checks whether the iterator is before the first element of the list.

  Returns: true if the iterator is not before the first element of the list

- E **previous**()

  This method moves the iterator over the previous element in the linked list. This method throws an exception if the iterator is before the first element of the list.

  Returns: The object that was just skipped over

- void **set**(E element)

  This method replaces the element that was returned by the last call to next or previous. This method throws an exception if there was an add or remove operation after the last call to next or previous.

  Parameters: element The element that replaces the old list element

Interface java.util.Map<K, V>

- V **get**(K key)

  This method gets the value associated with a key in this map.

  Parameters: key The key for which to find the associated value

  Returns: The value associated with the key, or null if the key is not present in the table

- Set<K> **keySet**()

  This method returns all keys in the table of this map.

  Returns: A set of all keys in the table of this map

- V **put**(K key, V value)

  This method associates a value with a key in this map.

  Parameters: key The lookup key

  value The value to associate with the key

  Returns: The value previously associated with the key, or null if the key was not present in the table

- V **remove**(K key)

  This method removes a key and its associated value from this map.

  Parameters: key The lookup key

  Returns: The value previously associated with the key, or null if the key was not present in the table

Class java.util.NoSuchElementException

This exception is thrown if an attempt is made to retrieve a value that does not exist.

Class java.util.Scanner

- **Scanner**(File in)
- **Scanner**(InputStream in)
  These construct a scanner that reads from the given file or input stream.
  Parameters: in   The input stream or reader from which to read
- void **close**()
  This method closes this scanner and releases any associated system resources.
- boolean **hasNext**()
- boolean **hasNextDouble**()
- boolean **hasNextInt**()
- boolean **hasNextLine**()
  These methods test whether it is possible to read any non-empty string, a floating-point value, an integer, or a line, as the next item.
  Returns: true if it is possible to read an item of the requested type, false otherwise (either because the end of the file has been reached, or because a number type was tested and the next item is not a number)
- String **next**()
- double **nextDouble**()
- int **nextInt**()
- String **nextLine**()
  These methods read the next white space-delimited string, floating-point value, integer, or line.
  Returns: The value that was read
- Scanner **useDelimiter**(String pattern)
  Sets the pattern for the delimiters between input tokens.
  Parameters: pattern   A regular expression for the delimiter pattern
  Returns: This scanner

Interface java.util.Set<E>

This interface describes a collection that contains no duplicate elements.

Class java.util.TreeMap<K, V>

- **TreeMap**<K, V>()
  This constructs an empty tree map. The iterator of a TreeMap visits the entries in sorted order.

Class java.util.TreeSet<E>

- **TreeSet**<E>()
  This constructs an empty tree set.

Package `javax.swing`

Class `javax.swing.AbstractButton`

- void **addActionListener**(ActionListener listener)
  This method adds an action listener to the button.
  Parameters: listener The action listener to be added

- boolean **isSelected**()
  This method returns the selection state of the button.
  Returns: true if the button is selected

- void **setSelected**(boolean state)
  This method sets the selection state of the button. This method updates the button but does not trigger an action event.
  Parameters: state true to select, false to deselect

Class `javax.swing.ButtonGroup`

- void **add**(AbstractButton button)
  This method adds the button to the group.
  Parameters: button The button to add

Class `javax.swing.ImageIcon`

- **ImageIcon**(String filename)
  This constructs an image icon from the specified graphics file.
  Parameters: filename A string specifying a file name

Class `javax.swing.JButton`

- **JButton**(String label)
  This constructs a button with the given label.
  Parameters: label The button label

Class `javax.swing.JCheckBox`

- **JCheckBox**(String text)
  This constructs a check box, having the given text, initially deselected. (Use the setSelected() method to make the box selected; see the javax.swing.AbstractButton class.)
  Parameters: text The text displayed next to the check box

Class `javax.swing.JComboBox`

- **JComboBox**()
  This constructs a combo box with no items.

- void **addItem**(Object item)
  This method adds an item to the item list of this combo box.
  Parameters: item The item to add

- Object **getSelectedItem**()
  This method gets the currently selected item of this combo box.
  Returns: The currently selected item

- `boolean` **`isEditable`**`()`
  This method checks whether the combo box is editable. An editable combo box allows the user to type into the text field of the combo box.
  Returns: `true` if the combo box is editable
- `void` **`setEditable`**`(boolean state)`
  This method is used to make the combo box editable or not.
  Parameters: `state` `true` to make editable, `false` to disable editing

Class `javax.swing.JComponent`

- `protected void` **`paintComponent`**`(Graphics g)`
  Override this method to paint the surface of a component. Your method needs to call `super.paintComponent(g)`.
  Parameters: `g` The graphics context used for drawing
- `void` **`setBorder`**`(Border b)`
  This method sets the border of this component.
  Parameters: `b` The border to surround this component
- `void` **`setFont`**`(Font f)`
  Sets the font used for the text in this component.
  Parameters: `f` A font

Class `javax.swing.JFileChooser`

- **`JFileChooser`**`()`
  This constructs a file chooser.
- `File` **`getSelectedFile`**`()`
  This method gets the selected file from this file chooser.
  Returns: The selected file
- `int` **`showOpenDialog`**`(Component parent)`
  This method displays an "Open File" file chooser dialog box.
  Parameters: `parent` The parent component or `null`
  Returns: The return state of this file chooser after it has been closed by the user: either `APPROVE_OPTION` or `CANCEL_OPTION`. If `APPROVE_OPTION` is returned, call `getSelectedFile()` on this file chooser to get the file
- `int` **`showSaveDialog`**`(Component parent)`
  This method displays a "Save File" file chooser dialog box.
  Parameters: `parent` The parent component or `null`
  Returns: The return state of the file chooser after it has been closed by the user: either `APPROVE_OPTION` or `CANCEL_OPTION`

Class `javax.swing.JFrame`

- `void` **`setDefaultCloseOperation`**`(int operation)`
  This method sets the default action for closing the frame.
  Parameters: `operation` The desired close operation. Choose among `DO_NOTHING_ON_CLOSE`, `HIDE_ON_CLOSE` (the default), `DISPOSE_ON_CLOSE`, or `EXIT_ON_CLOSE`
- `void` **`setJMenuBar`**`(JMenuBar mb)`
  This method sets the menu bar for this frame.
  Parameters: `mb` The menu bar. If `mb` is `null`, then the current menu bar is removed

- `static final int EXIT_ON_CLOSE`
  This value indicates that when the user closes this frame, the application is to exit.

Class `javax.swing.JLabel`

- `JLabel(String text)`
- `JLabel(String text, int alignment)`
  These containers create a `JLabel` instance with the specified text and horizontal alignment.
  Parameters: `text` The label text to be displayed by the label
          `alignment` One of `SwingConstants.LEFT`, `SwingConstants.CENTER`, or `SwingConstants.RIGHT`

Class `javax.swing.JMenu`

- `JMenu()`
  This constructs a menu with no items.
- `JMenuItem add(JMenuItem menuItem)`
  This method appends a menu item to the end of this menu.
  Parameters: `menuItem` The menu item to be added
  Returns: The menu item that was added

Class `javax.swing.JMenuBar`

- `JMenuBar()`
  This constructs a menu bar with no menus.
- `JMenu add(JMenu menu)`
  This method appends a menu to the end of this menu bar.
  Parameters: `menu` The menu to be added
  Returns: The menu that was added

Class `javax.swing.JMenuItem`

- `JMenuItem(String text)`
  This constructs a menu item.
  Parameters: `text` The text to appear in the menu item

Class `javax.swing.JOptionPane`

- `static String showInputDialog(Object prompt)`
  This method brings up a modal input dialog box, which displays a prompt and waits for the user to enter an input in a text field, preventing the user from doing anything else in this program.
  Parameters: `prompt` The prompt to display
  Returns: The string that the user typed
- `static void showMessageDialog(Component parent, Object message)`
  This method brings up a confirmation dialog box that displays a message and waits for the user to confirm it.
  Parameters: `parent` The parent component or `null`
          `message` The message to display

Class javax.swing.JPanel

This class is a component without decorations. It can be used as an invisible container for other components.

Class javax.swing.JRadioButton

- **JRadioButton**(String text)
  This constructs a radio button having the given text that is initially deselected. (Use the setSelected() method to select it; see the javax.swing.AbstractButton class.)
  Parameters: text   The string displayed next to the radio button

Class javax.swing.JScrollPane

- **JScrollPane**(Component c)
  This constructs a scroll pane around the given component.
  Parameters: c   The component that is decorated with scroll bars

Class javax.swing.JSlider

- **JSlider**(int min, int max, int value)
  This constructor creates a horizontal slider using the specified minimum, maximum, and value.
  Parameters: min   The smallest possible slider value
                        max   The largest possible slider value
                        value   The initial value of the slider

- void **addChangeListener**(ChangeListener listener)
  This method adds a change listener to the slider.
  Parameters: listener   The change listener to add

- int **getValue**()
  This method returns the slider's value.
  Returns: The current value of the slider

Class javax.swing.JTextArea

- **JTextArea**()
  This constructs an empty text area.

- **JTextArea**(int rows, int columns)
  This constructs an empty text area with the specified number of rows and columns.
  Parameters: rows   The number of rows
                        columns   The number of columns

- void **append**(String text)
  This method appends text to this text area.
  Parameters: text   The text to append

Class javax.swing.JTextField

- **JTextField**()
  This constructs an empty text field.
- **JTextField**(int columns)
  This constructs an empty text field with the specified number of columns.
  Parameters: columns The number of columns

Class javax.swing.Timer

- **Timer**(int millis, ActionListener listener)
  This constructs a timer that notifies an action listener whenever a time interval has elapsed.
  Parameters: millis The number of milliseconds between timer notifications
  listener The object to be notified when the time interval has elapsed
- void **start**()
  This method starts the timer. Once the timer has started, it begins notifying its listener.
- void **stop**()
  This method stops the timer. Once the timer has stopped, it no longer notifies its listener.

Package javax.swing.border

Class javax.swing.border.EtchedBorder

- **EtchedBorder**()
  This constructor creates a lowered etched border.

Class javax.swing.border.TitledBorder

- **TitledBorder**(Border b, String title)
  This constructor creates a titled border that adds a title to a given border.
  Parameters: b The border to which the title is added
  title The title the border should display

Package javax.swing.event

Class javax.swing.event.ChangeEvent

Components such as sliders emit change events when they are manipulated by the user.

Interface javax.swing.event.ChangeListener

- void **stateChanged**(ChangeEvent e)
  This event is called when the event source has changed its state.
  Parameters: e A change event

Package javax.swing.text

Class javax.swing.text.JTextComponent

- String **getText**()
  This method returns the text contained in this text component.
  Returns: The text

- boolean **isEditable**()
  This method checks whether this text component is editable.
  Returns: true if the component is editable

- void **setEditable**(boolean state)
  This method is used to make this text component editable or not.
  Parameters: state true to make editable, false to disable editing

- void **setText**(String text)
  This method sets the text of this text component to the specified text. If the text is empty, the old text is deleted.
  Parameters: text The new text to be set

GLOSSARY

Terms used in the **graphics programming** chapters are set in a different color.

Abstract class   A class that cannot be instantiated.

Abstract method   A method with a name, parameter types, and return type but without an implementation.

Access specifier   A reserved word, such as private or public, that indicates the accessibility of a feature.

Accessor method   A method that accesses an object but does not change it.

Actual parameter   The expression supplied by the caller to be the value of a formal parameter of a method.

Aggregation   The *has-a* relationship between classes.

Algorithm   An unambiguous, executable, and terminating specification of a way to solve a problem.

Anonymous class   A class that does not have a name.

Anonymous object   An object that is not stored in a named variable.

API (Application Programming Interface)   A code library for building programs.

Applet   A graphical Java program that executes inside a web browser or applet viewer.

Argument   An actual parameter in a method call, or one of the values combined by an operator.

Array   A collection of values of the same type stored in contiguous memory locations, each of which can be accessed by an integer index.

Array list   A Java class that implements a dynamically growable array of objects.

Assignment   Placing a new value into a variable.

Asymmetric bounds   Bounds that include the starting index but not the ending index.

Auto-boxing   Automatically converting a primitive type value into a wrapper type object.

Balanced tree   A tree in which each subtree has the property that the number of descendants to the left is approximately the same as the number of descendants to the right.

Binary file   A file in which values are stored in their binary representation and cannot be read as text.

Binary operator   An operator that takes two arguments, for example + in $x + y$.

Binary search   A fast algorithm to find a value in a sorted array. It narrows the search down to half of the array in every step.

Binary search tree   A binary tree in which each subtree has the property that all left descendants are smaller than the value stored in the root, and all right descendants are larger.

Binary tree   A tree in which each node has at most two child nodes.

Bit   Binary digit; the smallest unit of information, having two possible values: 0 and 1. A data element consisting of n bits has 2^n possible values.

Block   A group of statements bracketed by {}.

Boolean operator   See **Logical operator**

Boolean type   A type with two possible values: true and false.

Border layout   A layout management scheme in which components are placed into the center or one of the four border areas of their container.

Boundary test case   A test case involving values that are at the outer boundary of the set of legal values. For example, if a function is expected to work for all nonnegative integers, then 0 is a boundary test case.

Bounds error   Trying to access an array element that is outside the legal range.

break statement   A statement that terminates a loop or switch statement.

Bucket   In a hash table, a set of values with the same hash code.

Bug   A programming error.

Byte   A number made up of eight bits. Essentially all currently manufactured computers use a byte as the smallest unit of storage in memory.

Bytecode   Instructions for the Java virtual machine.

Case sensitive   Distinguishing upper- and lowercase characters.

Cast   Explicitly converting a value from one type to a different type. For example, the cast from a floating-point number x to an integer is expressed in Java by the cast notation (int) x.

catch clause   A part of a try block that is executed when a matching exception is thrown by any statement in the try block.

Character   A single letter, digit, or symbol.

Check box   A user-interface component that can be used for a binary selection.

Checked exception   An exception that the compiler checks. All checked exceptions must be declared or caught.

Class   A programmer-defined data type.

Collection   A data structure that provides a mechanism for adding, removing, and locating elements.

Combo box   A user-interface component that combines a text field with a drop-down list of selections.

Command line   The line the user types to start a program in DOS, UNIX, or a command window in Windows. It consists of the program name followed by any necessary arguments.

Comment   An explanation to help the human reader understand a section of a program; ignored by the compiler.

Compiler   A program that translates code in a high-level language (such as Java) to machine instructions (such as bytecode for the Java virtual machine).

Compile-time error   An error that is detected when a program is compiled.

Component   See **User-interface component**

Computer program   A sequence of instructions that is executed by a computer.

Concatenation   Placing one string after another to form a new string.

Concrete class   A class that can be instantiated.

Console program   A Java program that does not have a graphical window. A console program reads input from the keyboard and writes output to the terminal screen.

Constant   A value that cannot be changed by a program. In Java, constants are defined with the reserved word final.

Construction   Setting a newly allocated object to an initial state.

Constructor   A method that initializes a newly instantiated object.

Container   A user-interface component that can hold other components and present them together to the user. Also, a data structure, such as a list, that can hold a collection of objects and present them individually to a program.

Content pane   The part of a Swing frame that holds the user-interface components of the frame.

CPU (Central Processing Unit)   The part of a computer that executes the machine instructions.

De Morgan's Law   A law about logical operations that describes how to negate expressions formed with *and* and *or* operations.

Debugger   A program that lets a user run another program one or a few steps at a time, stop execution, and inspect the variables in order to analyze it for bugs.

Directory   A structure on a disk that can hold files or other directories; also called a folder.

Documentation comment   A comment in a source file that can be automatically extracted into the program documentation by a program such as javadoc.

Dot notation   The notation *object.method(parameters)* or *object.instance variable* used to invoke a method or access an instance variable.

Doubly linked list   A linked list in which each link has a reference to both its predecessor and successor links.

Dynamic method lookup   Selecting a method to be invoked at run time. In Java, dynamic method lookup considers the class of the implicit parameter object in order to select the appropriate method.

Editor   A program for writing and modifying text files.

Encapsulation   The hiding of implementation details.

Escape character   A character in text that is not taken literally but has a special meaning when combined with the character or characters that follow it. The \ character is an escape character in Java strings.

Escape sequence   A sequence of characters that starts with an escape character, such as \n or \".

Event   See **User-interface event**

Event class   A class that contains information about an event, such as its source.

Event adapter   A class that implements an event listener interface by defining all methods to do nothing.

Event handler   A method that is executed when an event occurs.

Event listener   An object that is notified by an event source when an event occurs.

Event source   An object that can notify other classes of events.

Exception   A class that signals a condition that prevents the program from continuing normally. When such a condition occurs, an object of the exception class is thrown.

Exception handler   A sequence of statements that is given control when an exception of a particular type has been thrown and caught.

Explicit parameter   A parameter of a method other than the object on which the method is invoked.

Expression   A syntactical construct that is made up of constants, variables, method calls, and any operators combining them.

Extension   The last part of a file name, which specifies the file type. For example, the extension .java denotes a Java file.

Fibonacci numbers   The sequence of numbers 1, 1, 2, 3, 5, 8, 13, . . ., in which every term is the sum of its two predecessors.

File   A sequence of bytes that is stored on disk.

`finally` **clause**   A part of a try block that is executed no matter how the try block is exited.

Flag   See **Boolean type**

Floating-point number   A number that can have a fractional part.

Flow layout   A layout management scheme in which components are laid out left to right.

Folder   See **Directory**

Font   A set of character shapes in a particular style and size.

Formal parameter   A variable in a method definition; it is initialized with an actual parameter value when the method is called.

Frame   A window with a border and a title bar.

Garbage collection   Automatic reclamation of memory occupied by objects that are no longer referenced.

Generic class   A class with one or more type parameters.

Generic programming   Providing program components that can be reused in a wide variety of situations.

Graphics context   A class through which a programmer can cause shapes to appear on a window or off-screen bitmap.

Grid layout   A layout management scheme in which components are placed into a two-dimensional grid.

GUI (Graphical User Interface)   A user interface in which the user supplies inputs through graphical components such as buttons, menus, and text fields.

Hard disk   A device that stores information on rotating platters with magnetic coating.

Hardware   The physical equipment for a computer or another device.

Hash code   A value that is computed by a hash function.

Hash collision   Two different objects for which a hash function computes identical values.

Hash function   A function that computes an integer value from an object in such a way that different objects are likely to yield different values.

Hash table   A data structure in which elements are mapped to array positions according to their hash function values.

Hashing   Applying a hash function to a set of objects.

Heapsort algorithm   A sorting algorithm that inserts the values to be sorted into a heap.

High-level programming languages   A programming language that provides an abstract view of a computer and allows programmers to focus on their problem domain.

HTML (Hypertext Markup Language)   The language in which web pages are described.

HTTP (Hypertext Transfer Protocol)   The protocol that defines communication between web browsers and web servers.

IDE (Integrated Development Environment)   A programming environment that includes an editor, compiler, and debugger.

Implementing an interface   Implementing a class that defines all methods specified in the interface.

Implicit parameter   The object on which a method is invoked. For example, in the call x.f(y), the object x is the implicit parameter of the method f.

Importing a class or package   Indicating the intention of referring to a class, or all classes in a package, by the simple name rather than the qualified name.

Inheritance   The *is-a* relationship between a more general superclass and a more specialized subclass.

Initialization   Setting a variable to a well-defined value when it is created.

Inner class   A class that is defined inside another class.

Instance method   A method with an implicit parameter; that is, a method that is invoked on an instance of a class.

Instance of a class   An object whose type is that class.

Instance variable   A variable defined in a class for which every object of the class has its own value.

Instantiation of a class   Construction of an object of that class.

Integer   A number that cannot have a fractional part.

Integer division   Taking the quotient of two integers and discarding the remainder. In Java the / symbol denotes integer division if both arguments are integers. For example, 11/4 is 2, not 2.75.

Interface   A type with no instance variables, only abstract methods and constants.

Internet   A worldwide collection of networks, routing equipment, and computers using a common set of protocols that define how participants interact with each other.

Iterator   An object that can inspect all elements in a container such as a linked list.

javadoc   The documentation generator in the Java SDK. It extracts documentation comments from Java source files and produces a set of linked HTML files.

JDK   The Java software development kit that contains the Java compiler and related development tools.

JVM   The Java Virtual Machine.

Layout manager   A class that arranges user-interface components inside a container.

Lazy evaluation   Deferring the computation of a value until it is needed, thereby avoiding the computation if the value is never needed.

Lexicographic ordering   Ordering strings in the same order as in a dictionary, by skipping all matching characters and comparing the first nonmatching characters of both strings. For example, "orbit" comes before "orchid" in lexicographic ordering. Note that in Java, unlike a dictionary, the ordering is case sensitive: Z comes before a.

Library   A set of precompiled classes that can be included in programs.

Linear search   Searching a container (such as an array or list) for an object by inspecting each element in turn.

Linked list   A data structure that can hold an arbitrary number of objects, each of which is stored in a link object, which contains a pointer to the next link.

Literal   A constant value in a program that is explicitly written as a number, such as –2 or 6.02214115E23, or as a character sequence, such as "Harry".

Local variable   A variable whose scope is a block.

Logical operator   An operator that can be applied to Boolean values. Java has three logical operators: &&, ||, and !.

Logic error   An error in a syntactically correct program that causes it to act differently from its specification.

Loop   A sequence of instructions that is executed repeatedly.

Loop and a half   A loop whose termination decision is neither at the beginning nor at the end.

Machine code   Instructions that can be executed directly by the CPU.

Magic number   A number that appears in a program without explanation.

main **method**   The method that is first called when a Java application executes.

Map   A data structure that keeps associations between key and value objects.

Memory location   A value that specifies where data is located in computer memory.

Method   A sequence of statements that has a name, may have formal parameters, and may return a value. A method can be invoked any number of times, and with different values for its parameters.

Method signature   The name of a method and the types of its parameters.

Modulus   The % operator that computes the remainder of an integer division.

Mutator method   A method that changes the state of an object.

Name clash   Accidentally using the same name to denote two program features in a way that cannot be resolved by the compiler.

Nested loop   A loop that is contained in another loop.

Networks   An interconnected system of computers and other devices.

new **operator**   An operator that allocates new objects.

Newline   The '\n' character, which indicates the end of a line.

Null reference   A reference that does not refer to any object.

Object   A value of a class type.

Object-oriented design   Designing a program by discovering objects, their properties, and their relationships.

Object-oriented programming   Creating programs that consist of interacting objects.

Object reference   A value that denotes the location of an object in memory. In Java, a variable whose type is a class contains a reference to an object of that class.

Off-by-one error   A common programming error in which a value is one larger or smaller than it should be.

Operating system   The software that launches application programs and provides services (such as a file system) for those programs.

Operator   A symbol denoting a mathematical or logical operation, such as + or &&.

Operator associativity   The rule that governs in which order operators of the same precedence are executed. For example, in Java the - operator is left-associative because a - b - c is interpreted as (a - b) - c, and = is right-associative because a = b = c is interpreted as a = (b = c).

Operator precedence   The rule that governs which operator is evaluated first. For example, in Java the && operator has a higher precedence than the || operator. Hence a || b && c is interpreted as a || (b && c).

Overloading   Giving more than one meaning to a method name.

Overriding   Redefining a method in a subclass.

Package   A collection of related classes. The import statement is used to access one or more classes in a package.

Panel   A user-interface component with no visual appearance. It can be used to group other components.

Parallel arrays   Arrays of the same length, in which corresponding elements are logically related.

Parameter   An item of information that is specified to a method when the method is called. For example, in the call System.out.println("Hello, World!"), the parameters are the implicit parameter System.out and the explicit parameter "Hello, World!".

Parameter passing   Specifying the expression(s) to be the actual parameter value(s) for a method when it is called.

Parameter value   The expression for initializing a parameter variable of a method that is supplied by the caller.

Parameter variable   A variable of a method that is initialized with a parameter value when the method is called.

Partially filled array   An array that is not filled to capacity, together with a companion variable that indicates the number of elements actually stored.

Polymorphism   Selecting a method among several methods that have the same name on the basis of the actual type of the implicit parameter.

Primitive type   In Java, a number type or boolean.

Project   A collection of source files and their dependencies.

Prompt   A string that tells the user to provide input.

Pseudocode   A high-level description of the actions of a program or algorithm, using a mixture of English and informal programming language syntax.

Pseudorandom number   A number that appears to be random but is generated by a mathematical formula.

Public interface The features of a class (such as methods, instance variables, and nested types) that are accessible to all clients.

Queue A collection of items with "first in, first out" retrieval.

Radio button A user-interface component that can be used for selecting one of several options.

RAM (Random-Access Memory) Electronic circuits in a computer that can store code and data of running programs.

Random access The ability to access any value directly without having to read the values preceding it.

Recursion A method for computing a result by decomposing the inputs into simpler values and applying the same method to them.

Recursive method A method that can call itself with simpler values. It must handle the simplest values without calling itself.

Redirection Linking the input or output of a program to a file instead of the keyboard or display.

Reference See **Object reference**

Regular expression A string that defines a set of matching strings according to their content. Each part of a regular expression can be a specific required character; one of a set of permitted characters such as [abc], which can be a range such as [a-z]; any character not in a set of forbidden characters, such as [^0-9]; a repetition of one or more matches, such as [0-9]+, or zero or more, such as [ACGT]; one of a set of alternatives, such as and|et|und; or various other possibilities. For example, "[A-Za-z][0-9]+" matches "Cloud9" or "007" but not "Jack".

Relational operator An operator that compares two values, yielding a Boolean result.

Reserved word A word that has a special meaning in a programming language and therefore cannot be used as a name by the programmer.

Return value The value returned by a method through a return statement.

Reverse Polish notation A style of writing expressions in which the operators are written following the operands, such as 2 3 4 * + for 2 + 3 * 4.

Roundoff error An error introduced by the fact that the computer can store only a finite number of digits of a floating-point number.

Run-time error See **Logic error**

Run-time stack The data structure that stores the local variables of all called methods as a program runs.

Scope The part of a program in which a variable is defined.

Selection sort A sorting algorithm in which the smallest element is repeatedly found and removed until no elements remain.

Sentinel A value in input that is not to be used as an actual input value but to signal the end of input.

Sequential access Accessing values one after another without skipping over any of them.

Sequential search See **Linear search**

Set An unordered collection that allows efficient addition, location, and removal of elements.

Shadowing Hiding a variable by defining another one with the same name.

Shell window   A window for interacting with an operating system through textual commands.

Short circuit evaluation   Evaluating only a part of an expression if the remainder cannot change the result.

Software   The intangible instructions and data that are necessary for operating a computer or another device.

Source code   Instructions in a programming language that need to be translated before execution on a computer.

Source file   A file containing instructions in a programming language such as Java.

Spiral model   An iterative process model of software development in which design and implementation are repeated.

Stack   A data structure with "last in, first out" retrieval. Elements can be added and removed only at one position, called the top of the stack.

Stack trace   A printout of the call stack, listing all currently pending method calls.

State   The current value of an object, which is determined by the cumulative action of all methods that were invoked on it.

Statement   A syntactical unit in a program. In Java a statement is either a simple statement, a compound statement, or a block.

Static method   A method with no implicit parameter.

Static variable   A variable defined in a class that has only one value for the whole class, which can be accessed and changed by any method of that class.

Stepwise refinement   The process of solving a problem that starts out with a subdivision into steps, then continues by further subdividing those steps.

String   A sequence of characters.

Stub   A method with no or minimal functionality.

Subclass   A class that inherits variables and methods from a superclass but may add instance variables, add methods, or redefine methods.

Substitution principle   The principle that a subclass object can be used in place of any superclass object.

Superclass   A general class from which a more specialized class (a subclass) inherits.

Swing   A Java toolkit for implementing graphical user interfaces.

Symmetric bounds   Bounds that include the starting index and the ending index.

Syntax   Rules that define how to form instructions in a particular programming language.

Syntax error   An instruction that does not follow the programming language rules and is rejected by the compiler.

Text field   A user-interface component that allows a user to provide text input.

Text file   A file in which values are stored in their text representation.

Throwing an exception   Indicating an abnormal condition by terminating the normal control flow of a program and transferring control to a matching catch clause.

`throws` **specifier**   Indicates the type(s) of the checked exception(s) that a method may throw.

Tree   A data structure consisting of nodes, each of which has a list of child nodes, and one of which is distinguished as the root node.

try block   A block of statements that contains exception processing clauses. A try block contains at least one catch or finally clause.

Two-dimensional array   A tabular arrangement of elements in which an element is specified by a row and a column index.

Type   A named set of values and the operations that can be carried out with them.

Type parameter   A parameter in a generic class or method that can be replaced with an actual type.

Unary operator   An operator with one argument.

Unchecked exception   An exception that the compiler doesn't check.

Unicode   A standard code that assigns code values consisting of two bytes to characters used in scripts around the world. Java stores all characters as their Unicode values.

Unified Modeling Language (UML)   A notation for specifying, visualizing, constructing, and documenting the artifacts of software systems.

Uninitialized variable   A variable that has not been set to a particular value. In Java, using an uninitialized local variable is a syntax error.

Unit test   A test of a method by itself, isolated from the remainder of the program.

URL (Uniform Resource Locator)   A pointer to an information resource (such as a web page or an image) on the World Wide Web.

User-interface component   A building block for a graphical user interface, such as a button or a text field. User-interface components are used to present information to the user and allow the user to enter information to the program.

Variable   A symbol in a program that identifies a storage location that can hold different values.

Virtual machine   A program that simulates a CPU that can be implemented efficiently on a variety of actual machines. A given program in Java bytecode can be executed by any Java virtual machine, regardless of which CPU is used to run the virtual machine itself.

void reserved word   A reserved word indicating no type or an unknown type.

Walkthrough   A step-by-step manual simulation of a computer program.

White space   Any sequence of only space, tab, and newline characters.

Wrapper class   A class that contains a primitive type value, such as Integer.

INDEX

Page references followed by a letter code indicate illustrations, tables, or examples as follows: *p* = photo, *t* = table, *ex* = example, *d* = diagram, *cs* = coding sample.

ILLUSTRATION CREDITS

Preface Page vii: iStockphoto.

Chapter 1 Page 1, 2: Sebastian Duda/iStockphoto.
Page 3, 22: Copyright © 2008, Intel Corporation.
Page 4: PhotoDisc, Inc./Getty Images.
Page 5: Courtesy of Sperry Univac, Division of Sperry Corporation.
Page 6: Courtest of Sun Microsystems, Inc.
Page 11, 22: Tatiana Popova/iStockphoto.
Page 12, 23: Josh Hodge/iStockphoto.
Page 15, 23: Martin Carlsson/iStockphoto.
Page 17: iStockphoto.
Page 18, 23: Claudia DeWald/iStockphoto.
Page 19: David H. Lewis/iStockphoto.
Page 21: Robert Ban/iStockphoto.
Page 26: Peter Macdiarmid/Getty Images, Inc.

Chapter 2 Page 31, 32 (top): Chad Anderson/iStockphoto.
Page 32 (middle): travis manley/iStockphoto.
Page 32 (bottom), 67: Javier Larrea/Age Fotostock.
Page 33, 67: © JupiterImages/Ablestock/Stockphotopro, Inc.
Page 35: Eric Isselée/iStockphoto.
Page 37, 67: james steidl/iStockphoto.
Page 42, 67: © Media Bakery.
Page 46 (top): Finn Brandt/iStockphoto.
Page 46 : Yunus Arakon/iStockphoto.
Page 47, 68: Michael Flippo/iStockphoto.
Page 50, 68: Rich Koele/iStockphoto.
Page 53: Joe McDaniel/iStockphoto.
Page 54: Gennagy Kudelya/iStockphoto.
Page 56: Photos.com/Jupiter Images.
Page 59 (top), 68: jason walton/iStockphoto.
Page 59 (bottom): Larry Hoyle, Institute for Policy & Social Research, University of Kansas.
Page 62, 68: Sven Larsen/iStockphoto.
Page 63, 68: Rich Legg/iStockphoto.
Page 66 (left): Paul Vachier/iStockphoto.
Page 66 (center): Joel Carllet/iStockphoto.
Page 66 (right): iStockphoto.
Page 67, Screencast: Jan Rysavy/iStockphoto.
Page 72: iStockphoto.
Page 73: Steve Snyder/iStockphoto.
Page 74: José Luis Gutiérrez/iStockphoto.

Chapter 3 Page 77, 78: iStockphoto.
Page 78: Oleksandr Gumerov/iStockphoto.
Page 79, 112: Creatas/Media Bakery.

Page 82: Timothy Large/iStockphoto.

Page 83: Photo by Vincent LaRussa/© John Wiley & Sons, Inc.

Page 84, 112: iStockphoto.

Page 87: iStockphoto.

Page 88, 112: Corbis Digital Stock.

Page 89: iStockphoto.

Page 91: Bob Daemmrich/Getty Images.

Page 92, 113: Kevin Russ/iStockphoto.

Page 95: iStockphoto.

Page 96: iStockphoto.

Page 99: Derek Thomas/iStockphoto.

Page 101: Bananastock/Media Bakery.

Page 102 (left), 113: Cusp/SuperStock.

Page 102 (right): Sidney Harris/ScienceCartoonsPlus.com.

Page 104: Alamy.

Page 107: Stig Andersen/iStockphoto.

Page 108: Tetra Images/Media Bakery.

Page 111 (top), 113: Bruce M. BEEHLER/AFP/Getty Images.

Page 111 (bottom): Vaughn Youtz/Zuma Press.

Page 112, Screencast: Benjamin Albach Galan/iStockphoto.

Page 118: Nick Schlax/iStockphoto.

Page 119: iStockphoto.

Page 120: iStockphoto.

Page 121: Charles Schultz/iStockphoto.

Chapter 4 Page 125, 126 (top): iStockphoto.

Page 126 (middle): Jarek Szymanski/iStockphoto.

Page 126 (bottom) 162: Fermi National Accelerator Laboratory/Photo Researchers, Inc.

Page 132: Karen Town/iStockphoto.

Page 133: M.C. Escher's "Ascending and Descending" © 2008 The M.C. Escher Company-Holland. All rights reserved. www.mcescher.com.

Page 134: Naval Surface Weapons Center, Dahlgren, VA.

Page 135, 162: Enrico Fianchini/iStockphoto.

Page 141, 162: iStockphoto.

Page 143, 162: Altrendo Travel/Getty Images.

Page 147: Dietmar Klement/iStockphoto.

Page 148: iStockphoto.

Page 149: matt matthews/iStockphoto.

Page 150: Tommy Ingberg/iStockphoto.

Page 151: Steve Geer/iStockphoto.

Page 154 (top): iStockphoto.

Page 154, 163: david kahn/iStockphoto.

Page 159, 163: Kiyoshi Takahase/iStockphoto.

Page 160: Tim Starkey/iStockphoto.

Page 161: Don Bayley/iStockphoto.

Page 162, Screencast: Rick Rhay/iStockphoto.

Page 167: david franklin/iStockphoto.

Page 168: Anthony Rosenberg/iStockphoto.

Page 169: Eric Isselée/iStockphoto.

Page 171: Michael O Flachra/iStockphoto.
Page 172: Erik Dreyer/Stone/Getty Images, Inc.

Chapter 5   Page 177, 178: Joselito Briones/iStockphoto.
Page 179, 208: Yenwen Lu/iStockphoto.
Page 180: dieter Spears/iStockphoto.
Page 181, 208: Nina Shannon/iStockphoto.
Page 184 (top): Lawrence Sawyer/iStockphoto.
Page 184 (collage), 208: Klaudia Steiner/iStockphoto (cherries); christine balderas/ iStockphoto (cherry pie); iStockphoto (apples); dieter Spears/iStockphoto (apple pie).
Page 187, 208: Natalia Bratslavsky/iStockphoto.
Page 189: Holger Mette/iStockphoto.
Page 190, 208: james steidl/iStockphoto.
Page 192, 208: Rob Belknap/iStockphoto.
Page 193: iStockphoto.
Page 199 (top): iStockphoto.
Page 199 (bottom): paul kline/iStockphoto.
Page 201 (collage), 209: Joan Champ/iStockphoto (Railway and Main); Steven Johnson/iStockphoto (Main and N. Putnam); Jeffrey Smith/iStockphoto (Main and South).
Page 203: Janice Richard/iStockphoto.
Page 204, 209: Nicolae Popovici/iStockphoto.
Page 207: Reprint Courtesy of International Business Machines Corporation, copyright © International Business Machines Corporation.
Page 208, Screencast: Kenneth C. Zirkel/iStockphoto.
Page 210: Stacey Newman/iStockphoto.
Page 214: Matjaz Boncina/iStockphoto.

Chapter 6   Page 219, 220: graham kiotz/iStockphoto.
Page 222, 261: Max Dimyadi/iStockphoto.
Page 224, 261: Jarek Szymanski/iStockphoto.
Page 227, 261: Steve Cole/iStockphoto.
Page 229 (top): matt matthews/iStockphoto.
Page 229 (bottom): Michal Kram/iStockphoto.
Page 230, 261: Yegor Korzh/iStockphoto.
Page 236: Vladimir Karpenko/iStockphoto.
Page 243: Thierry Dosogne/The Image Bank/Getty Images, Inc.
Page 245: Kiyoshi Takahase/iStockphoto.
Page 246 (top), 261: Chris Burt/iStockphoto.
Page 246 (bottom): Gian Mattia D'Alberto/LaPresse/Zuma Press.
Page 251, 261: Michael Brake/iStockphoto.
Page 252, 262: Danijel Micka/iStockphoto.
Page 256, 262: Sandra O'Claire/iStockphoto.
Page 260: Topham/The Image Works.
Page 260, Screencast: Henrik Jansson/iStockphoto.
Page 269: Leonid Nyshko/iStockphoto.
Page 269: Kathy Muller/iStockphoto.
✚ Worked Example 6.1: Ryan Ruffatti/iStockphoto.

Chapter 7   Page 273, 274: Stephanie Strathdee/iStockphoto.
Page 274 (bottom), 310: Michael Shake/iStockphoto.
Page 275, 310: Damir Cudic/iStockphoto.
Page 276, 310: Photo by Gary Lee/UPPA/Zuma Press. © Copyright 2006 by UPPA.
Page 277: James Richey/iStockphoto.
Page 279: iStockphoto.
Page 281, 310: Mark Evans/iStockphoto.
Page 282: Glow Images.
Page 284, 310: Ann Marie Kurtz/iStockphoto.
Page 289, 310: iStockphoto.
Page 291: Mark Evans/iStockphoto.
Page 295 (left): David Young-Wolff/PhotoEdit.
Page 295 (right): Lisa F. Young/iStockphoto.
Page 296, 310: Oleg Prikhodko/iStockphoto.
Page 297, 311: Anastaslya Maksymenko/iStockphoto.
Page 300, 311: Jacob Wackerhausen/iStockphoto.
Page 303, 311: Diane Diederich/iStockphoto.
Page 306, 311: Don Wilkie/iStockphoto.
Page 309: Courtesy of Richard Stallman, www.stallman.org.
Page 309, Screencast: Pavel Mitrofanov/iStockphoto.
Page 314: Miklas Voros/iStockphoto.
Page 314: Steve Dibblee/iStockphoto.

Chapter 8   Page 321, 322: Photo courtesy of Erik Vestergard, http://www.matematiksider.dk/enigma_eng.html.
Page 323, 350: Chris Price/iStockphoto.
Page 331, 350: iStockphoto.
Page 333: Anna Khomulo/iStockphoto.
Page 334: Oksana Perkins/iStockphoto.
Page 336: age fotostock/SUPERSTOCK.
Page 337, 350: Lisa F. Young/iStockphoto.
Page 339, 351: Andraz Cerar/iStockphoto.
Page 341, 351: iStockphoto.
Page 342, 351: iStockphoto.
Page 345: © AP/Wide World Photos.
Page 350, Screencast: iStockphoto.

Chapter 9   Page 357, 358: Lisa Thornberg/iStockphoto.
Page 358, 394: Tony Tremblay/iStockphoto (vehicle); Peter Dean/iStockphoto (motorcycle); nicholas belton/iStockphoto (car); Robert Pernell/iStockphoto (truck); Clay Blackburn/iStockphoto (sedan); iStockphoto (SUV).
Page 359: paul kline/iStockphoto.
Page 363, 394: Ivan Cholavov/iStockphoto.
Page 373, 394: Aleksandr Popov/iStockphoto.
Page 381: Sean Locke/iStockphoto.
Page 387, 395: gregory horler/iStockphoto.
Page 390: Janis Dreosti/iStockphoto.
Page 393: Greg Nicholas/iStockphoto.
Page 394, Screencast: Courtesy of John Reid.

Chapter 10   Page 403, 404: nicholas belton/iStockphoto.
Page 405 (left), 439: Filip Fuxa/iStockphoto.
Page 405 (middle), 439: iStockphoto.
Page 405 (right), 439: Vladimir Trenin/iStockphoto.
Page 4406, 439: david franklin/iStockphoto.
Page 407, 439: andrea laurita/iStockphoto.
Page 412: iStockphoto.
Page 414, 439: Photodisc/Punchstock.
Page 416: Courtesy of Nigel Tout.
Page 418, 439: Alfredo Ragazzoni/iStockphoto.
Page 419: Volkan Ersoy/iStockphoto.
Page 425, 439: Tom Hahn/iStockphoto.
Page 427, 440: iStockphoto.
Page 431, 440: Ken Brown/iStockphoto.
Page 436, 440: iStockphoto.
Page 439, Screencast: Ermin Gutenberger/iStockphoto.
Page 443: Luis Carlos Torres/iStockphoto.
Page 444: Jerry Moorman/iStockphoto.

Chapter 11   ✚ Chapter opener: iStockphoto.
✚ How To 11.1: Punchstock.

Icons   Animation icon: james steidl/iStockphoto.
Common Error icon: John Bell/iStockphoto.
How To icon: Steve Simzer/iStockphoto.
Programming Tip icon: iStockphoto.
Random Fact icon: © Media Bakery
Self-Check icon: Nicholas Homrich/iStockphoto.
Special Topic icon: iStockphoto.
Worked Example icon: Tom Horyn/iStockphoto.